EMPLOYMENT TRIBUNAL REMEDIES

FOURTH EDITION

EMPLOYMENT TRIBUNAL REMEDIES

FOURTH EDITION

ANTHONY KORN

Barrister, No 5 Chambers

MOHINDERPAL SETHI

Barrister, Devereux Chambers

OXFORD

UNIVERSITY PRESS

OXFORD

UNIVERSITY PRESS

Great Clarendon Street, Oxford OX2 6DP

Oxford University Press is a department of the University of Oxford.
It furthers the University's objective of excellence in research, scholarship,
and education by publishing worldwide in

Oxford New York

Auckland   Cape Town Dar es Salaam   Hong Kong   Karachi
Kuala Lumpur Madrid Melbourne Mexico City   Nairobi
New Delhi Shanghai Taipei Toronto
With offices in
Argentina Austria Brazil Chile Czech Republic France Greece
Guatemala Hungary Italy Japan South Korea Poland Portugal
Singapore Switzerland Thailand Turkey Ukraine Vietnam

Oxford is a registered trade mark of Oxford University Press
in the UK and in certain other countries

Published in the United States
by Oxford University Press Inc., New York

ISBN 978-0-19-958641-7

Printed and bound by CPI Group (UK) Ltd, Croydon, CR0 4YY

PREFACE

Employment tribunals, until 1998 known as 'industrial tribunals', comprise the main forum for resolving employment disputes. Of the tens of thousands of claims that are brought each year, most result in either some form of financial settlement or a tribunal award of compensation. This book aims to give a detailed, practical, and balanced account of the remedies available in employment tribunals and, in particular, the tribunal's power to award compensation and other remedies. The book has been retitled *Employment Tribunal Remedies* for this reason.

The overall structure of the book is the same as the third edition of *Employment Tribunal Compensation*, but for ease of reference, some of the material has been split into separate chapters. The book is divided into seven parts. The first deals with the tribunal's jurisdiction to award compensation for breach of contract and wrongful dismissal. The second part, which is the longest, examines the statutory remedies for unfair dismissal, both in terms of the various elements that make up an award of unfair dismissal compensation and the circumstances in which such an award may be reduced. The text of the first two parts of the book incorporates the original text of *Compensation for Dismissal*, originally published by Blackstone's, but has been reviewed and fully updated to reflect the many developments since the last edition.

The third part of the book looks at the remedies available in cases of all types of unlawful discrimination. Detailed consideration is given to the power of tribunals to award compensation for injury to health, injury to feelings, and aggravated and, exceptionally, exemplary damages, as well as other factors relating to quantum, including the rules on interest. This part has been substantially rewritten to take account of the Equality Act 2010, the relevant provisions of which came into force on 1 October 2010, and case law developments since the last edition.

The sixth part of the book covers compensation for other employment claims excluding redundancy payments, which is considered in the fifth part. The final two parts of the book look at the relevant tribunal procedures in relation to compensation claims and the issues that arise in relation to settlement of such claims.

As with the previous edition, there are a number of people who have made very helpful comments on the text. Some have made significant contributions to the book. In particular, we would like to acknowledge the contributions of: Raymond Jeffers, formerly head of the Employment and Benefits Group at Linklaters, who contributed and updated the section on pension loss; Tim Cox and Simon Kerr-Davis, also of Linklaters, who reviewed and updated the section on stock options; Jonathan Schwarz of 3 Temple Gardens, for commenting on the tax material; Roger Smith of No 5 Chambers, for his helpful comments on the application of the Ogden tables; and the conciliation section at ACAS for reviewing the chapter on settlement in the previous edition. We would also like to thank the editorial team at OUP for their contribution. Last—but by no means least—we express our appreciation and thanks to our respective families for their patience and support.

Appendices 1, 2 and 3 are reproduced with the permission of the Tribunals service.

We also welcome comments by readers, particularly those who draw our attention to any relevant unreported case law.

The book therefore represents the authors' understanding of the law as at 30 September 2010.

Anthony Korn and Mohinderpal Sethi
September 2010

CONTENTS

PART III REDUNDANCY

PART VI TRIBUNAL PROCEDURES IN
COMPENSATION CLAIMS

PART VII SETTLEMENT

TABLE OF CASES

TABLE OF LEGISLATION

EC LEGISLATION

Treaties

Directives

NON-STATUTORY CODES

LIST OF ABBREVIATIONS

AC	Appeal Cases
ACAS	Advisory, Conciliation, and Arbitration Service
Ad & El	Adolphus and Ellis Reports
ADR	alternative dispute resolution
All ER	All England Reports
AVCs	additional voluntary contributions
CA	Court of Appeal
Cab & EI	Cababe & Ellis' Queen's Bench Reports
CARE	career average revalued earnings
Ch D	Chancery Division
COIT	Central Office of the Industrial Tribunals
CPR	Civil Procedure Rules 1998
CSOP	company share option plan
DDA 1995	Disability Discrimination Act 1995
DHSS	Department of Health and Social Security (now the DWP)
DPA 1998	Data Protection Act 1998
DWP	Department for Work and Pensions
EA 1980	Employment Act 1980
EA 1982	Employment Act 1982
EA 2002	Employment Act 2002
EA 2008	Employment Act 2008
EAT	Employment Appeal Tribunal
ECJ	European Court of Justice
EEAR 2006	Employment Equality (Age) Regulations 2006
EP(C)A 1978	Employment Protection (Consolidation) Act 1978
EIM	Employment Income Manual
EMI	enterprise management incentive
EOR	Equal Opportunities Review
EPA 1975	Employment Protection Act 1975
EP(C)A 1978	Employment Protection (Consolidation) Act 1978
EqA 2010	Equality Act 2010
EqPA 1970	Equal Pay Act 1970
ERA 1996	Employment Rights Act 1996
ERelA 1999	Employment Relations Act 1999
ER(NI)O 1996	Employment Rights (Northern Ireland) Order 1996
ETA 1996	Employment Tribunals Act 1996
ET Regulations 2001	Employment Tribunals (Constitution and Rules of Procedure) Regulations 2001

ET Regulations 2004	Employment Tribunals (Constitution and Rules of Procedure) Regulations 2004
ETS	Employment Tribunal Service
EWHC	England and Wales High Court
EWCA Civ	England and Wales Court of Appeal Civil Division
Exch	Exchequer Reports
FIS	Family Income Supplement
FTER 2002	Fixed-term Employees (Prevention of Less Favourable Treatment) Regulations 2002
GAD	Government Actuary's Department
HGV	heavy goods vehicle
HL	House of Lords
HMRC	HM Revenue and Customs
ICE Regulations 2004	Information and Consultation of Employees Regulations 2004
ICR	Industrial Cases Reports
ICTA 1988	Income and Corporation Taxes Act 1988
IDS	Income Data Services
ILEX	Institute of Legal Executives
ILJ	Industrial Law Journal
Interest Regulations	Employment Tribunals (Interest on Awards in Discrimination Cases) Regulations 1996
IRA 1971	Industrial Relations Act 1971
IRLB	Industrial Relations Law Bulletin
IRLR	Industrial Relations Law Reports
IRS	Industrial Relations Services
ISA	individual savings account
IT(EP)A 2003	Income Tax (Earnings and Pensions) Act 2003
ITR	Industrial Tribunal Reports
JSA	Jobseeker's Allowance
JSB	Judicial Studies Board
KIR	Knights Industrial Reports
NHS	National Health Service
NIC	National Insurance Contributions
NICA	Northern Ireland Court of Appeal
NIRC	National Industrial Relations Court
NLJ	New Law Journal
NMWA 1998	National Minimum Wage Act 1998
NMWR 1999	National Minimum Wage Regulations 1999
PAYE	pay-as-you-earn
PAYE Regulations	Income Tax (PAYE) Regulations 2003
PHI	permanent health insurance
PIDA 1998	Public Interest Disclosure Act 1998
PIQR	Personal Injuries and Quantum Reports
PPP	personal pension plan
PSA 1993	Pension Schemes Act 1993
PTSD	post-traumatic stress disorder

PTWR 2000	Part-time Workers (Prevention of Less Favourable Treatment) Regulations 2000
QB	Queen's Bench
RBR 2003	Employment Equality (Religion or Belief) Regulations 2003
Recoupment Regulations	Recoupment of Jobseeker's Allowance and Income Support Regulations 1996
RRA 1976	Race Relations Act 1976
S2P	State Second Pension
SAP	Statutory Adoption Pay
SAYE	save-as-you-earn
SDA 1975	Sex Discrimination Act 1975
SERPS	State Earnings-Related Pension Scheme
SIP	share incentive plan
SJ	Solicitors' Journal
SMP	Statutory Maternity Pay
SOR 2003	Employment Equality (Sexual Orientation) Regulations 2003
SPP	Statutory Paternity Pay
SSCBA 1992	Social Security Contributions and Benefits Act 1992
SSP	Statutory Sick Pay
STC	Simon's Tax Cases
TICER 1999	Transnational Information and Consultation of Employees Regulations 1999
TLR	Times Law Reports
TUC	Trades Union Congress
TULR(C)A 1992	Trade Union and Labour Relations (Consolidation) Act 1992
TUPE 1981	Transfer of Undertakings (Protection of Employment) Regulations 1981
TUPE 2006	Transfer of Undertakings (Protection of Employment) Regulations 2006
UCTA 1977	Unfair Contract Terms Act 1977
UKEAT	UK Employment Appeal Tribunal
WHO	World Health Organization
WLR	Weekly Law Reports
WTR 1998	Working Time Regulations 1998

PART I

COMPENSATION FOR BREACH OF CONTRACT AND WRONGFUL DISMISSAL

INTRODUCTION

Three forms of financial compensation may be open to employees on dismissal: damages for wrongful dismissal (a common law remedy); compensation for unfair dismissal (a statutory remedy); and compensation for unlawful discrimination (a statutory remedy).

Jurisdiction over wrongful dismissal claims is concurrent with the ordinary courts. Such claims are more commonly brought in the High Court or county court, because the sums involved often exceed the jurisdiction of the employment tribunal. Employment tribunals have exclusive jurisdiction over claims for unfair dismissal and discrimination in employment.

Statutory and common law claims are not, however, mutually exclusive since the rules governing liability for each claim are distinct; a dismissal can therefore be wrongful or unfair, both, or neither. Furthermore, although a dismissal for a discriminatory reason is highly likely also to be unfair, it will not necessarily be wrongful.

A major drawback of the common law action for wrongful dismissal is that the courts or, in appropriate cases, the employment tribunal cannot award compensation beyond the time at which the contract could have been brought to an end in accordance with its terms. This principle was confirmed by the House of Lords in *Eastwood and another v Magnox Electric plc; McCabe v Cornwall County Council* [2004] IRLR 733, although the Court of Appeal's ruling in *Edwards v Chesterfield Royal Hospital NHS Trust* [2010] IRLR 702 (see **1.43**), which, at the time of writing is on appeal to the Supreme Court, suggests that a former employee may be able to sue for loss arising as a result of a breach of an express term of the disciplinary procedure.

Nonetheless, in most cases, this means that compensation will not be awarded beyond the time at which the notice period would have expired. Such an action therefore offers limited financial compensation for many employees. But such claims are still important for those employees who do not meet the statutory qualifications to bring an unfair dismissal claim, and for highly paid directors and other senior employees (whose claims under their service agreements will often exceed the amount that tribunals are permitted to award by statute). Furthermore, even for those whose earnings are smaller, it will be possible to bring an employment tribunal claim for damages for wrongful dismissal in addition to any claim that they may have for unfair dismissal compensation or compensation for discrimination.

This section deals primarily with compensation for wrongful dismissal. However, in addition, compensation may be awarded for sums due to employees on termination of their employment, such as outstanding wages, sick pay, or maternity pay. This may form part of a wrongful dismissal claim or may be the subject of a separate claim under Pt II of the Employment Rights Act 1996 (ERA 1996—considered in Part V of this book).

A. Contractual Claims

Subject to the restriction referred to above, a claim for breach of contract can be made in an employment tribunal for outstanding contractual payments such as arrears of salary, pension payments, holiday pay, maternity pay, sick pay, and any other contractual sums due to an employee on the termination of employment.

Arrears of salary

In *Item Software (UK) Ltd v Fassihi* [2004] IRLR 928, the Court of Appeal ruled that the High Court judge was wrong not to award the defendant, who was paid monthly in arrears, the arrears of salary due to him on the termination of his employment. Such a payment could be claimed under ss 2 and 3 of the Apportionment Act 1870, which provide that, unless otherwise stated, payments (such as salary) accrue from day to day and become due when the entire portion would be paid. The Court ruled that the judge had wrongly considered himself bound by the Court of Appeal's ruling in *Boston Deep Sea Fishing and Ice Co Ltd v Ansell* (1888) 39 Ch D 339 to the effect that an employee whose service is terminated before the end of the stated period is not entitled to recover a proportionate amount of his salary. As the Court of Appeal pointed out, in the *Ansell* case, no reliance was placed on the Apportionment Act and therefore it is not authority for the effect of that Act. In *Fassihi,* there was no suggestion that the payment of the defendant's salary was conditional on him working the whole of the month or that he failed to provide services up to the date of his dismissal. He was therefore entitled to his outstanding salary up to that date. The same principle may be relied on in relation to other accrued payments such as holiday pay.

Bonus payments outstanding on termination

It is not uncommon for the issue of bonus payments to be unresolved on termination. In situations in which the 'contractual right' to bonus has arisen either prior to or on termination of employment, a contractual claim for loss of bonus can be brought in the employment tribunal, particularly if the bonus is guaranteed (*Horkulak v Cantor Fitzgerald International* [2004] IRLR 942).

A claim may also be made in cases in which the bonus is discretionary, because it is assumed (and implied) that such discretion will be exercised in a 'genuine' and 'rational' manner as 'it is presumed to be the reasonable expectation and therefore the common intention of the parties that there should be a genuine and rational, as opposed to an empty or irrational, exercise of discretion' (*Horkulak*). The judge's role is to put himself or herself in the shoes of the employer, and to decide how much the employer would have awarded if it were to have acted rationally and in good faith. It follows that no award will be made where an employer acts rationally and in good faith (*Humphreys v Norilsk Nickel International (UK) Ltd* [2010] EWHC 1867).

A more detailed consideration of the *Horkulak* decision and the principles on which such claim is quantified is considered at **1.51–1.52** below. For the position regarding 'non-contractual' bonuses, see **7.16**.

Pension payments

A claim can also be made for pension contributions that are outstanding on the termination of employment.

There may be an issue as to whether such a claim should be based on the amount of the employer's contribution during the relevant period or the actuarial value of the contribution (see **1.75** below), particularly in cases in which the employee is long-serving.

Shares and stock options

The duty to act rationally and in good faith has also been held to apply where an employer purports to cancel stock options that have matured at the time of dismissal (see *Mallone v BPB Industries plc* [2002] IRLR 452, **1.64** below).

PHI schemes

Where an employee has a contractual right to payments under a permanent health insurance scheme, these may be recoverable in an action for breach of contract in an employment tribunal, but where such a claim has arisen prior to or on termination, it is more likely to be brought under Pt II of the ERA 1996, because the jurisdiction is not subject to the £25,000 limit (see, for example, *Jowitt v Pioneer Technology (UK) Ltd* [2002] IRLR 790; [2003] IRLR 356).

Other claims

Other claims that have arisen or are outstanding on the termination of employment may be brought before the employment tribunal except claims for personal injuries (even if these were the result of a breach of the duty of trust and confidence, as in *Gogay v Hertfordshire County Council* [2000] IRLR 703).

1

COMPENSATION FOR WRONGFUL DISMISSAL AS A REMEDY IN EMPLOYMENT TRIBUNALS

A. What is Wrongful Dismissal?

The law of wrongful dismissal is essentially an extension of the ordinary common **1.01** law rules that govern the termination of a contract. A dismissal is therefore wrongful if the employer either terminates the contract in a manner that is contrary to its terms or does some other act that shows an intention not to be bound by it. Essentially, any termination by an employer that is not lawful will be wrongful. Apart from exceptional cases, in which a contract of employment can be terminated on specified grounds, the law of wrongful dismissal is concerned with the mode of termination rather than the reasons for termination.

Dismissal without proper notice

1.02 The most common example of a wrongful dismissal is the failure of an employer to give an employee the correct period of notice that is required to terminate the employment contract lawfully. This period of notice may be expressly agreed between the parties or it may be implied. As regards the latter, there is a common law presumption that a contract for an indefinite period may be terminated by 'a reasonable period of notice'.

1.03 What is a reasonable period of notice depends on all of the circumstances of the employment. Particular importance is attached to such factors as the type of job, the employee's status, and the period by which pay is calculated—for example, weekly, monthly, etc. The courts also take into account any custom or practice established in an industry or profession (*Clark v Fahrenheit 451 (Communications) Ltd* EAT/591/99). It has been held that a clerk paid fortnightly was entitled to one month's notice (*Vibert v Eastern Telegraph Co* (1883) 1 Cab & EI 17), whereas a 'superior' clerk was entitled to three months' notice (*Mulholland v Bexwell Estates Co Ltd* [1950] TLR (Pt 2) 764). A controller of cinemas was entitled to six months' notice (*Adams v Union Cinemas Ltd* [1939] 3 All ER 136), whereas a director and company secretary of a small firm was entitled to three months' notice (*HW Smith (Cabinets) Ltd v Brindle* [1973] ICR 12). In the rather special circumstances that existed in *Hill v CA Parsons Co Ltd* [1971] 3 All ER 1345, the court considered that a chartered engineer was entitled to at least six months' notice. However, it is always open to employees to waive their rights to notice—for example, as part of a voluntary redundancy package—and in such circumstances it will not be open to them to seek damages for wrongful dismissal (*Baldwin v British Coal Corp* [1995] IRLR 139).

1.04 Employers are under a duty to specify the length of notice that an employee is entitled to receive. They are obliged to give the employee this information in the written statement of particulars of employment that they must provide within two months from the commencement of employment (Employment Rights Act 1996 [ERA 1996], s 1(2)).

Failure to give statutory notice

1.05 Whatever period of notice is stated in the contract, whether express or implied, the notice actually given to the employee must not be less than the statutory minimum periods of notice laid down by the ERA 1996.

1.06 The statutory periods are as follows (ERA 1996, s 86(1)):

(a) not less than one week's notice for an employee who has been continuously employed for one month or more (before 2 January 1983, four weeks or more), but less than two years;

(b) not less than one week's notice for each year of continuous employment for an employee who has been continuously employed for two years or more, but less than 12 years;

(c) not less than 12 weeks' notice for an employee who has been employed for 12 years or more.

An agreement that purports to reduce the periods of notice guaranteed by the statutory provisions is void (ERA 1996, s 203). **1.07**

See **1.105** below for calculating the statutory notice entitlement. **1.08**

Exceptions

The right to be given the statutory minimum period of notice does not apply to the following classes of employment: **1.09**

(a) overseas employment (other than certain employments in territorial waters or on the continental shelf) (s 196);

(b) certain merchant seamen (s 199(1));

(c) employment in the armed forces (s 192);

(d) casual workers are not normally entitled to minimum notice (s 86(5)), except those who are taken on an indefinite or periodic contract;

(e) Crown employees (s 191), and House of Lords and House of Commons staffs (ss 194 and 195);

(f) where the period of contractual notice exceeds the statutory minimum (*Scotts Company (UK) Ltd v Budd* [2003] IRLR 145).

Restrictions on the right to terminate with notice

In general, there are no restrictions on the right to terminate by giving the appropriate period of contractual or statutory notice (*Reda v Flag Ltd* [2002] IRLR 747). It follows that where there is an express and unequivocal power to terminate without reason, the contract will come to an end should such a power be exercised. **1.10**

However, the position may be different where the power to terminate is restricted by the express terms of the contract. For example, there may be an express provision that provides that the contract may only be terminated by following an express procedure, or termination may be restricted to certain specified circumstances. In certain highly exceptional circumstances, there may be implied restrictions on the right to terminate. **1.11**

Dismissal in breach of disciplinary procedures

Today, it is quite common for a disciplinary procedure to form part of the contract of employment and, in such circumstances, a failure to follow the disciplinary procedure may amount to a serious breach of contract (*The Post Office v Strange* [1981] IRLR 515). It has been held that where an employer fails to follow a disciplinary **1.12** procedure prior to termination, damages may be awarded for the length of time that it would have taken to complete the procedure (*Gunton v London Borough of Richmond upon Thames* [1980] 3 All ER 577; *Boyo v London Borough of Lambeth* [1995] IRLR 50; and *Edwards v Chesterfield Royal Hospital NHS Foundation Trust* [2009] IRLR 822, [2010] IRLR 702, in which the challenge to the *Gunton* principle was rejected by the Court of Appeal—but also see **1.43** below). However, in *Focsa Services (UK) Ltd v Birkett* [1996] IRLR 325, the Employment Appeal Tribunal (EAT) ruled that this will be appropriate only where the evidence shows that the use of the disciplinary procedure would have extended the length of employment beyond the notice period. The EAT's reasoning is open to doubt on the ground that an employee will not normally be given notice until the disciplinary process is completed.

Fixed-term contracts

1.13   Termination by an employer of a fixed-term contract before the term has expired can also constitute wrongful dismissal. For example, if a scientist were employed on a project for a fixed term of four years, any unlawful termination by the employer before that time would amount to a breach of contract and give rise to an action for wrongful dismissal (*Isleworth Studios Ltd v Rickard* [1988] IRLR 137). Normally, the possibility of early termination will be taken into account by the inclusion of a provision that the contract may be terminated by either side giving a specified period of notice. However, an employee who is employed under a fixed-term contract of one month or less and who has been continuously employed for three months or more is entitled to the minimum statutory periods referred to in **1.06** above (ERA 1996, s 86(4)).

Express restrictions on the right to terminate

1.14   Sometimes, the parties may restrict the grounds on which the contract may be terminated to certain defined situations by providing for circumstances in which notice will not be necessary, such as misconduct or incapacity. If an employee is dismissed where the grounds have been so restricted, such dismissal will be lawful only if the employer can justify it on one of the grounds specified in the contract. However, the precise effect of a failure to do this is uncertain.

1.15   In *McClelland v Northern Ireland General Health Services Board* [1957] 2 All ER 129, the House of Lords appears to have held that a dismissal for a reason other than one expressly permitted was of no legal effect. This decision involved the rather special rules of administrative law and the more likely interpretation is that the employer's action would amount to a breach of contract, with damages being quantified in the usual way. This interpretation appears to be supported by both the High Court's [2004] IRLR 279 and Court of Appeal's ruling [2005] IRLR 40 in *Kaur v MG Rover Group*, in which it was held that an express term in a contract that restricts the employer's right to terminate will prevail over a general right to terminate.

The issue that divided the courts was whether a provision in a collective agreement that there would be no compulsory redundancy was incorporated into the claimant's contract. The High Court ruled that it was incorporated, whereas the Court of Appeal ruled that it was not, because the statement was merely aspirational and not intended to have contractual effect. For the effect of disciplinary procedures, see 1.43 below.

Implied restrictions on the right to terminate

As stated above, the general rule is that there can be no implied restriction on an **1.16** express right to terminate as provided for in the contract of employment. However, in highly exceptional circumstances, the courts have been prepared to imply such a restriction on the basis of the presumed intentions of the parties. For example, in *Aspden v Webbs Poultry & Meat Group (Holdings) Ltd* [1996] IRLR 521, the High Court ruled that, except for situations in which summary dismissal may be justified, there was an implied term that an employer would not terminate the contract of employment during a period of incapacity so as to prevent an employee from qualifying for an entitlement to payments under a permanent health insurance scheme (notwithstanding that the written contract included a general power to terminate). As stated above, the claimant would be entitled to general damages for breach of contract in such circumstances. The Court's ruling was followed in slightly different circumstances by the High Court in *Jenvey v Australian Broadcasting Corp* [2002] IRLR 520.

The analysis in *Aspden* was endorsed, but distinguished, by the Privy Council in **1.17** *Reda v Flag Ltd* [2002] IRLR 747 and by the House of Lords in *Johnson v Unisys Ltd* [2001] IRLR 279. The argument that the implied duty of trust and confidence could also act as a restriction on the express power to terminate a contract was rejected in both of these cases on the basis that the implied duty only applies whilst the employment relationship subsists and therefore does not restrict the power to terminate. This was confirmed by the House of Lords in *Eastwood v Magnox Ltd and McCabe v Cornwall County Council* [2004] IRLR 733.

Contract for a specific task

An action for wrongful dismissal may lie if a contract for a specific task is termi- **1.18** nated prematurely—that is, before the task is complete. Here, again, the employer will often take this into account by reserving the right to dismiss on certain grounds before the task is complete. A dismissal will not be wrongful if the employer is able to show that one or more of these grounds existed at the time of termination. The statutory minimum periods of notice do not apply where it is contemplated that the specific task will last for less than three months unless the employee has, in fact, been continuously employed for more than three months (ERA 1996, s 86(5)).

Repudiation and breach of fundamental term

1.19   An action for wrongful dismissal also arises where the employer is found to have 'repudiated' the contract or is in breach of one of the fundamental contractual obligations. The two concepts are often used by the courts interchangeably to describe the same kind of conduct. For example, a failure to give proper notice is both a breach of a fundamental term and a repudiation.

Repudiation

1.20   A repudiation occurs where the employer, by its conduct, displays an intention not to be bound by the contract. For example, in *Shove v Downs Surgical plc* [1984] 1 All ER 7, the defendant company admitted liability for repudiating its contract of employment with Mr Shove, its managing director, when it passed a motion of no confidence in him and suggested that he should make 'a dignified exit on grounds of ill health'.

1.21   Employers may also repudiate the contract if they act beyond the powers conferred on them by the contract itself. Thus, in *Bliss v South East Thames Regional Health Authority* [1985] IRLR 308, the Court of Appeal ruled that the Authority had repudiated the contract by insisting that a consultant underwent a medical examination because the contract did not give it power to insist on a medical examination without just cause.

1.22   Employers may also repudiate the contract if they insist on imposing new terms and conditions of employment on their employees without their consent (see *Burdett-Coutts and others v Hertfordshire County Council* [1984] IRLR 91).

Breach of a fundamental term

1.23   A claim for wrongful dismissal will also arise where the employer is shown to be in breach of a fundamental term of the contract of employment, such as pay, location, status, etc. Thus, in some of the decisions cited above, the employers were also found to be in breach of their essential contractual obligations. For example, in *Bliss v South East Thames Regional Health Authority* [1985] IRLR 308, the Authority was found to be in breach of the duty of mutual trust and confidence. This implied term has since been confirmed and recognized as a fundamental term of the employment relationship (*Malik v BCCI* [1997] IRLR 462).

1.24   There is a difference of judicial opinion as to the effect of a breach of a fundamental term on the contract of employment. Some judges take the view that the wrongful dismissal ends the contract automatically (*per* Shaw LJ in *Gunton v London Borough of Richmond upon Thames* [1980] 3 All ER 577), whereas other judges are of the opinion that the dismissal will not terminate the contract of employment if the employee elects to affirm it (*per* Buckley LJ in *Gunton*). At the heart of the argument is the question of whether the rules relating to contracts generally (which provide that a unilateral repudiation does not terminate a contract) can be applied to employment contracts in view of the special relationship that exists between employer and employee. The Court of Appeal appears to have affirmed that the 'elective' theory applies at least in cases of anticipatory breach—that is, cases in which one of the parties indicates an intention not to abide by the terms of the contract before the time fixed for performance (*Harrison v Norwest Holst Group Administration Ltd* [1985] IRLR 240). See also *Thomas Marshall (Exports) Ltd v Guinle* [1978] IRLR 174; *R v East Berkshire Health Authority, ex p Walsh* [1984] IRLR 278; *Irani v Southampton & South-West Hampshire Area Health Authority* [1985] IRLR 203; *Dietmann v London Borough of Brent* [1987] IRLR 146; and *Boyo v London Borough of Lambeth* [1995] IRLR 50.

In practical terms, if the courts decide that the 'elective' theory is correct, this may **1.25** lengthen the period over which damages for wrongful dismissal are awarded. It may also encourage the development of other equitable remedies for wrongful dismissal that are outside the jurisdiction of employment tribunals.

B. Lawful Termination of Contract

An employment may be lawfully terminated by: **1.26**

(a) giving proper notice;
(b) expiry (a contract for a fixed term—that is, a specified period—will terminate automatically at the end of that period and a contract for a specified task will terminate automatically on the completion of that task);
(c) agreement—at common law, the employer and the employee may agree to terminate the employment contract and thereby release each other from their obligations thereunder; such agreements will, however, be void under ERA 1996, s 203 if they purport to exclude the rights conferred on all employees by employment protection legislation (*Igbo v Johnson Matthey Chemicals Ltd* [1986] IRLR 215);
(d) summary dismissal—a dismissal without notice may be lawful if the employer can prove that the employee has committed a serious act of misconduct (see **1.27** below);
(e) dismissal for cause—some contracts confer power on the employer to terminate the contract lawfully in a specified set of circumstances (for example, incapacity—see **1.16** above); and
(f) frustration—that is, where circumstances beyond the control of either party to the contract make it impossible to perform the contract in the manner originally contemplated by the parties (see **1.33** below).

Summary dismissal

At common law, an employer may dismiss an employee summarily—that is, without **1.27** notice—in the event of a serious breach of contract on the part of the employee.

This rule applies to all contracts of employment and is specifically preserved by ERA 1996, s 86(6) in relation to the statutory minimum notice requirements.

1.28 Whether the employee's conduct is sufficiently serious to justify summary dismissal depends on the particular circumstances and, to some extent, reflects changes in judicial attitudes to certain kinds of conduct, as well as changes in the ordinary expectations of employers and employees. Typical examples of situations in which summary dismissal would normally be justified include theft of the employer's property, disobedience to lawful orders, gross negligence, gross insubordination, and other forms of gross misconduct.

1.29 An employee may be summarily dismissed for a single serious incident or a series of incidents. However, as a general rule, 'one act of disobedience or misconduct can justify dismissal only if it is of a nature which goes to show (in effect) that the servant is repudiating the contract, or one of its essential conditions' (*per* Lord Evershed in *Laws v Chronicle (Indicator Newspapers) Ltd* [1959] 2 All ER 285). Lord Evershed added that, in other words, there must be a 'deliberate flouting of the essential contractual conditions'.

1.30 Such conduct must so undermine the relationship of trust and confidence that the employer can no longer be expected to retain the services of the employee, although account should be taken of the nature of the employer and the role of the employee. Normally, this will involve a 'deliberate flouting of the essential contractual conditions'. However, in certain circumstances—particularly where the employment involves a high degree of trustworthiness—financial wrongdoing short of deliberate dishonesty or deceit may suffice (*Neary v Dean of Westminster* [2000] IRLR 288), as will a deliberate and persistent failure to following mandatory instructions (*Dunn v AAH Ltd* [2010] IRLR 709).

Reasons for dismissal

1.31 The law of wrongful dismissal is primarily concerned with the form of dismissal rather than its substance. Employers may therefore exercise their right to dismiss without giving any reasons. As Lord Denman said in *Ridgway v The Hungerford Market Co* (1835) 3 Ad & El 171: '[I]t is not necessary that a master, having a good ground of dismissal should either state it to the servant or act upon it. It is enough if it exist, and if there be improper conduct in fact.'

1.32 One consequence of this rule is that an employer who wrongly dismisses an employee for reason X may justify the dismissal by reason Y even if the employer was unaware of reason Y at the time of dismissal (*Boston Deep Sea Fishing and Ice Co v Ansell* (1888) 39 Ch D 339, confirmed by *Cyril Leonard & Co v Simo Securities Trust Ltd* [1971] 3 All ER 1313, and applied by the EAT in *A v B* [2010] IRLR 844). This contrasts with the position in unfair dismissals in which employers may rely only on the reason that they put forward at the time of dismissal (see *W Devis &*

Sons Ltd v Atkins [1977] 3 All ER 40). Employers are also under a statutory duty to give written reasons for dismissal to employees who have two years' continuous employment (ERA 1996, s 92).

C. Frustration

There can be no claim for wrongful dismissal if the contract is terminated by **1.33** frustration. This occurs when circumstances beyond the control of either party to the contract make it impossible to perform the contract in the manner originally contemplated by the parties. Thus it has been held that a contract of employment may be frustrated as a result of a sentence of imprisonment being imposed on an employee (see *F C Shepherd & Co Ltd v Jerrom* [1986] IRLR 358), but not necessarily where an employee is charged with a criminal offence, but released on bail (*Four Seasons Healthcare Ltd v Maughan* [2005] IRLR 324). A contract may also be frustrated as a result of the employee suffering from a serious illness that renders him or her incapable of performing the contract (*Notcutt v Universal Equipment Co (London) Ltd* [1986] IRLR 218), but not simply because the employee has been on a period of extended absence (*Gryf-Lowczowski v Hinchingbrooke Healthcare NHS Trust* [2006] IRLR 100).

A detailed consideration of the common law rules on frustration is beyond the **1.34** scope of this book, but it should be noted that where frustration is shown, the contract terminates automatically and therefore there can be no claim for wrongful or unfair dismissal.

D. Assessing Compensation for Wrongful Dismissal

The usual remedy for wrongful dismissal is an action for damages. The rules governing **1.35** the assessment of compensation for wrongful dismissal are simply an extension of the ordinary rules that govern an award of damages for breach of contract. These differ in certain significant respects from the statutory rules that apply in assessing compensation for unfair dismissal.

Every breach of contract gives rise to a claim for damages. The basic object of **1.36** damages for breach of contract is to put the plaintiff 'so far as money can do it . . . in the same situation . . . as if the contract had been performed' (*Robinson v Harman* (1848) 1 Exch 850, 855). In the context of wrongful dismissal, this involves a consideration of two factors: first, the period over which damages are awarded— 'the damages period'; and second, the items that can be included in such a claim.

In order to ensure that an employee is not better off than he or she would have been **1.37** had the contract been performed and to prevent him or her from making a profit out of the employer's breach, an employee must give credit for payments received since dismissal, such as earnings from a new job or state benefits. These payments go towards reducing the employer's liability.

The damages period

1.38   The first stage in the calculation of damages for wrongful dismissal is to determine the 'damages period'. In determining this period, the courts assume that the employer would have brought the contract to an end 'in the way most beneficial to himself, which is to say, that he would have determined the contract at the earliest date at which he could properly do so' (*per* Buckley LJ in *Gunton v London Borough of Richmond upon Thames* [1980] 3 All ER 577, 589). This means that the period of loss ends at the time at which the employer could have terminated the contract lawfully (*Alexander and others v Standard Telephone & Cables Ltd (No 2)* [1991] IRLR 286).

Damages for the notice period

1.39   Where the contract is terminable by notice, the damages period is fixed by reference to the period of notice. For example, in cases in which an employee receives insufficient notice, the damages period is the difference between the period of notice that the employee should have been given and the period that he or she is actually given. If no notice is given, then the damages period is the full period of notice.

> **Example**
>
> An employee is entitled to receive four weeks' notice, but is given two weeks' notice. The damages period is therefore two weeks.
>
> See **1.02** for dismissal without proper notice.

Fixed-term contracts

1.40   If the contract is for a fixed term without express provision for earlier termination by notice, the earliest date on which the employer could bring the contract to an end is the end of the term. Therefore, subject to the duty to mitigate, damages may be awarded for the remainder of the term. For example, in *Gill and others v Cape Contracts Ltd* [1985] IRLR 499, the Northern Ireland High Court awarded Mr Gill and his colleagues six months' wages in compensation for breach of a collateral contract to work at Sullom Voe for six months (see also **1.13** above). However, if the fixed-term contract is terminable by notice, damages will be limited to the notice period.

> **Example**
>
> A scientist is employed on a research project under a contract for a fixed term of four years. If the contract were terminable on three months' notice, the damages period would be limited to three months.

Breach of contractual procedures

In *Gunton v London Borough of Richmond upon Thames* [1980] 3 All ER 577, the Court of Appeal ruled that, where the employers had failed to follow an established disciplinary procedure, the measure of damages should be based on the length of time that it would have taken for the employment to have been terminated lawfully if the employers were to have followed the procedure correctly. The Court therefore allowed 'a reasonable period' for carrying out those procedures plus the one month's notice provided for by the contract. (See also *Dietmann v London Borough of Brent* [1987] IRLR 259 and *Boyo v London Borough of Lambeth* [1995] IRLR 50, in which the Court of Appeal upheld the county court judge's ruling that five months was a reasonable period for carrying out the disciplinary procedure in the particular circumstances of the case; contrast this decision with that of the EAT in *Focsa Services (UK) Ltd v Birkett* [1996] IRLR 325, in which no damages were awarded.)   **1.41**

However, the Court did not deal with situations in which, had a disciplinary investigation been carried out, the employee would not have been dismissed.   **1.42**

This point arose in *Alexander and others v Standard Telephones & Cables Ltd (No 2)* [1991] IRLR 286, in which it was argued that the employer's failure to follow a redundancy selection procedure whereby persons other than the plaintiffs would have been selected for redundancy meant that therefore damages should reflect the plaintiffs' loss of earnings for the remainder of their working lives, allowing for contingencies. By analogy, it could be argued, in disciplinary cases, that compensation should be awarded beyond the notice period if it can be shown that, had a proper procedure been followed, the employee would not have been dismissed. The argument was, however, rejected in *Alexander* by Hobhouse J, who invoked the orthodox view that damages for breach of contract are assessed on the assumption that the contract breaker would have terminated the contract by giving the minimum period of notice necessary to terminate the contract lawfully. A similar argument was also rejected by the Court of Appeal in *Boyo v London Borough of Lambeth* [1995] IRLR 50 and *Focsa Services (UK) Ltd v Birkett* [1996] IRLR 325, in which the EAT overturned a tribunal's decision to award damages by way of unfair dismissal compensation for the same reason. Similarly, in *Edwards v Chesterfield Royal Hospital NHS Foundation Trust* [2009] IRLR 822, the High Court confirmed that loss in cases of wrongful dismissal is limited to the sums payable to the employee had the employment been lawfully terminated   **1.43** under the contract and that it was irrelevant to consider what might have happened had the contractual disciplinary procedure been followed. But doubt has now been cast on these cases because the High Court's ruling in *Edwards* was subsequently overturned by the Court of Appeal ([2010] IRLR 702). The Court of Appeal's ruling has been interpreted by some to suggest that where an employer is in breach of the express terms of a disciplinary procedure, damages may be awarded for any loss that flows from the breach of this express term both in terms of the process followed and its outcome (at [44] of the judgment). However, quite apart from issues of mitigation and causation, it is clear from [36] of the Court's judgment that Mr Edwards was seeking to recover damages for the loss of the opportunity to hold another full-time appointment with the National Health Service (NHS) as a consultant surgeon. It is unclear how far the ruling goes beyond the claim under consideration by the court. It therefore remains a moot point whether damages are recoverable under ordinary contractual principles if it can be established that the claimant would not have been dismissed had the employer followed the express terms of its disciplinary procedure (which formed part of the contract). On a broad interpretation of the ruling in *Edwards*, the same point may also be arguable wherever there is an express or implied restriction on the right to terminate (see *Kaur v MG Rover Group* [2004] IRLR 279, [2005] IRLR 40). The award may also include damages for loss of professional status (see **1.102** below).

Payments that count

1.44   Once the damages period has been identified, the second stage in the calculation is to consider which items of loss may be included in a claim for damages. Damages are awarded only for payments and benefits to which the employee is contractually entitled. In the past, this meant that discretionary or other payments that the employee had only a reasonable expectation of receiving could not be recovered by way of damages in a wrongful dismissal claim (see *Lavarack v Woods of Colchester Ltd* [1967] QB 278). This 'traditional' view probably still applies to non-contractual benefits (that is, benefits for which there is no provision in the contract of employment), but as far as discretionary contractual provisions are concerned, the principle must now be read in the light of the Court of Appeal's ruling in *Horkulak v Cantor Fitzgerald International* [2004] IRLR 942.

1.45   In *Horkulak*, the Court of Appeal ruled that even where the contractual provision is discretionary, this is subject to an implied term that the discretion will be exercised 'genuinely and rationally' since this is presumed to be the 'reasonable expectation' and common intention of the parties (see also *Small v Boots Co plc* [2009] IRLR 328, in which the EAT stressed that there may be two elements to the discretion—that is, whether the bonus is payable at all and the amount that is payable). Furthermore, the Court stated that the broad principle that an employer in an action for breach of contract is not liable for doing that which it is not bound to do is not applicable 'willy nilly' in a case in which the employer is bound to exercise such discretion in good faith in awarding or withholding a benefit provided for under the contract. Where an employer fails so to do, the employee is entitled to compensation for such failure. It is important to note, however, that the basis of the claim remains the contractual 'right' that the discretion be exercised in a genuine and rational manner rather than the basis of a reasonable expectation as such and that, at least in theory, the presumed intention that forms the basis of the Court of Appeal's reasoning in *Horkulak* could be overridden by an express provision to the contrary in the contract of employment (*Commerzbank AG v Keen* [2007] IRLR 132).

It may also be open to the court, or (in a claim before an employment tribunal) the **1.46** tribunal, to imply a reasonable amount where the contract makes no express provision for a particular rate or level of payment. Sometimes, however, an agreement to agree will be void for uncertainty. This issue arose in *Fontana (GB) Ltd v Fabio* EAT 140/01, in which an employment tribunal considered that a 15 per cent contribution to Mr Fabio's pension was 'reasonable' where the parties had failed to agree the rate of pension contributions. The EAT overturned the tribunal decision because, on the facts, as found by the employment tribunal, the agreement was void for uncertainty:as the parties had not defined what the level of pension contributions should be either when they met or in the correspondence that they exchanged. Therefore there was no evidential basis to support the tribunal view of what was reasonable. However, it is clear on the case law referred to by the EAT that it may be open to imply such a 'reasonable' provision in appropriate cases (see, in particular, the summary in *Mamidoil-Jetoil Greek Petroleum Company SA v Okta Crude Oil Refinery AD* [2001] 2 Lloyd's Law Reports 89).

Pay

Normally, the largest item in a claim for damages is the amount in respect of the pay **1.47** that the employee would have earned during the damages period. This should be relatively easy to calculate, but special rules apply in a claim for statutory notice pay (see **1.110** below). If, for some reason, the contract does not specify a rate of pay, the court will imply a 'reasonable' rate for the job.

A further difficulty may arise where a pay increase takes effect during the damages **1.48** period—that is, a case in which annual pay negotiations are concluded outside the damages period, but the agreement is backdated. This point arose indirectly in *Leyland Vehicles Ltd v Reston* [1981] 1 IRLR 19, in which the EAT had to decide whether a backdated pay increase counted for the purpose of calculating a week's pay. The EAT ruled that it did not (see **5.66** below), but Slynn J suggested that Mr Reston might have been able to sue for back pay had his contract so provided. (On the facts, there was some doubt as to whether the terms of the collective agreement had been incorporated into Mr Reston's contract.) Thus it would seem that an employee whose contract provides for a pay increase to be backdated should receive damages that allow for the increase from the time at which the increase takes effect to the end of the damages period.

1.49 Similarly, effect will be given to an inflation-proofing clause in a service agreement (*Re Crowther and Nicholson Ltd* (1981) 125 SJ 529) or a clause that provides for an annual review and an increase in salary 'by such amount as the board shall in its absolute discretion determine' (*Clark v BET plc and another* [1997] IRLR 348) on the basis that the powers conferred by such clause must be exercised rationally and in good faith. The *Clark* decision was approved by the Court of Appeal in *Horkulak*. This will normally entitle an employee to the same increase in salary as was awarded to employees in a comparable position over the notice period (although this may not be the case if the entire salary—or part of it—is performance-related).

1.50 A separate claim may be brought in the same action to recover back pay or holiday pay that was outstanding at the time of dismissal or, in cases in which it is appropriate, the amount may be recovered as an unlawful deduction from wages (under the Wages Act 1986, now Pt II of the ERA 1996) that an employee would have contributed to his or her employer's pension scheme and should not be included in a claim for lost earnings (*Dews v National Coal Board* [1987] IRLR 330).

Commission and bonus

1.51 If the employee would have been entitled to a bonus or commission during the damages period, that sum should be included in the award of damages (*Addis v Gramophone Co Ltd* [1909] AC 488; *Clark v BET* [1997] IRLR 348; *Horkulak v Cantor Fitzgerald International* [2004] IRLR 942, in which part of the bonus was guarantee), or if he or she will be entitled to commission calculated in accordance with the express terms of the scheme.

1.52 Damages may also be awarded where the bonus is discretionary in accordance with the principles set out in the *Horkulak* case—that is, on the assumption that the employer would have exercised its discretion as a reasonable employer in good faith and in a rational manner. Where the bonus scheme sets out the criteria that will determine the level of the bonus, judges (or tribunals) will be expected to place themselves in the position of the employer and apply those criteria to the evidence. For example, in *Clark v Nomura International plc* [2000] IRLR 766, Mr Justice Burton awarded the claimant, a senior proprietary trader, the sum of £1.35m for loss of bonus based on his individual performance. This, as defined by the terms of the scheme, included the claimant's profitability and his contribution to the team, but did not include factors such as the need to retain and motivate the employee. The relevant criteria may include such factors where, as in *Horkulak*, the bonus scheme is completely discretionary. For example, it may be relevant to consider the bonuses awarded to other comparable employees either in global terms or as a percentage of salary. (In the *Horkulak* case, the judge awarded Mr Horkulak, who was employed as a senior managing director of interest derivatives, a bonus of £180,000 in the first year of his employment and £450,000 in the second year—the latter award being remitted for reconsideration by the judge.) It follows that no award will be made where an employer acts rationally and in good faith in determining the amount of bonus to be awarded in accordance with the scheme's criteria (*Humphreys v Norilsk Nickel International (UK) Ltd* [2010] IRLR 976). There may also be an arguable case for damages where an employer prevents an employee from attaining the targets to qualify for a bonus by acting in a manner that amounts to a breach of trust and confidence (*Takacs v Barclays Services Jersey Ltd* [2006] IRLR 877). Some schemes give the employer the right to 'cap' the amount of bonus payable in any given period, but the extent of the employer's discretion in such circumstances will depend on the terms of the scheme. So, for example, in *GX Networks Ltd v Greenland* [2010] IRLR 991, the employer's decision to cap the claimant's bonus, thereby reducing the amount due from £163,503 to £37,980, failed because the terms of the scheme stated that the discretion to cap the bonus at the end of every quarter was only to be exercised in 'exceptional' circumstances and 'there were no exceptional circumstances which could justify the exercise of that power'.

1.53 However, as stated above, an employee's contractual right to claim such a bonus during the notice period may be excluded by the express terms of the contract. For example, it is not uncommon for a contract to provide that bonus payments will not be made if the employee resigns or is dismissed for serious misconduct. In such circumstances, a bonus payment could not be claimed (*Commerzbank AG v Keen* [2007] IRLR 132). Nonetheless, where the right to a bonus is expressed in mandatory terms, then a court is likely to hold that the employer is bound to observe the terms of the bonus scheme for the stated period (*Khatri v Cooperative Centrale Raiffeizen-Borenleendbank BA* [2010] IRLR 715).

Share schemes generally

1.54 Share schemes are an increasingly frequent and important part of the remuneration package. Several forms of employee share scheme have specific tax advantages: the share incentive plan (SIP); the approved save-as-you-earn (SAYE) option scheme; the approved company share option plan (CSOP); and the enterprise management incentive (EMI).

1.55 Outstanding options and awards under employee share plans will, under the plan rules, typically lapse on termination of employment. An employee may therefore claim damages in respect of such lost options or awards. He or she may also claim for damages in respect of future options and awards that he or she would have been granted during the notice period. Whether an employee will be successful in such claims will largely depend on the wording of the plan rules, whether the employee has a contractual entitlement (either express or implied) in respect of such options or awards, and whether the plan rules contain effective exclusion of liability wording. The case law in this area relates primarily to share options (see **1.59** below).

Share incentive plans

1.56 A SIP is a plan, approved by HM Revenue and Customs (HMRC) under Sch 2 to the Income Tax (Earnings and Pensions) Act 2003 [IT(EP)A 2003], under which a company can allocate employees free shares, partnership shares, and/or matching shares on a tax-favourable basis. The company has to allocate shares to all employees of a participating company on similar terms. Further details can be found online at the HMRC's website.

1.57 Depending on the plan rules, free shares and matching shares may be forfeited on termination of employment and the employee may be deprived of the opportunity to receive shares on a tax-favourable basis. Subject to any exclusion wording, the employee should be able to claim damages in respect of the loss of the shares and favourable tax treatment that he or she would otherwise have received.

1.58 Given that a SIP has to be operated on an all-employee and similar terms basis, the employee may also be able to claim in respect of any future allocations of shares during the notice period.

SAYE savings-related share option plans

1.59 A SAYE savings-related share option plan (sharesave) is a plan, approved by the HMRC under Sch 3 to IT(EP)A 2003, under which a company grants employees options, linked to a savings contract, on a tax-favourable basis. As with the SIP, sharesave options have to be offered to all employees on similar terms. Further details can be found online at the HMRC's website.

1.60 Sharesave options will lapse on termination of employment. Subject to any exclusion wording, the employee should be able to claim damages in respect of options that would otherwise have been exercisable. The quantification of such damages is discussed below (see **1.69**).

1.61 Given that a sharesave plan has to be operated on an all-employee and similar terms basis, the employee may also be able to claim in respect of future grants of options. Whether such grants will have any value will depend on whether they would have become exercisable during the employee's notice period.

Discretionary plans: Share option plans, long-term incentive plans, etc

1.62 Companies operate a wide range of share plans under which the company has discretion as to which employees can participate and the extent of their participation. Such plans include discretionary option plans (including option plans approved by the HMRC under Sch 4 to IT(EP)A 2003) and long-term incentive plans, under which a company will typically award employees free shares subject to the satisfaction of certain conditions over a specified period. Such discretionary plans can provide very significant benefits.

Outstanding options and awards will, typically, lapse or may be subject to cancellation **1.63**
on termination of employment. The duty to act rationally and in good faith has also
been held to apply where an employer purports to cancel stock options that have
matured at the time of dismissal.

In *Mallone v BPB Industries plc* [2002] IRLR 452, the claimant successfully recovered **1.64**
damages for the loss of a matured share option (that is, an option that had been granted
three years before his employment was terminated), which his employers purported to
rescind on termination of his employment. The Court of Appeal ruled that, under the
particular terms of the scheme operated by the employer, the power to rescind the option
continued to apply (even after the option had matured), but that a reasonable employer
would not have cancelled the options when the claimant left its employment.

The Court left open the possibility that the number of shares granted could be **1.65**
reduced by an 'appropriate proportion' (as provided for by the scheme) to reflect
'poor performance' prior to termination, but pointed out that the options were
granted to reward past performance, and to encourage future loyalty and performance.
It would therefore be highly unusual for the discretion to be exercised in such a
manner as to deprive an employee of options that had already matured and vested
other than in cases of gross misconduct.

In principle, therefore, an employee should be able to claim damages in respect of **1.66**
options and awards that would otherwise have been exercisable or have vested
during the notice period, but this is subject to any exclusion wording.

Most discretionary plans contain exclusion wording purporting to exclude any **1.67**
right to be compensated for lost rights under the plan. The validity of such wording
was judicially considered for the first time by John Mowbray QC in *Micklefield v
SAC Technology Ltd* [1992] 1 All ER 275. Mr Micklefield held a share option that
was exercisable from 19 February 1988. On 11 February 1988, he was summarily
dismissed and received six months' salary in lieu of his contractual notice. The hearing concerned the preliminary issue of whether, if Mr Micklefield had been
wrongfully dismissed, he was entitled to damages for loss of his share option. The
judge upheld the validity of the exclusion clause in the share option plan and therefore
ruled in favour of the employer.

Nevertheless, one case suggests that the reasoning in *Micklefield* may be open to **1.68**
challenge. The judge in *Micklefield* decided that the Unfair Contract Terms Act
1977 (UCTA 1977) did not strike out the exclusion clause because the Act does not
apply to any contract relating to 'the creation or transfer of securities' (UCTA 1977,
Sch 1, para 1(e)). In the Scottish case of *Chapman v Aberdeen Construction Group
plc* [1992] IRLR 505, the Court of Session upheld a claim for a lost share option
on the basis that the UCTA 1977 did nullify the exclusion clause. The decision is
not necessarily inconsistent with *Micklefield* because Sch 1, para 1(e) does not
apply in Scotland. However, the Court of Session treated the share option contract
as a secondary contract (the service contract being the primary contract) and, even

in England, Sch 1, para 1(e) applies only to primary contracts. It is worth noting that the Unfair Terms in Consumer Contracts Regulations 1999, SI 1999/2083, do not (unlike the preceding 1994 Regulations) contain a specific exclusion for contracts relating to employment. However, such contracts (which, arguably, cover share plans) are specifically excluded from the underlying directive and therefore it seems likely that contracts relating to employment are not caught by the 1999 Regulations on the basis that they are not 'consumer contracts'. This would appear to be confirmed in *Commerzbank AG v Keen* [2007] IRLR 132.

1.69 Assuming that an entitlement to damages for a lost option can be established, the question of how to value the option will then need to be considered. The straightforward approach, and the one that was apparently adopted by the plaintiff in *Micklefield v SAC Technology Ltd* [1992] 1 All ER 275 (see above), is simply to calculate the profit that the holder of the option would have realized had he or she exercised the option at the date of termination of employment and then immediately sold the shares for their market value. For example, if an executive has an option to acquire 10,000 shares at 50p per share and the share value on termination is 75p, the loss would be £2,500 (10,000 × 25p). However, this method disregards the 'time value' of an option, which can often be quite considerable. To take account of that value, a more sophisticated approach would be required. Various valuation techniques have been evolved for use in the traded options market of the stock exchange (of which the most popular is the Black-Scholes formula). Companies also have to calculate the fair value of options for accounting purposes. However, any valuation of an option to include its time value is likely to be very subjective. Furthermore, the valuation techniques for traded options are not particularly appropriate for employee options. A court may therefore prefer to adopt the simpler approach of calculating the gain in the option at the time of termination of employment, ignoring the time value. Awards under long-term incentive plans could be valued in a similar way by taking the market value of the underlying shares at the time of termination.

1.70 The position is even less certain in relation to future options and awards that would have been granted to an employee. It seems clear that an employee who, at the date of termination, has no more than a promise from his or her employer that he or she will be considered for the grant of options will not be able to recover damages for loss of those options (*O'Laoire v Jackel International Ltd* [1991] IRLR 170). However, an employee may, subject to any exclusion wording, be able to argue that he or she has a contractual entitlement (either express or implied) to receive future grants. Whether such grants will have any value will depend on whether they would have become exercisable or vested during the employee's notice period.

Perks

1.71 'Perks' are an increasingly important part of an employee's remuneration package and damages may be awarded to cover the loss of any 'perk' to which the employee is contractually entitled.

Company car   Damages may be awarded for the loss of a company car. In making   **1.72**
such an award, the court will have to assess the value of the benefit that the use of
the car gives to the employee. Thus there would be no claim if the car were used
exclusively for business purposes. Very often, however, the use of a company car is
not subject to any restriction and, in such circumstances, the judge will have to
assess the ratio of private use to business use. For example, in *Shove v Downs Surgical
plc* [1984] 1 All ER 7, Mr Shove successfully recovered £10,000 for the loss of use
of a Daimler over a period of 30 months, the notice period under Mr Shove's
contract. The judge based his assessment on the AA's estimate of the weekly cost of
running a car of this kind and also took into account the ratio of private use to
business use. The judge also found that Mr Shove was entitled to free petrol and
included this in his award (see also **8.12**).

Other perks   Damages may also be awarded for the loss of other perks such as free   **1.73**
travel passes, rent-free accommodation (*Ivory v Palmer* [1975] ICR 340), free medical
insurance (*Shove*), and subsidized loans or mortgages. The loss of such perks must
be measured in monetary terms—that is, the cost to the employee of making equivalent arrangements. It should always be remembered that damages for the loss of
these perks is limited to the damages period.

The assessment of compensation for loss of fringe benefits is considered in greater   **1.74**
detail in Chapter 8.

Pensions

Damages may be awarded for the loss of pension rights in wrongful dismissal if   **1.75**
there is a contractual right to a pension, provided that the loss is not too remote. In
Silvey v Pendragon plc [2001] IRLR 685, the Court of Appeal ruled that an employee
is entitled to claim damages for any enhanced pension rights lost as a result of
the employer's repudiation. Such loss was not too remote, because it was within the
reasonable contemplation of the parties when the contract was made (that is, at
the time, it was not unlikely that, if the employer gave 12 weeks' notice to the
employee as he approached his 55th birthday and he was a member of the scheme,
he would lose pension rights on his 55th birthday—but note *Beach v Reed Corrugated
Cases Ltd* [1956] 1 WLR 807, in which the plaintiff was not entitled to certain
pension benefits and so his claim that these should be taken into account in assessing
damages for wrongful dismissal was rejected).

Traditionally, the loss (which can conveniently be called 'future loss') has been seen   **1.76**
as the difference between the value of the pension at the date of leaving (namely, the
date on which the employee was wrongfully dismissed and employment ended)
and the value of what the pension would have been at the date on which the
contract could have been lawfully terminated (usually, the end date of the period of
notice required lawfully to terminate the employment contract or the expiry date
of a fixed-term contract)—that is, the normal 'damages period'. It is not correct
to use the period to normal retirement date if this is beyond the damages period

(see *Bold v Brough Nicholson & Hall Ltd* [1963] 2 All ER 849). Accordingly, the damages award should be a cash sum that reflects that difference in value (subject to any relevant adjustments referred to below and grossing up for any tax payable on the damages award). In calculating this amount of loss, it is necessary to distinguish between a defined-contribution scheme—typically a money-purchase scheme—and a defined-benefits scheme—typically a final salary scheme (see Chapter 9 for a brief description of varieties of pension scheme).

1.77 In relation to a defined-contribution scheme, the loss is generally calculated by adding the total lost contributions over the damages period. A number of deductions should be made: first, an appropriate allowance for mitigation; second, the possibility of withdrawal (namely, the fact that the employee might have left the job for some reason during the damages period) and other contingencies (such as death); third, a reduction to represent accelerated receipt (see **1.174**).

1.78 In relation to a defined-benefits scheme, it is suggested that the correct way to calculate the difference between what the pension was worth at the time of dismissal and what it would have been worth at the end of the damages period is to assess the capital value of the difference between the two. Another way to put this is: calculate what sum the claimant needs in order to purchase an annuity that will put him or her in the position in which he or she would have been at the end of the damages period (taking into account any pension benefits provided by the erstwhile employer). This will usually be the difference between a deferred pension at the date of dismissal and what a deferred pension would have been at the end of the damages period. In the case of a final-salary scheme, pension often accrues annually on a specified fraction of final salary. Thus, in simple terms, if the damages period is one year and the fraction is 1/60th, one would need to calculate the cost of purchasing an annuity that will provide 1/60th of final salary from normal retirement date. However, in practice, the position may well be more complicated than this. In particular, because the employer will be required to revalue the ex-employee's deferred pension, the difference between what the pension would have been and the deferred pension on leaving is to this extent reduced. Also, as with a defined-contribution scheme, relevant adjustments will have to be made for mitigation, withdrawal, contingencies, and accelerated receipt (although note that, in calculating the loss of an annuity, accelerated receipt may already have been taken into account).

Expert evidence

1.79 An actuary will usually be required to make the calculation described in **1.78** above. A simpler method would be to use the 'contributions' method as described at **1.77** above. Indeed, where the damages period is relatively short (see *Silvey v Pendragon plc* [2001] IRLR 685), this method may produce an outcome that is not materially different from that produced by the method described at **1.77** above (see *The Halcyon Skies* [1976] 1 All ER 856 and *Bold v Brough, Nicholson and Hall Ltd* [1963] 2 All ER 849). But the contributions method is a very rough-and-ready method of valuing pension loss and becomes increasingly unreliable the longer the damages period.

Calculating future loss of pension

(a) Ascertain the damages period (subject to the duty to mitigate) by reference to: **1.80**
  • the period of notice; or
  • the remainder of the term where there is a fixed-term contract without express provision for early termination.
(b) Loss equals either the lost contributions during the damages period or the cost of an annuity to make up the shortfall between the pension benefits provided to the claimant and what the pension would have been worth at the end of the damages period. (Note that an adjustment may have to be made to take account of any contributions that the employee would have been required to make during the damages period.)
(c) Make deductions (if any) for the possibility of withdrawal from the scheme and other contingencies.
(d) Apply a discount for accelerated receipt (unless already taken into account at (b) above—for example, in the cost of the annuity).
(e) Gross up for any tax payable on the damages award.

There is a further issue as to the extent to which one should take into account salary **1.81** increases during the damages period. To the extent that increases are taken into account for loss of salary, then it is submitted that the same should apply to pension loss (see *Gunton v London Borough of Richmond* [1980] 2 All ER 577, in which no salary increase was awarded, and *Clark v BET* [1997] IRLR 348, in which it was).

Damages for past loss?

The compensatable loss so far reviewed has been described as 'future loss'. This is **1.82** because it relates to loss of pension arising from not being employed during the damages period. Is compensation available for 'past loss'—namely, loss of all or part of the pension accrued as at the date of wrongful dismissal?

There is unlikely to be any 'past loss' in respect of a defined-contribution scheme **1.83** unless the claimant suffers a penalty on leaving the scheme. But even here, it is likely that the loss would have been suffered at the end of the damages period in any event.

In the case of a defined-benefits scheme, it is submitted that there is an argument **1.84** for such compensation in at least two situations. First, where the claimant is only entitled to repayment of contributions, but would have been entitled to a deferred pension at the end of the damages period, the loss would be the difference between the repaid contributions and the value of the deferred pension. Second, where even though the claimant would not have had an increase in salary during the damages period, it would be the case that, had he or she been employed during the damages period, the claimant's pension in respect of the period to the date of dismissal would have increased in value. For example, a deferred pension in a final-salary scheme may be based on salary during the last year of employment. Assume that a claimant's salary has been increased during the last six months prior to dismissal and the claimant was entitled to six months' notice. It follows that, had the claimant been employed during the notice period at this level of salary, the deferred pension would be larger because the last year's salary would have increased. A similar situation could arise where the pension is based on, say, an average of the last three years' salary or even an average calculated over the whole career. This loss should be compensatable. Again, the loss would be the difference between the deferred pension and what the deferred pension would have been had it been higher to reflect the salary.

1.85 The issue of pension loss in unfair dismissal and discrimination cases before employment tribunals is considered in Chapter 9, where fundamentally different principles apply. The chapter considers making an award in respect of the State Second Pension (S2P) element of State Pension. Arguably, a wrongfully dismissed employee has the right to such an award. Of course, if a claimant pursues a wrongful dismissal claim and an unfair dismissal claim, there should not be double recovery for the same loss.

Expenses

1.86 Expenses cannot be recovered as damages for wrongful dismissal because such payments are mere reimbursement for expenditure incurred by the employee on the employer's behalf. The payment of 'phoney' expenses may result in the contract being held illegal, thereby preventing the employee from recovering any damages at all (see *Napier v National Business Agency Ltd* [1951] 2 All ER 264).

Other items

1.87 Damages for wrongful dismissal may include compensation for the loss of other rights either arising out of or connected with the employment so long as the loss is foreseeable within the rule in *Hadley v Baxendale* (1854) 9 Exch 341.

Loss of chance of redundancy pay

1.88 Damages may be awarded for loss of redundancy pay where it is shown that the employee would have been made redundant in the damages period. For example, in *Basnett v J & Jackson Ltd* [1976] IRLR 154, Mr Basnett was wrongfully dismissed on the basis of redundancy three years before his fixed-term contract was due to expire. He argued that if he had been kept on, he would have been entitled to an enhanced payment at the end of that period due to his longer service. The judge, having heard evidence as to the fluctuating state of the building industry, concluded that there was 'half a chance' of this happening and awarded half the enhanced payment.

For a claim to succeed, it must be shown that the risk of redundancy was a real **1.89** one—that is, that the employee was likely to be made redundant at the relevant time. The more remote the possibility, the lower the award.

Loss of right to bring an unfair dismissal claim

At one time, it was suggested that, where an employer dismisses an employee with **1.90** no notice or less notice than that required and thereby prevents the employee from being able to bring an unfair dismissal claim successfully, damages may be recovered to compensate him or her for the loss of his or her statutory rights (*per* Browne-Wilkinson J in *Robert Cort & Son Ltd v Charman* [1981] IRLR 437). However, in *Virgin Net Ltd v Harper* [2004] IRLR 390, the Court of Appeal emphatically rejected this argument. In *Harper*, the employment tribunal found that the claimant had been wrongfully dismissed and awarded her compensation for her loss of notice pay and £30,844.57 by way of damages for the amount that she would have recovered had she qualified to bring an unfair dismissal claim, which it held would have been successful. The EAT allowed the employer's appeal against the award of damages for the loss of a chance of recovering compensation for unfair dismissal ([2003] IRLR 831). The Court of Appeal upheld the EAT's ruling, saying that it was not open to the courts through the machinery of an award for damages for wrongful dismissal to circumvent the statutory time limits laid down by Parliament for bringing an unfair dismissal claim—particularly where it had been open to Parliament to extend those time limits in cases in which an employee had been wrongfully dismissed, but it had chosen not to do so. In the present case, the claimant did not lose the right to bring an unfair dismissal claim because, in the judgment of the Court of Appeal, she never had the right, as she fell short of the one-year continuous service requirement.

The decision in *Harper* reflects the current judicial policy in resisting the develop- **1.91** ment of common law remedies for breach of contract where Parliament has provided for a statutory remedy for unfair dismissal (*Johnson v Unisys* [2001] IRLR 279), but the reasoning is not entirely convincing and may be open to challenge in the light of the Court of Appeal's ruling in *Edwards v Chesterfield Royal Hospital NHS Foundation Trust* [2010] IRLR 702, in which the *ratio* of *Johnson* is restricted to cases in which the claimant seeks to rely on the implied duty of trust and confidence as a contractual restriction on the right to dismiss. It is also inconsistent with the principles on which damages are normally assessed (see, for example, the Court of Appeal's approach to pension rights accruing in the notice period in *Silvey v Pendragon plc* [2001] IRLR 685): if the employee had been given notice, she would have qualified for the right to bring an unfair dismissal claim. The reason why she did not qualify was her employer's wrongful act and the damages awarded by the employment tribunal reflected that loss. It may be questioned whether Parliament's failure to extend the effective date of termination in such circumstances has any relevance to ordinary principles on which damages for breach of contract are calculated.

Nonetheless, the Court of Appeal's ruling (which, at the time of writing, is under appeal to the House of Lords) is binding on employment tribunals in cases in which dismissal is wrongful in the sense that the employer has failed to give the correct period of statutory notice.

1.92   Logically, the same reasoning should apply where an employer fails to follow a contractual disciplinary procedure and the 'damages' period is extended to reflect the length of time that it would have taken had such procedure been followed (see breach of contractual procedures above). In *Raspin v United News Shops Ltd* [1999] IRLR 9, the EAT ruled that it was open to an employment tribunal to make an award for the loss of the opportunity to bring an unfair dismissal claim where the claimant would have qualified to bring an unfair dismissal claim had the employer followed its disciplinary procedure. Moreover, the EAT indicated that such an award may be substantial if the employee could show that either, if he or she had been dismissed, the dismissal would have been unfair, or (assuming that the procedure had been complied with) that he or she would not have been dismissed.

1.93   The question whether the ruling in *Raspin* is still good law is open to debate: the decision was not overruled by the Court of Appeal in *Harper*. The EAT in *Harper* [2003] IRLR 831, 836, also refused to overrule it on the basis that it was unclear whether such a claim was based on the form and manner of the dismissal, or something that preceded the dismissal, but the House of Lords' ruling in *Eastwood v Magnox Electric plc*; *McCabe v Cornwall County Council* [2004] IRLR 733 would suggest that a dismissal in such circumstances would fall within the former rather than the latter, and therefore, applying the logic of the Court of Appeal in *Harper*, the claim for loss of a chance could fall within the exclusion area defined in *Johnson v Unisys*—but this must now been seen in the light of the Court of Appeal's ruling in *Edwards* (referred to in **1.43** above).

Damages for distress

1.94   As a general rule, no damages are awarded for the distress and vexation associated with a wrongful dismissal (*Addis v Gramophone Co Ltd* [1909] AC 488, confirmed in *Bliss v South East Thames Regional Health Authority* [1985] IRLR 308 and *O'Laoire v Jackel International Ltd* [1991] IRLR 70). The rule was confirmed by the House of Lords in *Johnson v Unisys* [2001] IRLR 279. The same rule applies to unfair dismissals (see below **6.10**).

Stigma damages

1.95   The main exception to the principle that damages will not be awarded for injury to feelings caused by the dismissal is where 'stigma' damages may be recovered.

1.96   The right to claim so-called 'stigma' damages was first recognized by the House of Lords in *Malik v Bank of Credit and Commerce International SA* (*in compulsory liquidation*) [1997] IRLR 462 (the *BCCI* case), in which the House of Lords ruled that such claims were possible where an employer conducted a corrupt and dishonest business, giving rise to a breach of the implied duty of trust and confidence, and the claimant could show that the loss was reasonably foreseeable as a 'serious possibility' as a consequence of the employer's actions. As Lord Steyn (with whom Lords Goff, Mackay, and Mustill agreed) said:

> [P]rovided a relevant breach of contract can be established, and the requirements of causation, remoteness and mitigation can be satisfied, there is no good reason why in the field of employment law recovery of financial loss in respect of damage to reputation caused by breach of contract is necessarily excluded.

Even so, it was recognized that the limiting principles of causation, remoteness, **1.97** and mitigation provide formidable obstacles to such claims succeeding. In practice, it may be difficult to show that an employee's employment prospects were, in fact, damaged by the employer's behaviour. In *Ali v Bank of Credit and Commerce International SA* (*in compulsory liquidation*) (*No 3*) [2002] IRLR 460, one of a number of test cases to have arisen in the context of the *BCCI* litigation, the Court of Appeal upheld the judge's ruling that BCCI's highly publicized dishonest conduct of its business amounted to a breach of trust and confidence, and placed a stigma on former employees who worked for the Bank, which hindered them from finding alternative employment and caused them financial loss, but ultimately concluded that, on the particular facts, the judge was entitled to conclude that there were other compelling explanations why the particular claimants had failed to find fresh employment (not least their own lack of honesty and integrity); therefore the judge had been entitled to conclude that the stigma was not the cause of their loss.

Nevertheless, the Court of Appeal considered that the judge had adopted what it **1.98** termed an 'over-elaborate' legal test in determining the issue of causation in relation to particular claimants. The Court ruled that, where an employee alleges that his or her job prospects have been affected by a breach of the implied duty of trust and confidence, the question to be determined is 'but for' the breach, what would the prospective employer have done and what would have been the outcome for the employee? This was, by definition, a hypothetical question that a court could sometimes answer with a high degree of confidence, but which, on other occasions, it would have to take 'a broad view on a number of imponderables' in order to answer. In each case, the central question was whether the stigma had a 'real or substantial' effect on the former employee finding new employment and, if so, how great the effect was. In answering the question, it may be necessary to consider the number of jobs for which the individual applied, whether the applications were sensibly targeted and well presented, how many interviews were obtained, how the interview went, and any stated reason for rejection. Although each application should be looked at separately, the question of stigma should be looked at in terms of the job search as a whole. It was not necessary, as a matter of law, for a former employee to call evidence from prospective employers as to the effect that the alleged stigma had on a particular application (although, from an evidential

31

point of view, such evidence would assist in proving the claim) provided that it could be shown that the stigma played a part in the overall failure to find employment. The Court also recognized that, in appropriate cases, it was open to a court to award damages on the basis of a 'loss of a chance' provided that the claimant could establish causation either by showing a 'general prejudice' amongst prospective employers or specific prejudice of a particular employer. In addition, it may be open to a judge to conclude that an employee would have found a job more quickly 'but for' the stigma suffered as a result of the dismissal.

1.99 There are many unresolved issues arising from the *BCCI* litigation, such as whether 'stigma' attaches to all employees who work for an organization guilty of corrupt and dishonest practices, or whether it is restricted to those who are employed in particular roles. Lord Nicholls (with whom Lords Mackay and Goff agreed) seems to suggest that this problem is likely to be particularly relevant to the issue of causation.

1.100 The decision also opens up the possibility that 'stigma' damages can be recovered for other breaches of the implied duty of trust and confidence. The answer to this question remains to be seen, but to date, the courts appear to have been unwilling to extend the *BCCI* ruling beyond situations in which the employer has behaved in a corrupt and dishonest manner, and have rejected the argument that damages can be recovered for any stigma associated with a peremptory and unfair dismissal (*Johnson v Unisys* [2001] IRLR 279).

Damages to career prospects

1.101 It is also possible that the general principle in *Addis* (see **1.94** above) does not apply where the pecuniary loss suffered by the employee is a foreseeable consequence of the breach of contract in accordance with normal contractual principles. Such cases include those in which the nature of the contract is to provide for status (for example, apprenticeships), or for the promotion or preservation of a reputation (for example, advertising), or for the opportunity to appear in a prestigious place or part.

1.102 The successful cases are almost all concerned with actors or writers who have argued that their career prospects were damaged as a result of the dismissal. For example, in *Marbe v George Edwardes (Daly's Theatre) Ltd* [1928] 1 KB 269, an American actress, wishing to establish her reputation in London, sued her employers when, in breach of contract, they refused to give her a part in a play. The Court of Appeal awarded her damages for the duration of the contract plus an amount representing the loss to her reputation that had been caused by the defendant's action. (See also *Joseph v National Magazine Co Ltd* [1958] 3 All ER 52.) The same principle may apply to other employments in which such an opportunity is an essential part of the consideration, or in the rather exceptional cases in which the employer is under an obligation to provide the employee with work as well as wages. But the Court of Appeal's refusal to strike out the claimant's claim for damages in *Edwards* [2010] IRLR 702, based on the damage to a doctor's reputation (that is, loss of professional status) when dismissed for gross misconduct that had not been substantiated in a properly conduct disciplinary process, suggests that the principle is by no means limited to the reputations of performers or writers (see also *Chagger v Abbey National plc* [2010] IRLR 47, referred to at **19.48** in Part IV).

As stated above, damage to career prospects is foreseeable in contracts of appren- **1.103** ticeship. For example, in *Dunk v George Waller & Son Ltd* [1970] 2 QB 163, it was held that an apprentice who was wrongfully dismissed was entitled to recover damages for the unexpired period of the apprenticeship and for a period of nearly two years thereafter as compensation for the damage to his future prospects caused by the loss of tuition and training. It is unclear whether the same principles would apply to a young person on a youth training scheme.

A possible further exception is where damages for distress are contemplated by the **1.104** contract itself. This is suggested by the High Court's decision in *Cox v Philips Industries Ltd* [1976] 3 All ER 161, in which the employer offered Mr Cox promotion to stop him from leaving and joining a rival. Subsequently, he was dismissed and became ill as a result. The judge awarded Mr Cox £500 for vexation and distress on the ground that it was in the contemplation of the parties that a breach of the agreement might cause him the anxiety, frustration, and sickness that he did, in fact, suffer. However, a real question mark hangs over the correctness of this decision in the light of the critical comments made by the Court of Appeal in *Bliss v South Thames Regional Health Authority* [1985] IRLR 308 and subsequent case law developments.

E. Calculating the Statutory Notice Entitlement

Statutory notice periods

There are special statutory rules that apply to the calculation of the periods of notice **1.105** guaranteed by ERA 1996, s 86.

The following table sets out the minimum periods of notice that an employee, other **1.106** than an excepted employee (see **1.09** above), is entitled to receive for each year of employment.

Period of continuous employment (years)	Minimum period (weeks)
Less than 2 (but one month or more)	1
At least 2, but less than 3	2
At least 3, but less than 4	3

Period of continuous employment (years)	Minimum period (weeks)
At least 4, but less than 5	4
At least 5, but less than 6	5
At least 6, but less than 7	6
At least 7, but less than 8	7
At least 8, but less than 9	8
At least 9, but less than 10	9
At least 10, but less than 11	10
At least 11, but less than 12	11
12 or more	12

The statutory formula

1.107   Statutory minimum notice is calculated in accordance with the rules set out in the ERA 1996, ss 87–91, and depends on whether the employee has normal working hours or no normal working hours.

1.108   Where the employee has normal working hours, an employer has to pay him or her a week's pay, or an appropriate proportion thereof, for each week (or part-week) of the statutory notice period during which the employee is:

(a) ready and willing to work, but is not given work by his or her employer;
(b) incapable of work through sickness or injury; or
(c) absent from work wholly or partly because of pregnancy, childbirth, adoption leave, parental leave, or paternity leave; or
(d) absent from work in accordance with the terms of his or her employment relating to holidays (ERA 1996, s 88(1)).

1.109   Where there are normal working hours, a week's pay shall be 'not less than the amount of remuneration for that part of normal working hours calculated at the average hourly rate of remuneration produced by dividing a week's pay by the number of normal working hours' (ERA 1996, s 88(1)–(3)). This formula takes account of the different patterns of employments with normal working hours.

1.110   Where the employee has no normal working hours, he or she is entitled to 'a sum not less than a week's pay' for each week of the statutory notice period during which he or she is ready and willing to do work of a reasonable nature to earn a week's pay. This latter condition does not apply where the employee is incapable of work due to sickness, is absent because of pregnancy or childbirth, or is absent from work in accordance with the terms of his or her employment relating to holidays (ERA 1996, s 89(1) and (2)). Holiday pay and sick pay are set off against the employer's liability (see below).

1.111   See Chapter 7 for the meaning of 'normal working hours', 'a week's pay', and 'remuneration'.

Any sick pay, Statutory Sick Pay (SSP), Statutory Maternity Pay (SMP), maternity **1.112** pay, or holiday pay paid to the employee may go towards meeting the employer's statutory liability, as may any payment for sickness or injury benefit (ss 88(1) and (2), 89, and 90). Payments that the employer has already made in respect of the statutory liability may also be set off. So, for example, if the employer wrongly terminates the contract halfway through the notice period, the employee is entitled to recover only those damages that relate to the outstanding period (ERA 1996, s 91(3)).

The employer is not under an obligation to make payments in respect of periods **1.113** when the employee has requested time off work for public duties, trade union duties or activities, or job seeking (ERA 1996, s 91(1)). Neither is the employee entitled to statutory notice pay if he or she takes part in a strike during the notice period (ERA 1996, s 91(2)).

The right to notice pay ceases if the employee breaches the contract and the employer **1.114** rightfully treats the breach as terminating the contract. So, for example, the employer's obligation ceases if an employee commits an act of gross misconduct during the notice period (ERA 1996, s 91(3)).

Damages may also be reduced if the employee has failed to mitigate his or her loss **1.115** (*Westwood v Secretary of State for Employment* [1984] 1 All ER 874). See **1.152** below.

Calculating statutory notice pay

> **Damages period = Statutory notice period (subject to duty to mitigate)**   **1.116**

£

Number of weeks' statutory notice period × Amount of one week's pay =
Less

— Sick pay
— Holiday pay
— Other payments made by the employer
— State benefits
Final award =

Relationship with contractual notice

ERA 1996, ss 87–91 do not apply if the notice 'to be given' by the employer is 'at **1.117** least one week more' than the notice required by s 86(1) of the ERA 1996 (ERA 1996, s 87(4)). Thus, if the contractual notice, express or implied, exceeds the employee's statutory entitlement, the statutory provisions do not apply. For example, if a clerk has been employed for six months and the contract states that the contract may be terminated by one month's noice, the employee's entitlement is based on the contractual one-month period, not the statutory period of one week (see **1.06**).

F. Pay in Lieu of Notice

1.118 It is common practice for employers to make a 'payment in lieu of notice' but, as Lord Browne-Wilkinson has pointed out in *Delaney v Staples* [1992] IRLR 191, the expression 'payment in lieu' may be used 'to describe many types of payment the legal analysis of which differs'. His Lordship identified four principal categories, as follows.

(a) *Where the employer gives proper notice of termination to the employee, but does not require the employee to attend his or her place of working during the notice period* This is commonly referred to as 'garden leave'. The wages due to the employee during such a period of garden leave may be either paid as a 'lump sum'—that is, as a payment in lieu—or payments may continue to be made on a weekly or monthly basis.

(b) *Where the contract of employment itself provides for the employment to be terminated on notice or on payment in lieu of notice* Such a provision is common in service agreements of more senior executives, because it enables the employer both to terminate lawfully by making such a payment and to continue to enforce any contractual provisions that take effect after the termination, such as restrictive covenants.

(c) *Where the contract of employment itself provides that an agreed sum is payable on termination* Known as an 'agreed damages clause', in this case, there will be no breach of contract provided that the employer pays the agreed sum.

(d) *Where the employer terminates the contract without notice* The employer may dismiss the employee summarily and at the same time tender a payment in lieu of proper notice. In *Delaney*, the House of Lords confirmed that such a payment is an advance payment of damages for wrongful dismissal and cannot be regarded as 'wages' (*Dixon v Stenor Ltd* [1973] ICR 157).

See also *Leech v Preston Borough Council* [1985] IRLR 337, in which the EAT classified Lord Browne-Wilkinson's fourth category as the 'technical' meaning of a payment in lieu and the first as its 'colloquial' meaning, and *Abrahams v Performing Rights Society* [1995] IRLR 486, in which the Court of Appeal appears to have treated a clause that gave the employer a right to terminate a contract by giving two years' notice or an equivalent payment in lieu as falling within Lord Browne-Wilkinson's second category. Similarly, in *Jenkins v City Index* (ELA Briefing July/August 2000), an employment tribunal concluded that a contract that provided for a six-month termination period, but gave the employer the right to terminate summarily with a payment in lieu, fell within Lord Browne-Wilkinson's second category.

1.119 Below, the phrase 'payment in lieu' is used to cover both its technical and more colloquial usage, but not cases in which the payment is provided for by the contract itself.

What the payment should cover

Although it is customary for a payment in lieu to cover wages or salary only, the **1.120** payment should in fact cover all of those items that could have been included in a claim for damages unless the contract provides to the contrary. Thus the loss of fringe benefits, use of a company car, mortgage subsidy, etc should all be taken into account, and an approximate value calculated and added to the payment. Any contractual bonuses, overtime, or shift premia that would have been earned during the notice period should also be included. For example, in *Silvey v Pendragon plc* [2001] IRLR 686, the Court of Appeal ruled that the fact that the employee had accepted a 'payment in lieu of notice' (where no provision was made for such a payment in his contract) did not prevent him from suing for damages for lost pension rights. However, where an employee accepts a payment consisting of wages alone in full and final settlement of his or her contractual claims, the acceptance is likely to be seen as a binding agreement not to sue in respect of the outstanding common law claims and therefore precludes a claim for any further sums due. Such acceptance may be express or implied (*Greene v Church Commissioners for England* [1974] Ch D 467; *Callisher v Bischoffshein* [1870] 5 QB 449). On the other hand, mere acceptance of a termination payment of itself will not necessarily prevent an employee from claiming damages for other losses consequent upon dismissal.

The acceptance of a redundancy payment under a government compensation scheme **1.121** does not necessarily preclude a dockworker from suing for his or her statutory notice pay (*Trotter v Forth Ports Authority* [1991] IRLR 419). In *Trotter*, the Court of Session rejected the employer's argument that acceptance of a redundancy payment itself meant that the employee had waived his rights to his statutory notice pay.

Taxation of payment in lieu

The tax regime for employment income is now to be found in Pts 2–7 of IT(EP)A **1.122** 2003 (which replaces the Income and Corporation Taxes Act 1988 [ICTA 1988]).

The term 'employee' is defined to include 'office holder' in s 5 of IT(EP)A 2003. **1.123**

'Earnings' are defined as 'any salary, wages or fee', 'any gratuity or other profit or **1.124** incidental benefit of any kind obtained by the employee', or 'anything else that constitutes an emolument of the employment' (IT(EP)A 2003, s 62(2)).

It was well established under the old law that to qualify as an emolument, the **1.125** payment must be made with 'reference to the services the employee renders by virtue of his office, it must be something in the nature of a reward for services past, present or future' (*Hochstrasser v Mayes* (1960) AC 376, 388, and *Shilton v Wilmhurst* [1991] 1 AC 684).

The HMRC's views on the taxation of such payments are set out in the Employment **1.126** Income Manual (EIM) available online at the HMRC website.

1.127   The four categories identified by Lord Browne-Wilkinson in *Delaney v Staples* are a useful starting point in considering how this principle applies to the taxation of payments in lieu.

Garden leave

1.128   Payments falling within the first category (payments made to an employee on 'garden leave') clearly amount to 'earnings' for the purpose of IT(EP)A 2003, s 62(2)(a). National Insurance contributions (NICs) will also fall to be paid on such payments in the normal way (s 6(1) of the Social Security Contributions and Benefits Act 1992 [SSCBA 1992]).

Payment in lieu of notice clauses

1.129   Payments falling within the second category (payments made pursuant to a contractual right to make a payment in lieu of notice) also count as earnings for the purpose of IT(EP)A 2003, s 62(2). For example, in *EMI Group Electronics Ltd v Coldicutt* (*HM Inspector of Taxes*) [1999] IRLR 630, the Court of Appeal ruled that payments in lieu of notice made pursuant to a clause that provided that 'the Company reserves the right to make payments of the equivalent salary in lieu of notice' were taxable because they were made 'in return for acting as or being an employee'. The payment is regarded as 'security or continuity of salary which the employee required as an inducement to enter employment'. Such payments are taxable under ITEPA 2003, s 62 (see EIM 00515 and EIM 00670) and are also subject to NICs under the statutory provisions referred to above.

1.130   The approach taken in the *EMI* case is also likely to apply where the contract gives an employer a discretion to make a payment in lieu (even though the payment is not guaranteed) either on termination or at any stage during the notice period and the employer exercises the discretion conferred by the contract. In such circumstances, the fact that the payment is made in accordance with such a provision will mean that there is no breach of contract (*SCA Packaging Ltd v Revenue and Customs Commissioners* [2007] EWHC 270).

1.131   The position is less clear where the employer elects not to exercise that discretion because, on the face of it, any subsequent payment may be regarded as damages for breach of contract (*Cerberus Software Ltd v Rowley* [2001] IRLR 160), but it is clear from the guidance referred to in **1.124** that the HMRC will scrutinize such payments carefully and may conclude that, in reality, the employer has exercised the rights conferred by the payment in lieu of notice clause.

1.132   In some circumstances, it may also be possible to imply such a provision, for example, that such payments are routinely made and amount to 'custom and practice' (see EIM 12977), although HMRC accepts that the normal principles will apply in determining whether such a custom or practice is established—that is, where there is a procedure for making a critical assessment in the particular circumstances and the payment is not made automatically, then a custom is unlikely (see *Solectron Scotland Ltd v Roper* [2004] IRLR 4). Nonetheless, where a custom or practice is established, the payment will be treated in the same way as if there is an express right.

However, it would appear from the HMRC guidance that HMRC takes the view **1.133** that such a payment will be taxable where an employee has a 'reasonable expectation' of receiving such a payment even where there is no express or implied right to receive such a payment, and HMRC takes the view that such a payment may be taxable under IT(EP)A 2003, s 62 (EIM 00640). The problem with this approach is that it blurs the distinction between categories (b) and (d) in *Delaney*, and it is certainly arguable that, even if there is a reasonable expectation, so long as the payment is a non-contractual payment, it is not taxable, although much will depend on the circumstances.

Agreed payments

Payments falling within the third category (where the contract itself provides for an **1.134** agreed sum payable on termination) count as earnings for the purpose of IT(EP)A 2003, s 62(2). For example, in *Williams v Simmonds* [1981] STC 715, Mr Simmonds received an agreed sum determined in accordance with the terms of his service agreement as 'compensation for loss of office'. It was held that the sum was subject to income tax in the ordinary way as an emolument from Mr Simmonds' employment.

More controversially, it has been held that, where there is a payment in lieu of notice **1.135** by agreement, the proceeds may be taxable. This issue arose in *Richardson v Delaney* [2001] IRLR 663, in which an employee, who was under notice on 'garden leave', received an 'agreed' payment for the balance of the notice period as part of the terms of settlement that were mutually agreed prior to termination. The High Court ruled that this payment was an 'emolument' under what was then ICTA 1988, s 19 (now IT(EP)A 2003, s 62) and was therefore taxable. The key finding in the case appears to have been that there had been no breach of the contract of employment in the making of the payment, because Mr Delaney was initially given notice in accordance with the terms of the contract and subsequently his employment was terminated by mutual agreement. In effect, the parties had agreed a payment in lieu of notice clause before the employment terminated. Concerns were raised in the aftermath of the *Delaney* decision that the Court's reasoning might extend to any situation in which a compromise agreement was reached prior to termination of employment. This led the HMRC's Tax Policy Unit to issue a statement clarifying its position. This states that:

> in the absence of a payment in lieu of notice clause in the contractual arrangements (and assuming that no expectation to receive such a payment otherwise existed) [HMRC] would not have argued that s. 19 of ICTA 1988 applies in this case. The reason that s. 19 ICTA was argued was . . . that the package received by the employee was essentially the same as would have been paid had the employer formally exercised its discretion to make a PILON [payment in lieu of notice]. In the absence of a breach

of contract in the events surrounding the termination, the reasonable inference was that the source of the payment lay in that provision, albeit in this case that the employer chose to instigate negotiations concerning the form and amount of payment.

1.136 The Sch E manual (now the EIM) has been amended to refer to *Delaney*. It should be noted, however, that this is a statement of general policy and that each case will be judged according to its own factual circumstances. Therefore, despite this guidance, some uncertainty remains.

1.137 Such payments are also subject to NICs under the statutory provisions referred to above.

Damages

1.138 Payments falling within the fourth category (that is, where the employee is wrongfully dismissed, but an employer either at the time of dismissal or subsequently offers a payment in lieu of notice) are not taxable under IT(EP)A 2003, s 62. However, where the payment is in excess of £30,000, it is taxable under IT(EP)A 2003, s 403(1).

1.139 It is clear from all of the above that the borderline between a payment that is taxable and one that is not is uncertain, but a payment will be treated as damages where:

(a) there is no express or implied payment in lieu of notice clause in the contract, nor, according to HMRC, any expectation of such a payment; or

(b) the employer makes an *ex gratia* payment ('golden handshake') in excess of the amount due under the contract, or makes a payment that is less than that which would be made as a payment in lieu; or

(c) the employer elects not to exercise its rights under such a clause as in *Cerberus Software Ltd v Rowley* [2001] IRLR 160.

1.140 HMRC accepts that, following *Cerebus*:

> [I]t can no longer be assumed . . . that the employer has chosen to make a payment under those contractual provisions if notice is not given. The effect of *Cerebus* is then that whether the discretion has been exercised is a question of fact in each case. The [HMRC] will consider all the surrounding circumstances in making a decision and the *Richardson* case is relevant in that context where it indicates that where the package equates to what would have been paid by the exercise of discretion, there will be a strong presumption that the source of the payment lies in the same place . . .

That context falls within what is now IT(EP)A 2003, s 62(2). So where an employer has a discretion whether or not to make a payment in lieu of notice and elects not to do so and a settlement is reached where the package is along the same lines, there is a risk that HMRC will treat the payment as taxable, although much will depend on the circumstances (see also *Wilson (HM Inspector of Taxes) v Clayton* [2005] IRLR 108).

NICs are not payable on damages for wrongful dismissal and are likewise not payable **1.141** on a payment in lieu offered in settlement of such damages.

Right to sue for payment in lieu

In *Abrahams v Performing Rights Society* [1995] IRLR 486, the Court of Appeal **1.142** ruled that, where there is a contractual right to a payment in lieu of notice, the employee has a right to sue for the payment and is not under a duty to mitigate, the claim being one for liquidated damages, but where an employer has a discretion to make such a payment and elects not to do so, as in *Cerberus Software Ltd v Rowley* [2001] IRLR 160, the employee will be required to sue for damages in the normal way and the rules on mitigation (considered below) apply.

Payment gross or net

It is not unusual for employers to make a payment in lieu of notice on the basis of an **1.143** employee's gross wage or salary. This is only lawful where the payment can be regarded as damages. Where the payment is taxable and subject to NICs, these sums must be deducted in accordance with pay-as-you-earn (PAYE) and NIC regulations.

Furthermore even where the payment represents damages for wrongful dismissal, **1.144** the employer's strict legal obligation is simply to pay the sum that would have been awarded as damages by a court—that is, the net amount that the employee would have received after deduction of tax and NICs (*Jackson v Foster Wheeler (London) Ltd* [1989] IRLR 283). In exceptional cases, however, it may be established that the employer is under an obligation to pay gross rather than net. For example, in *Gothard v Mirror Group Newspapers* [1988] IRLR 396, it was shown that a lump-sum payment in lieu of notice was made as part of an early retirement scheme that was expressed to be 'tax-free' and was accepted by Mr Gothard on that basis. The court held that there was a clear intention, and consequently a contractual obligation, to make the payment gross rather than net.

In any event, there is nothing to prevent an employer from paying the gross amount **1.145** and there may be sound reasons for doing so—for example, to maintain good industrial relations and/or as a financial inducement not to bring a claim for wrongful dismissal.

G. Reduction of Damages

General principles

The object of contractual damages is to compensate employees for the loss caused **1.146** by the employer's breach of contract, but the award should not result in the employee making a profit (*British Guiana Credit Corp v Da Silva* [1965] 1 WLR 248). Thus the third stage in the calculation of damages for wrongful dismissal is to take account of the different factors that might lead to an award being limited to a certain period of time. These include the duty to mitigate, contingencies, such as the possibility that the employee would have left the job anyway, and the fact that payments due under the contract are being received earlier than would otherwise have been the case. Allowance must also be made for tax liabilities.

1.147 Some of these factors, such as the duty to mitigate, apply even where the contract is terminable by a relatively short period of notice, but in general the factors considered in this section are more important where the 'damages period' is substantial.

Mitigation

1.148 The common law requires a dismissed employee to take all reasonable steps to reduce the loss caused by the wrongful dismissal.

1.149 There are two elements to the duty to mitigate are as follows.

(a) Employees are not entitled to sit back and wait until the time at which the contract could have been lawfully terminated and then sue for the loss that accrues during that period; they must take positive steps to find alternative employment. If they fail to do this, the award will be limited to the time before which the court believes that they should have found a new job.

(b) Employees must give credit for any benefits that accrue as a result of dismissal. For example, credit must be given for any income received from a new job during the notice period or for any state benefits received during that time. It is possible that credit should also be given for payments received under an early retirement scheme (*Smoker v London Fire and Civil Defence Authority* [1991] IRLR 271).

1.150 Lawyers often refer to the first element as the 'duty to mitigate in law' and the second element as the 'duty to mitigate in fact', but it should be stressed that both are aspects of what is essentially the same general duty. The distinction is used below purely as a matter of convenience.

1.151 The duty to mitigate also applies to the assessment of unfair dismissal compensation (see Chapter 13, in which the case law is considered in greater detail).

Mitigation in law

1.152 The duty to mitigate means that the employee must take reasonable steps to minimize the loss caused by the dismissal by seeking other employment. If he or she fails to do this, he or she will be penalized. What is reasonable is essentially a question of fact for the court to determine. On the one hand, the employee is not bound to accept the first offer that comes along—particularly if it involves a change of work, reduction in status, or a reduction in pay or other terms and conditions. On the other hand, the employee may, in some circumstances, be required to accept an offer of re-employment from the old employer or even less favourable employment elsewhere if there is no prospect of obtaining a similar position. The following case decisions illustrate the above principles.

(a) The plaintiff was dismissed as a result of a change in the partnership. The new partners offered him his old job back, but he declined their offer.

    Held: He was unreasonable in turning down the offer and was therefore awarded only nominal damages (*Brace v Calder* [1895] 2 QB 253).

(b) The plaintiff was dismissed from his position as managing director of the defendant company. The company offered to re-employ him as assistant managing director in the same company at the same salary, but he refused because acceptance would have meant 'a significant step down'. The judge was satisfied that the plaintiff had acted reasonably in turning down the offer and found that he had also taken other reasonable steps to look for work.

    Held: Full damages would be awarded up to the trial, but would be limited thereafter, because the plaintiff had agreed to look for a new job at a lower salary, which he was likely to find soon after the trial (*Yetton v Eastwoods Froy Ltd* [1966] 3 All ER 353).

(c) The plaintiff was dismissed from his job as managing director of the defendant company. The parent company offered to re-employ him at the same salary. He turned down its offer because he would have had to work with people with whom he had had major disagreements and it was a condition of the offer that he drop his wrongful dismissal claim.

    Held: It was reasonable for him to reject the company's offer on these grounds (*Shindler v Northern Raincoat Co Ltd* [1960] 2 WLR 1038).

1.153 On the positive side, employees may be held to have satisfied their duty to mitigate their loss by setting up a business or becoming self-employed. For example, in *Shove v Downs Surgical plc* [1984] 1 All ER 7, the judge held that Mr Shove had taken reasonable steps to mitigate his loss by setting himself up as a consultant even though the consultancy was not expected to make a profit until its third year.

1.154 **The duty to mitigate and statutory notice** In *Westwood v Secretary of State for Employment* [1984] 1 All ER 874, the House of Lords ruled that the duty to mitigate applies to statutory notice. Their Lordships said that the reference to the employer's 'liability for breach of contract' in s 51 of the Employment Protection (Consolidation) Act 1978 [EP(C)A 1978] (now ERA 1996, s 91(5)) showed that the ordinary common law rules for assessing damages for breach of contract also applied to an employer's liability under the statutory provisions.

1.155 **Assessing the deduction** The effect of a failure to mitigate is that the award of damages will be reduced. The reduction may be made in one of the following ways:

(a) it may be taken into account in determining the appropriate multiplier (see 7.83 below); or

(b) damages may be awarded only in respect of the period up to the time at which the court considers that the employee should have found a new job on equivalent terms.

1.156 It is also open to the court to reduce damages on the grounds that the employee should have found a new job even if it meant a drop in salary. In these circumstances, the recoverable loss will be the difference between the old salary and the new one.

1.157 **The duty to mitigate and payments in lieu of notice**   The duty to mitigate does not apply where an employee sues for the recovery of a payment in lieu of notice. This was the rather surprising conclusion of the Court of Appeal in *Abrahams v Performing Rights Society* [1995] IRLR 487, in which the Court classified such a payment as a 'sum due under a contract' (that is, a contractual debt) rather than damages for wrongful dismissal. Furthermore, Hutchinson LJ stated that the duty to mitigate did not apply even if (as the employers had contended) the sum should be regarded as liquidated damages.

1.158 **Onus of proof**   The burden of showing that the employee has failed to mitigate his or her loss is on the employer (*Fyfe v Scientific Furnishings Ltd* [1989] IRLR 331). As a result, the employer is entitled to particulars of any attempts (successful or otherwise) that the employee has made to find other employment since dismissal.

Mitigation in fact

1.159 The second element to the duty to mitigate is that the employee must give credit for any benefits received as a result of the dismissal.

1.160 **Earnings from a new job**   The main effect of this rule is that the employee must give credit for any earnings received during the damages period. This may include giving credit for other benefits received from the new employment. For example, in *Lavarack v Woods of Colchester Ltd* [1967] 1 QB 278, the court held that it was entitled to take into account the income that Mr Lavarack had received as a result of acquiring shares in his new employer's company. It is also open to the court to take into account the value of other benefits received by the employee in making its overall assessment. Credit must also be given for earnings received in the period of statutory notice (*The Secretary of State for Employment v Wilson* [1977] IRLR 483).

1.161 However, in working out what proportion of the earnings should be taken into account, allowance will be made for any reasonable expenses incurred by the employee in looking for work or setting up in business on his or her own account. This may even include expenditure incurred outside the damages period (see *Westwood v Secretary of State for Employment* [1984] 1 All ER 874).

Example: Mitigation of loss—Earnings from new job

Ms Firth is engaged to work as a designer in London for a fixed term of one year. She is dismissed after six months. She finds a new job in Cheltenham three months after her dismissal. She used to take home £400 net a week and now takes home £300 net a week. She claims £200 as expenses in looking for a new job.

Her damages claim is calculated as follows.

		£
Loss of earnings	26 weeks @ £400 a week	10,400
Less earnings from new job	13 weeks @ £300 a week	3,900
		6,500
Add expenses		200
Total claim (subject to further reduction in respect of such items as state benefits (see below))		£ 6,700

State benefits   Credit must be given for Jobseeker's Allowance (JSA) and other **1.162** state benefits received during the damages period.

It has been held therefore that JSA must be deducted from the award (*Parsons v* **1.163** *BNM Laboratories Ltd* [1963] 2 All ER 658). The same rule applies to supplementary benefit (now income support) (*Lincoln v Hayman* [1982] 1 WLR 488). However, some state benefits are excluded. For example, mobility and attendance allowances have been held to be non-deductible (*Bowker v Rose* (1978) 122 SJ 147). In relation to Family Income Supplement (FIS), it has been held that FIS that has been received is deductible, but FIS that is to be received in respect of loss of future earnings is ignored because of the difficulty in valuing the future benefits (*Gaskill v Preston* [1981] 3 All ER 427). Other statutory payments, such as redundancy pay, have been held to be too remote to be deductible (see **1.173** below).

State benefits and statutory notice pay   Credit must be given for state benefits **1.164** received during the statutory notice period (*Westwood v Secretary of State for Employment* [1984] 1 All ER 874).

This ruling led to a particular problem in relation to the long-term unemployed. **1.165** It was argued that, in deducting the full benefit received during the statutory notice period, no account was taken of the fact that employees would exhaust their entitlement to state benefits sooner than they would have done had employers fulfilled their statutory or contractual obligations. This problem was considered by the House of Lords in *Westwood*, in which the employee was dismissed without the statutory notice or pay in lieu, owing to the insolvency of his employers. Their Lordships held that although the duty to mitigate applied to the provisions guaranteeing minimum periods of notice, and hence the benefits fell to be deducted from the entitlement, the employee need give credit only for the net gain received during the notice period. In the particular circumstances, the net gain was not the sum of the actual benefits received in the notice period of 12 weeks, but the difference between the sum and the lesser amount of supplementary benefits received as a result of his entitlement to unemployment benefit being prematurely curtailed.

1.166 Following the House of Lords' decision in *Westwood*, the Department of Health and Social Security (DHSS—now the Department for Work and Pensions [DWP]) issued new regulations that deal specifically with employees who claim benefit at a time when they have a valid legal claim against their employers for lost notice pay. The Social Security (General Benefit) Amendment Regulations 1984, SI 1984/1259, provide that days covered by payments under the insolvency provisions of the ERA 1996 do not count in determining eligibility for JSA.

1.167 **Payments in lieu of notice**   Despite the decision in *Abrahams v Performing Rights Society* [1995] IRLR 487, a payment in lieu of notice is deductible if it is made by an employer in discharge of the employer's liability to an employee under the employment contract.

1.168 *Ex gratia* **payments**   If these are intended to discharge the employer's liability for wrongful dismissal, they should be deducted from the assessment of damages.

1.169 **Unfair dismissal compensation**   The compensatory element in an award for unfair dismissal is deducted in computing a wrongful dismissal award if it covers the same loss—namely, notice pay and other benefits (*O'Laoire v Jackel International Ltd* [1991] IRLR 70). On the other hand, it will not be deducted if it can be shown that the compensatory award relates to loss suffered outside the notice period, since there would be no 'double' recovery in such circumstances (*O'Laoire*). It may be open to an applicant who is bringing both unfair and wrongful dismissal proceedings to ask the employment tribunal not to make an award in respect of notice pay so as to retain the right to claim these sums in wrongful dismissal proceedings and to preserve the right to recover maximum compensation within the statutory limits. It is doubtful whether the basic award is deductible, because it represents compensation for loss of job security and not damages for dismissal (see *Wilson v National Coal Board* (1980) 130 NLJ 1146).

Remoteness

1.170 Credit need not be given for benefits that are too remote or that accrue to the employee independently of the employer's breach. These are known as 'collateral benefits'. Often, the dividing line between these non-deductible benefits and those discussed above is a narrow one.

1.171 **Collateral employment benefits**   In *Lavarack v Woods of Colchester Ltd* [1967] 1 QB 278, the Court of Appeal rejected the company's argument that, because Mr Lavarack had been released from a restriction that prohibited him from making investments in other companies quoted on the stock exchange whilst in its employment, he should give credit for the profits that he had made on all of his investments in other companies. The Court said that these benefits did not arise as a 'direct result of the dismissal', but were 'collateral' to it and so non-deductible.

Disability insurance and other private pensions   Payments received from a private   **1.172**
pension scheme or disability insurance (*Lewicki v Brown & Root Wimpey Highland
Fabricators Ltd* [1996] IRLR 565) are considered to be collateral benefits and are
not therefore deductible from damages for wrongful dismissal. In *Parry v Cleaver*
[1970] AC 1, the House of Lords held that a policeman's compensation for personal
injuries should not be reduced by the amount that he received as a disablement
pension from the police pension fund. Their Lordships did not think that it made any
difference whether the pension was payable as of right or discretionary. A contro-
versial issue is the extent to which the claimant must give credit for any early
payment of pension during the damages period. The Court of Appeal case of
Hopkins v Norcros [1994] IRLR 18 is authority for the proposition that no credit
need be given. It is questionable whether this is so where the early payment requires
the consent of the employer. On the other hand, where the claimant has a contractual
right to the early pension (such as an ill health pension) it would seem correct that
no deduction should be made (see, by analogy, *Smoker v London Fire and Civil
Defence Authority* [1991] 2 AC 502, HL).

Redundancy payments   It has been held by the House of Lords that it is not nor-   **1.173**
mally reasonable to deduct a redundancy payment in the assessment of damages for
wrongful dismissal since it represents compensation for the loss of an established job
and not compensation for loss of earnings (*Wilson v National Coal Board* (1980)
130 NLJ 1146). It is uncertain whether the same is true where the redundancy
package includes an enhanced notice entitlement, although it is likely that credit
should be given for the additional payment in such circumstances (see *Aspden v
Webbs Poultry and Meat Group (Holdings) Ltd* [1996] IRLR 521). Similarly, in
Baldwin v British Coal Corp Ltd [1995] IRLR 95, the High Court held that credit
should be given for a 'special' incentive redundancy payment where the employee
would not have received that payment but for the failure to receive proper notice.
In such circumstances, the payment received was a direct consequence of the
employer's breach and therefore was not too remote.

Contingencies and accelerated receipt of payments

Some reduction is made for contingencies such as the possibility that the employee   **1.174**
might have died or resigned before the date on which the contract could have been
lawfully terminated. This is likely to arise only where the period of notice, or the
unexpired period of the contract, is substantial. A further reduction is made to take
into account the accelerated receipt of the payment. This acknowledges the fact that
the employee receives the payments due under the contract sooner than would
otherwise have been the case.

Two methods are commonly used to make the reduction, as follows.   **1.175**

(a) *The annuity method* This involves finding out the current value of an annuity
    that would yield the same income annually as that which the employee would

have received during the damages period. The effect of the duty to mitigate may be taken into account by reducing the period covered by the annuity.

(b) *The multiplier* This method takes account of all of the relevant contingencies by discounting them from the maximum period of the employee's contractual entitlement. For example, if the damages period were five years, the multiplier may be limited to three years on account of the contingencies outlined above and the accelerated receipt of the payments. Accordingly, the award would be three times the employee's annual salary.

1.176 The need to use one of the above methods is likely to arise only if the damages period is considerable. In other cases, allowance for the accelerated receipt of the payment is based on a simple percentage reduction—for example, in *Shove v Downs Surgical plc* [1984] 1 All ER 7, the award was reduced by 7 per cent for this reason.

Contributory fault

1.177 In assessing the employer's liability, no reduction will be made for contributory fault since liability for breach of contract is strict. Thus the courts are not interested in whether the employee was partly to blame for the dismissal. See Chapter 12 for the position in unfair dismissal cases.

Deducting tax from damages

1.178 Tax liability is taken into account both in the assessment of damages and in the final award of damages (see Chapter 2).

2

TAX AND MISCELLANEOUS MATTERS

A. Tax

Deducting tax from damages

2.01 The principle that employees should be placed in no better position than that in which they would have been had the contract been performed means that damages for wrongful dismissal are awarded net of tax and National Insurance contributions (NICs). This is known as 'the *Gourley* principle' (see *British Transport Commission v Gourley* [1955] 3 All ER 796, a personal injuries case, which was applied to wrongful dismissal by the Court of Appeal in *Parsons v BNM Laboratories Ltd* [1963] 2 All ER 658).

Deducting tax from the final award

2.02 At the time of the decision in *Gourley*, post-cessation receipts such as damages for wrongful dismissal were not taxable in the hands of the employee. The law was subsequently changed and the present position is that payments on the termination of an office or employment (including damages for wrongful dismissal) are taxed on a sliding scale (Income Tax (Earnings and Pensions) Act 2003 [IT(EP)A 2003], s 401). This general statutory liability is, however, subject to a number of exemptions and reliefs. Furthermore, special provisions apply to employees who work overseas (IT(EP)A 2003, ss 401(1), 413, and 414). The position is as follows.

(a) The first £30,000 is tax-free.

(b) The balance may be taxed at the higher rate of tax, which, for the tax year 2010–11, is 20 per cent on income up to £37,500, 40 per cent on income above £37,500 but less than £150,000, and 50 per cent on any payment over £150,000.

2.03 These provisions also apply to 'payments in lieu of notice' (see Chapter 1) if they are not regarded as ordinary emoluments. Where such payments are taxable—that is, exceed £30,000—and are made prior to termination taking effect, tax should be deducted in the ordinary way under normal pay-as-you-earn (PAYE) arrangements. On the other hand, where the payment is made after termination (that is, after the P45 has been issued), the employer should deduct basic rate tax (currently 20 per cent) and leave the employee to account to the tax authorities for the balance. This means that the employee is entitled to the benefit of the use of the money in the meantime (Income Tax (PAYE) Regulations 2003—SI 2003/2682—reg 37). Special rules apply to the taxation of payments made on death or retirement (IT(EP) A 2003, ss 406 and 407). Where the P45 has been issued, it is for the individual taxpayer to account for the tax on any payment.

The *Gourley* principle and payments above £30,000

2.04 A problem arises where the lump-sum payment or an award of damages exceeds the tax-free exemption. The excess is taxable even though, in line with the *Gourley* principle, tax liability has already been included in the assessment of damages. In theory, this means that an employee could be placed in the unfortunate position of being taxed twice. However, the court said, *per curiam*, in *Parsons v BNM Laboratories Ltd* [1963] 2 All ER 658, that where this situation arises, the two amounts of tax should be left by way of set-off against each other.

2.05 The simplest way of achieving this effect is as follows.

(a) First, deduct the full tax that would have been payable on the earnings that an employee would have received during the damages period.

(b) Then, add back a sum that is equivalent to the tax payable under IT(EP)A 2003, s 401, so that this additional sum cancels out the amount of that tax.

2.06 This involves a kind of grossing-up of the tax liabilities that needs to take account of the differing rates of tax referred to in **2.05** above. The employee is therefore left with the net amount after the tax has been deducted from the damages. This approach was applied by the courts in *Shove v Downs Surgical plc* [1984] 1 All ER 7 and *Stewart v Glentaggart Ltd* 1963 SLT 119.

2.07 However, in assessing the employer's tax liability under **2.05(a)** above, it is important to take into account the following factors.

(a) *Future changes in rates of tax* Movements in the rates of tax in the period covered by the award are unknown at the time that the damages are assessed and it may therefore be difficult to work out the employee's net liability over the period.

(b) *Personal allowances* The employee's own personal allowances may change in future years and this may affect his or her tax liability over the period.

(c) *Other income* The employee may have other income that affects tax liability.

(d) *Employment overseas* There are special rules that govern the taxation of employees who spend a considerable amount of time overseas.

The task of adding back the tax that is going to be paid on the award (see 2.05(b) **2.08** above) is not quite as difficult, because the tax falls due in the tax year during which the dismissal took place, and therefore the employee's other income and the other variable factors will generally be known at the time of the assessment.

B. Miscellaneous Matters

Payments to directors

Payments made to a director by way of compensation for loss of office are unlawful **2.09** unless they are first disclosed to, and approved by, the company (Companies Act 2006, s 217). However, this provision does not apply to any payment made in good faith 'by way of settlement or compromise of any claim arising in connection with the termination of a person's office or employment or by way of pension in respect of past services' (Companies Act 2006, s 220(1)(c)–(d)).

Interest

The High Court and county court may award interest on damages for wrongful **2.10** dismissal from the date on which the cause of action arose to the date of judgment, or, in the case of a payment made before that date, the date of the payment (Supreme Court Act 1981, s 35A; County Courts Act 1984, s 69; Administration of Justice Act 1982, s 15(1)). The statutory rate of interest is currently 8 per cent, but this is subject to variation by statutory instrument. All claims for interest must be pleaded (RSC Order 18, r 8; County Court Rules 1981, Order 6, r 1A). A higher rate of interest may be awarded if the contract so provides.

The Court of Appeal (civil division) also has the power to award interest on damages **2.11** for wrongful dismissal (Law Reform (Miscellaneous Provisions) Act 1934, s 3).

Court proceedings

An action for wrongful dismissal may be brought in the High Court or county **2.12** court. The upper limit on the county courts' jurisdiction has now been abolished. All claims below £25,000 must now be commenced in the county court (High Court and County Courts Jurisdiction Order 1991, SI 1991/724). Such claims may be transferred to the High Court if one or more of the grounds for transfer specified in reg 7(5)(a)–(d) of the Order apply—for example, if it can be shown that complex points of law or fact are involved.

Time limits

2.13 The time limit for bringing a claim for wrongful dismissal is six years from the date on which the cause of action accrues (normally the date of the employer's breach of contract), although special provision is made for certain persons under disability (Limitation Act 1980, ss 2 and 28).

C. Employment Tribunal Jurisdiction

Employment Tribunals Act 1996

2.14 The power to determine contractual disputes in employment tribunals is now to be found in s 3 of the Employment Tribunals Act 1996 (ETA 1996), which replaced s 131 of the Employment Protection (Consolidation) Act 1978 (EP(C)A 1978).

2.15 This gives the Secretary of State for Trade and Industry (now the Secretary of State for Business, Innovation and Skills) power to confer on employment tribunals jurisdiction to determine:

(a) a claim for damages for breach of a contract of employment or other contract connected with employment (ETA 1996, s 3(2)(a));

(b) a claim for a sum due under such a contract (ETA 1996, s 3(2)(b)); and

(c) a claim for the recovery of a sum in pursuance of any enactment relating to the terms of performance of such a contract (ETA 1996, s 3(2)(c)).

2.16 Reference to breach of contract includes a reference to a breach of a term implied in a contract by or under any enactment or otherwise, a term of a contract as modified by or under any enactment or otherwise, and a term that, although not contained in a contract, is incorporated in the contract by another term of the contract—for example, in which terms of a collective agreement are incorporated into a contract of employment (ETA 1996, s 3(6)).

2.17 There is no power to include a claim for damages or for a sum due in respect of personal injury (ETA 1996, s 3(3)).

Employment Tribunals (Extension of Jurisdiction) Orders

2.18 Somewhat confusingly, the actual jurisdiction of employment tribunals to determine contractual claims is set out in the Employment Tribunals (England and Wales) (Extension of Jurisdiction) Order 1994, SI 1994/1623, and the Employment Tribunals (Extension of Jurisdiction) (Scotland) Order 1994, SI 1994/1624, both of which preceded the ETA 1996, but which have effect as if made under s 3(1) of that Act.

Claims by employees

2.19 Article 3 of the 1994 Order extends the jurisdiction of employment tribunals in respect of any claim by employees for the recovery of damages or other sums (other than a claim for personal injury) that 'arises or is outstanding on the termination of the employee's employment', provided that it is a claim in respect of which a court of law would have jurisdiction and does not fall within the scope of one or more of the excluded categories in art 5.

In *Sarker v South Tees Acute Hospitals NHS* [1997] IRLR 328, the Employment Appeal Tribunal (EAT) held that, in the context of what is now the Employment Rights Act 1996 (ERA 1996), these words were wide enough to cover claims brought by a prospective employee whose employment is terminated before commencing work for the employer. **2.20**

Such claims must be brought within three months of the effective date of termination of the employee's employment, or within three months of the last day of work, unless it was not reasonably practicable to do so (art 7(a) and (b)). Special provision is made for the impact of the statutory dispute resolution procedures in art 7(ba), in which an extension of time may be permitted under reg 15 of the Employment Act 2002 (Dispute Resolution) Regulations 2004, SI 2004/752. **2.21**

Counterclaims by employers

Article 4 of the 1994 Order, which is in identical terms to art 3, allows employers to make a counterclaim for damages against the former employee where a claim is brought under art 3. **2.22**

Such a claim must be brought within six weeks of the employer receiving the tribunal claim from the tribunal unless it is not reasonably practicable to do so (art 8(c)). It is conditional on the employee not having withdrawn or settled the contract claim at that time (art 8(a)), but the subsequent withdrawal, settlement, or dismissal of the employee's claim does not preclude the counterclaim from proceeding. So, for example, in *Patel v RCMS Ltd* [1999] IRLR 161, the employer's counterclaim was allowed to proceed even though the employee's claim had been rejected on the basis that it was out of time. The counterclaim must arise out of the contract with the employee and must not fall within one of the excluded categories in art 5 or relate to a claim for personal injuries. **2.23**

Claims excluded by art 5

Article 5 of the 1994 Order excludes claims for breach of a contractual term of any of the following descriptions: **2.24**

(a) a term requiring the employer to provide living accommodation for the employee (reg 5(a));
(b) a term imposing an obligation on the employer or the employee in connection with the provision of living accommodation (reg 5(b));
(c) a term relating to intellectual property (reg 5(c));
(d) a term imposing an obligation of confidence (reg 5(d)); or
(e) a term that is a covenant in restraint of trade (reg 5(e)).

2.25 For this purpose, 'intellectual property' is defined as including copyright, performance rights, moral rights, design rights, registered design rights, patents, and trade marks (reg 5)).

Extent of jurisdiction

2.26 It is important to stress that jurisdiction is conferred under the 1994 Order only where the claim arises, or a sum is outstanding, on the termination of employment. This would include a claim for contractual or statutory notice pay and may cover payments agreed under a compromise agreement entered into before termination (see *Rock-IT Cargo Ltd v Green* [1997] IRLR 581), but does not include any payments that are agreed after the termination date. In *Miller Bros and F P Butler Ltd v Johnston* [2002] IRLR 386, the EAT ruled that the employment tribunal had erred in awarding damages for breach of contract in a case in which negotiations for an agreement began before, and were outstanding on, the date of termination, but the agreement itself was not reached until after that date, since the jurisdiction of an employment tribunal was limited to claims that had arisen prior to termination. The EAT also ruled that termination of employment for this purpose means the date on which the employee ceases to work for the employer in the practical sense and corresponds to the 'effective date of termination', as provided for in ERA 1996, s 97. This decision also has the practical result that it will normally be necessary to sue in the ordinary courts where an employer breaches a compromise agreement (*Byrnell v British Telecommunications plc* EAT 0383/04), although in exceptional circumstances it may be possible to reinstate the claim before the employment tribunal.

Statutory maximum

2.27 Article 10 of the 1994 Order limits an employment tribunal's jurisdiction to contract claims that do not exceed £25,000. Rather surprisingly, this amount has remained unchanged since 1994. In *Fraser v HLMAD Ltd* [2006] IRLR 687, the Court of Appeal ruled that it is an abuse of process for a party to bring proceedings for damages for wrongful dismissal in the employment tribunal up to the statutory limit and then sue for the balance in the High Court. The cause of action, said the Court, cannot be split into two causes of action: one for damages up to £25,000 and another for the balance. Claimants and their advisers must therefore take care to assess the value of such claims properly, or limit the employment tribunal claim to compensation for unfair dismissal.

D. Calculating Damages for Wrongful Dismissal

2.28 The table below sets out the way in which an award for wrongful dismissal is assessed.

(1) Damages for loss of earnings
  (a) Work out the damages period by reference to
    — contractual period of notice, or
    — statutory period of notice, or
    — unexpired period of fixed term.
  (b) Calculate net pay in accordance with (a) above.   £
    Add overtime, bonuses, commission
(2) *Add* damages for loss of benefits by reference to   £
    same damages period as before in respect of loss of
    — company car
    — loans
    — subsidized mortgage
    — pension
    — profit-sharing scheme
    — medical insurance
    — other contractual benefits.
Total additions   £
(3) *Deduct*
    — earnings from new job
    — state benefit payments received in the damages period
    — payment in lieu
    — *ex gratia* payments
    — award of unfair dismissal compensation (but not basic award or redundancy
      payments).
Total deductions   £
Add
Total additions
Balance   £
Add/deduct tax adjustment and, if appropriate, gross up
Add interest
Final award   £

PART II

UNFAIR DISMISSAL

INTRODUCTION

The right to complain of unfair dismissal was established by the Industrial Relations Act 1971 (IRA 1971) and introduced in 1972. In substance, the law has remained relatively unchanged since its introduction.

In the year ending 31 March 2010, there were 57,400 complaints of unfair dismissal (ETS Annual Report 2009–10). However, not all employees qualify for protection against unfair dismissal: the right to complain is subject to a number of qualifying conditions and certain categories of worker are excluded altogether. The most important qualifying requirement is that the complainant, at the 'effective date of termination' (Employment Rights Act 1996 [ERA 1996], s 97(1) and (2)), must have worked for a period of one year or more, although this qualifying period does not apply if an employee is dismissed for one of the inadmissible or automatically unfair reasons set out in ERA 1996, ss 99–105.

In unfair dismissal cases, unlike in cases of wrongful dismissal, it is necessary for employers to establish a *valid* reason for dismissal—that is, a reason that falls within one of the five categories of valid reasons permitted by ERA 1996, s 98(1) and (2), and to show that it was 'reasonable' to dismiss for that reason.

The following reasons for dismissal are permitted by statute:

(a) a reason relating to the capability or qualifications of the employee for performing the work that he or she is employed to do;
(b) a reason relating to the conduct of the employee;
(c) redundancy;
(d) the fact that the employee cannot continue to do his or her job without contravening a statutory duty or requirement; and
(e) some other substantial reason of a kind such as to justify the dismissal of an employee holding the position that the employee held.

Having established a valid reason for dismissal, ERA 1996, s 98(4) provides that a tribunal must be satisfied that the employer acted 'reasonably or unreasonably in treating it [the reason for dismissal] as a sufficient reason for dismissing the employee' and that question 'shall be determined in accordance with equity and the substantial merits of the case'. In approaching the question of reasonableness, tribunals attach greater importance to the procedure by which employers reach their decision rather than to the merits of the decision itself. This trend has been strengthened by a series of Court of Appeal and Employment Appeal Tribunal (EAT) decisions that have stressed that a tribunal should not substitute its view for a decision that lies within the 'range of reasonable responses' of a reasonable employer. In the vast majority of cases, the critical question is whether the procedure followed by the employer was a reasonable one. In *Polkey v A E Dayton Services Ltd* [1987] IRLR 503, the House of Lords reasserted the importance of procedural fairness and stressed that a failure to follow a fair procedure will be justified only in the most exceptional of circumstances.

Certain reasons for dismissal are deemed to be automatically unfair, such as dismissals for family-related reasons (ERA 1996, s 99), dismissals for the assertion of statutory rights (ERA 1996, s 104), and dismissals as a result of whistleblowing (ERA 1996, s 103A). A dismissal is also automatically unfair if it is for a reason connected to the transfer of an undertaking unless the employer can establish an 'economic, technical or organisational reason entailing changes in the workforce', in which case the dismissal must still be shown to be 'reasonable' in accordance with ordinary unfair dismissal principles (Transfer of Undertakings (Protection of Employment) Regulations 2006 [TUPE 2006], SI 2006/246, reg 7), although it should be noted that the one year's service qualification applies in these circumstances.

Special provisions also apply where the dismissal is for union-related reasons,—that is, situations in which the reasons for dismissal relate to union membership or non-membership, or relate to an employee's participation in the activities of an independent trade union, and where the dismissal is for health and safety reasons contrary to ERA 1996, s 100. A dismissal for one or more of these reasons is automatically unfair and the usual qualifying requirements do not apply (Trade Union and Labour Relations (Consolidation) Act 1992 [TULR(C)A 1992], s 152; ERA 1996, ss 108–109). The same protection has been extended to elected employee representatives who are performing (or proposing to perform) the functions and activities as such, or candidates for election as employee representatives (ERA 1996, s 103). Special rules apply to the 'mass' dismissal of strikers and, in certain circumstances, the tribunal will have no jurisdiction to determine such claims.

As far as discrimination is concerned, although there is no specific statutory provision relating to dismissals for reasons connected with a person's race, gender (or sexual orientation), or religion, it is clear that such reasons are not 'valid' reasons for dismissal and therefore it is unfair to dismiss someone because of their 'protected characteristics' i.e. sex, race, sexual orientation, religion, disability, or subject to statutory qualifications, age.

The rules governing the remedies for unfair dismissal are laid down in ss 112–126 of the ERA 1996. An award of unfair dismissal compensation is usually limited to a basic award (ERA 1996, ss 119–122) and a compensatory award (ss 123–124). However, should an employment tribunal make an order for reinstatement or re-engagement pursuant to ss 113 and 114, and an employer fail to comply with it, the tribunal has the power to make an additional award (s 117). The power to make a special award has been repealed by s 33 of the Employment Relations Act 1999 (ERelA 1999).

Chapters 3–16 describe how each of these awards is calculated and the circumstances in which the statutory award may be reduced. Each of the statutory awards is subject to prescribed maxima. These statutory maxima are reviewed annually by the Secretary of State for Employment in September and, subject to the approval of Parliament, are increased (or decreased) in line with changes in the retail price index over the previous year (ERelA 1999, s 34). The new rates apply to any dismissals that take effect after 1 February in the following year.

The median award for unfair dismissal in 2010 was £4,903, whereas the average award was £9,120 (ETS Annual Report 2010).

3

RE-EMPLOYMENT ORDERS AND THE ADDITIONAL AWARD

A. Introduction

3.01 A novel feature of the statutory provisions relating to unfair dismissal is the power of tribunals to order reinstatement or re-engagement. Specific performance of an employment contract is a legal remedy that is rarely available in other circumstances.

3.02 As a result of the recommendation of the Donovan Commission that tribunals be given the power to order re-employment, a power to recommend re-engagement was included in the Industrial Relations Act 1971 (IRA 1971). The statutory powers were strengthened by the Employment Protection Act 1975 (EPA 1975) and remain in the form laid down in that Act to the present day.

3.03 It was Parliament's intention that reinstatement or re-engagement should be the primary remedy for unfair dismissal, but, in practice, there has been a noticeable reluctance on the part of employees to request re-employment and an even greater reluctance on the part of tribunals to make such orders when requested to do so. The result is that, in 2008–09, re-employment orders were made in only seven of all unfair dismissal cases that proceeded to a hearing and accounted for a mere 1.0 per cent of cases upheld (ETS Statistics 2010). Thus, instead of being the primary remedy, such orders are a rarity. Nonetheless, the statutory powers are still important, since failure to comply with such orders gives rise to an enhanced right to compensation—the additional award.

This chapter looks at the circumstances in which reinstatement and re-engagement **3.04** orders are made, the circumstances in which an additional award becomes payable, and how it is calculated.

B. Orders for Re-employment

Employment tribunals can make two types of permanent re-employment order: an **3.05** 'order for reinstatement', or an 'order for re-engagement'.

An order for reinstatement requires an employer to 'treat the complainant in all **3.06** respects as if he had not been dismissed'. This means that the employee must be restored to his or her former position (Employment Rights Act 1996 [ERA 1996], s 114(1)).

An order for re-engagement is a more flexible remedy. The order, which can be **3.07** made against either the employer, a successor of the employer, or an associated employer, requires the ex-employee to be taken on 'in employment comparable to that from that he was dismissed or other suitable employment' (ERA 1996, s 115(1)). Civil servants are regarded as being employed by the department in which they work rather than by the civil service as a whole. However, in exceptional circumstances in which, for example, two departments are linked for historical reasons, a re-engagement order may be made against a different government department (*Department of Health v Bruce and the Department of Social Security* EAT 14/92).

Employment tribunals may also make an interim re-employment order in certain **3.08** circumstances (see **3.61** below).

Statutory procedure

The statutory provisions lay down a detailed procedure that tribunals should **3.09** normally follow in deciding which of the statutory remedies to award.

The first step is to explain to the claimant what orders for reinstatement and **3.10** re-engagement can be made under ERA 1996, ss 114 and 115. The tribunal must then ask the claimant whether he or she wishes to be reinstated or re-engaged (ERA 1996, s 112(2) and (3)).

The second step is for the tribunal to decide whether to order reinstatement. The **3.11** tribunal has a general discretion whether or not to order reinstatement (*Port of*

London Authority v Payne and others [1992] IRLR 447) but, in reaching its decision, the tribunal must take into account the following considerations (s 116(1)):

(a) whether the claimant wishes to be reinstated;
(b) whether it is practicable for the employer to comply with an order for reinstatement; and
(c) where the claimant has caused or contributed to some extent to the dismissal, whether it would be just to order his or her reinstatement.

3.12 The third and final step is for the tribunal to decide whether to order re-engagement. The tribunal has a general discretion whether or not to order re-engagement (*Port of London Authority v Payne and others*) but, in reaching its decision, the tribunal must take into account the following considerations (s 116(3)):

(a) any wish expressed by the claimant as to the nature of the order to be made;
(b) whether it is practicable for the employer, or, as the case may be, a successor or associated employer, to comply with an order for re-engagement; and
(c) where the claimant has caused or contributed to some extent to the dismissal, whether it would be just to order re-engagement and, if so, on what terms.

3.13 Tribunals may take other factors into account. For example, in *Port of London Authority v Payne and others* [1992] IRLR 447, the Employment Appeal Tribunal (EAT) thought that the tribunal should have taken account of the applicants' ability to repay the £35,000 severance payments that they had received from their employers. On the other hand, the EAT accepted that employer objections or one or more of the grounds referred to above are not necessarily conclusive at this stage.

Wishes of the complainant

3.14 No order can be made if the employee does not want to be reinstated or re-engaged (ERA 1996, s 112(2) and (3)). For this reason, tribunals are under a statutory duty both to explain their powers to make such orders and to find out whether the employee wishes to be reinstated or re-engaged.

3.15 It has been held that the tribunal's duty in this respect is mandatory and applies even where the employee is represented (*Pirelli General Cable Works Ltd v Murray* [1979] IRLR 190). However, the EAT went on to rule that the terms of s 68(1) of the Employment Protection (Consolidation) Act 1978 (EP(C)A 1978)—now ERA 1996, s 112(2) and (3)—were discretionary only and need not be followed where either the employee had found another job and was not seeking re-employment, or the tribunal found the employee 100 per cent to blame for the dismissal, since it is 'pointless' to consider re-employment in these circumstances (see *Richardson v Walker* EAT 312/79 and *Pratt v Pickford Removals* EAT 43/86). These unreported authorities do not appear to have been placed before the Court of Appeal in *Cowley v Manson Timber Ltd* [1995] IRLR 153. However, the Court appears to have taken the view that a tribunal's failure to comply with the statutory provisions may be challenged only where this failure causes unfairness or injustice to the claimant. Furthermore, the Court ruled that a failure to comply with the statutory procedure will not nullify its decision on compensation. Nonetheless, a failure to consider reinstatement where this is requested by the claimant may still amount to an error of law. For example, in *Cruickshank v London Borough of Richmond* EAT 483/97, in overturning the employment tribunal's refusal to make such an order, the EAT criticized the employment tribunal for failing to give reasons for not making an order for reinstatement when this was requested by the claimant.

Practicability of compliance

Assuming that the employee wishes the tribunal to make an order of re-employment, **3.16** the central issue is whether it is practicable for the employer to comply with the order. The requirement of practicability must be considered both in relation to reinstatement and re-engagement. Although 'impracticability' is also a defence where the employer fails to comply with such an order (see **3.52** below), a tribunal must consider the issue at each stage. It should not postpone its consideration of practicability until the enforcement hearing, but by necessity any determination at the first hearing will be provisional (*Port of London Authority v Payne and others* [1992] IRLR 447 (EAT); [1994] IRLR 9 (CA)).

The issue of practicability is primarily a question of fact and the EAT has recom- **3.17** mended that tribunals adopt a 'broad common sense view' of the question and avoid trying to analyse the word 'practicable' in too much detail (*per* Kilner Brown J in *Meridian Ltd v Gomersall and another* [1977] IRLR 425). In *Port of London Authority v Payne and others*, the EAT suggested that the question of practicability must be judged by the standards of a 'reasonable employer' and tribunals must take care not to substitute their own judgment for that of a reasonable employer, but this approach does not appear to have been accepted by the Court of Appeal.

In deciding whether a re-employment order is practicable, the tribunal should **3.18** consider whether, having regard to the industrial relations realities of the situation, it is capable of being put into effect with success (*per* Stephenson LJ in *Coleman and Stephenson v Magnet Joinery Ltd* [1974] IRLR 343). Thus, what is practicable should not be equated with what is 'possible'. A tribunal may take into account the fact that its order may lead to serious industrial strife (see *Coleman*, above, and *Bateman v British Leyland UK Ltd* [1974] IRLR 101) or cause resentment amongst the workforce (*Meridian Ltd v Gomersall and another* [1977] IRLR 425). However, mere 'inexpediency' is no bar to re-employment (*Qualcast (Wolverhampton) Ltd v Ross* [1979] IRLR 98). Thus employers' fears that a re-employment order will undermine their authority or lead to embarrassment as a result of adverse publicity are irrelevant (*George v Beecham Group* [1977] IRLR 43 and *Ayub v Vauxhall Motors Ltd* [1978] IRLR 428). Similarly, the manner in which the claimant has conducted the case will not necessarily mean that it is not practicable to order reinstatement or re-engagement. For example, in *Cruickshank v London Borough of Richmond* EAT 483/97, the fact that the claimant had made unfounded allegations against his former employer was not considered to be a bar. Likewise, in *Wimbledon & District YMCA v Vardnell* EAT 467/98, the fact that the claimant alleged in the course of the hearing that the real reason for her dismissal was that she was a 'troublesome employee' did not render re-engagement impracticable.

3.19 It should also be remembered that the tribunal is only required to 'consider' the question of 'practicability' at this stage and may make an order to test whether employers' claims of impracticablity are justified (*Timex Corporation Ltd v Thomson* [1981] IRLR 522 and *Freemans plc v Flynn* [1984] IRLR 486). A tribunal may therefore order re-engagement even where the employer claims that there is no existing vacancy (*Electronic Data Processing Ltd v Wright* EAT 292/83) or where the employee was originally dismissed for redundancy (*Polkey v A E Dayton Services (formerly Edmund Walker (Holdings) Ltd)* [1987] IRLR 503), but such an order is unlikely if there is no prospect of a suitable vacancy arising in the near future. Such orders are also unlikely where the employer believes that the employee is incapable of doing the job (*SMT Sales & Services Ltd v Irwin* EAT 485/79) or is not qualified for the job (*Rose v RNIB COIT* 26830/91), or has a genuine fear that the employee will not be able to do the job without endangering those in his or her care (*ILEA v Gravett* [1988] IRLR 497). Similarly, in *London Borough of Greenwich v Dell* EAT 166/94, the EAT overturned an industrial tribunal's decision to order the re-engagement of a member of the National Front in a position that did not involve contact with ethnic minorities on the ground that such an order was impracticable and offensive to the Borough Council as an equal opportunities employer.

3.20 An order is also unlikely where there has been a fundamental loss of trust between the parties (for example, *Nothman v London Borough of Barnet (No 2)* [1980] IRLR 65, in which the employee believed that there had been a conspiracy against her by her employers). Similarly re-employment is unlikely in circumstances in which the dismissal has been held unfair on procedural grounds alone (*Wood Group Heavy Industrial Turbines Ltd v Crossan* [1998] IRLR 680). However, in *The Boots Company Ltd v Lees-Collier* [1986] ICR 728, a tribunal ordered reinstatement despite the employer's lingering belief in the employee's dishonesty. Re-employment was considered impracticable where compliance with an order might result in a withdrawal of funding for the employer (*Akram v Lothian Community Council* IRLIB 371).

3.21 Tribunals will also take the size of the employer organization into account, particularly where the employment involves a close working relationship between the dismissed employee and the employer (*Enessy Co SA t/a The Tulchan Estate v Minoprio* [1978] IRLR 489).

Contributory fault

Tribunals must also consider whether re-employment is appropriate in the light of   **3.22**
the employee's contributory conduct. The EAT has said that the test to be applied
is the same as that under what is now ERA 1996, s 123(6) (see *The Boots Company
Ltd v Lees-Collier* [1986] ICR 728). Thus an employee will not be held to have caused
or contributed to the dismissal unless he or she has been guilty of 'blameworthy'
conduct (see Chapter 14).

A finding of contributory fault does not necessarily preclude a tribunal from making   **3.23**
an order of reinstatement or re-engagement. Such orders are not uncommon where
the employee is to blame only to a small extent. More exceptionally, in *Automatic
Cooling Engineering Ltd v Scott* EAT 545/81, the EAT upheld an industrial tribunal's
order of reinstatement despite a finding that the employee, an apprentice, had been
75 per cent to blame for the dismissal. But, in *Nairne v Highlands & Islands Fire
Brigade* [1989] IRLR 366, the EAT held that re-engagement was impracticable in
a job that required a driving qualification where the employee had been disqualified
from driving for three years as a result of a second offence of drink-driving within a
two-year period. The EAT held the employee 75 per cent to blame for his dismissal
and overturned the tribunal's order of re-engagement. The EAT's decision was later
confirmed by the Court of Session ([1989] IRLR 366).

The extent of the employee's contributory conduct may, however, be reflected in the   **3.24**
terms of an order of re-engagement and, in particular, in a tribunal's refusal to
award compensation for loss of back pay (see **3.39** below).

Permanent replacements

Reinstatement or re-engagement is not considered impracticable simply because   **3.25**
the employer has taken on a permanent replacement, although it may be held
impracticable for this reason in the circumstances set out in ERA 1996, s 116(6):

> (5) Where . . . an employer has engaged a permanent replacement for a dismissed
>   employee, the tribunal shall not take that fact into account in determining . . .
>   whether it is practicable to comply with an order for reinstatement or re-engagement.
> (6) Subsection (5) does not apply where the employer shows—
>   (a) that it was not practicable for him to arrange for the dismissed employee's
>   work to be done without engaging a permanent replacement, or
>   (b) that—
>   (i) he engaged the replacement after the lapse of a reasonable period,
>   without having heard from the dismissed employee that he wished to
>   be reinstated or re-engaged, and
>   (ii) when the employer engaged the replacement it was no longer reason-
>   able for him to arrange for the dismissed employee's work to be done
>   except by a permanent replacement.

The effect is that large employer organizations which cannot invoke s 116(6)   **3.26**
successfully will often be unable to resist a re-employment order and may have to

consider the possibility of dismissing the permanent replacement in order to comply with it. The effect of this provision appears to have been overlooked by the EAT in *Cold Drawn Tubes Ltd v Middleton* [1992] IRLR 160.

Duty to give reasons

3.27 The tribunal must give reasons for exercising or declining to exercise its discretion under ERA 1996, s 116(1)–(4). Thus it should say why it considers re-employment to be practicable or impracticable in the particular circumstances (*Port of London Authority v Payne and others* [1992] IRLR 447). However, where a tribunal directs itself properly on the law, hears and accepts evidence on impracticability, and sets out its reasons clearly and fully, a plea that the tribunal's decision was nonetheless perverse is 'virtually impossible' (see *Clancy v Cannock Chase Technical College* [2001] IRLR 331).

C. Terms of Re-employment

Terms of reinstatement

3.28 On making an order of reinstatement, the tribunal must specify (ERA 1996, s 114(2)):

(a) any amount payable by the employer in respect of any benefit that the employee might reasonably be expected to have had but for the dismissal, including arrears of pay, for the period between the date of termination of employment and the date of reinstatement;

(b) any rights and privileges, including seniority and pension rights, which must be restored to the employee; and

(c) the date by which the order must be complied with.

3.29 The tribunal can therefore require the employer to award full back pay, holiday pay, etc between the date of dismissal and the date of reinstatement. This may include any improvement in an employee's terms and conditions (for example, a pay rise) that takes effect during the above period, since it is provided that the claimant is to be treated as if 'he had benefited from that improvement from the date on which he would have done so but for being dismissed' (s 114(3)). There is no statutory limit to the amount that the tribunal can award in this regard, because the statutory limit in ERA 1996, s 124, does not apply to awards under s 114(2).

3.30 However, in calculating the amount payable by the employer, tribunals must deduct (s 114(4)):

(a) wages in lieu of notice or any *ex gratia* payment received by the employee from the employer in respect of the period between the date of termination and the date of reinstatement (see *Butler v British Railways Board* EAT 510/89);

(b) any payments received by the employee in respect of employment with another employer during the above period (that is, wages, etc); and

(c) such other benefits as the tribunal thinks fit in the circumstances.

No deduction should be made for contributory fault or a failure to mitigate (*City &* **3.31** *Hackney Health Authority v Crisp* [1990] IRLR 47).

The Employment Protection (Recoupment of Jobseeker's Allowance and Income **3.32** Support) Regulations 1996, SI 1996/2349 (the Recoupment Regulations), apply to the award, so Jobseeker's Allowance (JSA) and other state benefits are recovered by the state through the operation of the regulations dealing with recoupment (see Chapter 16).

Example

An employee who is earning £150 a week is unfairly dismissed. The hearing takes place three months after the dismissal. At the time of the dismissal, the employee receives one month's wages in lieu. He commences a temporary job two weeks before the hearing, from which he receives wages of £100 a week. The tribunal orders reinstatement.

The calculation of back pay is as follows.

	£
Total arrears	1,800
Less	
— payment in lieu	600
— earnings from new job	200
Balance of arrears	1,000

There is no statutory limit to the amount that a tribunal may award for loss of back **3.33** pay under these provisions (see *Foster Wheeler (UK) Ltd v Chiarella* EAT 111/82) and the statutory cap on compensation does not apply to this part of the tribunal's award (ERA 1996, s 124(3)).

Terms of re-engagement

On making an order of re-engagement, the tribunal must specify (ERA 1996, **3.34** s 115(2)):

(a) the identity of the employer;

(b) the nature of the employment;

(c) the remuneration for the employment;

(d) any amount payable by the employer in respect of any benefit that the claimant might reasonably be expected to have had but for the dismissal, including arrears of pay, for the period between the date of termination of employment and the date of re-engagement (noting that there is no statutory limit to the amount that the tribunal can award in this regard);

(e) any rights and privileges, including seniority and pension rights, which must be restored to the employee; and

(f) the date by which the order must be complied with.

3.35 There is no power to order re-engagement on significantly more favourable terms than the employee would have obtained if the employee had been reinstated (*Rank Xerox (UK) Ltd v Stryczek* [1995] IRLR 568, in which the EAT held that an industrial tribunal had erred in law when it ordered an employer to re-engage the claimant in a position that carried a substantially higher salary and the added benefit of a company car). In addition, it has been held that the tribunal should specify the employee's place of work if this differs from the employee's original place of work (*Electronic Data Processing Ltd v Wright* [1986] IRLR 8). But in general it is undesirable for a tribunal to order re-engagement in a specific job as distinct from identifying the nature of the proposed employment (*Rank Xerox (UK) Ltd v Stryczek*).

3.36 The tribunal is again entitled to award the full amount of back pay, etc that has accrued between the date of the dismissal and the date on which the re-engagement will take effect. The arrears are normally calculated on the basis of the employee's pre-dismissal rate of pay, even where the employee is to be re-engaged at a lower rate of pay (*Electronic Data Processing Ltd v Wright*).

3.37 It is likely that the employee is entitled to the benefit of any pay rise or other improvement in terms and conditions that takes effect between the date of the dismissal and the date of re-engagement by virtue of the tribunal's duty under ERA 1996, s 116(2)–(4). However, there is no authority on this point.

3.38 Credit must be given for payments that have been made to the employee since dismissal, such as wages in lieu, *ex gratia* payments, and any payments made by a new employer (see **3.30** above) (ERA 1996, s 115(3)), but no deduction should be made for a failure to mitigate (*City & Hackney Health Authority v Crisp* [1990] IRLR 47).

3.39 The tribunal's broad discretion in deciding the terms of re-engagement is subject to the restriction that it is under a duty to ensure 'so far as is reasonably practicable' that the terms of re-engagement are 'as favourable as an order for reinstatement'. This does not, however, apply where the employee is found to have contributed to the dismissal. In such circumstances, it is open to tribunals to penalize an employee for contributory fault in the terms of the re-engagement order (ERA 1996, s 116(1), (3), and (4)).

Tribunal's duty to state terms

3.40 The tribunal is under a duty to state the statutory terms of re-engagement. In effect, this means that it must write a new contract for the parties. It will not discharge its duty in this respect by leaving it to the parties to decide the terms of re-engagement (*Pirelli General Cable Works Ltd v Murray* [1979] IRLR 190), or by leaving the parties to agree the nature of the work and the rate of pay (*Stena Houlder Ltd v Keenan* EAT(s) 543/93). Similarly, it has been suggested that the practice adopted by some tribunals of making an 'offer direction'—that is, of directing the employer to make an offer of re-engagement within a stated period on certain terms specified by the industrial tribunal—is invalid for the same reason. (See *Lilley Construction Ltd v Dunn* [1984] IRLR 483, in which the distinction between an offer direction and a full re-employment order is explained.)

D. Enforcing a Re-employment Order

The penalty for non-compliance with an order for reinstatement or re-engagement is prescribed by ERA 1996, s 117 and is purely financial. It is not open to the applicant to seek to enforce the industrial tribunal's orders for back pay or any other ancillary matter in a High Court or county court action (*O'Laoire v Jackel International Ltd* [1990] IRLR 70), but the statutory cap on compensation does not apply in relation to arrears of pay (ERA 1996, s 124(3)). The statutory remedy is in the nature of compensation and depends on whether the employer has failed to comply with the order or has partially complied with it. This distinction is considered below.   **3.41**

Partial compliance

Where a re-employment order is made and the claimant (the employee) is reinstated or re-engaged, but the 'terms of the order are not fully complied with', then, subject to ERA 1996, s 124(1), which fixes the statutory limit on the compensatory award, the tribunal is empowered to award compensation of such amount as it thinks fit, having regard to the loss sustained by the claimant in consequence of the employer's failure to comply with the terms of the order (ERA 1996, s 117(2)). There is no power to make an additional award.   **3.42**

Failure to reinstate or re-engage

Where an order for reinstatement or re-engagement is made, 'but the complainant is not reinstated or re-engaged in accordance with the order', the tribunal is required, subject to the defence of impracticability (see **3.52** below), to make an additional award under ERA 1996, s 117(3), as well as the standard award of compensation for unfair dismissal under ss 118–127.   **3.43**

Partial compliance and failure to comply distinguished

The precise distinction between a failure to comply with the tribunal's order and a failure to reinstate or re-engage in accordance with it is not entirely clear from the   **3.44** wording of ERA 1996, s 117(1) and (3), but the point was considered by the EAT in relation to an order for reinstatement in *Artisan Press Ltd v Srawley and Parker* [1986] IRLR 126.

3.45   In that case, the tribunal ordered two security officers, who were found to have been unfairly dismissed on union membership grounds, to be reinstated by their employer. The employer purported to comply with the tribunal's order by re-employing the two employees as cleaners with minor security functions (that is, in a different job), but it argued that it had done enough to achieve partial compliance with the tribunal's order for reinstatement. The EAT, however, did not agree. It said that reinstatement on less favourable terms did not amount to reinstatement for the purpose of EP(C)A 1978, s 69(2)—now ERA 1996, s 114—and therefore held that the employers were in breach of EP(C)A 1978, s 71(2)—now ERA 1996, s 117(3). (In the particular circumstances, the employees qualified for a special award since the dismissal was for a union-related reason.) By way of contrast, the EAT said that an employer would be treated as having failed to comply fully with the tribunal's order for reinstatement if the employer had failed to comply with the 'ancillary matters' in EP(C)A 1978, s 69(2)(a)—now ERA 1996, s 114(2) (see **3.28** above)—for example, if the employers had merely failed to pay off arrears due to the employee.

Additional award

3.46   The additional award is fixed by ERA 1996, s 117(3)(b) as an amount of not less than 26 weeks' pay and not more than 52 weeks' pay. Therefore the current maximum is £20,800 (Employment Rights (Increase of Limits) Order 2010 SI 2010 No. 2926).

3.47   The statutory rules governing the calculation of a week's pay are considered in detail in Chapter 5.

Fixing the penalty: The employer's conduct

3.48   The additional award is a financial penalty for non-compliance with the tribunal's order and, in fixing its award, a tribunal is likely to adopt a 'tariff approach'. It follows that, if the employer is guilty of a flagrant violation of the order, the award is likely to be at the higher end of the scale, whereas if the employer fails to observe the order because of genuine re-employment difficulties that fall short of the impracticability defence, the award will be at the lower end (*Morganite Electrical Carbon Ltd v Donne* [1987] IRLR 363). Considerations of public policy may also play a part in discrimination cases.

Fixing the penalty: Other factors

3.49   Although it is clear that the employer's conduct is the most influential factor in determining the amount of an additional award, tribunals may also take account of other factors. One such factor is the extent to which the compensatory award fully compensates the applicant. For example, in *Initial Textile Services v Ritchie* EAT 358/89, the EAT reduced the additional award from 26 to 20 weeks' pay on account of the fact that the employee had already received full compensation for the loss that she suffered as a result of her dismissal; on the other hand, a higher additional award may be justified where the loss exceeds the statutory limit (see also *Morganite Electrical Carbon Ltd v Donne*). Another factor is whether the employer has complied with the ancillary parts of the order—for example, whether the employer has paid any of the back pay due to the employee under the order. These factors may be balanced against other general factors, such as whether the employee has taken steps to mitigate his or her loss (*Mabirizi v National Hospital for Nervous Diseases* [1990] IRLR 133) and the extent to which the employee contributed to the dismissal (*Ayub v Vauxhall Motors Ltd* [1978] IRLR 428). However, a failure to mitigate should not lead to a quantifiable reduction in the additional award (see *Mabirizi*). Another relevant factor is whether the employee would have been fit and able to return to work on the date specified in the order had the employer complied with it (see *McQueen v Motherwell Railway Club* EAT 652/88).

3.50 It has been suggested that the award may, to some extent, include compensation for injury to feelings, but whilst this may be a relevant factor, it is unlikely to play a significant part because the main purpose of the award is to compensate the employee for the loss of reinstatement or re-engagement (see Bowers and Lewis, 'Non-economic loss in unfair dismissal cases: What's left After *Dunnachie*?' (2005) 34 ILJ).

Relationship between compensation for re-employment and the compensatory award

3.51 Where re-employment is ordered and it is practicable to comply with the order, the employment tribunal has the power to award compensation in excess of the statutory maximum for the compensatory award (currently) where the employer either fails to comply with the order or fails to comply fully with the order so as to fully reflect the terms of the order for reinstatement or re-engagement under ERA 1996, ss 114(2)(a) or 115(2)(d), and those arrears exceed the statutory maximum (ERA 1996, s 124(3) and (4)).

Example

An employee is unfairly dismissed. Re-engagement is ordered. The arrears are assessed at £60,000. The employer fails to comply with the order. The tribunal can award £60,000 representing the arrears due to the claimant, because this sum is 'necessary to reflect the amount specified as payable' in compliance with the order for re-engagement.

But it is clear from the wording of ERA 1996, s 123(4) that such an award is not self-standing and therefore it is not open to the tribunal to also make a compensatory award as well as an additional award if this would exceed the statutory maximum (*Selfridges Ltd v Malik* [1997] IRLR 577 and *Parry v National Westminster Bank plc* [2005] IRLR 193).

Example

So, for example, where (as in *Parry v National Westminster Bank plc*) the claimant received £21,188.72 for loss of arrears as well as an additional award of £13,500, it was not open to the employment tribunal to make a compensatory award of £53,500 (the then maximum) on top of this (although it could have made a compensatory award of the balance), since the limit may only be exceeded to the extent necessary to enable the aggregate of the compensatory and additional awards to reflect fully the amount specified as payable in compliance with the order for re-engagement.

Defence of impracticability

3.52 No additional award is payable if the employer can show that 'it was not practicable to comply with the order' (ERA 1996, s 117(4)(a)).

3.53 In determining whether the defence is made out, the tribunal is not restricted to considering the events that have taken place since the order was made. Thus the tribunal may take account of all of the relevant facts both before and after the date of the order (*Freemans plc v Flynn* [1984] IRLR 486).

3.54 This provision gives the employer 'a second bite at the cherry' since the employer is entitled to raise the same arguments twice—both at the time at which the order is made and at the enforcement stage (*Port of London Authority v Payne and others* [1994] IRLR 4). However, it should be noted that 'practicability' is only a 'consideration' under ERA 1996, s 116(1)–(4), whereas it is a complete defence under s 117(4)(a).

3.55 It follows that where the original order is made to put pressure on the employer to reinstate or re-engage the employee, it will still be open to the employer to argue that it was not practicable to comply with the order in the light of what happened subsequent to the order being made. For example, if, at the time that the order was made, there was no vacancy and this is still the case when an application is made to enforce the order, it will still be open to the employer to argue that it was not practicable to comply with the order for this reason.

3.56 Employers are not under a duty to create a special job for the employee or to dismiss existing employees to enable them to re-employ the claimant (*Freemans plc v Flynn*

[1984] IRLR 486). Neither will it be practicable to comply with the order if this would result in overstaffing or a redundancy situation (*Cold Drawn Tubes Ltd v Middleton* [1992] IRLR 161, in which the EAT rejected the argument that the applicant should have been reinstated and then, if necessary, the employers should have gone through a proper redundancy selection exercise). Furthermore, as the Court of Appeal pointed out in *Payne and others v Port of London Authority* [1994] IRLR 9, employers cannot be expected to explore every possible avenue that ingenuity might suggest. On the other hand, tribunals will scrutinize the genuineness of the employer's attempts to look for a vacancy and, in redundancy dismissals, may consider it appropriate for an employer to seek volunteers for redundancy if this is practicable. Some employer objections—for example, that non-compliance is justified on the ground of inexpediency—are unlikely to meet with any greater success the second time round. Similarly, the fact that the employer has taken on a permanent replacement does not necessarily mean that it is impracticable to comply with the order (see **3.25** above).

3.57 An additional award will be made even though, unknown to the employer, the employee would not have been able to return to work had the employer complied with the order. Thus, in *McQueen v Motherwell Railway Club* EAT 652/88, the EAT upheld an additional award of 20 weeks' pay when, unknown to the employers, one of the applicants would not have been able to start work on the day specified in the order on health grounds. The EAT said that this factor did not justify the employers' failure to comply with the order, although it did justify the award being limited to 20 weeks' pay rather than the full 26 weeks' pay.

3.58 Lodging an appeal against an industrial tribunal decision does not make it impracticable to comply with the order (*Initial Textile Service Ltd v Ritchie EAT* 358/89).

Non-compliance by employee

3.59 Where the tribunal finds that the claimant has unreasonably prevented an order under ERA 1996, ss 114 or 115 from being complied with, it must treat the employee's conduct in this respect as a failure to mitigate under s 123(4) (ERA 1996, s 117(8)).

3.60 This provision would seem to be aimed at the employee who changes his or her mind after an order for reinstatement or re-engagement has been made. Similar provisions apply where the employee unreasonably refuses an employer's offer of reinstatement or re-engagement.

E. Interim Re-employment

3.61 At present, there is no general statutory right to interim re-employment in unfair dismissal cases—that is, re-employment on an interim basis until the complaint is determined at the hearing. However, special provision is made for a form of interim re-employment in cases in which the dismissal is for a protected disclosure under the whistleblowing provisions or for union-related reasons or, in the case of employees with designated health and safety responsibility, or health and safety representatives or committee members, for carrying out health and safety responsibilities. This is known as 'interim relief'.

Interim relief

3.62   An application for interim relief (that is, interim re-employment) may be made where an employee claims to have been dismissed for union-related reasons, for union membership reasons, for reasons relating to carrying out health and safety responsibilities, or for reasons relating to 'protected disclosures' under the Public Interest Disclosure Act 1998 (PIDA 1998).

3.63   The procedure in trade union cases is set out in the Trade Union and Labour Relations (Consolidation) Act 1992 (TULR(C)A 1992), ss 161–163. The procedure in whistleblowing, and health and safety, cases is set out in ERA 1996, ss 128–129.

3.64   An application for interim relief must be made within seven days of the effective date of dismissal (TULR(C)A 1992, s 161(2); (ERA 1996, s 128(2)). In the case of dismissal for union membership, it must be supported by a certificate in writing signed by an authorized official of the independent trade union of which the employee was, or had proposed to become, a member stating that there are reasonable grounds for supposing that the reason or principal reason for dismissal was the one alleged in the complaint (TULR(C)A 1992, s 161(3)). There is no equivalent requirement in the ERA 1996. On receipt of the application, the employment tribunal is under a statutory duty to determine the matter 'as soon as practicable', although the employer must be given at least seven days' notice of the hearing (TULR(C)A 1992, s 161(2); ERA 1996, s 128(4)). Furthermore, where it is proposed to join the trade union as a party to the proceedings, the union must be given at least three days' notice of the hearing (TULR(C)A 1992, s 162(3)). The tribunal may postpone the hearing in special circumstances (TULR(C)A 1992, s 162(4); ERA 1996, s 128(5)).

3.65   If, at the hearing of the application for interim relief, the tribunal is satisfied that it is likely that, on determining the complaint to which the application relates, the tribunal will find that the claimant was unfairly dismissed, it must announce its findings and explain to both parties its powers under TULR(C)A 1992, s 163, and ERA 1996, s 129.

3.66   Broadly, these are:

(a) if the employer is willing to reinstate the employee, to order interim reinstatement until the case is heard or settled (TULR(C)A 1992, s 163(4); ERA 1996, s 129(3)(a));

(b) if the employer is willing to re-engage the employee, to order interim re-engagement until the case is heard or settled (TULR(C)A 1992, s 163(5); ERA 1996, s 129(3)));

(c) if the employer is unwilling to reinstate or re-engage the employee, to order that the contract of employment shall continue in force, irrespective of whether it has been terminated until the case is heard or settled (TULR(C)A 1992, ss 163(6) and 164(2); ERA 1996, s 130(1)). The tribunal is required to specify in its order 'the amount that is to be paid by the employer to the employee' (TULR(C)A 1992, s 164(2); ERA 1996, s 130(2)), although, in making the order, it will take account of any payment made by the employer such as payment in lieu of notice (TULR(C)A 1992, s 164(5) and (6); ERA 1996, s 130(5) and (6)).

3.67 On the application of either party, the tribunal may 'at any time between the making of an order' under these provisions and 'the determination or settlement of the complaint', revoke or vary its order on the ground of a relevant change in circumstances (TULR(C)A 1992, s 165; ERA 1996, s 131).

3.68 The penalty for a failure to comply with the terms of a continuation order is set out in TULR(C)A 1992, s 166, and ERA 1996, s 132. This provides that if, on the application of an employee, the tribunal is satisfied that the employer has failed to comply with an order of continuation of the contract—for example, by not paying the employee the amount stated under the order—the tribunal is required to determine the amount of pay owed by the employer and order that the sum due is paid to the employee by way of additional compensation at the 'full' hearing, In cases in which the employer has failed to comply with some other aspect of the tribunal's order—for example, in relation to pension rights or similar matters—the tribunal may award such compensation as it considers just and equitable in the circumstances.

3.69 In effect, these provisions enable the tribunal to ensure that the employee is either reinstated or re-engaged, or suspended on full pay, until the case is resolved. Any sums paid under these orders are not recoverable in the event that the employee loses the substantive complaint of unfair dismissal (*Initial Textile Services v Rendell* EAT 383/91).

3.70 As explained in **3.61** above, for such an order to be made, the employment tribunal must be satisfied that the automatic unfair dismissal is likely to succeed. In *Taplin v Shippam Ltd* [1978] ICR 1068, in which it was alleged that the claimant was dismissed for taking part in trade union activities, the EAT held that 'likely' meant that the claimant had a 'pretty good' chance of success. The same test was applied by the EAT in *Raja v Secretary of State for Justice* (UKEAT/0364/09), a whistleblowing case, in which it was stated that a claimant should show 'specific reason why his prospects of success are sufficiently strong to make interim relief appropriate'.

4

UNFAIR DISMISSAL: THE BASIC AWARD

A. Introduction

4.01 The basic award was introduced by the Employment Protection Act 1975 (EPA 1975) with the aim of compensating employees for the loss of job security brought about by dismissal. In a sense, the policy behind the award is similar to that underlying the redundancy payments scheme and this is reflected in the way in which the award is calculated. The award is normally calculated by reference to the employee's age and length of service at the effective date of termination, but in union-related dismissals, there is a statutory obligation to award a fixed amount as a minimum basic award. This amount is unrelated to the employee's age or length of service. The basic award is a separate statutory award and is not subsumed into an overall award of compensation in cases in which a discrimination complaint is upheld (*Visa International Ltd v Paul* [2004] IRLR 42).

B. Calculating the Basic Award

4.02 There are two main elements in the calculation of the basic award: the employee's length of service at the effective date of termination, and the employee's age at the time of dismissal—but this is not subject to any statutory age limit. The award is calculated by working out the number of reckonable years of continuous employment and then multiplying those years by the appropriate statutory factor. The employee is allowed (under the Employment Rights Act 1996 [ERA 1996], s 119(1) and (2)):

(a) one-and-a-half weeks' pay for each year of employment in which he or she was not below the age of 41;
(b) one week's pay for each year of employment in which he or she was below the age of 41, but not below the age of 22; and
(c) half a week's pay for each year of employment in which he or she was below the age of 22.

The method of calculation is illustrated below.   **4.03**

Examples

Example 1

An employee aged 30 has worked for the employer since the age of 20. The weeks' pay @ £150 at the calculation date is as follows.

Basic award:	One year × half a week's pay =	£75
	Nine years × one week's pay =	£1,350
	Total award =	£1,425

Example 2

An employee aged 50 has worked for the employer for 20 years. The weeks' pay @ £180 at the calculation date is as follows.

Basic award:	Ten years × one week's pay =	£1,800
	Ten years × one-and-a-half weeks' pay =	£2,700
	Total award =	£4,500

In both of these examples, we have assumed that the years spanning the 22nd and 41st years count at the higher rate.

Effective date of termination

The effective date of termination as defined by ERA 1996, s 97 depends on whether **4.04** or not the employee is dismissed with the requisite period of statutory notice (see **1.106** above).

Where an employer summarily dismisses an employee or gives him or her less than **4.05** the period of notice guaranteed by the statutory provisions, the effective date of termination is the date on which the statutory notice would have expired had it been given (ERA 1996, s 97(2)). Similarly, if an employee is constructively dismissed, the effective date of termination is extended by the minimum period of notice that the employer was required to give the employee by statute (ERA 1996, s 97(4)). However, where the employer gives the employee notice that is equivalent to or greater than the statutory minimum, the effective date of termination is the date on which that notice expires (ERA 1996, s 97(2)).

4.06 Establishing the correct effective date of termination can be important because extra years of employment may fall to be included in the calculation.

Straddling years of employment

4.07 Prior to the Employment Act 1980 (EA 1980), there was some doubt as to whether years of employment that spanned an employee's 22nd or 41st birthday counted. This was because years of service counted only if the employee was above the relevant age limit for the whole of the year. However, the new wording makes it clear that the years that span the 22nd or 41st birthday *do* count.

4.08 The problem now is whether the 'appropriate statutory factor' for such years is the higher rate (that is, one week's pay for a year that spans an employee's 22nd birthday and one-and-a-half weeks' pay for a year that spans an employee's 41st birthday) or the lower rate (that is, half a week's pay and one week's pay respectively). Before the EA 1980 was amended, it was thought that the lower rate applied because continuity of employment was calculated in weeks. Thus the higher rate would have applied only if the employee was above the age of 22 or 41 in each week of the relevant years, which plainly would not have been the case. However, Sch 2 to the Employment Act 1982 (EA 1982) deleted the crucial words 'which consist wholly in weeks' and substituted a calculation based on years of employment, with the result that it is now generally thought that such years now count at the higher rate.

Age

4.09 There is no minimum or lower age limit and no upper age limit (Employment Equality (Age) Regulations 2006, SI 2006/1031, Sch 8, Pt 2, para 25 and para 27). The provision is unchanged by the Equality Act 2010.

4.10 The previous provisions that provided for the scaling down of the award in the 64th year were repealed by the 2006 Age Regulations (Sch 8, Pt 2, para 27) SI 2006/1031. This provision is unchanged by the Equality Act 2010.

A week's pay

4.11 The rules governing the statutory calculation of a week's pay are set out in ERA 1996, ss 220–229 and are considered in Chapter 5.

C. Minimum Basic Award

Generally, there is no statutory right to a minimum basic award. However, statute **4.12** does provide for a minimum basic award in three specific situations.

Union-related and health and safety dismissals

The first relates to union membership dismissal—that is, dismissals that are **4.13** regarded as unfair by virtue of ss 152 and 153 of the Trade Union and Labour Relations (Consolidation) Act 1992 (TULR(C)A 1992) (equivalent protection is given to employee representatives by ERA 1996, s 103). This was extended to cases in which a health and safety representative is dismissed for carrying out his or her duties under ERA 1996, s 100(1)(a) and (b), and also applies to whistleblowing dismissals (s 103). The statutory minimum is currently £5,000 (Employment Rights (Increase of Limits) Order 2010 SI 2010 No 2926).

The statutory minimum is reviewed by the Secretary of State in September each **4.14** year and varied in line with increases (or decreases) in the retail price index (Employment Relations Act 1999 [ERelA 1999], s 34(1)–(2)). The new rate, subject to the approval of Parliament, takes effect from 1 February.

The intention behind these provisions is to ensure that the victims of union-related **4.15** dismissals receive a guaranteed minimum award. Thus employees will receive the guaranteed minimum if, having calculated the basic award in the ordinary way, the award would be less than the amount guaranteed by the statutory provisions. On the other hand, the statutory minimum is ignored if the award exceeds the minimum guaranteed by the statutory provisions.

Redundancy dismissals

An employee is not entitled to receive both a basic award and a redundancy pay- **4.16** ment. In cases of redundancy, therefore, the redundancy payment is deducted from the basic award (ERA 1996, s 122(4)). However, such a deduction will not be made if the tribunal finds that redundancy was not the real reason for dismissal (*Boorman v Allmakes Ltd* [1995] IRLR 553). For example, if an employer mistakenly makes a redundancy payment in circumstances in which the dismissal is automatically unfair under the Transfer of Undertakings (Protection of Employment) Regulations 2006 (TUPE 2006), SI 2006/246, reg 7, then the employee will be entitled to recover a basic award despite receiving a redundancy payment.

Union dismissals

This general exclusion does not apply where an employee is selected for redundancy **4.17** in breach of TULR(C)A 1992, s 153—that is, for a reason related to trade union membership, or where a workers' representative is selected for redundancy for carrying out health and safety duties pursuant to ERA 1996, s 100(1)(a) and (b). In such circumstances, an employee is entitled to a minimum basic award as well as a redundancy payment (TULR(C)A 1992, s 159). It also does not apply where the employee is dismissed for a reason other than redundancy, but receives a redundancy payment as part of the compensatory award (see *Addison v Babcock FATA Ltd* [1986] IRLR 388).

The 'unreasonable' employee

4.18 Where the principal reason for dismissal is redundancy, but the employee is not entitled to a redundancy payment because he or she has:

(a) unreasonably refused an offer of suitable employment (ERA 1996, s 141(2)); or

(b) unreasonably terminated or given notice to terminate a trial period of employment (s 141(4)(d)); or

(c) had his or her contract of employment renewed or is re-engaged under a new employment contract pursuant to ERA 1996, s 141(1), so that there is no dismissal,

the maximum basic award is limited to two weeks' pay. The purpose behind this is to prevent the 'unreasonable' employee from recovering the statutory equivalent to a redundancy payment in the form of a basic award.

Maximum basic award

4.19 The maximum basic award is fixed by reference to the maximum number of reckonable years of employment, the maximum multiplier provided for under the statutory provisions, and the maximum amount of pay that qualifies as a week's pay.

4.20 There is a maximum of 20 years' service at a maximum of one-and-a-half weeks' pay for each year of service, the limit of a week's pay being £400 on or after 1 February 2011 in cases in which the effective date of termination is on or after 1 February 2005. Thus the maximum award is £12,000 (Employment Rights (Increase of Limits) Order SI 2010 No 2926).

D. Reducing the Basic Award

Contributory fault

4.21 The basic award may also be reduced or further reduced where any conduct of the employee (including conduct that did not contribute to the dismissal) was such that it would be 'just and equitable' to reduce or further reduce the award (ERA 1996, s 122(2)).

4.22 This provision is wider than the similar provision in relation to the compensatory award under ERA 1996, s 123(6) (see Chapter 14), because it provides for any conduct to be taken into account if that would be just and equitable, whereas only conduct that contributes to the dismissal can be taken into account under s 123(6). In *Optikinetics Ltd v Whooley* EAT 1275/97, the Employment Appeal Tribunal (EAT) observed that this gives tribunals a broader discretion as to whether to make any, and if so what, reduction to the basic award in the light of the claimant's pre-dismissal conduct since the conduct in question need not be causally linked to the dismissal. As a result, misconduct that was not known at the time of the dismissal may be taken into account even though it did not contribute to the dismissal (see *Parker Foundry Ltd v Slack* [1992] IRLR 11).

> **Example**
>
> An employee is dismissed for fighting. Three weeks after the dismissal, the employer discovers that the employee was working for a trade rival in his spare time. The dismissal is found to be unfair because the employer failed to investigate the question of provocation. In deciding whether to reduce the basic award for contributory fault, the tribunal may take into account both the conduct that led to the dismissal and the conduct that was not known at the time of dismissal.

Apart from this wider power, the general principles are the same as those examined **4.23** in Chapter 14. Effectively, the award will not be reduced unless the employee is guilty of blameworthy conduct, as explained by the Court of Appeal in *Nelson v BBC (No 2)* [1979] IRLR 346. The amount of the reduction is a matter for the tribunal to decide and an appellate court is unlikely to interfere with the tribunal's decision on this point (*Hollier v Plysu Ltd* [1983] IRLR 260).

Unreasonable refusal of offer of reinstatement

The basic award may also be reduced by such extent as a tribunal considers just and **4.24** equitable having regard to its finding that the employee 'has unreasonably refused an offer by the employer which (if accepted) would have the effect of reinstating the complainant in his employment in all respects as if he had not been dismissed' (ERA 1996, s 122(1)). This provision will apply only where the employer makes an offer that complies with the statutory provisions. An invitation to 'discuss' the situation surrounding dismissal will not amount to such an offer (*McDonald v Capital Coaches Ltd* EAT 140/94). Furthermore, it would seem that the employer can rely on this provision only if the offer is one of reinstatement as defined by ERA 1996, s 114(1). Thus an offer of re-employment on less favourable terms will not amount to an offer of reinstatement; neither will an offer of a different job on the same salary (*Artisan Press Ltd v Srawley and Parker* [1986] IRLR 126). (See **13.11** below for factors that are taken into account in determining the reasonableness of the employee's refusal.)

Although a reduction will normally be made where the employee is found to have **4.25** acted unreasonably, the tribunal is not bound to make one if it feels that this would not be just and equitable. For example, in *Muirhead* & *Maxwell Ltd v Chambers* EAT 516/82, the EAT held that the tribunal was entitled to conclude that it was inequitable to reduce the award where the employee's reason for refusing the employer's offer of reinstatement was that he 'feared victimization'.

Restrictions in union membership dismissals

4.26 The same general principles as in ordinary dismissals apply in determining whether the basic award should be reduced for contributory fault in 'union-related' cases. No reduction, therefore, should be made unless the complainant is guilty of 'blameworthy' conduct that contributed to the dismissal (see Chapter 14). However, certain special statutory rules apply to the calculation of the basic award in union membership cases.

Matters to be disregarded

4.27 No reduction or further reduction in the basic award should be made where the employee's conduct amounts to a breach of a requirement to be a union member or non-member or to take part in trade union activities (TULR(C)A 1992, s 155). Tribunals should also ignore a refusal to comply with a requirement to make a payment in lieu of union subscriptions or an objection to deductions from pay for that purpose.

4.28 Thus an employee who previously agreed to such a payment may not be held to have contributed to the dismissal if that agreement is subsequently withdrawn. It is hard to imagine a case in which the employee would be held to have contributed to the dismissal under TULR(C)A 1992, ss 152 and 153.

Minimum award

4.29 As a general rule, there can be no reduction of the basic award for contributory fault where the reason or principal reason for dismissal is redundancy. This provision is intended to preserve an employee's full entitlement to a redundancy payment. However, the restriction does not apply where an employee would be entitled to receive a minimum basic award—for example, where a dismissal is automatically unfair under TULR(C)A 1992, s 153 due to selection on the grounds of trade union membership or non-membership (see **4.13** above). In such circumstances, the statutory minimum basic award may be reduced for contributory fault, but the reduction applies only to the amount of the basic award that is payable under ERA 1996, s 120.

> **Example**
>
> An employee with two years' service who earns £380 a week is selected for redundancy for union-related reasons. She would normally be entitled to a redundancy payment of £760, but is entitled to a minimum basic award of £5,000 and therefore would be entitled to an award of £4,240. In such circumstances, the award may be reduced for contributory fault to £4,240.

E. Deductions from the Basic Award

The basic award is a statutory award and may be reduced only where this is autho-   **4.30**
rized by the statutory provisions (*Cadbury Ltd v Doddington* [1977] ICR 982); it
therefore cannot be reduced where, for example, the employee has failed to mitigate
his or her loss (*Lock v Connell Estate Agents Ltd* [1994] IRLR 444) or where the
tribunal considers this to be 'just and equitable' (*Sahil v Kores Nordic (GB) Ltd*
EAT 379/90).

Deductions in respect of redundancy payments are dealt with at **4.16** above.   **4.31**

It has been held that where an *ex gratia* payment is specifically referable to the   **4.32**
employee's statutory right to unfair dismissal compensation, the payment may be
relied on as a defence to the employer's statutory liabilities (see *Chelsea Football
Club and Athletic Co Ltd v Heath* [1981] IRLR 73). (See also Chapter 15 for the
effect of an *ex gratia* payment on unfair dismissal compensation generally.)

5

A WEEK'S PAY

A. Problems of Definition

5.01 If an employee were asked to define what he or she thought his or her week's pay was, he or she would probably say that it was the amount that he or she earned in the course of a normal working week. In giving that answer, the employee would not be far from identifying the intention underlying the statutory provisions. However, what may appear to be a comparatively simple question is complicated by the different shift patterns and payment structures that exist in industry. For example, there are some workers, such as shift workers and piece workers, whose pay varies from week to week.

5.02 A further problem arises in relation to the number of hours of employment that count in the calculation of a week's pay; the hours an employee actually works do not necessarily count for the purpose of the statutory provisions. For example, most employees would probably include overtime payments as part of their week's pay, but overtime payments rarely count in the statutory calculation of a week's pay (see **5.18** below). In order, therefore, to determine what is meant by a week's pay it is necessary to turn to the Employment Rights Act 1996 (ERA 1996) and its relevant provisions to see how these have been interpreted by the courts and tribunals.

The statutory provisions governing the calculation of a week's pay are to be found **5.03** in ERA 1996, ss 220–229. These provisions apply whenever it is necessary to calculate a week's pay for statutory purposes (ERA 1996, s 220).

Central to the statutory provisions is the distinction between employments with **5.04** normal working hours and those with no normal working hours, since this determines which of the two basic statutory formulae applies. It should be noted that the formula used to work out a week's pay in cases in which there are no normal hours of work is potentially the more generous since it is based on an employee's average earnings over a 12-week period prior to the calculation date (see **5.78** below).

It would seem that the broad objective of the statutory provisions is to distinguish **5.05** between those employments that follow a fixed pattern of work and those in which the hours of work fluctuate with the demands of the business. However, the statutory provisions are technical and complex, and it is not always easy to determine which formula is appropriate.

B. Normal Working Hours

There is no general definition of normal working hours in ERA 1996, ss 220–229, **5.06** but some guidance for particular cases is given in s 234, which provides:

(1) Where an employee is entitled to overtime pay when employed for more than a fixed number of hours in a week or other period, there are for the purposes of this Act normal working hours in his case.

(2) Subject to subsection (3), the normal working hours in such a case are the fixed number of hours.

(3) Where in such a case—

    (a) the contract of employment fixes the number, or minimum number, of hours of employment in a week or other period (whether or not it also provides for the reduction of that number or minimum in certain circumstances), and

    (b) that number or minimum number of hours exceeds the number of hours without overtime,

the normal working hours are that number or minimum number of hours (and not the number of hours without overtime).

Thus the following are all examples of employments with normal working hours. **5.07**

> **Example**
>
> *Hours fixed by contract*
>
> An employee whose contract provides for 40 hours a week works a fixed number of hours—that is, 40 hours—and therefore the employment is one for which there are normal working hours.
>
> *Piece workers*
>
> Piece workers, whose rate of pay varies with output but who have hours of work that are fixed, are treated as having normal working hours despite the variation in the rate of pay. The particular statutory formula applicable to piece workers takes the variation in pay into account (ERA 1996, s 221(3)).
>
> *Rota workers*
>
> Less obviously, in the case of persons working on different shifts in accordance with a rota, provided that the shift pattern is fixed in advance, the employment will count as one for which there are normal working hours. Again, the statutory formula takes the different shift patterns into account (ERA 1996, s 222).

Regular overtime no bar to normal working hours

5.08 Regular overtime working does not prevent the employment from being one for which there are normal working hours. For example, in one case, a group of bakers claimed that they had no normal working hours because the hours that they worked depended upon how long the bread took to bake. However, the employers succeeded in their argument that their redundancy payments still fell to be calculated on the basis that the 40-hour week fixed by their contract was their normal working week (*Minister of Labour v County Bake Ltd* [1968] ITR 379).

Other employments with normal working hours

5.09 The statutory provisions quoted in **5.06** do not purport to give an exhaustive definition of employments with normal working hours and, as the Employment Appeal Tribunal (EAT) recognized in *Fox v C Wright (Farmers) Ltd* [1978] ICR 98, there may be other employments that are capable of being so regarded. In such circumstances, said the EAT, it is necessary to approach the matter 'according to general principles without the benefit of any statutory definition'. However, the EAT failed to spell out what factors tribunals should take into account in the determination of this issue. The matter is further complicated by a number of inconsistent decisions that make it difficult to predict on which side of the dividing line a particular employment is likely to fall.

For example, in *Fox*, the EAT held that an agricultural stockman who worked 'as   **5.10**
long as the work and the beasts demanded' was nonetheless in an employment with
normal working hours because, under the relevant order determining agricultural
wages, he was entitled to overtime pay if he worked more than 40 hours a week. The
EAT ruled that those were his 'normal working hours' even though he would often
work between 50 and 60 hours a week. The EAT's decision, however, has been criticized on the grounds that the order did not say what the normal hours of work were,
but simply stated when overtime rates became payable. Moreover, it is clear that the
reasoning in *Fox* may lead to arbitrary results. For example, if, on the same facts,
another stockman were to have worked only 35 hours a week, he or she would still
be entitled to receive a redundancy payment based on a 40-hour week. Indeed, it
may be thought that Mr Fox was a classic example of an employee who had no
normal hours of work.

By way of contrast, in *Cooper v Secretary of State for Employment* COIT 1717/223,   **5.11**
an industrial tribunal found that coach drivers who were on call 24 hours a day,
seven days a week, subject to the limitations of the regulations on drivers' hours, had
no normal working hours. The tribunal reached this conclusion despite evidence
that the drivers were paid overtime if they were required to work more than 40 hours
a week. The EAT's ruling in *Fox* does not appear to have been considered by the
tribunal and the two decisions would seem to be irreconcilable.

Employments with no normal working hours

The key feature that would seem to distinguish employment with no normal working   **5.12**
hours from employments with normal working hours is that, in the former, the
employee's hours of working fluctuate with the demands of the business—that is,
there is no fixed pattern of work. However, as indicated in **5.11** above, the EAT's
decision in *Fox v C Wright Farmers Ltd* [1978] ICR 98 makes it difficult to say with
certainty where the dividing line lies.

A good example of an employment with no normal working hours would be a   **5.13**
casual worker who is paid on commission, such as an ice cream vendor. There may
also be other similar kinds of employment in which the employee may be held to
have no normal working hours (see *Cooper v Secretary of State for Employment* COIT
1717/223—**5.11** above).

Which hours count as normal working hours

In practice, most employments fall within the concept of normal working   **5.14**
hours, so, in most cases, the real issue is what hours count as normal working
hours. However, rather confusingly, the answer to this question is to be found
in the same statutory provisions as those that have already been considered in
connection with the issue of whether the employment is one with normal working
hours.

5.15 Thus, to paraphrase the statutory provisions (ERA 1996, s 234, quoted in full at **5.06** above), the number of hours that count as normal working hours is the minimum number of hours of employment as fixed by the contract of employment. Where the contract clearly and unambiguously defines the employee's minimum hours of work, those hours will be the employee's normal working hours for the purpose of calculating a week's pay (*Gascol Conversions Ltd v Mercer* [1974] IRLR 155).

Overtime hours

5.16 As a general rule, overtime hours do not form part of an employee's normal working hours. This is because normal working hours are defined as the minimum number of hours specified in the contract of employment (s 234).

5.17 Thus, where overtime is voluntary on both sides, the normal working hours are the minimum number of hours that an employee is required to work under the contract of employment (*Tarmac Roadstone Holdings Ltd v Peacock* [1973] IRLR 157, CA). However, overtime hours do count when they form part of an employee's basic contractual hours. Thus, in *The Ouseburn Transport Co Ltd v Mundell* EAT 371/80, Mr Mundell's contract guaranteed a minimum of 45 hours' work a week and the EAT held that his redundancy payment should be calculated on the basis of a normal working week of 45 hours.

5.18 A problem arises where the employee is obliged to work overtime, but the employer's obligation to provide work is limited to the contractual minimum. This problem was considered by the Court of Appeal in *Tarmac Roadstone Holdings Ltd v Peacock*. Mr Peacock and his colleagues were employed by Tarmac Roadstone as maintenance fitters. Under their contracts of employment, they were obliged to work a minimum of 40 hours a week, but, in addition, they could be required to work overtime 'in accordance with the demands of the industry during the normal week and/or at weekends'. When they were made redundant, Mr Peacock and his colleagues claimed that their redundancy payment should have been calculated on the basis of the number of hours that they regularly worked—that is, 57 hours a week—but their employer based its calculation on the minimum number of hours as defined by the contract of employment—that is, 40 hours. The Court of Appeal held that the method used by the employers was correct. The reason, in Lord Denning's judgment, was that the contract did not guarantee work above the minimum, as required by Sch 2, para 2 of the Contracts of Employment Act 1963 (now see ERA 1996, s 234(3)) and therefore overtime hours were excluded by the wording of para 1 (now see ERA 1996, s 234(1)).

5.19 An alternative interpretation is that ERA 1996, s 234(3) does not require overtime to be compulsory on both sides; all that it requires is that the contract should fix the number of hours of employment including overtime. In *Mundell*, the EAT stressed that the crucial factor was whether the contract fixed the number of hours, not whether those hours were compulsory. However, the ruling in *Peacock* was confirmed and applied by the Court of Appeal in *Lotus Cars Ltd v Sutcliffe* [1982] IRLR 381 (see **5.23–5.24** below), so the present position is that overtime hours will be included in the calculation of a week's pay only where overtime is guaranteed by the employer and is compulsory on the employee.

Contracts and particulars of employment and other evidence of normal working hours

Normal working hours may be defined in a formal contract of employment or the statutory statement of written particulars of employment, which should state 'any terms and conditions relating to . . . normal working hours' (ERA 1996, s 1(4)(c)). Note, however, that a written statement is not conclusive proof of the terms agreed between the parties and can be challenged if it is inaccurate (*Systems Floors (UK) v Daniel* [1981] IRLR 475 and *Alexander and others v Standard Telephone & Cables Ltd (No 2)* [1991] IRLR 286).   **5.20**

In the absence of a formal written contract or a statement of particulars of employment, the tribunal will have to look at other evidence of normal working hours. Thus, in *Fox v C Wright Farmers Ltd* [1978] ICR 98, the EAT relied on the terms of a wages council order to establish Mr Fox's normal working hours.   **5.21**

Where the contractual provisions relating to normal working hours are unclear, the court or tribunal will be required to construe the contract carefully in order to determine the precise nature of the respective obligations of the parties.   **5.22**

For example, in *Lotus Cars Ltd v Sutcliffe* [1982] IRLR 381, Mr Sutcliffe's contract included two terms relating to his working hours. His 'basic' working week was 40 hours, but his 'standard' week was 45 hours, the extra being regarded as 'normal extra time' and carrying a supplementary pay increment. The staff handbook also included a profit-sharing scheme based on production levels that could only be achieved by working a 45-hour week. When he was made redundant, Mr Sutcliffe argued that his redundancy pay should be calculated on the basis that his normal hours of work were 45 hours a week. However, the company based its calculation on his basic 40-hour week.   **5.23**

Both the industrial tribunal and the EAT agreed with Mr Sutcliffe, but their rulings were overturned by the Court of Appeal, which found in favour of the company. The Court said that, on a true construction of the contract, the provision of work during 'normal extra time' was at the discretion of the employers.   **5.24**

Variation in normal working hours

Another problem arises where it is alleged that there has been a variation in the terms of the contract. Thus employees who have been required to work overtime   **5.25** over a long period may argue that their contractual working hours are the hours that they actually work. In general, tribunals are unlikely to accept this argument.

5.26 In *The Darlington Forge Ltd v Sutton* (1968) 3 ITR 196, Mr Sutton, a foundry worker, claimed that his normal working hours should be the average number of hours that he worked rather than the 40 hours specified by his contract, because it was essential that the furnaces were kept going. However, the High Court said that there had been no variation in his contract of employment and that the fact that overtime working was essential to the company did not mean that it was guaranteed by the contract. The employer was therefore correct to calculate his redundancy payment on a basic 40-hour week. Similarly, in *FMC (Meat) Supply Ltd v Wadsworth, Dey and Scrimshaw* EAT 20/83, the EAT said that regular working beyond the hours fixed by the contract did not affect normal working hours for the purpose of calculating a week's pay.

Agreed variation

5.27 In exceptional circumstances, however, courts and tribunals will give effect to an agreed variation in contractual hours where this is clearly established by the evidence (see *Saxton v National Coal Board* (1970) 5 ITR 196, in which a local agreement was held to take precedence over a national agreement). Such a variation may be shown to have been agreed expressly between the parties or agreement to it may be implied from their conduct.

5.28 For example, in *Barrett v National Coal Board* [1978] ICR 1101, a national agreement fixed the normal working week for surface workers at 40 hours, but it also provided that an 'arrangement' to work extra shifts could be made locally. Mr Barrett, a fan attendant, worked 56 hours a week in accordance with an informal local arrangement. When he was made redundant, he claimed that his redundancy payment should be calculated on the hours specified by the informal arrangement—that is, that his normal working hours were 56 hours a week. The EAT remitted the case to the industrial tribunal, saying that the absence of a written agreement was not fatal to Mr Barrett's case, because there might have been a more informal arrangement to the same effect.

Implied variation

5.29 A variation may also be implied. *Armstrong Whitworth Rolls Ltd v Mustard* [1971] 1 All ER 598 is one of the few reported cases in which the argument that there had been an implied variation was successful. In that case, Mr Mustard's contract was subject to a national agreement that specified a 40-hour week. However, after one of his colleagues left, Mr Mustard was told by his foreman to work a 12-hour shift instead of an eight-hour one. The industrial tribunal ruled that the foreman's instruction to work extra hours resulted in a variation in the contract, raising the required minimum to 60 hours a week. However, this decision (although correct on the facts) is very much the exception to the general trend.

Short-time working

Short-time working is all too common a feature of the current industrial climate, **5.30** since it is often seen as preferable to redundancy. In such cases, the general reluctance of courts and tribunals to find a variation in contractual arrangements works to the employee's advantage in relation to short-time working.

Thus, in *Friend v PMA Holdings Ltd* [1976] ICR 330, during the 'three-day week', **5.31** a group of employees came to a temporary arrangement with their employers to work as and when work was available. When they were made redundant, the company said that this arrangement amounted to a variation in their contractual hours of work and therefore their redundancy payment should be calculated on the basis of their average working hours, in accordance with ERA 1996, s 224. The EAT, however, said that the arrangement was designed to meet an emergency, with the result that there was no variation in the contract.

Nonetheless, care should be taken in relation to formal agreements between trade **5.32** unions and employers on short-time working, since such an agreement, which is incorporated into an individual employee's contract, may well result in a change to contractual provisions on normal working hours. The status quo may be preserved by including a clause in the collective agreement. For example, the TUC model clause states:

> This agreement is for a temporary period only and is being introduced solely in order to avoid redundancies. This agreement does not affect the existing contracts of employment of any employees: these contracts will remain in force for the duration of short-time working. Should any redundancies still occur during this short-time agreement, then entitlements to redundancy payment shall not be adversely affected by these short-time arrangements and, in particular, the amount of a week's pay used in the statutory calculation for redundancy payments shall be the amount payable under the contract of employment relating to normal working hours.

In essence, this wording preserves the contractual entitlement to a full week's pay during a period of short-time working in the event of redundancy. Where so desired, it should be extended to cover other statutory rights, such as the calculation of statutory notice pay, which may also be affected by short-time working agreements.

C. Remuneration

The other key difference between the meaning of a week's pay under statute and the **5.33** actual amount that an employee takes home in his or her pay packet relates to the statutory definition of 'pay', since some payments received by an employee do not count towards a week's pay. Essentially, a week's pay is the amount of 'remuneration' payable by the employer under a 'contract of employment in force on the calculation date'. The meaning of 'remuneration' is considered below; the meaning of 'calculation date' is dealt with at **5.61** below.

Meaning of 'remuneration'

5.34   There is no statutory definition of what payments count as remuneration but, as a general rule, remuneration includes all of the contractual payments that an employee receives from the employer for work done (*S & U Stores Ltd v Wilkes* [1974] 3 All ER 401).

5.35   In *S & U Stores Ltd v Wilkes*, the National Industrial Relations Court (NIRC) said that 'any sum that is paid as a wage or salary without qualification is part of an employee's remuneration'. In most cases, therefore, basic wages or salary will be the main element in a week's pay.

5.36   It may also include other payments regularly made to the employee. For example, in *A & B Marcusfield Ltd v Melhuish* [1977] IRLR 484, the EAT held that a bonus regularly paid to an employee formed part of her remuneration even though it was not included in her contract of employment. Discretionary payments, such as Christmas bonuses, will not normally qualify as remuneration. Similarly, benefits in kind will not count, because they do not qualify as remuneration. It should be noted that some disparity in tribunal decisions may be explained by the differences in wording under the different statutory formulae, with the result that certain payments may count for some workers, but not for others.

5.37   A week's pay is calculated on the basis of an employee's gross earnings (*Secretary of State for Employment v John Woodrow & Son's (Builders) Ltd* [1983] IRLR 11).

Rate of pay

5.38   The rate of pay is the real rate, rather than some artificial or notional rate (*Adams v John Wright & Sons (Blackwall) Ltd* [1972] ICR 463). For example, an employer who says to an employee that his or her rate of pay is 50p an hour, but that he or she will receive an additional 50p for every hour worked, is merely using an artificial way of saying that his or her real rate is £1 an hour (see *Mole Mining Ltd v Jenkins* [1972] ICR 282).

5.39   In employments that were covered by wages council orders, the minimum rate is that prescribed by the order, even if the employer pays less (*Cooner v PS Doal & Sons Ltd* [1988] IRLR 338). The same principle applies to workers covered by the National Minimum Wage Regulations 1999, SI 1999/584 (*Pagetti v Cobb* [2002] IRLR 861).

Productivity schemes

5.40   The principle laid down in *S & U Stores Ltd v Wilkes* [1974] 3 All ER 401 (see **5.35** above) has been applied to employees who receive incentive payments under productivity schemes. Employees who receive incentive payments over and above certain production levels will normally be able, therefore, to include such payments in their 'week's pay' (*Ogden v Ardphalt Asphalt Ltd* [1977] 1 All ER 267).

Bonus payments and commission

For the reason given at **5.40** above, bonus payments and commission to which an **5.41** employee is entitled usually fall to be included in a week's pay. In *Mole Mining Ltd v Jenkins* [1972] ICR 282, Mr Jenkins' contract provided that he would be entitled to a shift bonus of one-fifth of a shift for every shift that he worked, with the result that if he were to work five shifts, he would be credited with a payment for an extra shift. When he was made redundant, his redundancy payment did not include his shift bonus. His employer argued that the shift bonus was not a payment for work done, but both the industrial tribunal and the EAT disagreed, ruling that the shift bonus should have been included in the calculation of the redundancy payment. Similarly, in *Weevsmay Ltd v Kings* [1977] ICR 244, the EAT ruled that the commission received by a debt collector on the amount that he collected formed part of his remuneration.

Discretionary payments

Discretionary payments do not usually count as remuneration. However, follow- **5.42** ing the Court of Appeal's decision in *Nerva and others v RL & G Ltd* [1996] IRLR 461, a waiter's tips will normally be included in his or her week's pay unless the tips are paid in cash direct to the waiter (see *Palmanor Ltd t/a Chaplins Night Club v Cedron* [1978] IRLR 303 and *Tsoukka v Ptoomac Restaurants Ltd* (1968) 3 ITR 259). In *Tsoukka*, the employers operated a 'tronc', or pool, and the employees were held to be entitled to that share of the tips which formed part of their remuneration.

It is also possible that other discretionary bonuses, such as payments under a profit- **5.43** sharing scheme, do not count, although much depends on the contractual nature of the scheme. A discretionary bonus may be included if it is paid regularly (*A & B Marcusfield Ltd v Melhuish* [1977] IRLR 484).

Overtime pay

On the face of it, overtime payments clearly fall within the statutory definition of **5.44** remuneration and therefore, prima facie, should normally be taken into account in the calculation of a week's pay. However, overtime payments will count towards a week's pay only if overtime hours form part of an employee's normal working hours (see **5.06** above). Furthermore, in certain circumstances, overtime premiums— that is, additional payments received by an employee for working overtime—are excluded from the calculation of a week's pay. For example, where it is necessary to calculate the 'average hourly rate of pay' (including overtime hours—see 5.72 below), the calculation should be made as if the work had been done in normal working hours and the amount of that overtime remuneration reduced accordingly. The effect of this provision is that overtime premiums are ignored and overtime hours are rated at an employee's ordinary hourly rate.

5.45 This exclusion affects employees whose rate of pay varies with output, such as piece workers, and employees whose rate of pay varies with the number of hours that they work, such as shift workers or rota workers (see Example 1 below). It would appear that the statutory exclusion of overtime premiums does not apply to employees whose pay is constant (ERA 1996, s 222(1)). Thus, in such circumstances, provided that overtime hours form part of such an employee's normal working hours, overtime premiums are included in the calculation of a week's pay (see Example 2 below). Similarly, the statutory exclusion of overtime premiums would not seem to apply to employees whose employment is such that there are no normal working hours (ERA 1996, s 224).

Examples

Example 1

An employee works a 40-hour week in Week one, a 45-hour week in Week two, and a 39-hour week in Week three. All hours above 39 hours are overtime and are paid at time-and-a-half.

The additional premium rate does not count for the purpose of calculating a week's pay.

Example 2

An employee works a basic 40-hour week with a further four hours guaranteed overtime. All hours above 40 hours are paid at time-and-a-half.

The additional premium rate does count for the purpose of calculating a week's pay.

Holiday pay

5.46 Holiday pay is normally regarded as part of an employee's remuneration, but payments received in advance of a holiday are excluded. An example of such a practice is the 'stamp system' in the building trade whereby the employer purchases credit stamps from a management company and gives them each week to the employee. The stamps are cashed in when the holiday is taken and therefore do not count as part of the week's pay in the week in which they are given (*Secretary of State for Employment v Haynes* [1980] IRLR 270).

Allowances

5.47 Allowances cover a wide variety of payments, ranging from simple reimbursement of expenses to attendance allowances.

Allowances: General principles

In general, where the allowance is intended to be a reimbursement for expenses, it **5.48** will not count towards the calculation of a week's pay, but where an allowance is a way of paying additional wages or salary, it will.

For example, an attendance allowance will count as part of an employee's **5.49** remuneration (*London Brick Company Ltd v Bishop* EAT 624/78). Similarly, compensatory payments, such as London weighting, should be regarded as part of an employee's remuneration, although there is no reported case on this point. An allowance for working antisocial hours or for working in abnormal conditions has been held to count as part of a shift worker's remuneration (*Randell v Vosper Shiprepairers Ltd* COIT 1723/13 (IDS 323)).

Travelling time

It is more doubtful whether an allowance paid for travelling time counts as part of **5.50** a week's pay. In *NG Bailey & Co Ltd v Preddy* [1971] 3 All ER 225, the High Court ruled that, for the purpose of calculating a redundancy award, it did not, because such payments fell outside an employee's normal working hours. However, this reasoning would not apply to employments with no normal working hours (see **5.78** below). Moreover, the wording of the provisions has been slightly amended since the *Preddy* decision and now states that payments received by employees 'throughout normal working hours' are to be included in an employee's remuneration. Thus the better view is that payments for travelling time (as opposed to travel expenses) do count, provided that the travelling time is included in the employee's normal hours of work.

Expenses

Sums genuinely paid as expenses do not form part of an employee's remunera- **5.51** tion. Thus in *AM Carmichael Ltd v Laing* (1972) 7 ITR 1, it was held that a lodging allowance paid to a driver who worked on construction sites in the north of England and Scotland was reimbursement for lodging expenses and therefore did not form part of the driver's remuneration. Similarly, travel expenses will not normally form part of an employee's remuneration, because such payments are simply intended to be reimbursement for expenditure incurred by the employee in the course of travelling to and from work (*S & U Stores Ltd v Wilkes* [1974] 3 All ER 401).

A payment that exceeds the amount actually spent by the employee is still regarded **5.52** as expenses, provided that it is a genuine pre-estimate of the costs likely to be incurred. In *Josling v Plessey Telecommunications Ltd* IRLIB 243, August 1982, Mrs Josling received a weekly travel allowance of £28.41. The rate of her allowance was fixed by a collective agreement. However, because she travelled to work with a friend, she made considerable savings and she argued that those savings formed part of her week's pay. The industrial tribunal disagreed. It said that the allowance was a genuine attempt by her employer to assess her travel costs and that therefore the surplus did not form part of her remuneration (see also *London Borough of Southwark v O'Brien* [1996] IRLR 420).

5.53 If it is shown that expenses are, in reality, a disguised form of payment, they will count as part of an employee's remuneration, but, in such circumstances, there is a real danger of the payment (and, as a result, the whole contract) being illegal (see *Tomlinson v Dick Evans 'U' Drive Ltd* [1978] IRLR 77).

Fringe benefits

5.54 Remuneration covers only money payments and not fringe benefits. Tribunals have therefore refused to include the value of a company car as part of an employee's remuneration (*Skillen v Eastwoods Froy Ltd* (1966) 2 ITR 112) or the value of free accommodation (*Lyford v Turquand* (1966) 1 ITR 554). The rule was confirmed by the NIRC in *S & U Stores Ltd v Wilkes* [1974] 3 All ER 401.

Pensions

5.55 At one time, a pension was considered to be an *ex gratia* payment—that is, a gift to an employee from an employer as a reward for long service. In recent years, it has been argued that this view is out of date and that an employer's contribution to an occupational pension scheme should be regarded as part of an employee's remuneration, provided that the employee has a contractual right to such pension contribution from his or her employer. Support for the view that pension contributions form part of a week's pay may be found in a number of authorities involving the definition of pay for related purposes (see *Barber v Royal Guardian Exchange Assurance Group* [1990] IRLR 240, in which pension contributions were treated as 'pay' under Art 119 of the Treaty of Rome; *The Halcyon Skies* [1976] 1 All ER 856, in which employer contributions to an occupational pension scheme were held to form part of a seaman's wages for the purpose of a claim under s 1(1)(o) of the Administration of Justice Act 1956). It should also be noted that HM Revenue and Customs (HMRC) treats such contributions as 'remuneration' for tax purposes. However, in *Payne v Port of London Authority* 155560/89/LN/C, an industrial tribunal has held that pension contributions do not count towards a week's pay. The tribunal considered that although pensions contributions might be regarded as pay for some statutory purposes—for example, for equal treatment of women—pension contributions did not count towards a week's pay for this purpose because:

> they cannot be characterised as sums which an employee is entitled to receive under the contract of employment. They are (commonly) amounts paid by the employer to the pension fund. They may be varied from time to time at the behest of trustees who act on actuarial advice which itself depends on how the fund is prospering. The employee

is never entitled to receive the employer's contributions but only the product which they go towards purchasing for him.

Guarantee payments

Guarantee payments are excluded from the calculation of a week's pay by statute. **5.56** Thus, in relation to employees whose pay is constant, it is provided that remuneration is based on 'the amount payable by the employer . . . if the employee works throughout his normal working hours in a week' (s 221(2)). Similarly, in relation to piece workers and shift workers, it is provided that 'in arriving at the average hourly rate of remuneration, only—(a) the hours when the employee was working, and (b) the remuneration payable for, or apportionable to, those hours, shall be brought in' (s 223(1)).

However, employees who have no normal hours of work are not covered by the **5.57** statutory exclusion and it is possible that guarantee payments are included in the employee's remuneration in such circumstances.

State benefits

Remuneration does not cover payments made by a person other than the employer. **5.58** This means that state benefits do not count as remuneration. Thus in *Wibberley v Staveley Iron and Chemical Company Ltd* (1966) 1 ITR 558, it was held that Disablement Benefit and Special Hardship Allowance did not form part of a week's pay. The position may be different where the payment is made by the employer, but is subject to reimbursement by the government. Thus it is possible that statutory sick pay may count as part of an employee's week's pay, but other payments, such as Family Tax Credit, do not.

Remuneration in employments with no normal working hours

There are some authorities that suggest that some payments that do not count as **5.59** remuneration for employees with normal working hours do count where the employment is such that there are no normal hours of work. For example, in *S & U Stores Ltd v Lee* [1969] 2 All ER 417, the Court held that a £5 car allowance did form part of Mr Lee's remuneration, adding that ' "remuneration" is not mere payment for work done, but is what the doer expects to get as a result of the work he does in so far as what he expects to get is quantified in terms of money'. Such a payment would not normally have been included in a week's pay if the employee had normal working hours (see **5.06** above).

However, in *S & U Stores Ltd v Wilkes* [1974] 3 All ER 401, the NIRC thought it **5.60** 'improbable' that the different method of calculating a week's pay in cases in which there are no normal working hours showed that Parliament intended different standards to apply. The better view is that the meaning of remuneration is the same for both.

D. The Calculation Date

5.61 A week's pay is defined as the amount of weekly remuneration payable under the contract of employment in force on the 'calculation date'. The 'calculation date' is defined in ERA 1996, s 225; its meaning depends on the particular payment claimed under the statutory provisions.

5.62 These provisions were originally introduced by the Redundancy Payments Act 1965 with the object of protecting employees—particularly piece workers—from having their pay artificially reduced in the notice period. The provisions now apply to other statutory awards. Generally, the 'calculation date' is either, in unfair dismissal cases, the 'effective date of termination', or in redundancy cases, the 'relevant date', although special provision is made if the employer gives shorter notice than the statutory minimum. The detailed provisions are considered below.

Additional award

5.63 In relation to the additional award, the 'calculation date' is either the date on which the employee is given notice (s 226(2)(a)), or the effective date of termination—that is, the date of dismissal (s 226(2)(b)).

Basic award

5.64 In relation to the basic award, the position is slightly less straightforward: since the 'calculation date' depends on whether the notice that the employee gives or receives exceeds or is less than the statutory minimum (see **1.106** for the statutory minimum periods of notice). If the employee is dismissed or resigns in circumstances in which he or she should have received or given the statutory period of notice, the calculation date is the period of notice as defined by ERA 1996, s 97(2) or (4) (s 226(3)). In other cases, the calculation date is the date on which the notice required by ERA 1996, s 86 expires (ERA 1996, s 226(6)).

Examples

Summary dismissal

An employee with four years' service is summarily dismissed—that is, dismissed without notice—or summarily resigns—that is, resigns without notice.

The calculation date is the employee's last day of employment. The employee's week's pay will therefore be calculated on the rate of pay in force on the last day of employment.

Short notice

An employee with four years' service is given three weeks' notice or gives three weeks' notice.

The calculation date is the date on which the notice expires. Thus a week's pay will be calculated on the rate of pay in force on that day.

Statutory minimum notice

An employee with four years' service gives or is given four weeks' notice.

The calculation date is the date on which notice is given. Thus a week's pay is calculated on the rate of pay in force at the time.

More notice than statutory minimum

An employee with four years' service is given more than four weeks' notice.

The calculation date is fixed by deducting the employer's statutory minimum from the contractual notice. Thus, in the case of an employee who is given six weeks' notice, the calculation date is fixed at the beginning of the third week of the notice period.

Redundancy payment

In relation to a redundancy payment, the calculation date is determined in the same way as for the basic award (see **5.64** above) (ERA 1996, s 226(5) and (6)). Thus, if the employee is dismissed with no notice or with less than the statutory minimum period of notice, the calculation date is the date on which the employment ended, but where the notice exceeds or is equivalent to the statutory minimum, the calculation date is found by deducting the statutory minimum from the notice given. **5.65**

Backdated payments

A week's pay is calculated on the rate of pay in force on the calculation date. This means that any increase in the rate of pay that occurs after that date is ignored, even if it is backdated. Thus in *Leyland Vehicles Ltd v Reston* [1981] IRLR 19, the EAT held that Mr Reston's redundancy payment was based on the rate of pay prevailing at the time of his dismissal and therefore he was not entitled to the benefit of a pay increase awarded after his dismissal even though it was backdated. **5.66**

Similarly, an employee who agrees to a reduction in his or her rate of pay in order to avoid or defer redundancy, or as part of an agreement on short-time working, runs the risk that a subsequent redundancy payment or other statutory payment will be **5.67** calculated on the reduced rate of pay in force at the calculation date—that is, the reduced rate (*Valentine v Great Lever Spinning Co Ltd* (1966) 1 ITR 71). Some courts and tribunals may be prepared to mitigate the harshness of this rule by holding that a temporary variation does not amount to an agreed variation in the contractual rate of pay, but it should be noted that this is not possible in the face of a clear agreed variation. Thus employees who agree to a reduction in pay in such circumstances should take care to ensure that, by so doing, they do not prejudice their rights to a full redundancy payment (see **5.32**).

E. Methods of Calculating a Week's Pay

5.68 There are four different ways of calculating a week's pay. It is therefore important to identify which method is appropriate for the particular employees concerned. This will depend on their pattern of work.

Employees with normal working hours

5.69 The three different ways of working out a week's pay for employees with normal working hours cover workers whose pay is constant (time workers), workers whose pay varies with output (piece workers), and shift or rota workers whose pay varies with the hours that they work, but whose employment is still such that there are normal working hours (see **5.06** above).

Time rates

5.70 The formula for workers on time rates is relatively straightforward. A week's pay is simply the remuneration for working the normal working hours in the week (ERA 1996, s 221(3)). If payment is made monthly or yearly, or by reference to a period longer than a week, the tribunal must apportion the payment in the manner that it considers just (s 229(2)).

Examples

Example 1

An employee works a 40-hour week at £5 an hour. A week's pay is £200 a week.

Where the payment includes a variable element, such as a commission or bonus, one of the other formulae will apply, since the amount of pay will vary with the work done. However, where commission or bonus pay is constant, it should be added to the basic rate in the normal way. If the period of commission does not coincide with the period of payment, the remuneration or payments should be apportioned in such manner as may be just. Normally, this will be a constant rate of commission over the whole period (*J & S Bickley Ltd v Washer* [1977] ICR 425).

Example 2

An employee earns £500 commission in the first and third quarters of a year, and £800 commission in the second and fourth quarters. Total commission is £2,600.

The sum of £50 per week, which is the average weekly rate of commission, should be added to the employee's basic weekly rate.

Pay varying with output

The formula for workers whose pay varies with output (that is, piece workers) is rather more complicated, because it is necessary to work out their average hourly rate over a period of 12 weeks. **5.71**

The average hourly rate is worked out by taking the total remuneration for all of the hours actually worked, including overtime hours (ERA 1996, s 223(1) and (2)), over a period of 12 weeks prior to the calculation date and dividing it by the number of hours actually worked. **5.72**

Overtime premiums are ignored in the calculation of the average hourly rate (ERA 1996, s 223(3)), with the result that overtime hours are rated as basic hours. This can have the effect of artificially depressing the average hourly rate in cases in which an employee receives a guaranteed incentive bonus for work done in ordinary hours, but receives only an overtime premium for overtime hours. If that premium is ignored in the calculation, the result is that the rate for overtime hours is considerably lower than for ordinary hours and those who work overtime are penalized (see *British Coal Corporation v Cheesbrough* [1990] IRLR 148, HL). **5.73**

If the calculation date (see **5.61** above) does not coincide with the pay day, the period of 12 weeks is the period ending on the last pay day before the calculation date. For weekly employees, the 'pay day' is defined as the day on which they are paid; for other employees, it is a Saturday (ERA 1996, s 235(1)). **5.74**

After establishing the average hourly rate, the week's pay is arrived at by multiplying the average hourly rate by the normal working hours. **5.75**

Example

An employee receives £170 for working 45 hours in Weeks one, two, three, and seven, £180 for 45 hours in Weeks four, five and 12, £200 for a 45-hour week in Week 11, and £150 for working a 45-hour week in the remaining Weeks six, eight, nine, and ten. The normal working week is 40 hours. Hours above 40 hours are rated as normal working hours.

The total remuneration in the 12-week period is £2,020. The total number of hours worked in the 12 weeks is 540. The average hourly rate is worked out as:

$$\frac{£2,020}{540} = £3.75 \text{ (rounded up)}$$

The normal working week is 40 hours, so a week's pay is approximately £150.

This formula should be used to calculate a week's pay for piece workers or workers whose bonus or commission varies with output.

Variable hours

5.76 Where the hours of work vary from week to week over a fixed period (that is, shift workers), it is necessary to work out both the average hours worked in a given period and the average rate of remuneration received in those hours. The average hourly rate is worked out in the same way as for workers whose pay varies with output (see **5.71** above). The average number of normal working hours is determined by:

(a) ascertaining the pay day;
(b) ascertaining the calculation date (see **5.61** above);
(c) taking a period of 12 weeks prior to whichever of the two is the earlier and adding together the total number of hours worked, excluding overtime hours unless these form part of normal working hours;
(d) dividing the total by 12.

Example

An employee works a four-week shift. In Week one, the employee works 40 hours and is paid £150. In Week two, the employee works 60 hours and is paid £300 (including a special bonus). In Week three, the employee works 35 hours and is paid £120, and, in Week four, the employee works 45 hours and is paid £200. The shift pattern is identical for the whole of the 12-week period.

Average normal working hours	=	Total hours of shift × 3
	=	12 weeks
	=	540
	=	45

Average hourly rate is calculated as in **5.72** above (approximately £4.27 per hour), but remember to take the variation in hours into account—that is:

$$\frac{\text{Total pay} \div 12 \text{ weeks}}{\text{Average hours}} = \frac{£2,310 \div 12}{45} = \frac{£192.50}{45} = £4.27$$

This formula should be used to calculate a week's pay for shift workers.

Weeks without remuneration

5.77 In calculating a week's pay in the situations covered by **5.69** and **5.76** above, a week in which no remuneration is payable is ignored in the calculation and an earlier week is brought into the calculation in its place, until the total of 12 weeks is reached (ERA 1996, s 223(1) and (2)). Guarantee payments are ignored in the calculation.

Employees with no normal working hours

5.78 For employees with no normal working hours, such as casual workers, a week's pay is the average remuneration that they receive over a period of 12 weeks, including overtime hours and overtime rates. (The exclusion of overtime premiums does not apply to employees with no normal working hours.)

5.79 Again, the average remuneration is taken over the period of 12 weeks immediately before the calculation date or, if that date is not the same as the pay day, the pay day immediately before the calculation date. Weeks in which no remuneration was payable are ignored and earlier weeks brought in to make the total number of weeks up to 12.

Example

An employee with no normal working hours earns £2,000 in 12 weeks. A week's pay is £166.66 (that is, £2,000 ÷ 12).

Recent recruits

5.80 There is one further statutory formula that applies to recent recruits. This applies to employees who are dismissed shortly after they start a new job, but who still qualify for a statutory notice payment. It may also apply to employees who are dismissed shortly after starting work with an associated employer or the purchaser of a business, if continuity of employment is preserved by the statutory provisions or by the Transfer of Undertakings (Protection of Employment) Regulations 2006 (TUPE 2006), SI 2006/246.

5.81 In such circumstances, the tribunal must determine what 'fairly represents a week's pay', applying the statutory rules as it considers appropriate (ERA 1996, s 228(1)). The tribunal may take into account:

(a) any remuneration received by the employee;

(b) any amount offered as remuneration, whether it was paid or not; and

(c) any remuneration paid by the employer to employees in comparable positions in the same employment or other employments.

5.82 If continuity is preserved by statute, as it is where two employers are associated employers, the tribunal must take into account the average remuneration received by the employee from the previous employer that falls within the period of 12 weeks (ERA 1996, s 229(1)). The average rate is calculated in accordance with one of the formulae set out above.

F. Statutory Maximum

5.83 There is a limit to the amount of pay that counts as a week's pay. This is set by the Secretary of State and is currently fixed at £400 (Employment Rights (Increase of Limits) Order 2010 SI 2010 No 2926). The statutory maximum is reviewed by the Secretary of State annually in September and varies in line with the increase (or decrease) in the retail price index (Employment Relations Act 1999 [ERelA 1999], s 34(1) and (2)). The new rate, subject to the approval of Parliament, takes effect from 1 February. The statutory limit on a week's pay does not apply to the calculation of statutory notice pay.

6

THE COMPENSATORY
AWARD: GENERAL PRINCIPLES

A. Introduction

The third element in unfair dismissal compensation is the compensatory award. **6.01** Unlike the basic award, this is not based on a fixed statutory formula, but rests on the simple principle that employees should be compensated for the economic loss caused to them as a result of their dismissal. Thus, in most cases, the compensatory award will be the largest element in the total award. This chapter looks at the general principles that govern the compensatory award. Chapters 7–9 consider the types of payment and the benefits for which compensation may be awarded in detail.

The overriding aim of the compensatory award is to compensate employees for the **6.02** financial loss caused by their dismissal to the extent that a tribunal considers 'just and equitable', subject to the statutory maximum. To this effect, s 123(1) of the Employment Rights Act 1996 (ERA 1996) provides that:

> Subject to the provisions of this section and sections 124 and 126, the amount of the compensatory award shall be such amount as the tribunal considers just and equitable in all the circumstances having regard to the loss sustained by the complainant in consequence of the dismissal in so far as that loss is attributable to action taken by the employer.

6.03 This provision gives tribunals a wide discretion over the assessment of the compensatory award and they generally approach this task with the minimum amount of technicality. This approach has been encouraged by the Employment Appeal Tribunal (EAT) and the Court of Appeal. In *Fougère v Phoenix Motor Co Ltd* [1976] IRLR 259, for example, the EAT stressed that tribunals are 'bound of necessity to operate in a rough and ready manner and to paint the picture with a broad brush' rather than as skilled cost accountants or actuaries. However, it would be wrong to conclude that the assessment of the compensatory award is an arbitrary exercise, since it has been said that a tribunal must exercise its discretion 'judiciously and upon the basis of principle' (*per* Sir John Donaldson in *Norton Tool Co Ltd v Tewson* [1973] 1 All ER 183). Moreover, a tribunal must set out its reasons in sufficient detail to show the principles used in the assessment.

B. Compensation, not Punishment

6.04 The object of the compensatory award is to compensate employees for financial loss caused by their dismissal, not to punish employers for their wrongdoing. The EAT has therefore said that an award should not be increased either out of sympathy for the employee or as a means of expressing disapproval of the employer's industrial relations policy (*Lifeguard Assurance Ltd v Zadrozny* [1977] IRLR 56).

Exceptions

6.05 There is one well-established exception to the principle that the compensatory award is strictly limited to economic loss attributable to the dismissal—namely, the right to receive compensation for the loss of statutory rights (see Chapter 11).

6.06 There is currently a conflict of authority on the issue of whether, as a matter of justice and equity, a claimant should also be compensated for loss of notice pay. Prior to the EAT's ruling in *Hardy v Polk* [2004] IRLR 420, there was a body of case law that appeared to establish a further exception in relation to awards of compensation for the loss of notice pay. Both the National Industrial Relations Court (NIRC) and the EAT had previously ruled that, as a matter of justice and equity, as well as good industrial relations, employees should normally recover their lost notice pay either by way of a payment in lieu of notice from their employer or as a minimum award of compensation for unfair dismissal (see *Norton Tool Co Ltd v Tewson* [1973] 1 All ER 183; *TBA Products Ltd v Locke* [1984] IRLR 48). These decisions appeared to have been approved by the Court of Appeal in *Babcock FATA Ltd v Addison* [1987] IRLR 173, although Lord Donaldson recognized that the concept of good industrial relations is not a static one and, in the view of Ralph Gibson LJ, there may be exceptional circumstances in which an employer might not offend good industrial relations by tendering a lesser sum than the full contractual notice.

However, in *Hardy v Polk*, the EAT departed from these earlier authorities and **6.07** ruled that there was no 'right' under ERA, s 123(1) to receive a minimum payment equivalent to contractual or statutory notice, because the compensatory award was based strictly on compensating the victim of an unfair dismissal for his or her economic loss rather than penalizing the employer for its conduct and that the duty to mitigate arose from the moment of dismissal. In support of its reasoning, the EAT relied on the House of Lords' ruling in *Dunnachie v Kingston Upon Hull City Council* [2004] IRLR 727 (see **6.10** below).

The EAT followed this approach in *Morgans v Alpha Plus Security Ltd* [2005] IRLR **6.08** 234. However, the more 'traditional' view was followed by the EAT in *Voith Turbo Ltd v Stowe* [2005] IRLR 228. The issue was considered by the Court of Appeal in *Langley v Burlo* [2007] IRLR 145, in which the EAT's reasoning ([2006] IRLR 460) based on *Dunnachie* was rejected. In *Burlo*, the majority of the Court of Appeal appear to have accepted that the claimant was entitled to compensation for her notice period; the issue was how the loss should be calculated. The Court ruled that the amount of claimant's loss during her eight-week notice period should be calculated on her actual loss based on the loss of statutory sick rate of pay rather than on her contractual rate of pay. Nonetheless, Mummery LJ in particular accepted that the narrower principle in *Norton Tool* was still good law and this meant that the claimant did not need to account for earnings received during the notice period. On the other hand, Smith LJ doubted whether there was any principle that required a minimum award of compensation to be made based on the period of notice. Leveson LJ, rather confusingly, agreed with both judgments. Therefore, at the time of writing, the issue remains unresolved.

Whatever the rights and wrongs, as Smith LJ pointed out in *Burlo*, this exception is **6.09** anomalous (given the underlying compensatory purpose of the statutory provisions) and it has been held not apply to fixed-term contracts (*Isleworth Studios v Rickard* [1988] IRLR 173) or, more recently, to constructive dismissals (*Stuart Peters Ltd v Bell* [2009] IRLR 941). As regards the latter, this results in an inconsistent approach between cases in which the employment is terminated directly by the employer and constructive dismissals. In reaching its decision, the Court of Appeal justified the distinction on the basis that it is not 'a general practice, let alone good practice, for the employer to make a payment in lieu at the point when an employee resigns in response to an alleged repudiatory breach'.

C. Compensation for Economic Loss

It has now been firmly established by the House of Lords, in *Dunnachie v Kingston* **6.10** *Upon Hull City Council* [2004] IRLR 727, that the power to award compensation under ERA 1996, s 123 is limited to financial loss attributable to the dismissal, rather than non-economic loss, such as injury to health and injury to feelings.

This confirms the earlier case law referred to in Chapter 10. Nothing in the House of Lords' reasoning prevents employees from claiming compensation for additional economic loss that is attributable to the dismissal—for example, where ill health results in the employee being unable to find alternative work.

D. Date of Dismissal

6.11 The normal rule is that, for the purpose of calculating the compensatory award, the employee's loss is determined at the date of the hearing on quantum. This may not be at the same time as the hearing on liability, because it is not uncommon for there to be a split hearing—for example, *Iggesund Converters Ltd v Lewis* [1984] IRLR 431.

6.12 The normal rule applies even where the assessment of compensation is delayed because of an appeal to the EAT on the question of liability. For example, in *Ging v Ellward Lancs Ltd* (1978) 13 ITR 265, following a successful appeal by the employee, the case was remitted to the industrial tribunal. At the rehearing, which took place some 18 months after the date of dismissal, the tribunal found the dismissal to be unfair and proceeded to assess Mr Ging's loss as at the time of the second hearing. The EAT upheld the tribunal's decision. Mr Justice Arnold said:

> It seems to us that for better or for worse, whether it has an effect one way or whether it has an effect another way, the date to be taken must always be the date at which the assessment actually takes place, all matters which are uncertain then being assessed by the ordinary operation of forming an estimate as to what will happen in the future.

6.13 Similarly, in *Gilham v Kent County Council* [1986] IRLR 56, following the employer's unsuccessful appeal on liability, the Court of Appeal remitted the case to the industrial tribunal to assess compensation. The hearing on quantum took place two years and nine months after the date of dismissal. The industrial tribunal accepted the employer's argument that its liability to compensate the employees was limited to a period of one year following the date of dismissal. However, the EAT, allowing the appeal, ruled that the tribunal was entitled to take into account the employees' loss of earnings for the entire period up to the date of the hearing on quantum. In *NCP Services Ltd v Topliss* EAT 0147/09, the EAT has held that the same principle applies where there has been a successful remedy appeal and the case is remitted to the employment tribunal for a rehearing. In such circumstances, the EAT states that the tribunal should calculate loss on the basis of the facts known at the remitted hearing, rather than limiting itself to those known at the time of the original hearing. The EAT gave three reasons in support of its approach: first, it stated that this approach was 'just and equitable' because 'it has the result of substituting certainty for that which is uncertain'. Second, the EAT considered that there was no reason why a court knowing the situation as it existed at the time of the hearing should then ignore it and substitute a hypothetical one, and finally, the EAT considered that where it is known what the right calculation is, it is correct to assume that the calculation would have been the calculation that a court would have made. However, these decisions should be contrasted with *Qualcast (Wolverhampton) Ltd v Ross* [1979] IRLR 98, in which the EAT reached the opposite conclusion. That decision does not appear to have been referred to the EAT in *Topliss*, in which the EAT incorrectly believed that the point had not arisen previously for judicial consideration.

Implications

In *Gilham*, the rule that the loss is determined at the time of the hearing on quantum **6.14** worked to the employees' advantage, since Mrs Gilham and her colleagues were still out of work at the time of the second hearing. Sometimes, however, it will be to the employee's disadvantage for the hearing on quantum to be postponed—for example, if the employees receives earnings from a temporary job between the date of the first hearing and the hearing on quantum, those earnings will be set off against his or her loss of earnings claim. For example, in *Ging*, Mr Ging's earnings from a temporary job on an oil rig were set off against the loss of earnings that he suffered during two periods of unemployment. In such circumstances, it may be prudent for the employee to invite the tribunal to assess compensation as soon as liability is established. (This may also be desirable for the purpose of ensuring that interest starts to run from the earliest opportunity.) Similarly, in *Topliss* (referred to above), it is reported that, at the rehearing, the employment tribunal increased its award by £79,900 (Case No 2201995/08).

From the employer's point of view, it is generally better to seek to get the issue of **6.15** compensation determined as soon as possible, since, as the decision in *Gilham* illustrates, tribunals are likely to be more sympathetic to the employee in assessing past loss than future loss. Thus awards are likely to be higher if the hearing on quantum is delayed. In such circumstances, employers should ask the tribunal to assess compensation as soon as the decision on liability is known or before the 42-day time limit for an appeal has expired.

Exception

However, the EAT has held that, where the employee has found a permanent better- **6.16** paid job by the date of the hearing on quantum, the award will be based on the employee's loss up to the date on which the employee commenced the new job (*Lytlarch Ltd t/a The Viceroy Restaurant v Reid* [1991] ICR 216 and *Fentiman v Fluid Engineering Products Ltd* [1991] IRLR 150).

E. Remoteness

Compensation cannot be recovered if the loss suffered by the employee is too **6.17** remote—that is, if it does not arise as a 'consequence of dismissal'. For this reason, it has been argued that an employer's liability to pay compensation should cease once the employee has started a 'permanent' new job at an equivalent or better rate of pay, even if the employee is later dismissed from the new job or voluntarily leaves the new job, because any subsequent loss is not a 'consequence of dismissal' attributable to the employer's action. The same argument has been relied on to oppose the payment of compensation where, after dismissal, the employee goes on a training course instead of looking for work. The approach of the EAT and employment tribunals to this question is considered below.

Permanent new employment

6.18   It is accepted, as a matter of principle, that an employer's liability to compensate an employee for loss should cease once the employee obtains a permanent new job at an equivalent or better rate of remuneration, which includes the total value of pay and other benefits (*Aegon UK Corporation Services Ltd v Roberts* [2009] IRLR 1042). The problem is whether liability continues where what was thought to be a permanent job turns out to be a temporary one.

6.19   A strict approach to the issue of causation was adopted by the EAT in *Courtaulds Northern Spinning Ltd v Moosa* [1984] IRLR 43. In that case, the EAT held that the employer was not required to compensate an employee beyond the time at which he started his new job, even though he had been dismissed from the new job by the time the hearing on compensation took place. The EAT ruled that, where an employee obtained permanent new employment, but was later dismissed from his or her new job, any loss flowing from the dismissal from the new job was not attributable to the original dismissal and therefore was not the responsibility of the original employer. The EAT's decision in *Moosa* was followed by the Scottish EAT in *Simrad Ltd v Scott* [1977] IRLR 147, in which the applicant voluntarily gave up her new job to retrain as a nurse, and was also followed by the EAT in *Whelan v Richardson* [1998] IRLR 114.

6.20   However, the EAT's reasoning may be open to criticism on the ground that it introduces the common law concept of causation into the rules on unfair dismissal compensation. If followed, this could lead to complex legal argument as to when a new job can be regarded as sufficiently permanent to break the chain of causation, thereby bringing the old employer's liability to an end. It is not unusual for a job to turn out to be less 'permanent' than was hoped at the time that the employee was engaged and the employee may not be to blame for his or her subsequent dismissal. For example, the employee may be selected for redundancy on a 'last in, first out' basis. Another potential difficulty with the approach in *Moosa* is at what stage a job should be regarded as 'permanent'. The EAT suggested that a new job should be regarded as permanent if the employment lasts long enough for the employee to re-qualify for protection against unfair dismissal. This may be fair enough if the qualifying period is one year, but is more questionable if the qualifying period is two years or more, or less than one year.

In *Dench v Flynn & Partners* [1998] IRLR 63, the Court of Appeal rejected the   **6.21**
'causation' approach in favour of one based on 'justice and equity'. Ms Dench was
found to have been unfairly dismissed on grounds of redundancy. During her
notice period, she found a job with another firm of solicitors, subject to a probationary period. She was not kept on after completing her probationary period.
Nonetheless, the tribunal found that her losses were no longer 'attributable to the
actions' of her former employers and therefore limited its award to the period
between the end of her employment with her old employer and the start of her
employment with her new employer. Allowing the appeal, the Court of Appeal
ruled that the loss consequent on an unfair dismissal does not necessarily cease
when the employee finds a new job of a permanent nature at an equivalent or
higher salary, because this would not be 'just and equitable'. What the tribunal has
to determine, in the words of Staughton LJ, is whether the loss in question was
caused by the unfair dismissal or by some other cause. In the *Dench* case, the tribunal
should have asked itself whether the original dismissal could be seen as a continuing
cause of the claimant's loss following her subsequent dismissal from her new job,
and whether it was just and equitable for her to recover that loss. The Court's
approach is consistent with the more pragmatic approach adopted by the EAT in
the earlier cases of *Morgan Edwards Wholesale Ltd/ Gee Bee Discount Ltd v Hough*
EAT 398/78, *Dundee Plant Co Ltd v Riddler* EAT 377/88, and *Fentiman v Fluid
Engineering Products Ltd* [1991] IRLR 150.

Any lingering doubts as to which of these two approaches should be followed by   **6.22**
tribunals were set aside by the EAT's ruling in *Salvensen Logistics Ltd v Tate* EAT
689/98, in which the Court of Appeal's ruling in *Dench* was described as 'the most
authoritative judgment on this whole topic'. The EAT stated that:

> [The] current position essentially establishes that what is important is that the tribunal
> should look . . . at all the facts in deciding the effect that intervening employment
> should have where it has come to an end before the calculation date . . . even where the
> remuneration is as great or greater than that enjoyed in the employment under
> consideration.

The effect of the *Dench* decision is, therefore, to focus on whether it is just and   **6.23**
equitable for the complaint to be compensated if the claimant is still out of work at
the time of the remedies hearing, having lost the new job. Relevant factors that a
tribunal is likely to consider include the nature of the new job, whether it was
intended to be temporary or permanent, how long the new employment lasted, the
claimant's reasons for leaving, and whether the claimant is able to bring an unfair
dismissal claim against the new employer. (In *Tate*, the tribunal held that the fact
that the new job lasted for nine months did not bar a claim for compensation for
losses after the new job came to an end.)

It should be noted that this issue will arise only where the employee obtains a   **6.24**
permanent new job. The chain of causation will not be broken where it is clear
from the outset that the employment is to be on a temporary basis. For example, in

Ging v Ellward Lancs Ltd (1978) 13 ITR 265 (see **6.12**), the industrial tribunal accepted that Mr Ging was entitled to recover compensation for his second period of unemployment because the job on the oil rig turned out to be a temporary one. For similar reasons, the EAT has held that a post-dismissal illness does not cut off an employee's right to compensation under ERA 1996, s 123(1). In such circumstances, a tribunal should consider how long the employment would have lasted but for the dismissal, and the claimant should be compensated for the loss of pay and benefit that would have been received during that period (*Wood v Mitchell SA Ltd* EAT 0018/10).

6.25   On the other hand, where the employment tribunal concludes that the 'new' job brings to an end the former employer's liability, it is not open to the tribunal to award compensation for any loss that arises subsequently as a result of the claimant losing the new job. Therefore, in *Aegon UK Corp Ltd v Roberts* [2009] IRLR 1042, the Court of Appeal ruled that the tribunal had erred in awarding the claimant compensation for loss of pension rights in relation to her subsequent employment when it had concluded that the claimant's new job brought her loss to an end. It was not open to the tribunal to apply different principles of causation to different parts of the remuneration package. In particular, the tribunal cannot carve out pensions for special treatment. The position would have been different if the new job had not been on equivalent terms, (thereby bringing the loss to an end), or if the tribunal had concluded that the new job had not broken the chain of causation (as illustrated by *Dench* above).

Period of training

6.26   A similar problem arises where the employee decides to undergo a period of retraining rather than to look for a new job. In such circumstances, a tribunal must consider the question of mitigation (see Chapter 13), as well as whether the employer's liability to pay compensation ceases under ERA 1996, s 123(1). This has also led to a conflict of authority.

6.27   In *Pagano v HGS* [1976] IRLR 9, an employment tribunal ruled that an employer's liability ceases when the employee starts the training course, because any loss suffered by the employee during that time is caused by the employee's own actions and not those of his or her former employer. Thus the tribunal limited its award of compensation to the period of 12 weeks before Mr Pagano commenced his course of study. The employment tribunal's ruling is consistent with the approach taken by the EAT in *Courtaulds Northern Spinning v Moosa* [1984] IRLR 43. Similarly, in *Simrad v Scott* [1997] IRLR 147, it was successfully argued that the employer's liability ceases where an individual chooses to undergo a period of training prior to embarking on a new career, because any continuing loss was too remote to be attributable to the conduct of the employer.

6.28   However, in *Khanum v IBC Vehicles Ltd* EAT 785/98, the EAT held that, in the particular circumstances of the case, the employment tribunal should not have refused to award compensation for the losses suffered by the claimant after she had embarked on a full-time university course, because those losses were a direct result of her dismissal and therefore not too remote. In the EAT's opinion, the ruling in *Simrad* did not establish any rule of law or binding principle that the pursuit of education subsequent to dismissal necessarily broke the chain of causation. A similar approach was applied by the EAT in *Larkin v Korean Airlines Ltd* EAT/1241/98, in which the claimant's decision to embark on a training course for a new career did not preclude her from recovering compensation from her old employers. These cases are consistent with a number of earlier authorities in which a pragmatic approach has been applied. For example, in *Sealey v Avon Aluminium* [1978] IRLR 285, an industrial tribunal rejected the argument that an employer's liability under what is now ERA 1996, s 123(1) came to an end in such circumstances, pointing out that 'these are hard times even for a young man to find other work and we do not propose to cut short his recoverable loss because meanwhile he has decided to use the time to some purpose'. Similarly, in *Glen Henderson Ltd v Nisbet* EAT 34/90, the EAT upheld an industrial tribunal's decision to award compensation to an employee for the time during which she attended a five-week business enterprise course.

Tribunals seem to prefer this more pragmatic approach to the one based on causation, **6.29** because it accords more with justice and equity. But this does not mean that compensation will be awarded in every case. For example, in *Holroyd v Gravure Cylinders Ltd* [1984] IRLR 259, an industrial tribunal refused to award compensation for the period during which the applicant attended a one-year postgraduate course. Upholding the tribunal's ruling, the EAT took the view that it was the applicant's decision to take himself out of the labour market for 12 months and therefore it was correct not to award him compensation during that period. The EAT considered that any loss in the period after the course finished was 'so remote as to be . . . incapable of calculation'. Compensation therefore may not be awarded where a course is long or is not of a vocational nature, or where the employee's decision to retrain is taken after having found a new job (*Simrad v Scott* [1997] IRLR 147), since the 'loss' is no longer attributable to the dismissal or any action of the dismissing employer.

The reasoning in *Pagano v HGS* and *Simrad v Scott* is also open to the more funda- **6.30** mental objection that it is inconsistent with the more pragmatic approach taken by the Court of Appeal in *Dench v Flynn & Partners* that, subject to the issue of mitigation, the tribunal should approach the issue of whether the loss is attributable to the conduct of the employer on the basis of what is just and equitable in the circumstances.

Consequential loss

The extent of liability imposed by ERA 1996, s 123(1) for consequential loss flowing **6.31** from the dismissal would seem to be substantial. For example, in *Royal Court Hotel Ltd v Cowan* EAT 48/84, an employment tribunal held that compensation could be claimed for the loss to the family's budget arising out of the dismissal of the applicant's spouse who was employed by a 'sister' company. On appeal, the employers argued that the claim should have been disallowed because the loss was too remote.

However, the EAT refused to interfere with the employment tribunal's ruling on the point, although the appeal was allowed on other grounds (see **6.34** below). This decision suggests that the employer is liable for any financial loss that flows directly from the dismissal, provided that it is 'attributable to the employer's action'.

6.32   On the other hand, loss suffered prior to dismissal is not considered to arise as a 'consequence of dismissal'. This can cause problems in constructive dismissals where it is argued that the repudiatory breach arises as a result of a sequence of events that ultimately gives rise to a breach of the implied duty of trust and confidence (often referred to as 'last straw' dismissals). In *GAB Robins (UK) Ltd v Triggs* [2008] IRLR 317, the Court of Appeal ruled that an employee could not recover compensation for financial loss post-dismissal as a result of personal injury suffered as a result of the employer's action prior to dismissal. In support of its approach, the Court relied on the House of Lords' rulings in *Eastwood v Magnox Electric plc*; *McCabe v Cornwall County Council* [2004] IRLR 733, in which it was held that the appropriate remedy for an employer's pre-dismissal conduct that was in breach of the duty of trust and confidence was an action for damages in the ordinary courts. The Court also relied on the House of Lords' ruling in *Johnson v Unisys Ltd* [1999] IRLR 279 as to the correct demarcation between employment tribunal claims and claims in the ordinary courts. The Court's reasoning, which is not free from difficulty, would appear to limit severely the compensation that can be awarded to an employee who suffers illness as a result of an employer's pre-dismissal conduct.

Attributable to the employer's action

6.33   The proviso that the loss must be caused by the employer's action—that is, the dismissal—is an important limitation on the employer's liability under ERA 1996, s 123(1).

6.34   It was relied on by the EAT when it overturned the employment tribunal's decision in *Royal Court Hotel v Cowan* EAT 48/84 (see **6.31** above). The EAT said that the employer could not be held responsible for the actions of its 'sister' company, with the result that the dismissal of Mrs Cowan's spouse was not attributable to action taken by it. (The EAT does not seem to have considered the possibility that the employer could have been liable if the sister company were an 'associated employer'.)

6.35   It also means that loss caused by the employee's impecuniosity is unlikely to be recoverable, since it arises from the employee's own action rather than that of the employer. For example, if, as a result of dismissal, an employee defaults on a loan, the employer is unlikely to be liable for the costs suffered by the employee in defending any consequential legal proceedings. (The position may be different if the employer knew about the loan or gave the employee financial assistance to pay it off.)

6.36   In *McDonald v Capitol Coaches Ltd* EAT 140/94, the EAT appears to have extended this reasoning when it upheld an employment tribunal's decision not to award any compensation to an employee who declined to take up the employer's invitation to discuss the situation surrounding his dismissal with his employer. The EAT held that the industrial tribunal was entitled to conclude that, had he taken up the offer, he would have been reinstated and therefore the loss was attributable to his, and not his employer's, actions. The decision, however, would appear to be inconsistent with the reasoning of the EAT in *Soros and Soros v Davison and Davison* [1994] IRLR 264 and *Lock v Connell Estate Agents* [1994] IRLR 444, in which the EAT stresses that employers cannot rely on the employee's actions after dismissal to reduce the award of compensation.

In considering the question of remoteness, tribunals should concern themselves only **6.37** with the actual consequences of dismissal and not with hypothetical ones (*Gilham v Kent County Council* [1986] IRLR 56). This rule means that, if a business is subsequently closed, employees who are unfairly dismissed at an earlier date cannot recover compensation for any loss that they suffer beyond the date of closure unless they are able to persuade the tribunal that the closure is not genuine (see *James W Cook & Co (Wivenhoe) Ltd v Tipper and others* [1990] IRLR 386).

F. Heads of Compensation

In *Norton Tool Co Ltd v Tewson* [1973] 1 All ER 183, the NIRC said that compensation **6.38** should be assessed under four main headings:

(a) *immediate loss of earnings*—that is, the loss of earnings between the date of dismissal and the date of the hearing;
(b) *future loss of earnings*—that is, anticipated loss of earnings in the period following the hearing;
(c) *loss arising from the manner of dismissal*; and
(d) *loss of statutory rights*—that is, compensation for being unable to claim unfair dismissal for a period of at least one year.

In *Tidman v Aveling Marshall Ltd* [1977] IRLR 218, the EAT said that it was the **6.39** duty of the employment tribunal to raise and inquire into each of the four heads of compensation established by *Norton Tool*, plus a fifth head—that is, loss of pension rights. The assessment of claims under this last head has proved to be rather complex (see Chapter 9).

Proof of loss

Whilst it is the duty of the tribunal to raise each of the heads mentioned at 6.38 **6.40** above, it is up to the employee to particularize his or her claim under each of them. This point was stressed by the EAT in *Adda International Ltd v Curcio* [1976] IRLR 425. In the context of a claim for loss of future earnings, Bristow J said: 'The tribunal must have something to bite on, and if an applicant produces nothing for it to bite on he will only have himself to thank if he gets no compensation for loss of future earnings.' This means that applicants should come to the tribunal well pre-pared with evidence that shows what their loss is under each head of compensation.

6.41   Employers should be requested to disclose any information relevant to the assessment of the employee's compensation claim. This will be particularly important in relation to a claim for loss of pension rights, in which case much, if not all, of the relevant information is likely to be in the employer's possession or control (see also *Benson v Dairy Crest Ltd* EAT 192/89). If employers refuse to disclose this information voluntarily, an application should be made to the industrial tribunal for an order of discovery. Employers may also be penalized if they fail to disclose the details of the new employers' pension scheme (*Bingham v Hobourn Engineering Ltd* [1992] IRLR 298).

6.42   Failure to make a claim under one of the heads or to quantify a particular type of loss properly cannot normally be rectified on appeal. For example, in *UBAF Bank Ltd v Davis* [1978] IRLR 442, the industrial tribunal awarded Mr Davis one year's loss of future earnings. On appeal, Mr Davis complained that the tribunal had ignored the fact that his dismissal meant that he would never be able to work in banking again. He argued that, consequently, the award should be increased. However, the EAT ruled that if Mr Davis had wanted the tribunal to take the point into account, he should have raised evidence before it to prove this (see also *Adda International Ltd v Curcio* [1976] IRLR 425).

6.43   Once an employee has produced evidence of loss suffered under one of the relevant heads of compensation, the evidential burden of proof will usually shift to the employer (*Barley v Amey Roadstone Corporation Ltd* [1977] IRLR 299).

Industrial pressure disregarded

6.44   In assessing the compensatory award, industrial tribunals must take no account of 'any pressure which, by . . . calling, organising, procuring or financing a strike or other industrial action, or . . . threatening to do so, was exercised on the employer to dismiss the employee . . .'. The question of compensation must be determined 'as if no such pressure had been exercised' (ERA 1996, s 123(5)).

G. Statutory Maximum

6.45   The compensatory award is subject to a statutory maximum of £68,400 (Employment Rights (Increase of Limits) Order 2010 SI 2010 No. 2926), which applies to all dismissals after 1 February 2010. The statutory maximum is reviewed by the Secretary of State in September each year and is varied in line with the increase (or decrease) in the retail price index (Employment Relations Act 1999 [ERelA 1999], s 34(1)–(2)). The new rate, subject to the approval of Parliament, takes effect from 1 February.

7

CALCULATING THE COMPENSATORY AWARD: LOSS OF EARNINGS

A. Introduction

This chapter looks at the two main heads of compensation established by *Norton*   **7.01**
Tool Co Ltd v Tewson [1973] All ER 183: immediate loss of earnings—that is, loss
of earnings between the date of dismissal and the date of the hearing; and future loss
of earnings—that is, compensation for any continuing loss after the hearing.
Tribunals are thus expected 'to glance both backward into the past and forward into
the future' (*per* Waite J in *Thompson v Smiths (Harlow) Ltd* EAT 952/83), but before
considering how tribunals approach this task, it is necessary to examine what sums
count as lost earnings for this purpose.

119

B. What Losses Count

7.02 The object of the compensatory award is 'to compensate, and compensate fully, but not to award a bonus', *per* Sir John Donaldson in *Norton Tool Co Ltd v Tewson* [1973] 1 All ER 183. Thus, in broad terms, an employee may claim compensation for any loss suffered as a consequence of the dismissal provided that it is 'attributable to the action taken by the employer' (see **6.02** above). At the same time, it should be remembered that compensation will be awarded only where the tribunal considers it 'just and equitable'. This means that some tribunals may ignore small payments, particularly if they are discretionary—for example, a Christmas bonus may be disallowed for this reason. For the same reason, tribunals may refuse to award compensation where a claim is made for loss of state benefits (see **7.36** below) or may reduce their award to take account of a small tax rebate (see **7.39** below). Bearing this is mind, the first part of this chapter looks at the sort of payments that are included in a claim for loss of earnings.

Pay

7.03 As the Employment Appeal Tribunal (EAT) points out in *Brownson v Hire Services Shops Ltd* [1978] IRLR 73, 'other things being equal, the first thing you lose in consequence of being dismissed is what you would have got in your pay packet'.

7.04 The 'pay packet' in this context includes both the payments that qualify as remuneration for the purpose of calculating a week's pay (see Chapter 5) and payments that are not included in that calculation. Thus it was held in *Brownson* that an employee can claim for the loss of any bonus or productivity payments, or any commission received, and for the loss of overtime payments at premium rates, if appropriate. The fact that the employee does not have a contractual right to such a payment is no bar to compensation being awarded so long as it can be shown that the payment is one that the employee might have reasonably been expected to have had but for the dismissal (Employment Rights Act 1996 [ERA 1996], s 123(2)(b)). The loss of regular tips may also be recovered for the same reason (*Palmanor Ltd t/a Chaplins Night Club v Cedron* [1978] IRLR 303).

7.05 In employments covered by wages council orders, the calculation will be based on the amount that the employer should have paid under the relevant order even if the employer was paying less at the time of dismissal (*Senelle v G Desai t/a Pizza Express* COIT 29552/85 LN and *Cooner v PS Doal & Sons* EAT 307/87). The same principle applies to workers covered by the National Minimum Wage Act 1998; see *Pagetti v Cobb* [2002] IRLR 861, in which it was held that the tribunal erred in not having regard to the national minimum wage in calculating the basic and compensatory award.

7.06 'Pay' is assessed as a net figure—that is, after the deduction of tax and National Insurance contributions (NICs).

Calculating pay

In contrast to the strict statutory rules that are used to work out the basic and special **7.07**
awards, there is nothing (apart from the words of ERA 1996, s 123) to guide tribunals
in working out a week's pay for the purpose of calculating the compensatory award.
It is therefore up to the tribunal to decide what method of calculation is just and
equitable in the particular circumstances.

For example, tribunals may adopt one of the formulae in ERA 1996, ss 221–229 **7.08**
(see **5.68** above). These formulae set out methods of calculating the weekly earnings
of groups of workers such as piece workers, whose pay varies with output, or shift
workers, whose pay varies with the shifts that they work. The problem with this
approach, however, is that the formulae in those sections are not intended specifically for the purpose of calculating a 'week's pay' for the compensatory award and
ignore certain payments that are included in the compensatory award.

A further problem arises in cases in which it is necessary to compensate employees **7.09**
for loss of payments that fluctuate from week to week, such as tips, bonuses, and
commission. In such circumstances, the normal practice is for tribunals to work out
the average amount that an employee was earning in this way during the 12 weeks
prior to dismissal, but there is nothing to prevent employees from arguing that the
tribunal should award either a lump sum or use a longer period of time for calculating
the average in cases in which the work is seasonal or the period of compensation
exceeds three months. (See **7.16** regarding bonus and commission payments.)

The rate of pay should be based on the amount that the employee is entitled to **7.10**
receive under his or her contract. It is for the tribunal to resolve any disputes relating
to the correct rate or level of pay to which an employee is entitled. Thus, in *Kinzley
v Minories Finance Ltd* [1987] IRLR 490, the EAT held that the employment tribunal
had erred in law when it refused to determine whether the applicant was entitled
to be compensated on the basis of her actual earnings at the time of her dismissal,
or, as she claimed, the earnings that she should have been receiving at that time.
The EAT held that loss of earnings should be assessed on what the employee was
entitled to receive irrespective of whether the employee was, in fact, receiving that
entitlement at the time of dismissal.

Pay rises

An important difference between the compensatory award and the basic award is **7.11**
the treatment of pay rises.

In *Leyland Vehicles Ltd v Reston* [1981] IRLR 19, the EAT ruled that a pay increase **7.12**
awarded after the calculation date could not be included in the basic award even if
it was backdated. The same principle applies to the additional award. However, in
assessing the compensatory award, a tribunal can take into account any pay increase
awarded up to the date of the hearing, including a backdated pay rise (*Leske v Rogers*

of *Saltcoats* (*ES*) *Ltd* EAT 520/82) and 'any benefit which [the employee] might reasonably be expected to have had but for the dismissal' (ERA 1996, s 123(2)(b)). This may include a future pay rise provided that there is a 'high probability that, in conformity with company policy, the company would increase the salary of an employee' in the period of assessment—that is, during the period covered by the future loss (*York Trailer Co Ltd v Sparkes* [1973] IRLR 348).

7.13   The size of the award depends on the tribunal's view of the likelihood of the increase. The greater the likelihood, the higher the award—see *Sparkes*.

Notice pay

7.14   ERA 1996, s 86 sets out the minimum periods of notice to which an employee is entitled on the termination of employment (see **1.106** above).

7.15   The primary remedy for a breach of these provisions is an action for damages in the ordinary courts (normally the country court), because the tribunal does not have jurisdiction to hear claims arising out of a breach of contract. However, a long line of authority, latterly confirmed in *TBA Industrial Products Ltd v Locke* [1984] IRLR 48, has established that such sums may also be included as part of the employee's lost earnings in the compensatory award.

Loss of bonus

7.16   As stated above, pay includes any bonus and commission that the claimant, on a balance of probabilities, is likely to receive during the compensation period.

7.17   In context of such payments, it is important to bear in mind that the loss under ERA 1996, s 123(1) is taken to include 'any benefit that he [the claimant] might reasonably be expected to have had but for the dismissal'. It is not therefore necessary for the claimant to show that he or she had a contractual right to the bonus (although, since the Court of Appeal's ruling in *Horkulak v Cantor Fitzgerald International* [1994] IRLR 942, the distinction is perhaps of less significance, because similar principles are likely to apply in determining the loss suffered by the claimant).

7.18   However, it is still necessary for the claimant to show, on a balance of probabilities, that he or she had an 'expectation' of receiving a bonus within the compensation period and that the expectation was 'reasonable'. Such an expectation may be generated by the contract or the conditions of employment, or (possibly) by representations made at an interview or at an annual performance appraisal.

7.19   Nonetheless, even where a reasonable expectation is established, there may still be difficulties in quantifying the amount of the bonus—particularly where the scheme is completely discretionary. Where the bonus is linked to targets, it will be open to the tribunal to find out whether the targets were actually achieved or would have been but for the claimant's dismissal. Evidence of bonuses received by other people in a comparable position may set an appropriate benchmark.

Tribunals may also base their awards on a percentage chance approach if liability is established (*Allied Maples Group Ltd v Simmons & Simmons* [1995] 1 WLR 1602).   **7.20**

Holiday pay

The primary remedy for loss of holiday pay is an action for damages in the ordinary   **7.21** courts. However, in certain circumstances, employees may be entitled to recover pay for lost holiday leave as part of the compensatory award (*Tradewinds Airways Ltd v Fletcher* [1981] IRLR 272), or as a claim for unpaid wages under ERA 1996, Pt II. In order to recover compensation, it must be shown that the employee has lost a period of paid holiday as a result of dismissal. This commonly occurs where the entitlement to paid holiday at a new job is service-related. For example, in *Wilson v Tote Bookmakers Ltd* COIT 15570/81, Mrs Wilson had booked her holiday before she was unfairly dismissed. By the time of the hearing, she had found a new job, but her new employer would not allow her to go on paid holiday until she had been with it for one year. She therefore claimed compensation for the loss of holiday pay from her old employer. The industrial tribunal upheld her claim.

The same principle would apply to employments in which the entitlement to paid   **7.22** holiday increases with length of service. Employees who have acquired extra holiday in such circumstances would be entitled to recover compensation for the loss of their holiday entitlement if the holiday entitlement in their new job were lower. The loss in such circumstances is the difference between the two.

In both of these situations, the claim is not for loss of holiday pay per se, but rather   **7.23** the loss of an entitlement to a period of paid holiday consequent upon dismissal. Such a claim will not normally arise where the employee is still out of work at the time of the hearing, since the claim for lost holiday pay would be absorbed by the general claim for loss of earnings. However, tribunal practice on this question is by no means universal—some tribunals are willing to ignore the legal niceties and award compensation for loss of holiday pay in itself.

Stock options

It has become increasingly fashionable to include stock options and profit-related   **7.24** pay as part of the remuneration package (see **1.62** for further details). The value of these schemes will vary depending on their nature and whether or not the option has vested. In *Leonard v Strathclyde Buses Ltd* [1998] IRLR 693, the EAT accepted that compensation could be awarded for the loss in value caused by the premature sale of stock options. The claimants successfully recovered the difference between the share price on termination and the share price that they would have received but for their unfair dismissal. Compensation may be awarded for the loss of the option itself provided that the employment tribunal is satisfied that the claimant would have been granted such an option but for the dismissal (*O'Laiore v Jackel International Ltd* [1991] IRLR 170), but the compensatable loss may be more difficult to quantify and prove where there is no more than a mere promise to grant such an option in the future. Nonetheless, where possible, tribunals will seek to place a value on these rights. For example, in *Casey v Texas Homecare Ltd* EAT/632/87, the employment tribunal had declined to estimate the value of an employee's share option because it regarded this as too 'speculative and indefinite', but the EAT awarded £1,000 for the loss on the basis of the evidence presented to it, making an allowance for the chance that the share price might fall. In the context of private companies, among the contingencies that may need to be considered in connection with the future exercise of share options is an assessment of flotation, the likely value of shares on flotation date, and the likelihood that the claimant would have purchased some or all of the shares allocated to him or her (*Selective Beauty (UK) Ltd v Hayes* EAT/058/04).

Redundancy payments

7.25 The statutory redundancy scheme sets the minimum level of payment that must be made to employees who are dismissed on the grounds of redundancy (see **17.15** below). Many employers simply incorporate these provisions into their employees' contracts of employment. In the event of an employee being unfairly dismissed, the loss of the employee's accrued rights in this respect will be reflected in the basic award.

7.26 However, some contractual redundancy arrangements make provision for enhanced redundancy payments—that is, payments in excess of the statutory minimum—and an employee who is dismissed in circumstances in which such arrangements exist may legitimately want to claim compensation for the loss of this benefit. This was recognized by the EAT in *Lee v IPC Business Press Ltd* [1984] ICR 306, in which it was said:

> . . . if it is shown that there was a term in the contract between Mr Lee and the company which was binding on the company and meant that, if Mr Lee was made redundant, he was entitled as a matter of contract to more than the statutory redundancy payment, which is something which he has lost as a result of being unfairly dismissed and it is one of the things which the industrial tribunal should take into account in arriving at their award of compensation if any.

7.27 The EAT added that the same principle would apply if the enhanced redundancy payment formed part of a collective agreement that was not incorporated into the individual employee's contract, but which was honoured in practice.

7.28 The EAT's conclusion in *Lee* is supported by the words of ERA 1996, s 123(3), which states that an employee's loss under s 123(1) includes:

> . . . any entitlement or potential entitlement to a payment on account of dismissal by reason of redundancy (whether in pursuance of Part XI or otherwise), or . . . any

expectation of such a 'payment' to the extent that the entitlement would have exceeded the basic award.

A claim for an enhanced redundancy payment may arise in one of three situations. **7.29** These three claims are alternatives—the same loss cannot be recovered twice.

(a) *An employee who is dismissed is entitled to an enhanced payment for redundancy, but does not receive it* Here, assuming that the scheme is contractual, the primary remedy is an action for breach of contract, but the decision in *Lee* shows that, in the alternative, the loss is recoverable as part of the compensatory award. Indeed, this is the only claim that can succeed, although there is an expectation of payment, but it is not enforceable in contract.

(b) *The employee is dismissed for some other reason, but is able to show that he or she would have been made redundant, and hence would have been entitled to the enhanced redundancy payment, within the period of the award* For example, in *Addison v Babcock FATA Ltd* [1986] IRLR 388, the EAT held that Mr Addison was entitled to an enhanced redundancy payment because he would have been dismissed for redundancy 13 months after he was actually dismissed. (The EAT's ruling on this point was not challenged by the employer in the Court of Appeal.) In other cases, the level of the award depends on the likelihood of a redundancy actually occurring.

(c) *There is no risk of the employee being made redundant, but the employee's claim is based on the loss of the benefit of the additional protection afforded by the enhanced redundancy provisions* Such a claim may arise even if the employee is lucky enough to find a new job with an equivalent scheme, because the employee will have lost the value of the years of service with the previous employer and will have to requalify under the new scheme.

The decision in *Lee* above casts little light on how compensation should be assessed **7.30** in this third situation. One possibility is that the employee should receive compensation for the full loss of the benefits incidental to the old employment, but this takes no account of the fact that the employee was under no risk of redundancy at the time of dismissal. The better view is that this type of compensation is analogous to awards for loss of employment protection rights (see Chapter 11) and so the figure should be based on a proportion of the value of the enhanced benefit—for example, 50 per cent.

Out-of-pocket expenses

Genuine tax-free reimbursement for expenses incurred in the course of employ- **7.31** ment are excluded from the compensatory award.

For example, in *Tradewinds Airways Ltd v Fletcher* [1981] IRLR 272, Mr Fletcher **7.32** claimed compensation for various tax-free allowances that he received from his previous employer. Although he also received similar allowances from his new employer, they were at a reduced rate. The industrial tribunal allowed his claim and awarded him the difference between his old allowance and his new allowance. The EAT, allowing the appeal on this point, ruled that the sums claimed represented genuine expenses incurred on the company's behalf and therefore did not form part of Mr Fletcher's pay.

7.33 However, the reimbursement of expenses must be distinguished from 'perks', such as a season ticket loan or travel expenses. The loss of the value of such perks could be included in the compensatory award if the new employer either made no provision for such payments or was less generous. Thus, in *Fletcher*, the EAT stressed that the position would have been different if there were an element of profit in the allowance.

7.34 Fringe benefits and expenses are considered more fully in Chapter 8.

7.35 The payment of 'bogus' expenses to evade tax liability may result in the contract becoming unenforceable on the grounds of illegality, thereby excluding an unfair dismissal complaint altogether (*Tomlinson v Dick Evans 'U' Drive Ltd* [1978] IRLR 77).

Loss of National Insurance contribution credits

7.36 Compensation may also be recovered for any lost NIC credits in the period covered by the compensation claim.

7.37 Such claims may arise because of the operation of social security law. Under reg 9(1) of the Social Security (Credits) Regulations 1975, SI 1975/556, unemployed persons are generally entitled to a Class 1 NIC credit for each week of unemployment. However, this entitlement may be lost for up to a year if a person receives compensation for unfair dismissal during that period (Social Security (Unemployment, Sickness and Invalidity Benefit) Regulations 1983, SI 1983/1598, reg 7(1)).

7.38 The loss of credited NICs for a short time is unlikely to affect the entitlement to state benefits because these are assessed on the employee's contribution record over the whole of the relevant contribution year. However, a prolonged period of disqualification is likely to affect an employee's entitlement. This problem may be partially overcome if the employee makes voluntary contributions. In *Allen v Key Markets Ltd* COIT 1425/41, the industrial tribunal suggested that compensation for lost credits should be awarded in any case in which the employee is unemployed for more than eight weeks. The amount of compensation is fixed by reference to the weekly Class 3 NIC rate.

Tax implications

7.39 Where, as a result of the dismissal, an employee is entitled to a tax rebate, the employer may argue that the amount of the award should be reduced to reflect this. Conversely, where the dismissal takes place towards the end of the tax year, an employee may argue that account should be taken of the fact that, had the correct disciplinary procedure been followed, the dismissal might have occurred in the next tax year leaving him or her with a larger tax rebate.

Initially, the EAT ruled that this was really a question of 'swings and roundabouts' **7.40** and that therefore tax liability should be completely ignored (*Adda International Ltd v Curcio* [1976] IRLR 425). However, in *Lucas v Laurence Scott Electromotors Ltd* [1983] IRLR 61, the EAT ruled to the contrary and decided that the tax implications should be taken into account, although in *MBS Ltd v Calo* [1983] IRLR 189, the EAT said that tax implications should be ignored unless the sums involved are large. A similar approach was taken by an employment tribunal to the loss of Working Tax Credit in *Mosse v Hastings and Rother Voluntary Association for the Blind* (1103096/06/NW).

Interest

There is no power to add interest to the award itself, but, in *Melia v Magna Kansei* **7.41** *Ltd* [2005] IRLR 449, the EAT has suggested that it may be appropriate to compensate the claimant for the loss of interest on the sums that it has awarded as a head of loss by applying the same premium as that used in making a deduction for alliterated payment (that is, 2.5 per cent).

C. Credits for Payments Received

In assessing the loss caused by the dismissal, credit must normally be given for **7.42** any payments received by the employee both at the time of dismissal and since dismissal. The rules on the treatment of *ex gratia* payments made by an employer are considered in Chapter 15.

Payments in lieu

In the absence of an express or implied agreement to the contrary, credit should be **7.43** given for any payment made by the employer to the employee on account of wages or other benefits, such as a payment in lieu of notice. This principle was confirmed by the Court of Appeal in *Babcock FATA Ltd v Addison* [1987] IRLR 173, which overturned the EAT's ruling that such a payment should be ignored in calculating an employee's loss of earnings. It should be noted, however, that the EAT's approach in *Addison* may still apply in Scotland, because the EAT based its ruling on the earlier decision in *Finnie v Top Hat Frozen Foods Ltd* [1985] IRLR 365, which has not been overruled by the Court of Session and therefore may still be good law.

Payments received from a new employer

As a general rule, credit must also be given for any payments received from a new **7.44** employer since dismissal, including income from part-time employment (*Justfern*

Ltd v D'Inglethorpe and others [1994] IRLR 164). The application of this principle requires special consideration in two situations: first, where, prior to the hearing on compensation, the employee has found a permanent new job at an equivalent or higher rate of pay; and second, in relation to earnings received during the notice period.

Permanent new employment

7.45　It has already been noted that an employer's liability to pay compensation will normally cease once an employee has started a permanent new employment at an equivalent or better rate of pay. A related issue is whether, in such circumstances, the applicant is required to offset the additional earnings received from the new job in the period up to the date of the hearing on compensation against the loss suffered during the period of unemployment.

7.46　This point was considered by the EAT in *Lytlarch Ltd t/a The Viceroy Restaurant Reid* EAT 296/90 and in *Fentiman v Fluid Engineering Products Ltd* [1991] IRLR 151. In *Fentiman*, the applicant was out of work for 29 weeks after his dismissal. He then found himself a new job that was better paid than his old job. The hearing on compensation took place some 68 weeks after dismissal—that is, 39 weeks after he had started his new job. The employment tribunal calculated Mr Fentiman's loss of earnings during the period for which he was unemployed, but set off against this loss the earnings that he had received from the date on which he started the new job to the date of the hearing. This produced a net loss of £2,373. The EAT, allowing the appeal, held that Mr Fentiman was entitled to £9,744, representing his full loss of earnings between the date of dismissal and the date when he started the new job, and was not required to give credit for the additional earnings that he had received from the new job. (The award of £9,744 was, in fact, reduced to £8,925 to take account of the statutory maximum that applied at the time.)

7.47　The EAT justified its decision on two grounds. First, it said that if this were not the case, employees would be discouraged from mitigating their loss by finding new employment prior to the tribunal hearing on compensation. Second, as a matter of justice and equity, it was unjust that an employer's liability should be reduced to 'a fraction of the loss sustained by the complainant during his period of unemployment' simply because the employee has found a better-paid job.

7.48　A number of points can be made both for and against the EAT's ruling. On the one hand, the EAT's decision is the mirror image of the ruling in *Courtaulds Northern Spinning Ltd v Moosa* [1984] IRLR 43: just as an employer's liability to compensate an employee will, in general, cease once equivalent employment has been obtained, so an employee will not be required to give credit for payments received from that time onwards. Furthermore, as a matter of justice and equity, it would seem arbitrary that the amount of the award should depend on when the compensation hearing happens to take place, because this may well vary from region to region. On the other hand, it may be considered unjust that an employee who obtains a permanent new job that is less well paid is required to give credit for all of the earnings that he or she receives up to the date of the hearing on compensation, whereas one who receives a better-paid permanent job does not. Moreover, as has already been noted, sometimes it may be difficult to determine when a new job is permanent.

The ruling in *Fentiman* applies only where the applicant has obtained a permanent new job. The general rule still applies where the job is temporary, part-time, or, as already noted, is permanent, but less well paid than the original employment. **7.49**

Payments during the notice period

Previously, there was a conflict of case law on the issue of whether a claimant has to account for payments received during the notice period. Prior to the EAT's ruling in *Hardy v Polk* [2004] IRLR 420, there was a body of case law that established that credit need not be given for such payments: both the National Industrial Relations Court (NIRC) and the EAT had previously ruled that, as a matter of justice and equity, as well as good industrial relations, a former employee should normally recover his or her lost notice pay either by way of a payment in lieu of notice from his or her employer, or as part of an award of compensation for unfair dismissal (see *Norton Tool Co Ltd v Tewson* [1973] 1 All ER 183 and *TBA Products Ltd v Locke* [1984] IRLR 48). These decisions appeared to have been approved by the Court of Appeal in *Babcock FATA Ltd v Addison* [1987] IRLR 173), although Lord Donaldson recognized that the concept of good industrial relations is not a static one and, in the view of Ralph Gibson LJ, there may be exceptional circumstances in which an employer might not offend good industrial relations by tendering a lesser sum than the full contractual notice. However, in *Hardy v Polk* (above), the EAT ruled that there was no 'right' under ERA 1996, s 123(1) to receive a minimum payment equivalent to contractual or statutory notice, because the compensatory award was based strictly on compensating the victim of an unfair dismissal for his or her loss, rather than penalizing the employer for its conduct, and that the duty to mitigate arose from the moment of dismissal. The EAT applied the same reasoning in *Morgans v Alpha Plus Security Ltd* [2005] IRLR 234, in which it ruled that the claimant had to account for Incapacity Benefit received during the notice period, because such benefits are not covered by the Employment Protection (Recoupment of Jobseeker's Allowance and Income Support) Regulations 1996, SI 1996/2349 (the 'Recoupment Regulations'—see Chapter 16). But in *Langley v Burlo* [2007] IRLR 145, the Court of Appeal ruled that credit need not be given for payments received from a new employer during the statutory notice period. **7.50**

As noted in **6.09** above, the principle in *Norton Tool* does not apply to fixed-term contracts or constructive dismissals. Thus, in *Isleworth Studios Ltd v Rickard* [1988] IRLR 137, the EAT overturned an industrial tribunal decision to compensate Mr Rickard for his lost earnings during the remaining 29 weeks of his fixed-term contract because his earnings from his new business exceeded the loss that he had **7.51** suffered as a result of his dismissal. The EAT was adamant that the *Norton Tool* principle applied only to contracts terminable by notice and that good industrial relations practice did not require it to be extended to fixed-term contracts, where compensation should be based strictly on the loss suffered by the applicant. The EAT's reasoning may be open to doubt on the ground that good industrial relations should not distinguish between an employee whose contract is terminable by six months' notice and one who is employed under a fixed-term contract for six months.

7.52 Credit must still be given for any payment received outside the notice period (*Vaughan v Weighpack Ltd* [1974] IRLR 105).

7.53 The way in which to ascertain how the tribunal will calculate the award is as follows.

(a) Calculate the amount of wages lost during:
    (i) the statutory notice period; and
    (ii) the contractual notice period (if any) without making any deductions.
(b) If the claim is for a higher amount than (i) above, then deduct from (ii) all of the sums earned since the dismissal. If the balance is still higher than the amount of (i), the tribunal should award the higher sum. If it is less than (i), the tribunal should award the statutory minimum.

Example

An employee, Mr Smith, is dismissed by his employer on 1 November after two-and-a-half years' service. His monthly pay was £1,000 and he was entitled to three months' notice. He was employed by a new employer on 1 January at an increased salary of £1,400 per month.

His statutory notice pay is two weeks' pay—that is, £500. His contractual notice pay is £3,000, less the £1,400 that he has received from his new job—that is, £1,600. Because this is more than the £500 statutory notice, Mr Smith will be awarded £1,600.

Pay rises in the new job

7.54 In working out whether the employee is better or worse off in the new job, the tribunal may take into account likely future increases in earnings in that job (*Gee Walker & Sons Ltd v Churchill* EAT 11/84).

7.55 This is the converse to the principle examined in 7.12 above—namely, that tribunals may increase the award by making allowance for possible future pay rises that the employee would have received had he or she not been dismissed. In theory, tribunals should set off the award that they make for one against the other. In practice, tribunals are unlikely to make the deduction unless they are certain that a pay increase is about to be awarded.

In addition, it should be remembered that, if the difference between the two sums **7.56** is small, the tribunal is unlikely to make an award at all. On the other hand, if the evidence shows that the employee would have definitely received an increase, it is unlikely to start weighing up the probabilities of a future pay rise from the new employers and will probably award the difference.

Are state benefits deductible?

State benefits received during the period of unemployment are not taken into **7.57** account until after the award has been fixed by the tribunal. This includes income support (*Savage v Saxena* [1998] IRLR 182). The deduction is then made in accordance with the procedures laid down by statutory instrument (the Recoupment Regulations—see Chapter 16). However, the position appears to be different in relation to other state benefits received by an employee after dismissal, which are not covered by the recoupment provisions. In *Puglia v C James & Sons Ltd* [1996] IRLR 70, the EAT ruled that, in assessing the loss caused by the dismissal, credit must be given for state incapacity/sickness benefits (*Sun & Sand Ltd v Fitzjohn* [1979] ICR 268) and invalidity benefit received by an employee after his or her dismissal. This contrasts with the EAT's earlier rulings in *Hilton International Hotels v Faraji* [1994] IRLR 267, in which the EAT ruled that such payments were an 'insurance-type' benefit and should be ignored, and *Rubenstein v McGloughlin* [1996] IRLR 557, in which the EAT rejected the 'all or nothing' approach and suggested that, as a matter of justice and equity, one half of the amount of the benefit received should be deducted. However, in *Morgans v Alpha Plus Security Ltd* [2005] IRLR 234, the EAT rejected this approach and came down firmly in favour of the EAT's approach in *Puglia*. The current position therefore is that the receipt of Incapacity Benefit, whilst not precluding an award of compensation for loss of earnings (*Sheffield Forgemasters International Ltd v Fox* [2009] IRLR 192), is not covered by the Recoupment Regulations and is therefore deductible from the tribunal's award. It is arguable, however, that credit should not be given for such payments received during the notice period (see 7.50 above).

It is unclear whether the EAT's ruling in *Morgans* applies to all other state benefits **7.58** not covered by the Recoupment Regulations. For example, in *Savage v Saxena* [1998] IRLR 182 (a case not cited to the EAT in *Morgans*), the EAT ruled that Housing Benefit should be excluded in the calculation in an award of unfair dismissal compensation because it would not be just and equitable for employers to benefit from such payments.

Remoteness

It is open to an employment tribunal to conclude, as a matter of discretion, that **7.59** certain state benefits that an employee receives after dismissal are either too remote or arise independently of the employer's wrong, with the consequence that credit need not be given for such payments. For example, in *Justfern Ltd v D'Inglethorpe and others* [1994] IRLR 164, the EAT upheld an industrial tribunal's decision not to give credit for a £4,000 educational grant received by the applicant in connection with a training course in its calculation of its award of compensation. The same principle is likely to apply to payments received by an employee under a private insurance scheme. In this context, see *Parry v Cleaver* [1970] AC 1 and *Savage v Saxena* [1998] IRLR 182, in which it was held that Housing Benefit is too remote to fall within the general common law principle that credit should be given for payments received post-dismissal, because the payment results from the employee's inability to meet housing needs from his or her resources and is paid in respect of the needs of the household rather than the individual. On the other hand, credit must be given for payments received under an employer's non-contributory permanent health insurance (PHI) scheme if such payments continue beyond the termination date (which is likely to depend on the terms of the employer's scheme). For example, in *Atos Origin IT Services UK Ltd v Haddock* [2005] IRLR 20, a disability discrimination case, the EAT held that an employment tribunal had erred in its assessment of future loss when it failed to take account of the payments that might be made to the claimant under the employer's PHI scheme under which the claimant was entitled to 75 per cent of his salary. (See also *Simrad Ltd v Scott* [1997] IRLR 147 for a somewhat unusual illustration in which an employee was not required to give credit for a loan that was made to her during her employment and was to be repaid by way of work. The EAT took the view that the employee had been denied the opportunity to repay the loan as a result of the actions of the employer, and that therefore it would not be 'just and equitable' for the employee to give credit for the loan even though it had been waived by the employer on dismissal.)

D. Assessing Loss of Earnings

7.60 As Lord Donaldson MR pointed out in *Babcock FATA Ltd v Addison* [1987] IRLR 173:

> the assessment of any compensation, whether in an industrial relations context or otherwise, must always involve a comparison between what was, is and will be and what would (or should) have been—between the actual past, present and future and the hypothetical past, present and future.

Immediate loss of earnings

7.61 The first head of compensation established by *Norton Tool Co Ltd v Tewson* [1973] 1 All ER 183 is the employee's immediate loss of earnings between the date of dismissal and the date of the hearing on compensation. This is calculated by assessing the total loss of earnings and benefits in the relevant period, and giving credit for payments received during that time, in accordance with the principles outlined above.

Example

Calculating immediate loss of earnings

Mr Jones is unfairly dismissed from his job as an electrician. He takes home £200 a week, including overtime and a bonus. He finds a new, slightly better-paid, job three months after the dismissal. He worked for his old employer for four years. The hearing takes place four months after the dismissal. The award for immediate loss of earnings is calculated as follows.

	£
Loss of earnings between dismissal and the hearing	2,400
Credit for earnings from new job @ £10 a week for a month	40
Total loss	2,360

E. Loss of Future Earnings

The second head of compensation established by *Norton Tool Co Ltd v Tewson* [1973] 1 All ER 183 is loss of future earnings. This requires the employment tribunal to assess the employee's ongoing loss and is inevitably, to a large extent, a speculative exercise, but, as the Court of Appeal stressed in *Scope v Thornett* [2007] IRLR 155, a tribunal cannot opt out of this task simply because it involves a certain amount of speculation. A tribunal will err in law if it simply 'plucks a figure from the air' and must give a rational basis for its decision (*NCP Services Ltd v Topliss* O147/09). This will involve a consideration of the factors identified at **7.63** below. Normally, tribunals adopt a fairly 'rough and ready' approach to the calculation of future loss—particularly in cases in which the award is limited to one year or less. However, since the increase in the compensation limit, it is becoming increasingly more common for tribunals to be faced with more substantial claims for future loss covering longer periods. This will involve the tribunal having to consider what the EAT in *Kingston Upon Hull City Council v Dunnachie (No 3)* [2003] IRLR 843 called 'old job facts' (that is, the chance that the old job would have come to an end) and 'new job facts' (that is, the chance of the employee finding a new job). It is clear from the EAT's ruling that tribunals must give a reasoned decision for the awards that they make, having taken these factors into account. However, so long as the tribunal takes all relevant factors into account, its decision is unlikely to be overturned on appeal. **7.62**

The tribunal is always faced with one of the following three situations: **7.63**

(a) the employee has found a new job by the time of the hearing in which he or she is better paid than, or at least as well paid as, he or she was in the old job; or

(b) the employee has found a new job by the time of the hearing, but he or she is less well paid than he or she was in the old job; or

(c) the employee is still out of work at the time of the hearing.

New job: Equivalent or better

7.64 If the employee has found a new job by the time of the hearing that is at least as well paid as the old job, there will be no continuing loss of earnings and hence no compensatory award for loss of future earnings.

7.65 In making the comparison, the tribunal looks not only at pay, but also at the fringe benefits in the new job (see Chapter 8).

New job: Less well paid

7.66 There will, however, be a continuing loss where the new job is less well paid. In such circumstances, the tribunal has to assess how long it will take before the employee earns the same as he or she was earning in the old job. Again, fringe benefits are taken into account.

7.67 It is open to the tribunal to conclude that this loss will last indefinitely—that is, that the employee's earnings in the new job will never match those in the old job. In such circumstances, compensation would be awarded for the remainder of the employee's working life. However, other than in cases in which the employee is close to retirement, such as *Kennard v Royal British Legion Industries* (15 April 2002), referred to by the EAT in *Dunnachie* (*No 3*), it is unlikely that the tribunal would reach this conclusion, since it fails to take into account the uncertainties of life and other factors that the EAT in *Dunnachie* (*No 3*) refers to as 'old job facts', such as whether the claimant would have remained in the old job for the period in question (see below). In most cases, tribunals are likely to place some limit on the length of the continuing loss.

7.68 The period of the award may also be limited for other reasons. (See Chapter 12 as to limits on full compensation.)

Unemployed claimants

7.69 Where a claimant is unemployed at the time of the hearing, the tribunal is faced with the task of having to decide how long the employee is going to remain unemployed and how long it will be before the earnings from the new job will match those of the old. In theory, for the reasons given above, the period of continuing loss could be indefinite, but, in practice, the award will normally be limited because of the various contingencies taken into account by the tribunal. (See Chapter 12 as to the limits on full compensation.)

Assessing future loss

7.70 The tribunal normally takes the personal characteristics of the employee and the state of the labour market into account in assessing future loss.

Personal characteristics of employee

In fixing the award for future loss, tribunals will take into account the personal **7.71** characteristics of the employee such as his or her age, state of health, and other personal circumstances.

This point is illustrated by the EAT's decision in *Fougère v Phoenix Motor Co Ltd* **7.72** [1976] IRLR 259. Mr Fougère was 58 years old at the time of his dismissal. Even though he was in a poor state of health, the tribunal based its award on the length of time that an average person in his position would have taken to find a new job. The EAT said that this was the wrong approach—the tribunal should have taken Mr Fougère's personal circumstances into account.

Similarly, in *Brittains Aborfield Ltd v Van Uden* [1977] ICR 211, the EAT held that **7.73** an employee who had defective eyesight would be at a disadvantage in the labour market and therefore would find it more difficult to get a new job.

Age is one of the most important factors influencing the tribunal's assessment. Thus **7.74** an applicant who is close to retirement may recover compensation for the remainder of the applicant's working life. For example, in *Isle of Wight Tourist Board v Coombes* [1976] IRLR 413, the industrial tribunal held that Mrs Coombes, who was dismissed at the age of 58, was entitled to recover compensation for her lost earnings until the date of her retirement—that is, for two years. Similarly, in *Penprase v Mander Bros Ltd* [1973] IRLR 167, Mr Penprase was three-and-a-half years away from retirement when he was dismissed. The industrial tribunal found that he would have remained in his job until he retired had he not been dismissed and therefore awarded him compensation for the full three-and-a-half years. (See also *Sandown Pier Ltd v Moonan* EAT 399/93, in which the EAT held that an industrial tribunal was entitled to conclude that an employee who was unfairly dismissed at the age of 50 was unlikely to work again given that there was a 20 per cent rate of unemployment in the area in which he lived and worked.) The extent to which age is relevant and the evidential basis of its relevance will give rise to some complex issues once the default retirement age is removed.

Moreover, if the evidence shows that the employee would have been kept on **7.75** beyond retirement age, additional compensation may be awarded. For example, in *Barrell Plating and Phosphating Co Ltd v Danks* [1976] IRLR 262, the industrial tribunal awarded compensation for an additional six months beyond Ms Danks' retirement age. On appeal, the employers argued that such a claim should be disallowed on the ground that the statutory provisions prevent employees over the normal retiring age from claiming unfair dismissal. Rejecting this argument, the EAT said that such a limitation on an award of compensation could not be implied from the statutory exclusion. On the facts, there was ample evidence to support the tribunal's conclusion that Ms Danks would have been kept on after reaching retirement age.

State of the labour market

7.76 The state of the labour market obviously has an important bearing on the tribunal's view of how long the applicant is likely to remain unemployed (*Perks v Geest Industries Ltd* [1974] IRLR 228).

7.77 In this context, the tribunal will consider the state of the labour market both at a national level and at a local level. It is open to either side to call consultants who specialize in job search to give expert evidence on the applicant's prospects of finding a new job. It is also open to the tribunal to rely on its own knowledge of the local labour market to assess the employment prospects of the applicant and it may even come to a different conclusion from that presented to it by the parties. For example, in *Eastern Counties Timber Co Ltd v Hunt* EAT 483/76, the applicant said in his evidence that he thought that he would find a new job in three months, but the industrial tribunal thought that this was too optimistic and assessed the future loss at six months. However, in *Hammington v Berker Sportcraft Ltd* EAT 344/79, the EAT said that the parties should be given an opportunity to comment at the hearing on an assessment based on the tribunal's own knowledge.

Contingencies

7.78 Assessing future loss involves a consideration of a number of factors: including: whether and how long the claimant would have remained in the job (that is, the possibility of leaving the job voluntarily or as a result of redundancy) and, if so, for how long; whether there were personal factors such as health, family situations or locations, or economic factors that might have a bearing on this issue; whether there was a possibility of promotion leading to an increase in earnings; or whether the level of earnings would have remained the same. Mr Justice Burton in *Dunnachie* (*No 3*) refers to these as 'old job facts'. For example, in *O'Donoghue v Redcar & Cleveland Borough Council* [2001] IRLR 615, the Court of Appeal upheld an employment tribunal decision to limit the compensation awarded to the claimant on the basis that she would have been fairly dismissed six months after her actual dismissal on the basis of her 'divisive and antagonistic approach to her colleagues'.

7.79 The tribunal is also required to consider what the EAT in *Dunnachie* (*No 3*) referred to as 'new job facts'. This involves a consideration of the 'new' (where the employee has found a new job), including the likelihood of promotion or improvement in salary and benefits over the compensation period, the possibility of the claimant moving to a better new job in the future either voluntarily or compulsorily, and what the new job might be, by what date it might be obtained, and what remuneration might be received by way of mitigation. Again, the tribunal's task in this respect is highly speculative, but it is important that the tribunal makes findings in relation to both 'old job facts' and 'new job facts'.

7.80 In *Cartiers Superfoods Ltd v Laws* [1978] IRLR 315, it was argued that the tribunal was wrong to base its award of future loss on a three-year period because it had ignored certain factors. These included the chances of Mrs Laws, who was 33 years of age, finding a new job in that period, or having a child, or being transferred to another part of the country. The EAT, dismissing the appeal, accepted that these factors were all relevant, but held that the tribunal had taken them into account in its decision:

> Nobody could say, of course, how long she would have continued to be employed by Cartiers Superfoods Ltd if she had not been dismissed; partly, it would depend on how long she wanted to work. But, as far as her wishes are concerned, it seems fair to summarise it and to say that the shortest period seems likely to have been two or three years, and the longest about ten; and it does not seem to us that we can say, as a matter of law, which the industrial tribunal misdirected themselves in making the judgment which they did on this point.

The next step is to establish whether there is a pay differential (or, in relevant cases, **7.81** a difference in value in the overall package) between the old job and the new job, and if so, whether that differential is likely to continue having regard to the factors referred to above. In *Dunnachie (No 3)*, the EAT stressed that a tribunal must not abdicate from the task of deciding what, on a balance of probabilities, is likely to happen and must give a reasoned decision for its conclusion. For example, in *Birmingham City Council v Jaddoo* EAT 10448/04, a disability discrimination case, the EAT ruled that the employment tribunal had erred in making a 'lifetime' loss award without properly addressing the issue of whether the future loss was as great as the claimant had suggested, given the claimant's many entrepreneurial activities.

Furthermore, as the EAT points out in *Dunnachie (No 3)*, if the tribunal is either **7.82** unable to speculate, or reaches the conclusion that it is impossible to speculate as to the future, then there would be 'no future loss proved rather than the establishment of the high multiplier followed by the immediate application of a substantial percentage deduction'. This is correct, to the extent that the burden of proof is on the claimant to satisfy the tribunal as to future loss, but it should be noted that the EAT's observations were made in the context of a claim for career-long loss and that if a tribunal was unable to reach that conclusion on the evidence, it still would be open to the tribunal to award compensation over a shorter period in such circumstances—that is, one that fell within the range of speculation.

The multiplier

The problem of putting a figure on future loss of earnings also arises in claims for **7.83** personal injuries. In those cases, it is common for the ordinary courts to use a multiplier—that is, a figure, be it in weeks, months, or years, which reflects the employee's likely continuing loss of earnings. Included in the multiplier are the contingencies outlined at 7.78–7.79 above, as well as other factors that actuaries take into account in working out premiums for life insurance policies. Some tribunals use a similar approach in working out the length of future loss of earnings.

But it is clear from the EAT's ruling in *Dunnachie (No 3)* that the approach to calculating future loss in unfair dismissal cases differs in certain respects from that in personal injury cases.

Use of Ogden tables

7.84   The Ogden tables are a set of actuarial tables with explanatory notes for use in personal injury and fatal accident cases. The tables, which are updated periodically, provide a multiplier to be used for calculating future loss of earnings up to retirement age (and beyond, if pension loss is appropriate) where a claimant will be in less remunerative employment for the rest of his or her working life owing to the continuing effect of the injury. The current tables for 2010–11 for loss of earnings (Tables 1–4) take account of the risk of mortality for men and women, and make allowance for the accelerated payment of any award at different rates of return. In addition, Table A4 makes allowance for the extent to which a person's future working life expectations are affected by factors such as educational attainment, disability, and employment status. However, other risks associated more directly with the employment relationship, such as the possibility that the level of earnings may have been affected by periods of illness or unemployment, or ceasing to work to care for children or other dependants, are not included in the tables. Furthermore, no allowance is made for specific risks associated with the particular employment, such as the risk of redundancy. A special discount has to be calculated and applied to the multiplier to take account of these contingencies.

7.85   The circumstances in which the Ogden tables may be used in the calculation of unfair dismissal compensation were considered by the EAT in *Dunnachie (No 3)*. The EAT ruled that the Ogden tables (and any similar such table that may be devised) should be relied upon by the employment tribunal only in the calculation of future loss in unfair dismissal claims where the tribunal has reached the conclusion that there is, prima facie, a career-long loss. In other words, it is only if the tribunal is satisfied, having considered the 'old job facts' and the 'new job facts' in line with the principles set out in **7.62** above, that the loss is a career-long loss that the Ogden tables may become 'helpful'. An example of such a case referred to by the EAT in *Dunnachie (No 3)* is *Kennard v Royal British Legion Industries* (15 April 2002). In that case, the claimant was found to have been unfairly selected for redundancy at the age of 58 and was disabled. The tribunal, having found that there was no possibility that he would secure comparable paid employment for the rest of his working life and that his previous employment was secure for the rest of his working life, went on to conclude that there was a lifelong loss and therefore used the multipliers in the Ogden table to calculate its award (see also the cases referred to in **7.81** above). But the EAT suggests that the use of the Ogden tables in assessing future loss in unfair dismissal will be rare. The position may be different in discrimination cases (*Abbey National plc v Chagger* [2009] IRLR 86, EAT; [2010] IRLR 47, CA) (see **19.48**).

As stated above, the multipliers in the Ogden tables are principally based on the **7.86** risk of mortality, although allowance is made for accelerated payment based on different rates of return as reflected in different multipliers. At the time of writing, the tables do not take account of any specific risk associated with the particular employment or with the particular individual (as in *Dunnachie (No 3)* referred to above) and, for the reasons given by the EAT in *Dunnachie*, it may well be inappropriate to use the tables in such circumstances.

The Ogden tables also do not take account of the many other contingencies that **7.87** may fall to be discounted in the calculation of future loss in an unfair dismissal case (as recognized by the EAT at [30] of its decision in *Dunnachie (No 3)*). So, even where the Ogden tables are considered relevant, the award will have to be discounted to take account of these factors. Experience of the use of these tables indicates that some of the many factors, such as regional variations and risks in different types of employment, are overemphasized and the discount for these factors is generally less than 1 per cent, although a higher discount may be justified in particular circumstances. Moreover, the EAT warns that, where the reduction for contingencies is too high, it is likely to have been inappropriate for the tribunal to have assessed its award on the basis of a career-long loss in the first place.

In *Dunnachie (No 3)*, the EAT also refers to other 'dangers' of using actuarial tables, **7.88** such as:

(a) difficulties in calculating loss of earnings over the relevant period, because the differential may be variable;
(b) the failure to address issues relating to tax and mitigation; and
(c) the risk of double counting.

(The EAT gives further guidance on the tribunal procedures to be followed where the claimant does wish to rely on the Ogden tables, or similar actuarial methods—see **22.48** below.)

Finally, it should be noted that the EAT expressly acknowledges that its ruling does **7.89** not apply to the calculation of pension loss where 'different considerations apply' and where an actuarial method is used when the 'substantial loss' approach is used to calculate pension loss.

Deducting contingencies

The alternative to a multiplier is to decide on the overall figure and then make a **7.90** deduction based on the various contingencies. Some early authorities suggested that five years was an appropriate starting point for this purpose, but the EAT has suggested one year as a rule of thumb (*Tidman v Aveling Marshall Ltd* [1977] IRLR 218). This approach appears to be more consistent with the EAT's ruling in *Dunnachie (No 3)* provided that the tribunal addresses the issue raised in the 'old job facts'/'new job facts' analysis and reaches a reasoned conclusion on those issues.

> **Example**
>
> *Calculating future loss of earnings*
>
> Mr Jones is unfairly dismissed from his job as an electrician. He takes home £200 a week including overtime and commission. He is unemployed at the time of the hearing, which takes place four months after the dismissal. The tribunal finds that he will find a new job in three months and would have received a 5 per cent pay increase three months after his dismissal. The award for loss of earnings is calculated as follows.
>
> | | £ |
> | --- | --- |
> | Loss of earnings for the first three months | 2,400 |
> | Loss of earnings for the next four months | 3,360 |
> | Total loss | 5,760 |

No set amount

7.91 It should be stressed that a tribunal has complete discretion to award what it considers to be appropriate in the particular circumstances of the case. Although, in practice, many tribunals limit their awards for future loss to 12 months and the EAT will only interfere with the award if the tribunal erred in law in its assessment or reached a perverse decision—that is, one to which no reasonable tribunal could have come—it is not required to do so and, subject to the statutory maximum, compensation may be awarded for such period as is considered appropriate in the circumstances (see *Morganite Electrical Carbon Ltd v Donne* [1987] IRLR 363, in which the EAT rejected the argument that a tribunal's award of 82 weeks' loss of earnings, made up of 30 weeks' loss up to the date of the hearing and 52 weeks thereafter, was excessive).

Power to review

7.92 The EAT has emphasized that the speculative nature of the tribunal's task in fixing an award for future loss means that it will rarely overturn its assessment on appeal. However, the industrial tribunal does have a power to review its own decisions if new evidence comes to light that could not have been known or reasonably foreseen at the time of the hearing (Employment Tribunals (Constitution and Rules of Procedure) Regulations 2004, SI 2004/1861, r 34).

7.93 This power may be relied on by either the employer or the employee if the forecast that formed the fundamental basis of the tribunal's decision has been falsified to a sufficiently substantial extent so as to invalidate the assessment (*Yorkshire Engineering Co Ltd v Burnham* [1974] ICR 77). For example, in *Dicker v Seceurop Ltd* EAT 554/84, the employer successfully applied for the award for future loss to be reviewed when Mr Dicker found a new job two days after the hearing. Similarly, in *Cichetti v K Speck & Son* COIT 2041/209, the industrial tribunal reviewed its original assessment that it would take Mr Cichetti 13 weeks to find a job when he found a new job with similar pay two weeks later. The same principle applies where there is a fundamental change in the employee's circumstances. In *Bateman v British Leyland* [1974] IRLR 101, Mr Bateman successfully applied for a review when he lost his new job two weeks after the hearing on compensation. An application for review is also possible where the award was based on the incorrect assumption that the payments received by the claimant would not be taxable (*Williams v Ferosan Ltd* [2004] IRLR 607). It is unclear whether this authority could be relied upon in support of an application that could be made to increase the award to the statutory limit where the tribunal awards the statutory maximum, but the award is then reduced as a result of taxation.

7.94 An application for review must be made within 14 days of the decision being sent to the parties, although an Employment Judge does have a discretion to allow late applications (Employment Tribunals (Constitution and Rules of Procedure) Regulations 2004, SI 2004/1861, r 35(1)).

8

CALCULATING THE COMPENSATORY AWARD: FRINGE BENEFITS AND EXPENSES

A. Introduction

8.01 Fringe benefits play an ever-increasing part in the employment package, and, although the loss of earnings claim is usually the more substantial element in the compensatory award, compensation may also be awarded for the loss of these benefits. This chapter looks at how compensation for the loss of such benefits is assessed and describes the circumstances in which it is possible to recover expenses incurred as a result of the dismissal.

B. General Principles

8.02 The loss of fringe benefits is included in the assessment of 'loss' under the Employment Rights Act 1996 (ERA 1996), s 123.

Section 123(2) states that the employee's 'loss' also includes: **8.03**

(a) any expenses reasonably incurred by the complainant in consequence of the dismissal; and
(b) subject to s 123(3), loss of any benefit that he or she might reasonably be expected to have had but for the dismissal.

Taken together, these provisions cover the loss of most of the common fringe benefits **8.04**
such as company cars, free or subsidized accommodation, subsidized mortgages, low-interest loans, and private health insurance (PHI). It may also cover the loss of benefits received under a profit-sharing scheme or a share option scheme. Some benefits, such as travel expenses, depend on the employee continuing to be in work and therefore cannot be claimed while the employee is out of work.

The statutory provisions also cover the loss of any benefit that an employee might **8.05**
reasonably expect to receive in the course of employment. However, compensation will be awarded only where the benefit is received on a regular basis (*Mullett v Brush Electrical Machines Ltd* [1977] ICR 829). As a result, some *ex gratia* benefits may be excluded. For example, the loss of a Christmas hamper is not the kind of perk for which compensation would normally be awarded. Moreover, some tribunals may refuse to compensate employees for the loss of benefits where the sums involved are small, although much will depend on the particular circumstances of each case.

The same general principles govern the assessment of loss of fringe benefits as **8.06**
govern a claim for loss of earnings. Thus, in *Textet v Greenhough Ltd* EAT 410/82, the Employment Appeal Tribunal (EAT) said that tribunals should first work out the net loss of earnings, and then add to that figure the weekly sum awarded for the loss of benefits (in the particular case, the loss of a company car).

The award will be calculated up to the date on which an employee finds a new job for **8.07**
which the package is either as good as or better than the old job. Moreover, credit must be given for the value of additional benefits received in the new job and may be set off against any loss suffered during the period that the employee was out of work.

C. Multiplier

Tribunals have to assess the length of time for which any loss is likely to continue— **8.08**
that is, future loss. This involves considering the same 'old job facts' and 'new job facts', and other contingencies (considered in greater detail at 7.78 above), such as the chances of the employee having left the old job anyway or finding a better-paid job in due course. The principles outlined by the EAT in *Kingston Upon Hull City Council v Dunnachie (No 3)* [2003] IRLR 843 equally apply to any award for future loss of benefits, as will the rules on causation (considered in greater detail at 7.83 above).

It is possible that the period covered by the claim for loss of benefits may exceed that **8.09**
of the loss of earnings claim. For example, in *Morgan Edwards Wholesale Ltd v*

Francis EAT 205/78, Mr Francis claimed compensation for the loss of his company car. Both sides agreed that this was worth £500 a year. The industrial tribunal held that this loss was likely to continue for a further five years and awarded £2,500. On appeal, it was argued by the company that the five-year period was too long. However, the EAT upheld the award, saying that, because Mr Francis did not have a car in his new job, the award was not excessive.

8.10   In most cases, however, the period covered by an award for loss of fringe benefits is unlikely to exceed the period covered by the award for loss of earnings, since the loss of fringe benefits must be seen in the context of an employee's overall loss and therefore, in the long run, is likely to be offset by the increase in earnings from the new job.

D. Valuing Fringe Benefits

8.11   A particular problem in relation to fringe benefits is how to calculate the value of the benefit in cash terms. Providing guidance on this subject is not an easy task since it is relatively uncommon for a tribunal to give reasons as to why it chose one method of valuation rather than another. The EAT has also been reluctant to lay down any guidelines in this area and will not overturn a tribunal's assessment unless it is obviously incorrect or completely unreasonable (see *UBAF Bank Ltd v Davis* [1978] IRLR 442). The result is that there are no hard-and-fast rules on quantifying the loss of particular benefits and much will depend on the nature of the evidence presented to the tribunal. However, there are a number of well-established methods that are often followed by tribunals in practice. These are considered in the context of the particular benefits discussed below.

E. Company Cars

8.12   Despite recent changes in taxation, the company car remains one of the most common perks received by employees as part of their benefits package. In addition (or sometimes in the alternative), employees often receive financial assistance in the running of the car, such as petrol allowances.

8.13   It is important to recognize at the outset that compensation will be awarded only for the loss of the private use of the car. If the car is used exclusively for business purposes or if private use is minimal, as may be the case where the employee has only the use of a 'pool' car for business purposes, or if the use of the car is subject to other restrictions, little or no compensation will be awarded. On the other hand, if the car is a 'perk' of the job and business use is minimal, compensation may be substantial. That loss will be greater if, in addition to the use of the car, the employee also receives free maintenance, tax, insurance, and petrol.

Valuing use

The biggest problem is to value the use of the car. There is no single or universal **8.14**
method of valuing the loss of the use of a car. Indeed, in many cases, tribunals do
not give any clear indication of their reasons for making an award or the method
used in choosing a particular figure. For example, in *Gotts v Hoffman Balancing
Techniques Ltd* 1979 COIT 951/115, Mr Gotts claimed compensation for the loss
of a new BMW that he had retained until his notice expired. During that time, the
company had levied a charge of £820 per month and Mr Gotts claimed that this
was what the benefit was worth. The industrial tribunal disagreed. It pointed out
that this was a penal levy that was intended to put pressure on Mr Gotts to return
the car. The tribunal considered that £20 a week was a fair sum based on 'their own
knowledge in these matters' (see also *Bowness v Concentric Pumps Ltd* 1974 COIT
318/217). Both of these cases were decided some time ago, with the result that
some allowance must be made for inflation.

Personal injury cases favour a tariff approach to compensation for such claims, **8.15**
but, yet again, the judges' reasons for awarding a particular amount are rather
obscure. For example, in *Kennedy v Bryan*, The Times, 3 May 1984, a victim of
a motor car accident received a lump sum of £800 for the loss of her company
car. The High Court adopted a tariff approach, saying that the normal range for
the loss of such a benefit was between £700 and £1,000. However, the judge
gave no particular reason for choosing £800 in the particular circumstances of
this case. The tariff approach has also found favour with some industrial
tribunals.

Costs of running a car: AA and RAC estimates

One common method of establishing the value of being provided with a company **8.16**
car is to estimate the weekly cost of running a particular type of car. This calculation
may be based on the AA's or RAC's estimates, which are published annually. The AA
estimates can be found online at <http://www.theaa.com>.

This method was applied by Sheen J in *Shove v Downs Surgical plc* [1984] 1 All ER 7, **8.17**
a wrongful dismissal case. The judge awarded £10,000 for the loss of a Daimler
motor car over a period of 30 months—the notice period under Mr Shove's
contract. In reaching this conclusion, the judge relied on the AA estimates and
reduced the estimated cost by the ratio of private use to business use.

A further adjustment to these estimates would have to be made if the employee were **8.18**
to contribute to the running of the car.

This method of assessment normally leads to compensation being assessed on a **8.19**
weekly basis, partly because this makes it easier to calculate the overall loss (see *Textet
v Greenough Ltd* EAT 410/82). However, where the applicant remains unemployed
at the time of the hearing, the tribunal may opt for a lump-sum payment instead.

8.20 Some employers also have their own motor mileage allowances that are sometimes more generous than the estimates produced by the AA and RAC (see Industrial Relations Services [IRS], *Pay and Benefits Bulletin*, No 288). Where this is the case, it would be open to either the applicant or the employer to base its valuation of the loss on these figures.

HM Revenue and Customs scales

8.21 Another method of valuing the benefit of a company car is to rely on the scale charges drawn up by HM Revenue and Customs (HMRC) for tax purposes. The scale charges are based on the cylinder capacity and age of the car or, in the case of a more expensive car, its original market value and age.

8.22 The drawback of relying on the HMRC scales is that they are intended to value the perk for tax purposes and may therefore not give a true valuation of the benefit to the employee. Thus, in *Shove v Downs Surgical plc* [1984] 1 All ER 7, Sheen J rejected the employer's argument that he should use the HMRC scales to value Mr Shove's claim for the loss of the company car. Similarly, in *Kennedy v Bryan*, The Times, 3 May 1984, the judge distinguished the value of the car for tax purposes and the value for compensation purposes. On the other hand, despite recent changes, the HMRC scales represent a very conservative valuation and may therefore be favoured by employers in settlement negotiations.

Purchase and resale

8.23 Another possible way of valuing the loss of a company car is for the employee to buy or hire a car and claim a proportion of the cost from the employer.

8.24 This approach was successfully relied on by the applicant in *Nohar v Granitstone (Galloway) Ltd* [1974] ICR 273. Following his dismissal, Mr Nohar bought himself a new car that he then resold after he found a new job (in which a car was also provided as a perk). In addition to the loss on resale, which was £80, Mr Nohar claimed the cost of insuring the car—a further £20—and £18 for tax, making a total of £118. The industrial tribunal rejected his claim, but the National Industrial Relations Court (NIRC), allowing the appeal, held that an award of £100 was 'fair and reasonable'.

8.25 Such an approach should, however, be treated with caution because the loss on resale includes the depreciation in the value of the car rather than the 'pure' loss suffered as a direct result of the loss of employment, and therefore applicants who go for the 'purchase and resale' option will have to satisfy the tribunal that they acted reasonably.

8.26 Similarly, employees who seek to recover the cost of hiring an equivalent car should be aware that the hire charges include the profits of the hire company and therefore a claim for the full amount may be disallowed for this reason. Such a claim may be allowed in exceptional circumstances in which the car is necessary to enable the applicant to mitigate his or her loss.

Cars provided on hire purchase

The basis of assessment is different where the benefit takes the form of both the free **8.27** use of the car and its eventual ownership. This may arise if a car is bought on hire purchase in the employee's name, but the employer pays the whole, or part, of the hire purchase repayments. The assessment of loss in such circumstances raises similar problems to those raised in cases in which the employee is claiming compensation for the loss of an interest-free loan or a subsidized mortgage (see **8.34**).

One method is to award the employee a proportion of the outstanding hire purchase **8.28** payments. This approach was used by the industrial tribunal in *S & U Stores v Wormleighton* EAT 477/77. The industrial tribunal found that, at the time of dismissal, £820 was outstanding under the hire purchase agreement. It awarded Mr Wormleighton half of this amount. On appeal, the employer criticized the tribunal's assessment, saying that it did not make allowance for the continued depreciation in the value of the car over the remainder of the repayment period. It also challenged the tribunal's calculation of the repayments. Thus the employer argued that Mr Wormleighton should have received £390 rather than £410. The EAT, dismissing the appeal, said that although the tribunal's approach was rather unscientific, it was not unreasonable in the circumstances.

Calculating the value of the loss of a car: A summary

In summary, the following steps should be taken in assessing the value of a **8.29** company car:

(a) make sure that you know what you are trying to value—that is, the terms on which the benefit was provided;
(b) decide what method of valuation is appropriate;
(c) remember to take into account the ratio of private use to business use; and
(d) add the value of the lost benefit to the employee's overall loss.

F. Accommodation

Compensation may be awarded for the loss of rent-free or subsidized accommodation. **8.30** Here, again, the first task is to determine what kind of benefit is being provided, since the award will normally be greater if the accommodation is free than if it is subsidized. Furthermore, no compensation will be awarded if the employee pays the market rent (*Nohar v Granitstone (Galloway) Ltd* [1974] ICR 273). Having determined the nature of the benefit, it is then necessary to put a cash figure on it. In practice, tribunals apply a fairly rough-and-ready approach to the value they place on this benefit.

8.31 The most favourable method of assessment from an employee's point of view is the open-market value of the accommodation. This method seems to have been used by the industrial tribunal in *Butler v J Wendon & Son* [1972] IRLR 15, in which the open-market rental of a tied cottage was assessed at £3 a week (although clearly this is not a reliable guide to present-day values). Employees wishing to rely on this approach should be able to give evidence on the open-market value of the accommodation.

8.32 The alternative method of assessing the cost of suitable alternative accommodation is more favourable to employers. This method is commonly used where the employee has found new accommodation at the time of the hearing. In *Lloyd v Scottish Co-operative Wholesale Society* [1973] IRLR 93, the tribunal awarded the difference between the rent that Mr Lloyd paid in the council flat in which he lived at the time of the hearing and the rent that he previously paid to his employer for the occupation of tied accommodation. However, it has also been applied where the employee has not found a new place to live. Thus, in *Dandy v Lacy* EAT 450/77, the tribunal based its award on the difference in rent between a rent-free tied cottage and a council flat in the same area even though Mr Lacy had not found himself a council flat at the time of the hearing. Again, evidence should be presented to the tribunal by employers wishing to rely on this method.

8.33 On the other hand, where employees buy accommodation rather than look for suitable rented accommodation, it is arguable that they should be entitled to recover a pro-portion of the mortgage during the period of assessment. The notional sum should be based on the interest paid by the employee to the building society, thereby excluding the part of the repayment that relates to the purchase of the capital asset. The award will therefore rarely cover the full cost of the mortgage.

G. Company Loans

8.34 Many organizations, particularly in the banking and financial sectors, offer their employees the valuable perk of a cheap-rate loan or subsidized mortgage. The loss of such a benefit may be recovered as part of the compensatory award. The problem yet again is how to put a cash value on the benefit. In theory, the assessment should be fairly straightforward—the employee's loss is the difference between the cost of the perk and the comparable market rate for a mortgage or loan—but tribunals often opt for a broad-brush approach rather than a mathematical quantification of the award.

8.35 For example, in *UBAF Bank Ltd v Davis* [1978] IRLR 442, the industrial tribunal awarded Mr Davis £2,000 for all of the privileges that he had lost as a result of his dismissal. This included a low-interest mortgage. Mr Davis had produced evidence to show that he would have to pay a high street building society an extra £675 and argued that this was the annual value of the perk. On appeal, the bank argued that the tribunal's award was excessive because it had failed to take into account the fact that the loan from the bank did not have to be repaid for a year after the dismissal. The EAT said that the bank should have argued this point in mitigation before the tribunal and refused to interfere with the tribunal's award. The fact that the tribunal opted for a lump-sum payment does not, of course, mean that it ignored Mr Davis's evidence on quantum. Indeed, this evidence would appear to have influenced its decision.

H. Other Benefits

Food

Many companies have their own staff canteens; sometimes, the meals are provided **8.36** free, but more often they are subsidized. The loss of this perk has been claimed in a number of cases. For example, in *Fowler v Westcliffe* COIT 1001/164, a tribunal estimated that the weekly value of free food and drink was £10. In *Rippa v Devere Hotels* COIT 144/83, the value of free meals for one year was held to be £600.

Travel allowances

The loss of a travel allowance or other benefits relating to travel may be recovered as **8.37** part of the compensatory award. In *Dr Cruz v Airways Aero Association Ltd* COIT 6066/72, an industrial tribunal awarded £600 for the loss of a special travel allowance, even though the allowance was a privilege and not a contractual right.

Free telephone

Sometimes, employers pay for an employee's home telephone or mobile. Compen- **8.38** sation can be recovered for the loss of this benefit (see *Dundee Plant Co Ltd v Riddler* EAT 377/88, in which £160 was awarded for the free use of a telephone, covering both the rental and telephone charges). The same principle would apply to the free or private use of a company mobile or Blackberry or iPhone.

Medical insurance

Compensation may be awarded for the loss of private medical insurance, the loss **8.39** being measured in terms of the cost of providing equivalent or continued insurance cover (*Ross v Yewlands Engineering Co Ltd* COIT 17321/83/LN). Often, the cost to the individual will be greater than that to the employer under a group scheme. It will therefore be necessary for the claimant to produce evidence on the cost of obtaining an equivalent benefit in the open market. The same principles apply to claims for the loss of death-in-service benefits and other forms of life insurance. However, in *Knapton v ECC Card Clothing Ltd* [2006] IRLR 756, the EAT ruled that compensation is recoverable only for the loss of such benefits if the claimant actually suffers the loss in the period in question either through death or illness, or has bought such cover (in which case, the award would be based on the cost of such cover). Where, as in *Knapton*, the claimant survived for the period covered by the award and did not take out life insurance cover during that period, there was no financial loss and therefore compensation could not be award for the loss of life insurance. The position may be different regarding a claim for future loss because, in such circumstances, it would be open to the claimant to persuade the tribunal that he or she proposed to take out such cover in the future if awarded compensation.

Childcare benefits

8.40 It is not uncommon these days for employers to either offer free child care in the workplace or to make a contribution to childcare costs. Where the employer offers free or subsidized child care, the loss may be claimed as part of the compensatory award. From an employer's point of view (as with other benefits), the simplest way of calculating the loss will be the cost to the employer of providing the benefit, but, from the employee's point of view, the loss will be based on the 'reasonable' cost of providing equivalent child care. Where the employer makes a contribution to childcare costs, the financial loss will be the loss of that contribution (*Visa International Ltd v Paul* [2004] IRLR 42).

Share ownership

8.41 Some companies encourage their employees to buy shares in the business. The annual value of such benefits may well be considerable and the loss may be claimed as part of the compensatory award.

8.42 Compensation may be awarded for the loss of a stock option provided that the employment tribunal is satisfied that the applicant would have been granted such an option but for the dismissal (*O'Laoire v Jackel International Ltd* [1991] IRLR 170). But the loss may be difficult to prove and quantify where there is no more than a mere promise to grant such an option in the future. Nonetheless, where possible, tribunals should seek to place a value on these rights. In *Casey v Texas Homecare Ltd* EAT/632/87, an employment tribunal declined to estimate the value of an employee's share option because it was too 'speculative and definite'. The EAT, overturning the tribunal's ruling, awarded £1,000 on the basis of the evidence that had been presented to the tribunal after making allowance for the chance that the share price might fall. In some cases, the assessment may involve a separate consideration of uncertainties connected with the future exercise of share option such as the likelihood of flotation, the likely value of the shares on flotation, and the likelihood that the claimant would have exercised the option and bought some, or all, of the shares (*Selective Beauty (UK) Ltd v Hayes* UKEAT/0582/04/M). A problem may arise where such an option lapses on dismissal and the scheme excludes liability for compensation in such circumstances (see *Micklefield v SAC Technology Ltd* [1991] 1 All ER 275). Here, however, it is arguable that an exemption clause would contravene ERA 1996, s 203, and therefore has no effect. As to the valuation of lost stock options, see **1.67**.

Similarly, compensation may be claimed were an employee is compelled to sell **8.43** shares as a result of dismissal, and the shares increase in value between the date of dismissal and the date of the hearing. In *Leonard v Strathclyde Buses Ltd* [1998] IRLR 693, the EAT accepted that compensation could be awarded for the loss in value caused by the premature sale of the stock options. The claimant and his colleagues were compelled to sell their shares back to their employers when they were dismissed. Some months later, their former employer was taken over by another company and the shares rose. They successfully recovered the difference between the share price on termination and the share price that they would have received but for their unfair dismissal. Given the volatility in share prices, tribunals may have some difficulty in deciding when the claimants would have sold their shares. In the absence of an agreed valuation, the tribunal is likely to base its award on what is just and equitable in the circumstances.

I. Expenses

The assessment of loss also includes any expenses reasonably incurred by the **8.44** employee as a result of the dismissal. However, before such an award is made, the tribunal must be satisfied that (ERA 1996, s 123(2)(a)):

(a) the expenses were incurred as a result of the dismissal;
(b) the expenses were reasonably incurred; and
(c) the sums incurred were reasonable in themselves.

A claim for expenses should therefore be supported by evidence produced at the **8.45** tribunal hearing.

Cost of finding a new job

The most common kind of expenses allowed under this head are those incurred as a **8.46** result of looking for a new job. The expenses may include postal costs, phone calls, and other costs relating to the application. They also cover the cost of attending interviews (*Leech v Berger, Jensen & Nicholson Ltd* [1972] IRLR 58). Such expenses cannot be recovered if the costs are reimbursed by the prospective employer or the state.

Tribunals have also allowed employees to claim removal expenses and other costs **8.47** arising from the need to move home. For example, in *Lloyd v Scottish Co-operative Wholesale Society Ltd* [1973] IRLR 93 (see **8.32** above), the tribunal awarded Mr Lloyd £20 for the cost of moving out of the tied accommodation supplied by his employers. A claim for removal costs also succeeded in *Co-operative Wholesale Society v Squirrell* (1974) ITR 191, in which the tribunal considered that it was necessary for the employee to move home in order to secure another job. In one case, a tribunal thought that it was just and equitable to award compensation for other expenses connected with the sale of a house, such as the conveyancing costs and estate agents' fees (*Daykin v IHW Engineering Ltd* COIT 1440/117). This approach is consistent with the Court of Appeal's ruling in *Essa Ltd v Laing* [2004] IRLR 313.

8.48 Such expenses may include the cost of a car, if a car was provided as a perk of the old job (*Sparkes v E T Barwick Mills Ltd* 1977 COIT 611/68), and relocation costs. For example, in *United Freight Distribution Ltd v McDougall* EAT(S) 218/94, the EAT upheld an industrial tribunal's decision to award £550 to cover the legal fees necessary to sell Mr McDougall's house. The EAT also accepted that, in principle, an award of compensation could also include a loan to cover relocation expenses, provided that the loan was a reasonable estimate of the relocation expenses and was made for that purpose. (See **13.36** regarding the issues relating to mitigation.)

Expenses in starting up a business

8.49 In addition, tribunals have allowed employees to recover some of the costs incurred in setting up a business where they considered that this was a reasonable way of mitigating the loss flowing from the dismissal.

8.50 In *Gardiner-Hill v Roland Berger Technics Ltd* [1982] IRLR 498, Mr Gardiner-Hill claimed £500 worth of expenses that he had incurred in setting up a consultancy service. The tribunal held that Mr Gardiner-Hill had acted reasonably in setting up the consultancy service in mitigation of his loss and allowed his claim in respect of the expenses incurred by him. The EAT agreed, saying that the expenses were reasonably incurred as a result of the dismissal.

Legal expenses

8.51 The tribunal is entitled to award costs only in accordance with its own rules of procedure (Employment Tribunals (Constitution and Rules of Procedure) Regulations 2004, SI 2004/1861, rr 38–40). The legal and other expenses associated with bringing or defending a complaint of unfair dismissal are not recoverable as part of a compensation claim (*Raynor v Remploy* [1973] IRLR 3), although the cost of attending the tribunal hearing may be recovered from the tribunal itself.

8.52 The rules on costs are considered in at **22.68** below.

Credit for expenses saved

8.53 In principle, it may be open to a tribunal to reduce the amount claimed for loss of benefits and expenses by any significant sums saved as a result of the dismissal. For example, if it is no longer necessary for the claimant to incur childcare costs, this saving may be deducted from the overall loss suffered by the claimant, but tribunals are unlikely to make such deductions where the sums involved are relatively small or too remote, in accordance with the principles discussed at **6.17**.

9

CALCULATING THE COMPENSATORY AWARD: PENSIONS

A. Introduction and General Principles

In one sense, pension loss is no different from other monetary losses that flow from a dismissal or an act of discrimination. But it deserves special treatment not only because pension loss may be one of the claimant's most financially material losses, but also because defining and assessing such loss is not always straightforward. **9.01**

The right to recover compensation for loss of pension following an unfair dismissal was established as long ago as 1974 by the National Industrial Relations Court (NIRC) in *Copson v Eversure Accessories Ltd* [1974] IRLR 247. It is now a well-established component of the compensatory award. The relevant statutory authority is to be found in s 123 of the Employment Rights Act 1996 (ERA 1996). Section 123(1) provides that the 'amount of the compensatory award shall be such amount as the tribunal considers just and equitable in all circumstances having regard to the loss sustained by the [claimant] in consequence of the dismissal . . .'. Section 123(2) expressly states that the loss of any benefit that a claimant might reasonably be expected to have had but for the dismissal constitutes a loss sustained 'in consequence **9.02** of the dismissal' under s 123(1). Pension is such a benefit. Likewise, it has been recognized that pension loss is a head of claim in discrimination claims (see, for example, *Ministry of Defence v Mutton* [1996] ICR 590 and s 65(1)(d) of the Sex Discrimination Act 1975 [SDA 1975]). Unlike wrongful dismissal, pension loss is recoverable where pension is not a contractual benefit (see *Cables Maintenance & Engineering Ltd v Sudworth* EATS/0078/03, final paragraph).

9.03 However, as the Employment Appeal Tribunal (EAT) observed in *Benson v Dairy Crest Ltd* EAT 192/89, it remains one of the most difficult areas of compensation to assess and quantify. As a result, tribunals have often applied a 'broad-brush' approach to compensation. Inherent in this approach is a risk of inconsistency between cases and over/under-compensation. Perhaps this mattered less when tribunal awards were comparatively small.

9.04 In 1990, a committee of chairmen of industrial tribunals appointed by the President of the Industrial Tribunals (England and Wales), in consultation with the Government Actuary's Department (GAD), produced a set of guidelines for assessing pension loss entitled *Industrial Tribunals: Compensation for Loss of Pension Rights*. This built on the GAD's earlier guide to tribunals of 1980. A revised second edition appeared in 1991. The EAT in *Benson* described it as 'an excellent and careful study of the issues with some extremely useful suggestions on how Industrial Tribunals may be helped with the problems that appear before them'. But the second edition soon became out of date. Its limitations were exposed by the EAT in the case of *Clancy v Cannock Chase Technical College* [2001] IRLR 331, especially in the context of public sector schemes. Lindsay J, presiding, issued a plea for revised guidelines. This was answered in November 2003 when tribunal chairmen David Sneath and Colin Sara, together with Chris Daykin and Adrian Gallop from GAD, produced a revised set of guidelines and published them in a booklet entitled *Compensation for Loss of Pension Rights: Employment Tribunal*. This is available online at <http://www.employmenttribunals.gov.uk/Documents/Publications/Lossofpensionrights.pdf>. Tribunals are now applying the guidelines in this third edition (the Guidelines) and being encouraged by the EAT to do so (see, for example, *Orthet Ltd v Vince-Cain* [2004] IRLR 857). As will be seen, these revised Guidelines are more sophisticated and make greater use of actuarial tables. They are likely to lead to an increase in the quantum of pension awards. The limitations of the second edition led many claimants in discrimination cases to adopt the principles of assessing pension loss in personal injury cases (see, for example, the personal injury case of *Auty v National Coal Board* [1985] 1 WLR 785). In the light of the revised Guidelines, employment tribunals can be expected to prefer claimants in discrimination cases to use the new Guidelines (see *Griffin v West Midlands Police Authority* ET Case No 5208776/00, for an application of the third edition).

9.05 Nevertheless, as the EAT pointed out in *Benson* (commenting on the second edition), these Guidelines are not 'rules'. Similarly, in *Bingham v Hobourn Engineering Ltd* [1992] IRLR 298, it was said that there is no duty on employment tribunals to follow the second edition and that they will not err in law in failing to give effect to its recommendations. Even more forcefully, the EAT in *Port of Tilbury (London) Ltd v Birch and others* [2005] IRLR 92 held that it was an error of law for an employment tribunal to proceed entirely on the basis of the booklet, and to reject out of hand the evidence and submissions of the parties simply because they did not reflect the Guidance. The first duty of the tribunal is to consider such evidence and submissions in order to ascertain whether a fair and equitable assessment of the loss of pension rights can be worked out on the basis argued. The third edition is there to assist a tribunal only when there is little evidence forthcoming from the parties. Thus, the Guidelines may not be mandatory—but their influence is seen in the recent suggestion by the EAT in *Greenhoff v Barnsley Metropolitan Council* [2006] UK EAT 0093/06/3105 that employment tribunals should address pension loss by:

(a) identifying all possible benefits that the employee could obtain under the pension scheme;

(b) setting out the terms of the pension relevant to each possible benefit;

(c) considering in respect of each such possible benefit, first, the advantages and disadvantages of applying the simplified approach or the substantial loss approach (see **9.84–9.87** below), and also any other approach that might be considered appropriate by the tribunal or by the parties;

(d) explaining why they have adopted a particular approach and rejected any other possible approach; and

(e) setting out their conclusions and explaining the compensation that they have arrived at in respect of each head of claim, so that the parties and the EAT might then ascertain if they have made an error.

9.06 This chapter starts by explaining the types of occupational pension likely to be encountered. It then sets out the main principles that have been established by tribunal decisions on identifying and calculating pension loss (including where the employment had no pension scheme). Lastly, detailed consideration is given to the Guidelines, because they will understandably be an important port of call for tribunals and litigants alike.

9.07 It should be noted that 'pension benefits' are sometimes taken to include benefits that are occasionally treated by employers as part of a pension scheme although they are not strictly pensions. Such benefits include life assurance and permanent health insurance (PHI), but these benefits are not considered in this chapter. They are, however, benefits that might form part of a compensatory award.

B. Types of Pension

9.08 In order to assess pension loss, it is necessary to recognize and understand the various types of pension scheme. Reference is often made to the three pillars of pensions.

This refers to the three main sources of pensions. The employer and the state are the first two, while the third source of funding for pensions is the employee. All three are considered in turn below.

Occupational pension schemes and personal pensions

9.09 For many years, employers have provided two types of pension. These are called defined-contribution (or 'money-purchase') and defined-benefits (usually of the 'final-salary' type). It is possible for an occupational pension scheme to be a mixture of the two. If, under a defined-contribution or defined-benefits scheme, the employee is not obliged to contribute, this is called a 'non-contributory' scheme.

9.10 The defined-benefits scheme has been, until recent times, the most common occupational pension scheme. In a defined-benefits scheme, the aim is to provide a certain pension benefit on retirement. The level of the employer's contribution will be the amount necessary (together with any employee's contributions) to provide that benefit. The level of benefit in such a scheme is usually expressed as a specified fraction of the employee's salary at or near retirement (for example, 1/60th or, often in public sector schemes, 1/80th) multiplied by the number of years of pensionable service (usually with an adjustment for additional months). Such a scheme will be known as a 'final-salary' scheme. Thus, in a scheme with a 1/60th accrual rate, an employee with 40 years' service on retirement would be entitled to a pension of two-thirds of final salary. Note that the title 'final-salary' can, on occasion, be misleading. This is because not only may the pension not be based only on 'salary', but also some schemes base the pension on average pay over the last few years or possibly over all service.

9.11 It is important to appreciate that the contribution that the employer makes is dependent upon how likely it is that the accumulated funds will meet the pensions to be paid or in payment. Generally, the employer will pay a certain percentage of the total payroll (such as 15 per cent of payroll). So this number does not relate to a particular employee's pension. Further, in the public sector, schemes are often unfunded. They also differ from private sector schemes in which deferred pensions (that is, a pension that will become payable on a specified retirement date) and pensions in payment are generally increased on a more generous basis. In the public sector, increases are usually in line with the cost of living index. In private sector schemes, increases are usually lower and capped at a lower level (for example, 5 per cent per annum). In periods of low inflation, this will not be a major issue. Another difference is that most private sector schemes allow the employee to give up part of his or her pension for a retirement lump sum, whereas public sector schemes will often provide both a pension and a lump sum as two separate benefits; in such a public sector scheme, therefore, the true value of the retirement benefits is greater than that of the pension alone.

9.12 In a defined-contribution scheme, the scheme defines the contributions to be made by employer and employee (if any). On retirement, the employee receives whatever pension (usually an annuity) can be bought by the accumulated contributions. This type of scheme has grown in popularity because an employer knows exactly how much must be contributed to the scheme. By contrast, in a defined-benefits scheme, the employer has entered into an open-ended commitment.

An employee who leaves employment before retirement will usually be entitled **9.13** to the benefit of the accrued contributions under a defined-contribution scheme or to a deferred pension (payable from retirement) under a defined-benefits scheme. It will be seen below, however, that, notwithstanding the deferred pension, the early leaver will suffer a financial loss that tribunals have recognized as compensatable.

Recent times have seen the development of personal pension plans (PPPs) and **9.14** stakeholder pensions. These are varieties of defined-contribution scheme. A PPP is a plan under which employer and employee (or one of them) contributes to a private pension plan with an insurance company or other pension provider. The final pension on retirement will be an annuity purchased from the accumulated contributions. Such plans are 'portable' in the sense that if the employee changes employer, the plan stays with the employee rather than the employer. Another feature is that, sometimes, the employee can choose where the funds are invested. Stakeholder pensions were introduced in 1999. Stakeholder pensions are another form of personal pension whereby contributions are made to a policy with an insurance company or other pension provider. All employers (with some minor exceptions) must provide access to a stakeholder scheme for their employees (unless they already offer a suitable pension scheme). Significantly, employers are not required to contribute to the scheme (and so such a scheme will be irrelevant for pension loss purposes).

State Pension

The second pillar is a pension payable by the state. In the UK, this can comprise the **9.15** basic State Pension, a graduated retirement benefit, and an additional State Pension that is payable under either the State Earnings-Related Pension Scheme (SERPS) or, since April 2002, the State Second Pension (S2P). Pertinent for pension loss purposes is whether the amount of pension is dependent on earnings.

The basic State Pension is a flat-rate pension (that is, it is not earnings-related) payable **9.16** from the State Pension age. The amount does depend on the number of National Insurance contributions (NICs) paid or credited. The graduated retirement benefit is based on NICs paid by employer and employee between April 1961 and April 1975. SERPS is earnings-related, and varies according to NICs paid between April 1978 and March 2002—but a lower earnings limit and upper earnings limit applied (in the last year of SERPS, this was £72 per week and £575 per week, respectively). S2P replaced SERPS in April 2002 (under the Child Support, Pensions and Social Security Act 2000).

9.17 It has been possible for employers and employees to 'contract out' of SERPS, and now, S2P. Employees can use a PPP to contract out of S2P, in which case the state will contribute an amount equal to the saving in NICs that would have been made if the employee were contracted out under an occupational scheme, plus an additional age-related contribution. This now applies to S2P. Contracting out through defined-contribution schemes (that is, money-purchase, PPP, and stakeholder arrangements) is likely to be abolished. Although a date has not been agreed, it is likely to be with effect from 6 April 2012. Anyone contracted out of a defined-contribution scheme at that time will automatically be contracted back into S2P.

Additional voluntary contributions and other contributions by employees

9.18 The third pillar is funding by employees. Some employees are able to pay additional voluntary contributions (AVCs) into their employer's occupational pension scheme to provide benefits additional to the basic benefits under the scheme. These usually operate on a money-purchase basis, even where the occupational pension scheme is a final-salary scheme. However, AVCs are not portable and so the loss of this facility could be a financial loss to the employee. Employees can also contribute to PPP and stakeholder schemes (see **9.14**), and most occupational pension schemes are partly funded by employees' contributions.

C. Types of Loss

9.19 In *Copson v Eversure Accessories Ltd* [1974] IRLR 247, the NIRC recognized that compensation for pension loss falls to be considered under two heads: past loss and future loss. However, in some circumstances, it may be inappropriate to make an award at all. It is therefore necessary to review separately:

(a) no compensatable loss;
(b) compensatable past loss; and
(c) compensatable future loss.

9.20 The methods of calculating any identified loss are examined subsequently (see **9.45–9.60** below). The third edition of the Guidelines makes the case for awarding pension loss even where the ex-employment did not have a pension scheme. This is because of loss of S2P during unemployment (see **9.79** below).

No compensatable loss

9.21 In common with the other heads of compensation, an award will be made only if it can be shown that the claimant has suffered loss as a result of the dismissal. Unless the claimant is covered by an occupational pension scheme that confers greater benefits than those guaranteed by the state scheme, there will be no loss. This is subject to the point mentioned above that even in the case of no pension scheme there may be a loss of S2P.

Even where the claimant is covered by a pension scheme, there may be no **9.22** compensatable loss if the claimant does not qualify for a pension under the rules of the scheme (see *Jones v International Press Institute* EAT 571/81 and *Manning v R & H Wale (Export) Ltd* [1979] ICR 433), or if the claimant's rights under the scheme are valueless. In the case of *Samuels v Clifford Chance* EAT 559/90, the employer's pension scheme had a qualifying period of five years. Ms Samuels was unfairly dismissed after two-and-a-half years' service. The tribunal concluded that, because she would not have stayed with the employer for another two-and-a-half years, she would not have qualified for a pension and therefore no pension loss arose.

Past loss

The first type of compensatable loss is past loss—namely, loss of all or part of the **9.23** pension earned at the date of dismissal. This expression is possibly confusing because one might view loss up to the date of the tribunal award as past loss. But loss from the date of dismissal to the date of the award is best viewed as future loss. Perhaps it would be clearer if the term 'past service loss' were used. However, because the authorities and Guidelines use 'past loss', this is used here.

In the case of a defined-contribution scheme, the employer's commitment is to **9.24** contribute to the scheme in accordance with the rules of the scheme. It follows that if the employee receives the full value of those contributions, there is no past loss. However, if the employee suffers a penalty for early departure from the scheme, then that penalty is the past loss.

In the case of a defined-benefits scheme, the employee's entitlement is to a defined **9.25** benefit, so that, at the time of dismissal, the employee will have earned part of the benefit payable on retirement. To the extent that the claimant does not receive the benefit earned, there is clearly a loss, but, in most cases, there is an additional loss. It is still common (although less so than previously) for a defined-benefits scheme to offer a pension calculated as a percentage of the employee's final salary. If an employee leaves service early, the pension entitlement on retirement is almost always calculated by reference to the salary at the date of leaving. It follows that, if it is to be expected that the employee's salary would have increased prior to retirement, a loss will arise. This type of loss is often called 'loss of enhancement of accrued pension rights' and can be shown by the following example.

Example

A is aged 50 and was employed for 30 years with the benefit of a final-salary scheme that promises a pension of two-thirds of final salary after 40 years' service at age 60 (that is, an accrual rate of 1/60th). A was earning £20,000 per

---

annum at the date on which she left service, but had she worked another ten years (that is, until she was aged 60 and retired), her salary would have been £30,000 per annum immediately before retirement. At the date of retirement, her pension would have been:

$$\frac{40}{60} \times £30,000 = £20,000 \text{ per annum}$$

Looked at another way, the amount of pension attributable to her first 30 years of service would have been:

$$\frac{30}{60} \times £30,000 = £15,000 \text{ per annum}$$

However, because A left service at the age of 50, her pension at the age of 60 will be calculated by reference to salary at the leaving date. Therefore, her pension at the age of 60 will be:

$$\frac{30}{60} \times £20,000 = £10,000 \text{ per annum}$$

Thus, the failure to take account of the prospective increase in salary has produced a pension loss of £5,000 per annum.

9.26   In practice, the position is more complicated than this example. First, part of a member's deferred pension in a contracted-out scheme will typically be a guaranteed minimum pension. This must be revalued in line with statutory requirements and this will reduce the deficit in the example. Second, under the provisions of the Pension Schemes Act 1993 (PSA 1993), accrued pensions in excess of the guaranteed minimum pension on leaving service must be revalued up to retirement by the lower of 5 per cent (or 2.5 per cent for post-5 April 2009 accrual in some schemes) per year compound and the rise in retail prices (between leaving service and retirement). The extent to which these statutory revaluations increase the pension payable by less than the projected increase in salary is the extent to which the member still suffers a past loss. (For an example of a tribunal incorrectly failing to take account of enhancement of accrued pension rights, see the EAT decision in *Polyflor Ltd v Old* EAT/0482/02.)

9.27   Some of the factors that have to be taken into account in assessing past loss are set out below.

Transferability

There is no past loss if employees are offered the opportunity of transferring the full **9.28** value of their pension entitlement to a new fund (provided that this takes into account any projected increases in salary). Thus, in *Freemans plc v Flynn* [1984] IRLR 486, the EAT overturned a tribunal award for past loss on the ground that the employee had sustained no loss because the employee could either make such a transfer or leave the contributions in the original scheme, so that they would provide him with a pension at the age of 65. (See also *Yeats v Fairey Winches Ltd* [1974] IRLR 362, in which the fund was frozen and the benefits were therefore preserved.)

Until the mid-1980s, it was primarily a matter for the particular scheme's rules as **9.29** to whether employees could transfer the value of their existing pension entitlement to another fund. Since 1 January 1986, however, employees leaving occupational pension schemes have a statutory right to a 'transfer value' that is at least equal to the cash equivalent of the benefits to which the member leaving early would have been entitled had he or she remained in the scheme. Regulations prescribe the types of scheme that are acceptable recipients of transfer values and also set out certain requirements with regard to the calculation of transfer values (see the Occupational Pension Schemes (Transfer Values) Regulations 1996, SI 1996/1847). There is no obligation to provide for projected increases in salary (see above). It follows that it is necessary to check in the case of final-salary schemes whether a transfer value covers salary increase (although, for most individual transfers, it will not). If not, there is likely to be a past loss.

Withdrawal

The possibility that the dismissed employee would have withdrawn from the scheme **9.30** in any event before normal retirement has to be taken into account in the assessment of past loss. This is because the claimant would not then have received the increases that are the cause of the past loss. This reflects the chance that the employee would have left the job voluntarily, or might have been fairly dismissed due to redundancy or for some other reason, before retirement. There is also the issue of whether the employer would have continued the pension scheme. There has been a recent trend of employers closing final-salary schemes in respect of future service. In *Glen Dimplex UK Ltd v Burrows* EAT/0265/03, the EAT overturned the decision of a tribunal that had failed to consider this issue fully (see also *Polyflor Ltd v Old* EAT/0482/02).

It is for the tribunal to assess the chances of withdrawal and reduce the award **9.31** accordingly. A tribunal's failure to consider the possibility of withdrawal amounts to an error of law (*Manpower Ltd v Hearne* [1983] IRLR 281 and *Linvar Ltd v Hammersley* EAT 226/83). The GAD guide of 1980 included a table of percentage deductions based on an average chance of withdrawal. The third edition of the Guidelines deliberately refrains from producing a table, on the basis that this is a matter for each tribunal to determine. It is clear that it is open to the parties to call evidence to support a particular level of reduction. For example, in *Manpower Ltd v Hearne*, the company argued for a greater reduction than that specified in the GAD guide of 1980 on the ground that the industry had a high labour turnover. The tribunal rejected Manpower's argument. The EAT refused to disturb its ruling on this point, but implicitly accepted that it was open to the parties to call evidence in support of a higher or lower figure.

9.32 Factors that may lead a tribunal to increase the percentage reduction for withdrawal include where there is a higher than average chance of resignation (for example, a 'high flyer' may be considered to have a higher than average likelihood of changing jobs), or where there is a higher than average chance of fair dismissal.

Deferred pensions

9.33 Credit must be given for the receipt of a deferred pension in the calculation of past pension loss. As explained at **9.24–9.25** above, if an employee stays in service until retirement, the pension would often have been calculated as a percentage of final salary at retirement; in leaving early, the deferred pension is likely to be based on the employee's salary at the date of leaving and this is likely to be less. Recent statutory changes go some way to meeting this problem by requiring deferred pensions to be revalued (see **9.26** above). Another factor is the switch to career average revalued earnings (CARE) schemes, and steps taken by employer to limit the extent to which future pay increases are pensionable.

Return of contributions

9.34 Most schemes give employees the right to a refund of their own contributions if they leave the scheme before completing two years of service; after three months' membership, the employee has a statutory right to such a refund. The return of an employee's contributions does not in itself compensate employees for the pension to which they would have become entitled had they not been dismissed or for the loss of the sums contributed to the fund by the employer on their behalf (*Willment Bros v Oliver* [1979] IRLR 393 and *Smith, Kline & French Laboratories Ltd v Coates* [1977] IRLR 220). Nonetheless, some credit must be given for the return of the contributions in the assessment. This will be greater if compound interest is included in the returned contributions.

Mitigation of loss

9.35 Employees are under a general obligation to lessen the loss flowing from their dismissal. The question of whether an employee has taken reasonable steps to mitigate loss is essentially a question of fact. It is therefore, for example, open to tribunals to conclude that an employee is acting unreasonably if he or she chooses a refund of contributions where he or she could choose a deferred pension, in the absence of good reason for doing so. The deferred pension is usually more valuable.

An example of a case in which a tribunal decided that an employee was not in breach   **9.36**
of the duty to mitigate is *Sturdy Finance Ltd v Bardsley* [1979] IRLR 65. Mr Bardsley
refused to accept his employer's offer of a deferred pension and preferred to take a
refund of his contributions. Sturdy Finance argued that, by taking the less valuable
benefit, thereby increasing his loss, Mr Bardsley was in breach of this duty. Mr Bardsley
justified his refusal on the ground that the pension would not have been worth very
much and he needed the money to set up a new business. Both the tribunal and the
EAT accepted that his refusal was reasonable.

Future loss

The second type of pension loss is the loss of future pensions opportunity—   **9.37**
namely, the opportunity to improve on the pension earned at the time of
dismissal. In the case of a defined-contribution scheme, this is the loss of the
employer's contribution to the scheme. In the case of a defined-benefits scheme,
in which longer service is likely to lead to increased benefits, the loss is the benefits
forgone by reason of the shortened service.

Some of the factors that have to be taken into account in assessing future loss are set   **9.38**
out below.

Period of unemployment

As is the case when assessing loss of salary, the tribunal has to wrestle with the question   **9.39**
of how long the claimant will be unemployed. Furthermore, where it is thought
that the claimant will find new employment, will the employment carry with it
pension benefits? For a recent example, see *Bentwood Bros (Manchester) Ltd v
Shepherd* [2003] IRLR 364. Similarly, in the case of *Glasgow City Council v
Rayton* EATS/005/07, an employment tribunal was overruled by the EAT for
having failed to take account of future pension when it had concluded the claimant
had failed to mitigate loss by not taking up similar employment with one of four
neighbouring local authorities. Having concluded that such employment would be
pensionable, it was wrong for the tribunal to neglect to take this into account
when calculating pension loss. In other words, it is prima facie incorrect to apply
mitigation of loss to general earnings, but not loss of pension. As will be seen when
reviewing the Guidelines, the predicted length of employment is critically relevant
to determining the method of assessing pension loss. This is the issue of 'career
loss'—see **9.86**.

Where an employee finds a new job without an occupational pension scheme, the   **9.40**
tribunal will have to assess the chances of the employee finding a job with an equivalent scheme in the future. If the claimant finds a new job and is eligible to join the
new employer's occupational pension scheme, the tribunal is faced with the task of
comparing the 'old' and 'new' schemes. If the new scheme is broadly the same as
the old, there will be no future loss (*Sturdy Finance v Bardsley* [1979] IRLR 65). If the

new scheme is significantly less beneficial, the tribunal will have to value the consequential loss suffered by the employee. In making this assessment, the tribunal should take into account both the chances of the employee finding a different job with an equivalent pension to the one in the original scheme and the chances of improvements being made to the scheme that the claimant has now joined. It is also possible that, for example, a higher salary reflects the absence of a pension. However, tribunals are likely to adopt a fairly broad-brush approach to these matters.

Withdrawal

9.41 Tribunals must consider the possibility of withdrawal from the 'old' scheme as a result of resignation or fair dismissal. Tribunals often apply the same percentage reduction that they apply to past loss (see **9.30–9.32** above and the case of *Manpower Ltd v Hearne* [1983] IRLR 281).

Credit for future employee contributions

9.42 Allowance must be made for the contributions that the employee would have had to make to the pension scheme had the claimant remained in the former employment (see *Pringle v Lucas Industrial Equipment Ltd* [1975] IRLR 266).

9.43 **Allowance for accelerated payment**   As with the award generally, the award for loss of pension rights must take into account any accelerated receipt of benefits that would not otherwise have become payable until retirement (see *Smith, Kline & French Laboratories Ltd v Coates* [1977] IRLR 220; *Powermatic Ltd v Bull* [1977] IRLR 144; *Bentwood Bros (Manchester) Ltd v Shepherd* [2003] IRLR 364). However, the extent to which the award should be reduced for this reason is unclear. It is important to check whether any valuation of loss does reflect a discount. The present value of future payments will usually be less than the future value.

9.44 Allowance is made for accelerated payment in the tribunal Guidelines, but where an alternative basis is put forward, then the payment will have to be discounted to take this into account. For example, in *Yeats v Fairey Winches Ltd* [1974] IRLR 362 (a case described prior to the tribunal Guidelines), the award for pension loss was reduced by approximately 44 per cent to take account of the possibility of withdrawal and to make allowance for the accelerated payment in the form of a lump sum rather than a weekly payment. Unfortunately, the tribunal did not specify what proportion of this percentage reduction related to the latter factor. It is arguable that the reduction should be smaller as the employee nears retiring age. Of some interest, therefore, is the decision in *Page v Sheerness Steel plc* [1996] PIQR Q26, in which, in determining a discount rate for a lump-sum payment of damages for personal injury (which included pension loss), Dyson J applied a rate of 3 per cent, being the rate of return on index-linked gilt securities. More recently, in the case of *Benchmark Dental Laboratories Group Ltd v Perfitt* EAT/0304/04, an employment tribunal made a one-off reduction of 2.5 per cent for accelerated receipt of an award for loss of earnings for a period of loss of eight years and two months. The EAT commented on the practice in personal injury cases. It noted that the discount for accelerated repayment should reflect the fact that the employee would be able to invest the sum and that, without a discount, the claimant would be overcompensated. The tribunal's discount of 2.5 per cent was wrong. This did not recognize that the amount to meet the loss in the eighth year would be available for him to invest seven years before it was required and so on. The EAT noted that if the claimant's loss accrues in a straight line rateably over the whole period, receipt of this sum is, overall, accelerated for approximately half the period and so the discount rate should apply to the whole sum for approximately half the period. On that basis, the EAT decided that it would expect a discount of 10 per cent, but the parties were invited to refer the employment tribunal to 'an appropriate table'.

D. Methods of Calculating Loss

9.45 The problem of how to value pension loss was recognized soon after it became a permissible head of compensation (see *Scottish Co-operative Wholesale Society Ltd v Lloyd* [1973] ICR 137). In later cases, the EAT has said that there is no single correct method of assessing pension loss and that the choice of method is essentially a matter for the tribunal to determine. Moreover, provided that a tribunal exercises its discretion fairly and reasonably, its decision is unlikely to be overturned on appeal.

9.46 There are two common methods of calculating pension loss:

(a) *the contributions method*—where the loss is assessed by reference to the employer's contributions to the pension scheme in question; and

(b) *actuarial assessment (often called the 'benefits' method)*—where the loss is assessed by reference to the benefit to which the employee would have become entitled under the relevant pension scheme but for the dismissal.

9.47 The Guidelines consider both methods (see **9.66–9.88** below), with the third edition making a shift towards greater use of actuarial assessment in respect of defined-benefits schemes.

Contributions method

9.48 The contributions method calculates pension loss in terms of the contributions paid by the employer and employee, and then applies an appropriate multiplier. An illustration of the use of the contributions method can be seen in the Guidelines (see **9.100–101** below). The various elements in such an assessment are dealt with below.

Contribution rate and interest

9.49 If the scheme specifies a contribution rate (usually expressed as a sum equal to a specified percentage of salary), the loss should be determined at that rate. However, if the contribution rate is anomalous (for example, because the employer is taking a contribution holiday), a notional rate should be found. Consideration ought to be given to whether interest (simple or compound) should be added.

Multiplier

9.50 The multiplier represents the period over which the claimant's future loss should be computed. The multiplier is likely to be the period during which the claimant, but for the unfair dismissal, might have reasonably expected the employer to contribute to the pension scheme. Account must be taken of the prospect of the claimant leaving the scheme. Thus, in *Powermatic Ltd v Bull* [1977] IRLR 144, the claimant had 33 years until retirement at the age of 65. The EAT considered that a multiplier of 33 was inappropriate, bearing in mind the prospects of Mr Bull leaving the employer's service. It substituted a multiplier of 15.

Other elements

9.51 The prospects of withdrawal must be considered and it may be appropriate to make a discount for accelerated payment, as well as to give credit for a transfer payment to another scheme, deferred pension, a return of contributions, finding a new job with a pension scheme, and the claimant forgoing an obligation to pay contributions to the former employer's pension scheme (see **9.41** and **9.42** above).

Drawbacks to contributions method

9.52 The contributions method is self-evidently easy to apply and therefore has been much used by tribunals. In the case of a defined-contribution scheme, the contributions method will be appropriate. But in the case of a defined-benefits scheme, the claimant's loss can only be fully provided for by putting the claimant in the position in which he or she would have been but for the dismissal. The contributions method is unlikely to achieve this. In broad terms, it can be said that the contributions method tends to favour younger employees with short service and underestimates the value of the benefits of older employees with long service. Also, in relation to a defined-benefits scheme, past loss is generally a more important issue than in the relation to a defined-contribution scheme. But the contributions method does not specifically address the issue of past loss. In truth, for final-salary schemes, it is a rough-and-ready method.

Benefits method

9.53 The alternative and more accurate method of calculating pension loss (especially in the case of defined-benefits schemes) is the benefits method. This defines the loss in terms of the pension benefits that an employee has earned at the time of dismissal and then seeks to place a monetary value on what is needed to put the claimant in the pension position in which he or she would have been had there not been a dismissal. A number of different methods might be used. Some are more generous to employees than others.

Whichever method is adopted, consideration must be given to deductions or **9.54** discounts for benefits received by the claimant and similar factors, as discussed earlier in respect of the contributions method.

Cost of annuity

One way of assessing the loss is to work out (or to ask an insurance company to **9.55** calculate) the capital cost of purchasing an annuity that would yield an equivalent pension to that which the employee would have received but for the dismissal. From this is deducted what the claimant has received (such as a deferred pension). In *John Millar & Sons v Quinn* [1974] IRLR 107, Mrs Quinn was dismissed eight years before her 60th birthday. The NIRC assessed compensation as the cost of purchasing an annuity that would give her a pension equivalent to the one that she would have received at 60 years of age had she not been dismissed.

However, this approach is likely to be adopted only where the employee is close to **9.56** retirement. In other cases, an adjustment will have to be made to reflect the fact that the loss may not be a continuing one.

Effect of pension from new employment

In *Willment Bros v Oliver* [1979] IRLR 393, the EAT accepted that it was possible to **9.57** assess pension loss by comparing the difference in the annual value of the pension that an employee received in the new job with that in the old. The total loss would then depend on the multiplier adopted in a particular case. However, the EAT warned that it would normally be impossible to make this calculation with any certainty, since there were so many unknown factors to take into account. It would also create difficulties in assessing the possibility of withdrawal.

Partial discontinuance method

The GAD guide of 1980 used the 'partial discontinuance' method. This makes **9.58** some allowance for inflation and the prospects of an increase in real income before retirement.

Other factors

The benefits method of valuing pension loss (irrespective of actuarial method used) **9.59** still requires a tribunal to make:

(a) a discount for the possibility of withdrawal; and
(b) an allowance for the accelerated payment of the benefits (see *Copson v Eversure Accessories Ltd* [1974] IRLR 247)—but note that the present cost of a future annuity will already reflect a discount for early payment.

Moreover, if the scheme is contributory, the award must be reduced by the amount **9.60** of the employee's future contributions (see *Pringle v Lucas Industrial Equipment Ltd* [1975] IRLR 266). If the actuarial method adopted takes the salary earned on dismissal rather than the projected final salary, not all of the loss referred to at **9.25** will have been compensated.

E. Other Principles

Proof of loss

9.61   The tribunal must raise pension loss as a head of loss along with the other heads of compensation, but the actual burden of proving loss lies on the employee (*Tidman v Aveling Marshall Ltd* [1977] IRLR 218). Thus it is 'for Claimants . . . to present material to the tribunal upon which they desire an assessment to be made' (*Hilti (GB) Ltd v Windridge* [1974] IRLR 53). The EAT is unlikely to be sympathetic to parties who do not adduce evidence and then complain when the employment tribunal does the best it can to assess loss—see, for example, *Evans v Barclays Bank plc* EAT/0137/09. However, the problem is that the relevant information is normally in the hands of the employer, with the result that it is up to the employee to acquire the relevant documentation in advance of a remedies hearing. If necessary, tribunals may make an order of disclosure that compels employers to disclose the information in their possession (see Employment Tribunals (Constitution and Rules of Procedure) Regulations 2004, SI 2004/1861, Sch 1, r 10). Note that employees have the right to extensive information about their pension scheme (see Occupational Pension Scheme (Disclosure of Information) Regulations 1996, SI 1996/1655).

9.62   The importance of the employment tribunal having sufficient information and time to assess pension loss arose in the case of *Green v Metroline London Northern Ltd* EAT/0291/04. It seems that, at lunch during the employment tribunal hearing, it was discovered that the employer's pension scheme was a final-salary scheme and not, as both sides had thought at the outset of the hearing, a money-purchase scheme. Nonetheless, the tribunal proceeded to deal with the matter. In remitting the issue back to the employment tribunal, the EAT decided that 'in order for justice to have been done', both parties should have had the opportunity to produce further information. The claimant who fails at the employment tribunal stage to produce figures showing what the pension loss might be, meaning that the tribunal makes no award, is unlikely to find the EAT sympathetic to making an award even where the EAT accepts that there was a potential loss (see, for example, *Davis and Davis v Derbyshire* EAT/0099/03).

Actuarial evidence

9.63   The relevance and admissibility of evidence given by actuaries has been the subject of conflicting judicial rulings. In *Copson v Eversure Accessories Ltd* [1974] IRLR 247, the NIRC accepted that evidence from actuaries or pension brokers was relevant and admissible, but thought that it would not usually be necessary in the type of case with which tribunals are concerned. On the other hand, in *Tradewinds Airways Ltd v Fletcher* [1981] IRLR 272, the EAT went so far as to hold that a tribunal was wrong to prefer the evidence of a skilled actuary called on behalf of the claimant to the figures set out in the GAD guide of 1980. The EAT's conclusion is a little surprising. The preferable view is that actuarial evidence is admissible, but that parties who rely on such evidence do so at their own risk and their own expense (see *Manpower Ltd v Hearne* [1983] IRLR 281). This is implicit in the more recent decision of the EAT in *Glen Dimplex UK Ltd v Burrows* EAT/0265/03. But the EAT pointed out that the tribunal did not have to accept such evidence.

Relationship with other heads

The award for pension loss must be seen in the context of the claimant's overall **9.64** compensation claim. Thus, if a former employee's pay and other conditions in a new job either match or are superior to those in the old, there will be no continuing loss and hence no award for future loss will be made. This is a particularly important point where a claimant is dismissed from employment with a defined-benefits pension and then subsequently finds new employment, but with only a defined-contribution pension. As the number of employers offering defined-benefits pensions declines, this will become more commonplace. It follows that, where the new employment offers an overall higher remuneration package, it is necessary to determine whether this eliminates the loss flowing from losing future accrual of pension under the erstwhile employer's defined-benefits pension scheme. Thus, an employment tribunal was wrong to conclude that, in such a situation, while it would make no award on account of loss of earnings because the chain of causation of loss had been broken (in line with the principle in *Dench v Flynn & Partners* [1998] IRLR 653), nonetheless it would be appropriate to award compensation for loss of future accrual of pension under the defined-benefits pension scheme. The Court of Appeal, in overturning the EAT and employment tribunal, pointed out that it was not legitimate for pension loss to be carved out for special treatment. Once the employment tribunal had accepted that the new employment broke the chain of causation of loss (albeit the new employment had ended before the employment tribunal hearing) and that the overall remuneration package was better than that with the former employer (taking account of the loss of pension), no award should be made for loss of earnings including pension (*Aegon UK Corp Services Ltd v Roberts* [2009] IRLR 1042). However, it is submitted that it must still follow that an award for pension loss may yet be made if the employment package in the new job is as good as the old one in all respects, but inferior in relation to pension.

Contributory fault

The normal rules on contributory fault (see ERA 1996, s 123(6)) apply to compen- **9.65** sation for pension loss (see, for example, *Port of Tilbury (London) Ltd v Birch and others* [2005] IRLR 92).

F. Tribunal Guidelines

Introduction

9.66 As noted at **9.04** above, over the last 20 years, guidance has been available to tribunals (and litigants), originally from GAD and subsequently a committee of employment tribunal chairmen. November 2003 saw the publication of the third edition of *Compensation for Loss of Pension Rights: Employment Tribunals*. This booklet is available online—see **9.04** above. The third edition is materially different from the second edition. As will be explained further below, the third edition has introduced the concept of the substantial loss approach. This is said to be appropriate in those cases in which the tribunal is considering career loss. Other material changes are compensating for loss of S2P, updated GAD tables for the simplified approach (including separate tables for private sector and public sector employees), and the 'Appendix 7 adjustment' in which the contributions method is used in assessing loss in respect of defined-benefits schemes.

9.67 The second edition warned readers that the Guidelines would become 'tripwires if they [were] blindly applied without considering the facts of each case'. That edition also added that 'any party is free to canvass any method of assessment that he considers appropriate'. Those words do not appear in the third edition, but they remain valid. In particular, the Guidelines have no statutory force (see the discussion at **9.05** above), although tribunals and litigants will naturally turn to them first for guidance, especially as calculations can be readily made on information that the parties are likely to possess. The Guidelines consequently need to be reviewed in detail.

9.68 It is worth remembering that the Guidelines are based on 'mainstream' pension schemes and pursue a middle course between oversimplification and overelaboration. Thus they do not, and do not purport to, cover all pension loss. Litigants need to note that:

(a) simplicity may not always work in their favour and so they need to consider whether they should contend that the Guidelines do not apply to their particular facts;

(b) because the Guidelines will encourage tribunals to consider pension loss at the first hearing on remedies, the parties should be ready and able to argue a departure from the Guidelines (where relevant) or risk the tribunal applying them; and

(c) the Guidelines do not cover all possibilities and so a slavish adherence to them can produce mistakes—see the discussion at **9.109** below for an example of this.

Structure of the guidelines

9.69 The third edition begins by describing State Pension provision (Chapter 2) and occupational pension schemes (Chapter 3). It then moves on to describe pension loss and, very importantly, lays down when either the simplified approach or the substantial loss approach should be adopted (Chapter 4). The next three chapters are devoted to the simplified approach (Chapters 5–7). Chapter 8 then sets out the substantial loss approach. The appendices contain actuarial tables and background information on the tables. The booklet recognizes that these tables will become out of date and so recommends periodic review.

Helpfully, in Appendix 1, the Guidelines set out a checklist for assessing pension loss: **9.70**

(1) Was the Claimant a member of any personal or occupational pension scheme at the date of dismissal?
(2) If not, is it necessary to award compensation for loss of S2P rights?
(3) If the Claimant was a member of a personal pension scheme, did the respondent contribute to it?
(4) If the Claimant was a member of an occupational scheme, do the circumstances call for use of the simplified approach?
(5) If not, do the circumstances call for use of the substantial loss approach?
(6) If the scheme was not contracted out, is it necessary to award compensation for loss of both occupational pension and S2P?

While the Guidelines are not structured in terms of dealing with these questions **9.71**
in sequence, because progressing through the checklist is a practical way of proceeding, this route is followed below. Accordingly, each of the questions is now considered in turn.

Paragraph numbers noted below refer to the paragraphs in the third edition. The **9.72**
booklet tends to use the expression 'final-salary scheme' for defined-benefits schemes and 'money-purchase scheme' for defined-contribution schemes. To avoid confusion between the text below and the paragraphs referred to in the Guidelines, these labels are used below.

No pension loss

Before looking at each of the six questions, it is worthwhile noting when the **9.73**
Guidelines take the view that there is no pension loss. In summary, this is in respect of:

(a) basic State Pension; and
(b) employee contributions.

The second edition of the Guidelines recommended that 'the assumption is made **9.74**
that there is no pension loss in respect of a dismissed employee who is not in an occupational pension scheme'. However, the third edition departs from this view. Accordingly, the Guidelines are relevant even though the employee is not provided with a pension by the erstwhile employer. In particular, the Guidelines state that where a dismissed employee is not in a pension scheme or is in a scheme that is not contracted out, he or she is likely to lose the S2P element for the period during which he or she is out of work (para 2.14). The recommended method for calculating this loss is set out at **9.79** below.

9.75 By contrast, the third edition recommends 'the assumption that there is no loss of Basic State Pension in respect of a dismissed employee. The onus will . . . be on him to show otherwise'. The reasoning for this is that if an employee is re-employed 'without too long a delay', the loss of basic State Pension arising from the dismissal 'is likely to be nil or relatively small' (para 2.13).

9.76 An employee may have been making contributions to a money-purchase scheme (whether company or personal); once dismissed, the employee may not be able to do so. Is this a head of pension loss? The Guidelines state that it is not (para 4.2). If the claimant is re-employed, then he or she is likely to be able to make contributions to a pension scheme associated with the new employment. If not re-employed, then the claimant should still be able to make contributions to a stakeholder pension or enjoy similar advantages from investing in an individual savings account (ISA). While the third edition does not state this, presumably, if the new job does not involve a pension scheme, the writers of the third edition would say that there is no loss because of the ability to make contributions to a stakeholder pension. Most employers must provide access to a stakeholder pension. A person can always make a contribution to a stakeholder or PPP.

The six questions of the guidelines

Question 1: 'Was the Claimant a member of any personal or occupational pension scheme at the date of dismissal?'

9.77 This is the starting point for the journey through the remaining five questions. if the answer is 'no', then only question 2 need to be considered. If the answer is 'yes', the questions 3–6 will need to be addressed. In answering question 1, a claimant needs to review the type of pension scheme associated with his or her employment. Is there a scheme operated by the employer? If there is, is it of the defined-contribution or defined-benefits type? If not, does the employer contribute to a PPP or a stakeholder pension?

Question 2: 'If not, is it necessary to award compensation for loss of S2P rights?'

9.78 This question is relevant because even if a claimant were not in a pension scheme in the lost employment, the claimant may still suffer a loss (if earning over the lower earnings limit) owing to future S2P not accruing (para 2.14). S2P is accrued by employees earning over the lower earnings limit (unless in a pension scheme contracted out of S2P).

9.79 The Guidelines provide a formula and actuarial table (Table 3.2 in Appendix 3) to calculate this loss (para 7.5). Adjustments may have to be made to reflect ages and earnings not set out in Table 3.2. Appendix 2 of the booklet sets out the assumptions used in producing Table 3.2. The recommended formula for calculating loss of S2P is:

Compensation = Gross annual earnings × One year's accrual of S2P (taken from Table 3.2) × Estimated years of loss

Accordingly, to make the calculation, the information required is gross annual **9.80** earnings, State Pension retirement date, and, for the purposes of Table 3.2, age and gender. Table 3.2 will need to be updated every tax year because it is dependent upon lower and upper earnings limit thresholds, and these change most tax years.

Example

B, who is a male employee, is dismissed in 2003–04 at age 55 from private sector employment with gross earnings of £20,000 per annum and no prospect of re-employment before the State Pension age of 65. He was not a member of any pension arrangements run by his employer and hence was accruing S2P, since his earnings are above the lower earnings limit.

Loss for future accrual of S2P for B is calculated as:

$$£20,000 \times 0.065 \times 10 = £13,000$$

(In this calculation, '0.065' is taken from Table 3.2 and '10' is the number of years to retirement—namely, the period of unemployment to be covered.)

Question 3: 'If the Claimant was a member of a personal pension scheme, did the respondent contribute to it?'

By definition, a PPP is a scheme provided by a third party (not the employer) to which **9.81** the employer and/or the employee contribute. In other words, it is a variety of money-purchase scheme. As far as employee contributions are concerned, the Guidelines take the view there is no loss (para 4.2 and see **9.76** above). As far as employer contributions are concerned, there could be future loss, but generally no past loss.

Future loss, if short term, would be calculated as recommended in the simplified **9.82** approach for occupational pension schemes (see **9.88** below) in respect of loss from the date of dismissal to the date of the hearing and from the date of hearing onwards. However, where the loss is regarded as a career loss, the tribunal would use the Ogden tables to assess loss of future earnings. The Guidelines recommend that the employer's contributions to the personal pension should be added to the continuing loss of earnings before applying the appropriate multiplier in the Ogden tables and a deduction for any accrued S2P (para 8.13).

Questions 4 and 5: 'If the Claimant was a member of an occupational scheme, do the circumstances call for use of the simplified approach? If not, do the circumstances call for use of the substantial loss approach?'

Questions 4 and 5 of the checklist are best considered together since they are, in **9.83** effect, alternatives. Prima facie, a person who has been unlawfully dismissed will suffer a loss of pension. If the claimant was a member of a money-purchase scheme, the loss is generally the loss of future contributions by the respondent employer. Past loss arises only where there is a penalty for leaving the scheme early. If the claimant was a member of a final-salary scheme, he or she will generally be entitled to a deferred pension. In this case, the loss is likely to be the difference between the deferred pension and the pension that he or she would have received but for the unlawful dismissal. This is a combination of past loss and future loss; it is putting a monetary value on that difference that is so difficult. The third edition offers different methodologies depending upon whether the simplified approach or the substantial loss approach is adopted. But the substantial loss approach would not apply to the loss of a money-purchase pension.

9.84 **The simplified approach or the substantial loss approach?** As the third edition rightly states, the decision to adopt the simplified approach or the substantial loss approach is 'the key choice to be made by the tribunal' (para 4.7) and 'crucial' (para 4.10). As their respective names suggest, the substantial loss approach is more complex than the simplified approach. The former is based on actuarial tables that are similar to (but different from) the familiar Ogden tables for assessing future loss of earnings in typical personal injury cases. This is no accident because the substantial loss approach is based on looking at a whole career loss. The simplified approach uses a combination of actuarial tables and the contributions method. Because the choice between the approaches is 'crucial', it is worthwhile quoting at length from the third edition:

> 4.13 Experience suggests that the simplified approach will be appropriate in most cases. Tribunals have been reluctant to embark on assessment of whole career loss because of the uncertainties of employment in modern economic conditions. In general terms, the substantial loss approach may be chosen in cases where the person dismissed has been in the respondent's employment for a considerable time, where the employment was of a stable nature and unlikely to be affected by the economic cycle and where the person dismissed has reached an age where he is less likely to be looking for new pastures. The decision will, however, always depend on the particular facts of the case.

> More particularly, we suggest that the substantial loss approach is appropriate in the following circumstances:

> (a) when the [claimant] has found permanent new employment by the time of the hearing and assuming no specific uncertainties about the continuation of the lost job such as a supervening redundancy a few months after dismissal; further, the tribunal has found that the [claimant] is not likely to move on to better paid employment in due course (see for example *Sibbit v The Governing Body of St Cuthberts Primary School* UKEAT/0070/10 where the EAT ruled that the Tribunal should have adopted the substantial loss approach rather than the simplified method);

> (b) when the [claimant] has not found permanent new employment and the tribunal is satisfied on the balance of probabilities that he will not find new employment before State Pension Age (usually confined to cases of significant disability where the [claimant] will find considerable difficulty in the job market);

(c) when the [claimant] has not found new employment but the tribunal is satisfied that the [claimant] will find alternative employment (which it values, for example, with the help of employment consultants) and is required then to value all losses to retirement and beyond before reducing the total loss by the percentage chance that the [claimant] would not have continued to retirement in the lost career. See *Ministry of Defence v Cannock and ors* [1994] ICR 918.

In essence, the 'key choice' is whether the tribunal should look at career loss to **9.85** retirement or loss over a shorter period on the assumption that the claimant will find employment with a comparable pension scheme. It follows that if the tribunal decides that a person will return to a job at a comparable salary, but will never get a comparable pension, the substantial loss approach may be needed even where the future loss of earnings is for a short period (para 4.12). In such a case, however, it should be checked whether a lack of pension has been compensated for by an increase in salary.

The third edition suggests that, in determining whether it is appropriate to treat the **9.86** case as a career loss case, the judgment in *Kingston-upon-Hull City Council v Dunnachie* (*No 3*) [2003] IRLR 844 will be of assistance. In *Dunnachie* (*No 3*), the President of the EAT (Mr Justice Burton) stated that a tribunal, in deciding on the balance of probabilities whether there is a career loss, should decide this after matching the 'old job facts' and the 'new job facts'. [He continued (at [28]):

(i) Old job facts would include the following . . .
  - Would the [claimant] have remained in the job anyway: and if so for how long? Assuming he would otherwise have intended/wished to remain in such job, were there apparent factors, whether personal (health, family situations, locations) or economic (new technology, fall-off in orders, lay-offs, redundancies) which on the available evidence, including the experience of the employment tribunal as industrial jury, should be taken into account? Would he have taken early retirement, or considered a second career?
  - Would he have been promoted?
  - Would his earnings have remained stable (other than by reference to the cost of living)?
(ii) New job facts:
  (a) The first question is whether he would be likely (after using reasonable mitigation) to obtain a new job at all? If he has not yet obtained a new job, what steps (using reasonable mitigation) should he now take, and what new job is he likely to have obtained, by what date and at what remuneration?
  (b) The next question is whether (having taken reasonable steps and mitigation) he now has a job, but at a pay differential (or would have obtained a job at such differential if/when reasonable steps in mitigation were taken).
  In the latter case:
  - Will he stay in that job or (in accordance with the obligations of reasonable mitigation) change jobs to one which is better paid, thereby in whole or in part eliminating the differential?
  - Will he be promoted: to the same effect?
  - Will the earnings in the new job be stable (subject to the cost of living) or will they improve: to the same effect?

9.87 Interestingly, in the decision of *Orthet Ltd v Vince-Cain* [2004] IRLR 857, the EAT put the issue of choosing between the two approaches in terms of deciding whether the simplified approach is inappropriate. It noted that the Guidelines at para 7.1 stated that the simplified approach should not be used where the period of loss is likely to be more than two years. In other words, where the period of loss will be more than two years, the substantial loss approach should be used. It is submitted that this is a too-simplistic approach. The better analysis is to determine whether the substantial loss approach should be chosen, having regard to factors described in **9.83–9.85** above. (For an example of the EAT upholding an employment tribunal's adoption of the substantive loss approach, see *Network Rail Infrastructure Ltd v Booth* [2006] UK EAT 0071/06/2206.)

9.88 **The simplified approach**   Under the simplified approach, the Guidelines recognize three heads of loss:

(a) loss of enhancement of pension rights accrued prior to dismissal;
(b) loss of pension rights from the date of dismissal to the date of hearing; and
(c) loss of future pension rights from the date of hearing.

9.89 *Loss of enhancement of accrued pension rights: Money-purchase schemes*   The recommendations set out below apply only to final-salary schemes. However, the third edition does recognize that a claimant who was a member of a money-purchase scheme might be required to pay a penalty for leaving the scheme early and that this loss should be covered (para 4.3). The Guidelines do not mention the possibility that a penalty might have been incurred anyway on withdrawal before retirement.

9.90 *Loss of enhancement of accrued pension rights: Final-salary schemes*   As previously noted, the claimant who leaves a final-salary scheme is generally entitled to a pension payable as an annuity from what would have been the retirement date for the rest of their life (commonly called a 'deferred pension'). It was also noted that the claimant may suffer a loss of accrued pension benefits where the deferred pension is calculated as a percentage of final salary. This is sometimes called 'past loss' and the reason that the loss arises was explained in detail at **9.23–9.25**. Put briefly, if the claimant's deferred pension (calculated on the date of leaving) is not enhanced to reflect increases in salary that the claimant might have expected to receive had he or she stayed in employment, there will be a loss if salary would have increased. This potential loss is mitigated to some extent by the statutory obligation to revalue deferred pensions (see **9.26** above). However, because this revaluation is capped broadly speaking at the lower of 5 per cent (and, for some post-5 April 2009 services, 2.5 per cent) per annum compound and the rise in the retail prices index between withdrawal from the scheme (date of dismissal) and retirement, a claimant with an expected salary increase in excess of that amount will suffer a loss. Of course, it may be very difficult to predict what salary increases might have been received between dismissal and retirement, especially if this is a long period. For example, the claimant might have voluntarily left employment or been fairly dismissed in the future. The claimant might have been promoted or demoted. Nonetheless, there could be a substantial loss, assuming 'normal' salary increases.

9.91 Part IV of the PSA 1993 entitles a person to require his or her ex-employer to transfer the value of his or her accrued pension to a similar scheme run by a new employer or to personal pension arrangements meeting certain prescribed requirements. However, the Guidelines take the view that such a transfer value does not eliminate this head of loss (para 5.9). This is on the basis that the transfer value will usually not be based on salary increases, but rather represents the present value of the deferred pension. But the Guidelines do recognize that transfer values 'operate more favourably . . . between the public sector pension schemes' (para 5.9).

9.92 The Guidelines (paras 5.10 and 5.11) set out two circumstances in which they consider no compensation should be awarded for this head of loss:

- where the Claimant is within five years of retirement (this is because the difference between cost of living increases and anticipated increases in earnings has less cumulative effect over this shorter period); and
- where the tribunal finds as a fact that the employment would have terminated in any event within a period of one year.

9.93 Assuming that the claimant is not denied compensation for the reasons mentioned above, the Guidelines in the third edition recommend the use of actuarial tables produced by GAD. This is similar to the recommendations in the second edition, although the tables have been revised and augmented. Appendix 4 to the third edition sets out four tables: men in private sector schemes; men in public sector schemes; women in private sector schemes; and women in public sector schemes. The reason for drawing a difference between public and private sector schemes is that the former usually provide a pension of 1/80th of final salary plus a lump sum, whereas the latter usually provide 1/60th of final salary with the (tax-efficient) option of partial commutation, together with some other differences (para 5.12).

9.94 As with previous editions, the recommended formula for calculating this head of loss is:

Compensation = Deferred pension × Multiplier
(taken from the relevant table) – Appropriate percentage for withdrawal

9.95 It follows that, to make the calculation, one needs the deferred pension (without any allowance for anticipated cost of living increases or other benefits), and the claimant's gender, date of birth, and normal retirement date under the scheme. The deferred pension ought to be obtainable from the employer. The final element is the 'withdrawal factor'. The tables assume that the claimant would not have left employment before retirement for reasons other than death or disability. Accordingly, it is necessary to consider the percentage likelihood that the claimant would have left employment anyway before retirement other than by virtue of unfair dismissal or unlawful discrimination. This could be fair dismissal, resignation, or 'fair' redundancy. The GAD guide of 1980 provided a table showing reduction factors for withdrawal calculated by reference to age, gender, and the normal retirement date. However, consistently with previous editions, the third edition considers it is best to leave the withdrawal factor to the discretion of the tribunal (para 5.15, and see the discussion at **9.30** and **9.31**).

Example

C, a man, earned £20,000 per annum in the private sector. He is unfairly dismissed. His deferred pension is £1,000. He is 45 years old, with a normal retirement date of 65. The tribunal assess the withdrawal factor as 25 per cent.

C's loss of enhancement of accrued pension benefits is calculated as follows:

£1,000 × 3.17 (see Table 4.1) × 75 per cent = £2,378

9.96 The Guidelines recognize that some crude assumptions are made in assessing loss on this basis. They therefore admit that the parties may consider the Guidelines inapplicable in a particular case (para 5.20). They also recognize that the tables need to be reviewed periodically because the assumptions made are likely to change over time. Indeed, use of the tables has been successfully challenged (see, for example, *Bingham v Hobourn Engineering Ltd* [1992] IRLR 298). Accordingly, litigants must be ready not only to contend for the appropriate withdrawal factor, but also to challenge the tables if inappropriate. With regard to the latter, it is relevant to understand that the tables make various assumptions and that these may be inappropriate for the particular claimant.

9.97 The assumptions (para 5.18) are that:

(a) private sector pensions are based on a defined amount of pension (usually 1/60th of final salary), of which part can be commuted to a lump sum, while public sector pensions have a lump sum payable in addition to the pension—at an amount equal to three years of pension payments at the initial rate;

(b) there is a widow or widower's pension at 50 per cent of the member's rate;

(c) the maximum possible amount of pension is commuted for a lump sum;

(d) pensions after retirement are increased annually in line with the retail price index (subject to an annual limit of 5 per cent per annum for private sector pensions); and

(e) no allowance is made for the effects of contracting out.

9.98 The actuarial basis for the tables is set out in Appendix 2 of the third edition.

9.99 *Loss of pension rights from the date of dismissal to the date of hearing: Money-purchase schemes* For a money-purchase scheme, including a PPP or a money-purchase top-up, the claimant's loss is easy to calculate. It is the contributions the employer would have made during the period from dismissal to the date of hearing. Thus, the formula mentioned below for final-salary schemes can be used (but not the adjustment using the tables in Appendix 7 referred to below). While the Guidelines do not make the point, it would seem correct that regard should be had to any mitigation of loss by the claimant through securing pension benefits from a new employer during the period under review.

Loss of pension rights from the date of dismissal to the date of hearing: Final-salary **9.100**
schemes The Guidelines accept that the technically correct method for computing loss is to value the difference between the pension benefits to which the claimant is entitled at the date of leaving employment and the pension benefits to which the claimant would have been entitled had employment continued until the date of hearing (para 6.3). However, their recommendation is 'simply to include with the weekly loss [of earnings] a sum to represent what the employer would have contributed notionally towards the Claimant's pension had he still been employer' (para 6.4). In their view, this is 'the fairest and simplest way of calculating . . . continuing loss of pension rights' (para 6.7). This was the method used in the second edition, but a substantial change has been introduced. As noted, usually in a final-salary pension scheme, the employer does not make a specific contribution in relation to each employee's likely pension; rather, the employer pays a percentage of total payroll. But, in fact, the amount that should be paid in respect of an individual employee increases with age. Accordingly, the Guidelines recommend that tribunals apply the factors set out in Tables 1 and 2 of Appendix 7.

As a result, the recommended formula is: **9.101**

**Compensation per week = Gross weekly pensionable pay ×
Employer's pension contribution × Appendix 7 adjustment**

In order to calculate this, one needs gross weekly pensionable pay (which may **9.102**
not be the same as basic pay), employer's pension contribution, and, for the purposes of Appendix 7, the age, gender and normal retirement age of the claimant. The Guidelines suggest that if the employer's pension contribution rate is currently anomalous (for example, because of a 'contributions holiday'), the tribunal should apply the true 'standard rate of contribution'. This ought to be found in the report and accounts of the pension scheme, or in the statement of pension costs for inclusion in the accounts of the employer (para 6.6). If it happens that the percentage cannot easily be ascertained, the Guidelines suggest using a figure of 15 per cent or 20 per cent for a non-contributory scheme (para 6.7). (In the current climate, this looks on the low side.) The employee's itemized pay statement should reveal whether the scheme is contributory.

Example

D, a man aged 40, earns £400 a week gross, which is his pensionable pay. He contributed £20 a week (that is, 5 per cent) to the pension fund. His employer contributed 15 per cent of gross wage bill to the fund. D's normal retirement date is at the age of 65. The factor from Table 1 of Appendix 7 is therefore 0.95.

D's continuing loss of pension rights per week is calculated as:

$$£400 \times 0.15 \times 0.95 = £57 \text{ a week}$$

9.103 While the Guidelines do not state this, it would seem arguable that an allowance should be made to the extent that the claimant secures pension benefits from a new employer in respect of this period.

9.104 *Loss of future pension rights from the date of hearing* In essence, the approach is the same as loss of pension rights from the date of dismissal to the date of hearing.

9.105 *Loss of future pension rights from the date of hearing: Money-purchase scheme* The value of the loss during the fixed period is the aggregate of the contributions that the employer would have made to the scheme during this period. The Guidelines point out that, in view of the Court of Appeal in *Bentwood Brothers (Manchester) Ltd v Shepherd* [2003] IRLR 364, an allowance should be made for accelerated receipt. This could be done by using Ogden Table 38 (para 7.2).

9.106 *Loss of future pension rights from the date of hearing: Final-salary scheme* The Guidelines recommend the same formula as for loss of pension rights from the date of dismissal to the date of hearing. Therefore, in contrast with money-purchase schemes, the Appendix 7 adjustment applies. Again, there should be a discount for accelerated receipt.

Example

E, a woman aged 20 earned £200 a week gross, which is her pensionable pay. She contributed £10 a week (that is, 5 per cent) to the pension fund. Her employer contributed 15 per cent of gross wage bill to the fund. E's normal retirement date is the age of 60. The factor from Table 1.2 of Appendix 7 is 0.74.

E's continuing loss of pension rights per week is calculated as:

$$£200 \times 0.15 \times 0.74 = £22.20 \text{ a week}$$

9.107 **The substantial loss approach** As noted, this is the most radical change introduced by the third edition. Set out at **9.83–9.85** above are the factors that determine whether a tribunal should adopt the simplified approach or the substantial loss approach. The substantial loss approach does not apply to money-purchase schemes.

The recommended formula is as follows: **9.108**

Compensation = A – B – C – Relevant withdrawal factor for A, B, and C

where:

- A = value of prospective final-salary pension rights up to normal retirement age in former employment (assuming no dismissal);
- B = value of accrued final-salary pension rights to date of dismissal from former employment; and
- C = value of prospective final-salary pension rights to normal retirement age in any new employment.

C will be zero if the tribunal concludes that the claimant will not obtain further **9.109** pensionable employment. Less obviously, it will also be zero if the claimant joins a money-purchase scheme (including contributions to a stakeholder pension). The Guidelines recommend that the claimant's mitigation in this case should be dealt with by adjusting loss of earnings (as distinct from pension loss). Thus, loss of earnings (excluding pension) becomes the difference between net earnings in the old job (ignoring employer pension contributions) and net earnings in the new job (including employer pension contributions). See *Network Rail Infrastructure Ltd v Booth* [2006] UK EAT 0071/06/2206, in which the EAT ruled that an employment tribunal was incorrect in failing to take account of the provision of a money-purchase scheme by a new employer. It seems that the tribunal had made this error because it had not been called upon, when assessing loss of general earnings, to compare the difference between net earnings in the old job and the new job. Put another way, if, for whatever reason, the tribunal does not make an award in respect of loss of general earnings, the tribunal must still somehow take into account the benefit of the money-purchase scheme, even though the Guidelines do not mention this possibility. Of course, this leaves open the problem of how to calculate the value of the pension with the new employer. Interestingly, in the case of *Evans v Barclays Bank plc* EAT/0137/09, in which the parties had not made submissions to help the tribunal, the tribunal decided to treat the employer's contributions as a stream of 'income', applied Ogden Table 7 (6th edn) to find a multiplier, and then made a deduction to reflect the chance of the claimant staying in the new employer's pension scheme. Having done this, the tribunal took the same approach to calculating the loss of future accrual of service under the respondent employer's pension scheme (that is, it did not follow the tables in the Guidelines). On appeal by the claimant, the EAT refused to overturn this approach.

This calculation requires taking five steps. **9.110**

9.111　The first step is to determine the annual amount of pension for A, B, and C. This is:

$$\text{Pension fraction (eg 1/60th)} \times \text{Relevant period of service} \times \text{Pensionable salary}$$

A is the projected pension on retirement from the old job, B is the deferred pension on leaving the old job, and C is the final pension from the new job. In A and B, pensionable salary is the salary at the date of dismissal. In C, pensionable salary is the current pensionable pay in the new employment (or deemed pay, if new employment is assumed). In A, the relevant period of service is from the beginning of employment to normal retirement age. In B, it is service up to the date of dismissal. In C, it is from the start of the new job to the normal retirement date in the new job.

9.112　The second step is to determine the values of the relevant pensions. In the case of A and C, this is found by multiplying the respective annual amounts by the factors from Tables 1–4 of Appendix 5 corresponding to the age of the claimant. For B, one uses Tables 1–4 of Appendix 6. The tables require knowing the sex, gender, and normal retirement date of the claimant under the scheme. For the purposes of A and B, the relevant age will be the age at the date of dismissal. For C, it will be the age at the start of the new job.

9.113　The third step is to apply the withdrawal factor. Cases such as *Clancy v Cannock Chase Technical College* [2001] IRLR 331 (see **9.04** above) suggest that a withdrawal factor should be applied. Interestingly, the GAD has argued (at para 8.9):

> that a blanket withdrawal factor is wrong in principle because the tribunal might have material upon which to decide, for example, that the chance of the [claimant] losing his new job before retirement was not as great as that of losing the old job before retirement.

A and B should have the same withdrawal factor, but C may well be different. Issues relevant to the withdrawal factor percentage were noted at **9.30–9.31**. However, bearing in mind that the retirement date may be many years hence, one should also consider age, status, work record, health, and viability of the employer's business (para 8.4).

9.114　The fourth step to consider is whether the employee contributes to the pension scheme in the old job. If so, the Guidelines accept that another table ought to be devised to deal with this. But to simplify matters, the Guidelines suggest an alternative. This is that, when calculating loss of earnings (as contrasted with pension loss), any employee contributions should be subtracted from the net earnings before applying the appropriate multiplier. By the same token, if the new job offers a contributory final-salary scheme, when assessing the value of the net earnings in the new job, the tribunal should deduct the value of the claimant's contributions.

The final step is to consider whether the claimant obtains a new job in which S2P **9.115** accrues. If so, this value should be deducted from the value of A – B. The value of future accrual of S2P can be computed by using Table 3.2 in Appendix 3, calculated using earnings in the new employment (see **9.79** above).

Example

F, a female employee is dismissed in 2002–03 at age 40 from private sector employment, which had a contracted-out pension scheme offering a pension of 1/60th of final year's salary per year of service. Her pensionable pay in the year before she was dismissed was £20,000. She had completed 15 years of service before being dismissed and had a pensionable age of 65.

She is employed again one year later, at age 41, in a public sector job, with a salary of £15,000 and a contracted-out pension scheme offering a pension of 1/80th of final year's salary per year of service and a lump sum of three years' pension, payable at normal retirement age of 60.

Step 1: Determine the annual amount of pension for A, B, and C

For the calculation of A:	Pension expected at normal retirement age in former employment = 1/60th × 40 (ie 15 years' service + 25 years to retirement) × 20,000 = £13,333.33 a year
For the calculation of B:	Pension expected at normal retirement age in former employment with service cut short at date of dismissal = £ 1/60th × 15 × 20,000 = £5,000.00 a year
For the calculation of C:	Pension expected at normal retirement age in new employment = 1/80th × 19 × 15,000 = £3,562.50 a year

In addition, there is an expected lump sum at normal retirement age of three years' pension—namely £10,687.50—but no separate calculation is required for the lump sum in C, because this is incorporated within the factors for public sector schemes. The pension schemes in both employments are contracted out. No specific allowance is made for inflation or future career progression, since these factors are taken into account in the multiplier factors to be applied.

Step 2: Determine the values of the relevant pensions

(a) Factor for the calculation of the value of A = 11.45 from Table 5.3
(b) Factor for the calculation of the value of B = 7.56 from Table 6.3
(c) Factor for the calculation of the value of C = 17.54 from Table 5.4

The loss of pension rights can therefore be calculated as follows.

Pension amount × factor for A (£13,333.33 × 11.45)	= £152,667
Pension amount × factor for B (£5,000.00 × 7.56)	= £37,800
Pension amount × factor for C (£3,562.50 × 17.54)	= £62,486
Loss	= £52,381

Step 3: Apply the withdrawal factor

Assuming that the tribunal determines a 40 per cent withdrawal factor for the lost job and a 25 per cent withdrawal factor for the new job, the calculation is as follows.

A = £13,333.33 × 11.45 × 60%	= £91,600
B = £5,000.00 × 7.56 × 60%	= £22,680
C = £3,562.50 × 17.54 × 75%	= £46,865
Loss	= £22,055

Step 4

It may be necessary to deal with employee contributions to the pension scheme by way of deducting employee contributions from net earnings when calculating loss of earnings (see above).

Step 5: Taking account of S2P accruing in new job

Assume that F, instead of obtaining a public sector job, finds work in the private sector, but with no pension scheme and no prospect of one. She has no PPP, but pays NICs at the full rate, so as to entitle her to S2P. Her age at date of re-employment is 41 and her state retirement age is 65—because she was born after 1955 (see Table 3.2). The result is:

A – B (as before) – C (calculated in accordance with Appendix 3)

That is:

£15,000 × 5.0% (extrapolated from 4.8% rising to 5.6% between the ages of 40 and 45) × 24 = £18,000

The loss is calculated as:

£152,667 – £37,800 – £18,000 = £96,867

The amount will be smaller if withdrawal factors are applied.

(Another worked example can be found in *Occupational Pensions*, May 2004, p 13.)

Question 6: 'If the scheme was not contracted out, is it necessary to award compensation for loss of both occupational pension and S2P?'

In the same way as a claimant who is not in a pension scheme may suffer a loss **9.116** of S2P (see Question 2), a claimant whose pension scheme is not contracted out of S2P may also suffer a loss owing to his or her future S2P not accruing. This is calculated in the same way as mentioned when addressing Question 2 (para 7.5; see **9.79** above).

10

CALCULATING THE COMPENSATORY AWARD: MANNER OF DISMISSAL

A. Introduction

10.01   The third head of compensation established by *Norton Tool Co Ltd v Tewson* [1973] 1 All ER 183 is compensation for the manner of dismissal. At first, this was thought to include compensation for injured feelings, but, in *Dunnachie v Kingston Upon Hull City Council* [2004] IRLR 727, the House of Lords ruled that the loss contemplated by s 123(1) of the Employment Rights Act 1996 (ERA 1996) is economic loss rather than injury to feelings or other forms of non-economic injury. Nonetheless, compensation will be awarded where the manner of dismissal means that the employee is likely to be at a disadvantage in the labour market or causes psychological injury that prevents the claimant from looking for a new job. Furthermore, the compensatory award may be increased where the manner of dismissal does not comply with the ACAS Code on Discipline and Grievances at Work (see **10.11** below).

B. No Compensation for Injured Feelings

10.02   As a general rule, compensation will not be awarded for the distress or emotional upset caused by the dismissal itself. In *Vaughan v Weighpack Ltd* [1974] IRLR 105, the National Industrial Relations Court (NIRC) dismissed Mr Vaughan's claim for compensation for the injury to his feelings caused by the distressing circumstances of his dismissal. The NIRC also rejected the idea that his employment prospects would suffer if news of his dismissal spread through the small community in which he lived and worked. Similarly, in *Brittains Arborfield Ltd v Van Uden* [1977] ICR 211, the Employment Appeal Tribunal (EAT) ruled that a compensation claim would not lie even in cases in which gross misconduct had been alleged if the employer's allegation were subsequently shown to be false. This has now been confirmed by the House of Lords in *Dunnachie v Kingston Upon Hull City Council* [2004] IRLR 727.

Exceptions

Compensation for injured feelings may be awarded in rare cases in which the **10.03** manner of dismissal is so distressing that it seriously undermines the employee's capacity to look for work—that is, where it results in an illness that prevents the employee from looking for work. For example, in *John Millar & Sons v Quinn* [1974] IRLR 107, the industrial tribunal awarded Ms Quinn one year's loss of earnings after it had heard that it would take Ms Quinn that length of time before she would be fit to look for work. The NIRC refused to overturn this award on appeal, commenting that the tribunal had heard and seen Ms Quinn in the witness box, and was therefore entitled to reach its decision.

Similarly, in *Devine v Designer Flowers Wholesale Florist Sundries Ltd* [1993] IRLR 517, **10.04** the EAT held that the industrial tribunal was wrong not to award compensation to an employee who, as a result of her dismissal, suffered from anxiety and reactive depression. The EAT held that, in such circumstances, compensation could be awarded for loss of earnings until such time as the applicant could reasonably be expected to find other employment. However, the EAT warned tribunals against assuming that 'the whole of the period of unfitness thereupon' was attributable to the actions of the employer since 'there may, for example, be questions as to whether the unfitness might have manifested itself in any event'. Furthermore, the EAT pointed out that the fact the employee was not fit to look for work in her former capacity did not mean that she was necessarily unfit for any form of remunerative employment.

The correct approach to such situations was refined by the Court of Session in **10.05** *Dignity Funerals Ltd v Bruce* [2005] IRLR 189. In that case, the employment tribunal declined to award compensation to a claimant who suffered from reactive depression that was allegedly brought on by the disciplinary process between the date of dismissal and the date of the hearing, but did make an award for future loss. The EAT allowed the claimant's appeal. Confirming the correctness of the EAT's decision, the Court of Session ruled that if it could be shown that the depressive illness was caused by the dismissal and it was this that prevented the claimant from working, then a full award of compensation for loss of earnings should have been made (as in the earlier cases). On the other hand, if the dismissal is merely one of two or more concurrent causes of the claimant's loss, or where the dismissal is a cause of the loss for only part of the period, it is then necessary for the tribunal to consider what sum it is just and equitable to award; the Court indicated that, 'in all likelihood', this would be 'less than the full amount of the wage loss'. For this reason, the EAT had erred in awarding the claimant the full loss between the date of dismissal and the date of the tribunal hearing, because there were no findings as to the extent to which the depression had been caused by the dismissal and the extent to which this had prevented the claimant from finding work. The same approach may apply where the claimant finds a new job, but is either dismissed or resigns as a result of the continuing effects of the illness caused by the original dismissal (*Barton v Sheffield City Council*, Case No 2800284/00).

10.06 The employer's conduct may be taken into account in any event when considering future loss of earnings (see Chapter 8).

Disadvantage in the labour market

10.07 Compensation may also be awarded where it is shown that the manner of dismissal gives rise to a risk of financial loss in the future by making it more difficult for the employee to find a new job (*Vaughan v Weighpack Ltd* [1974] IRLR 105) or rendering the employee exceptionally liable to selection for dismissal.

10.08 An illustration of a successful claim in such circumstances is *Johnston t/a Richard Andrews Ladies Hairdressers v Baxter* EAT 492/82. Ms Baxter was employed as an apprentice hairdresser. She was dismissed one month before her apprenticeship expired. The industrial tribunal held that she had been unfairly dismissed and awarded her compensation of £765 for loss arising in the period after the expiration of the apprenticeship. The employer appealed, arguing that the tribunal was wrong to award compensation for that period because it was not under an obligation to employ her once the apprenticeship ended. The EAT, dismissing the appeal, ruled that the claim could either be regarded as compensation for consequential loss flowing from the dismissal (that is, that Ms Baxter's employment prospects might be affected as a result of not finishing her apprenticeship) or that the employer's conduct had actually been the cause of her inability to find a new job and hence it was appropriate to award compensation for the manner of dismissal.

10.09 It is unclear whether, following the Court of Appeal's ruling in *Abbey National plc v Chagger* [2010] IRLR 47, an employment tribunal can make an award for 'stigma' in an unfair dismissal case as well as in a discrimination case (see **19.69**). There is no reason in principle why compensation should not be awarded for any stigma attached to the dismissal, as in the *BCCI* case (see **1.96** above), however, apart from the circumstances outlined at **10.07** and **10.08** above, such an award is unlikely in an ordinary unfair dismissal case because it may be extremely difficult for an employee to show that he or she suffered such stigma as a result of bringing an unfair dismissal claim against his or her former employers, and any difficulties that the claimant has in mitigating his or her loss as a result of the dismissal is likely to be reflected in the award for loss of earnings. Nonetheless, by analogy to discrimination cases, such an award may be made in special categories of dismissal such as dismissals for trade union activities, pregnancy or maternity-related reasons, or whistleblowing.

Discrimination cases

An exception to the general rule that compensation will not be awarded for injured **10.10** feelings exists in discrimination cases in which special statutory provisions apply (see **19.01** below).

C. Power to Increase Compensatory Award

The previous statutory provisions, which continue to be applied to dismissals on **10.11** or before 5 April 2009 (Employment Act 2008 (Commencement No 1 Transitional Provisionals and Savings) Order 2008, Pt 1, para 2), required employment tribunals to increase the compensatory award where there was a failure to comply with the statutory disputes procedures. These provisions were repealed by the Employment Act 2008 (EA 2008).

EA 2008, s 3 inserted s 207A(2) into the Trade Union and Labour Relations **10.12** (Consolidation) Act 1992 (TULR(C)A 1992). This provides that the compensatory award may will be increased by up to 25 per cent where an employer 'unreasonably' fails to comply with the Advisory, Conciliation, and Arbitration Service (ACAS) 2009 Code of Practice on Discipline and Grievances at Work, and the tribunal considers this to be 'just and equitable'. ERA 1996, s 124A(1)(b) provides that the increase applies before any reduction is made for contributory fault under ERA 1996, s 123(6) or the payment of an enhanced redundancy payment under ERA 1996, s 123(7).

At the time of writing, there are no reported decisions of awards being increased for **10.13** this reason, but the example below is provided by way of illustration of the kind of circumstances in which an award may be increased.

Example

An employer dismisses an employee summarily for gross misconduct without following a disciplinary procedure or without giving the employee a proper opportunity to answer the allegations against him. In such circumstances, the tribunal may well consider it just and equitable to increase the award by 25 per cent.

11

CALCULATING THE COMPENSATORY AWARD: LOSS OF STATUTORY RIGHTS

A. Introduction

11.01 The final head of compensation established by *Norton Tool Co Ltd v Tewson* [1973] 1 All ER 183 is compensation for loss of statutory rights, such as the temporary loss of the right to claim unfair dismissal, redundancy, or maternity leave in future employment owing to the need to re-qualify for these rights. This head is somewhat inconsistent with the general principle that compensation should be awarded only for financial loss and it would appear from the decision of the Employment Appeal Tribunal (EAT) in *Harvey v The Institute of the Motor Industry (No 2)* [1995] IRLR 416 that industrial tribunals will not err in law if they fail to make such an award or fail to give reasons for not making such an award, although the latter must be open to doubt (*Meek v City of Birmingham* [1987] IRLR 250). However, awards under this head are likely to be fairly small. This chapter examines the principles underlying the assessment of compensation under this head.

B. Redundancy and Unfair Dismissal

11.02 In *Norton Tool Co Ltd v Tewson* [1973] 1 All ER 183, the National Industrial Relations Court (NIRC) held that an award of two weeks' salary was sufficient compensation for the need to re-qualify for statutory protection against unfair dismissal. In the past, tribunals used to award a nominal sum of £20. However, in *SH Muffett Ltd v Head* [1986] IRLR 488, the EAT ruled that this conventional award should be increased to £100 to reflect the diminution in the value of the pound since 1972. Because this case was decided over 20 years ago, tribunals may well award a higher amount (of around £350) to take account of the loss in the value of the pound since 1986 if they consider it just and equitable to do so.

It is not entirely clear whether this is also intended to cover the need to re-qualify **11.03** for redundancy protection. At the time of the NIRC's decision, this was covered by a separate head of claim that was abolished when the basic award was introduced in 1975. It could therefore be argued that a separate award should be made in respect of the need to re-qualify for a redundancy payment, but, in practice, this point is ignored.

C. Other Statutory Rights

Additional compensation may be awarded for the loss of other employment protection **11.04** rights. The most important of these is the right to statutory notice—that is, the minimum period guaranteed by s 86 of the Employment Rights Act 1996 (ERA 1996). This was accepted as a valid category of claim in *Hilti (GB) Ltd v Windridge* [1974] IRLR 53 (a case decided under the identical provisions of the Contracts of Employment Act 1972) and was confirmed by the EAT in *Daley v A E Dorsett (Almar Dolls) Ltd* [1981] IRLR 385. The EAT suggested that the award should be fixed at half the employee's statutory entitlement to take account of the risk that the employee may be dismissed before re-qualifying for statutory protection and of other contingencies. So, an employee with six years' service should receive three weeks' net pay. A tribunal that awards more than this conventional sum will err in law (see *Arthur Guinness & Son Co (GB) Ltd v Green* [1989] IRLR 288).

Awards may also be made for the loss of other service-related employment protection **11.05** rights, such as the right to maternity leave (*Barnes v Gee Hogan (Convertors) Ltd* EAT 198/77).

D. No Award

An award of compensation for loss of statutory rights will not be made if the loss is too **11.06** remote. Thus, in *Gourley v Kerr* EAT 692/81, the EAT said that no award should be made unless the applicant satisfies the tribunal both that he or she will get a new job and that he or she runs the risk of being dismissed from that job before re-qualifying for statutory protection. (For other applications of this principle, see *SH Muffett Ltd v Head* [1986] IRLR 488 and *Puglia v C James & Sons Ltd* [1996] IRLR 70.)

Of the two conditions put forward by the EAT, the first—that the applicant will get **11.07** a new job—is the more important, since the second—concerning the risk of dismissal—is already taken into account in fixing the conventional award. Thus, by awarding only 50 per cent of the lost period of notice, tribunals assume that employees have a 50:50 chance of being dismissed from the new job before re-qualifying for their full statutory protection.

11.08 As far as the first condition is concerned, tribunals may decline to make an award for loss of statutory rights if it is found that the employee is unlikely to be on the labour market for some time due to illness, or for some other reason. For example, in *Gourley v Kerr*, the EAT declined to make an award because it thought that Mr Gourley would not get another job for some time due to the illness that led to his dismissal. Moreover, even if he were to find another job, he was close to retirement and therefore would not have been entitled to statutory protection. (The EAT's reasoning on this second point seems unsound because s 49 of the Employment Protection (Consolidation) Act 1978, relating to statutory notice, did not contain an age qualification; see now ERA 1996, s 86.) Similarly, in *Pagano v HGS* [1976] IRLR 9, an industrial tribunal declined to make an award for loss of employment protection rights because Mr Pagano enrolled in a full-time course of study and therefore would be off the labour market for several years. A tribunal may also decline to make an award for loss of statutory rights if an employee becomes self-employed because he or she will no longer be eligible for statutory protection.

11.09 A further ground for refusing to award compensation for loss of statutory rights is that the employee is unlikely to benefit from the particular form of protection in the future. For example, in *Barnes (Convertors) Ltd* EAT 198/77, the EAT refused to make an award for the right to maternity pay because Mrs Barnes was aged 44 at the time of the hearing and was unlikely to have another baby. The claim was therefore considered to be too remote.

E. Reduced Award

11.10 The conventional figure may be reduced in the light of uncertainties surrounding the employee's future employment prospects. For example, in *Arthur Guinness & Son Co (GB) Ltd v Green* [1989] IRLR 288, the EAT limited its award to four weeks' net pay because of the uncertainty as to when Mr Green would be fit to return to work.

11.11 The award may also be reduced for contributory fault.

12

REDUCING UNFAIR DISMISSAL
COMPENSATION: JUSTICE AND EQUITY

A. Introduction

The grounds upon which an award of unfair dismissal compensation may be **12.01** reduced or limited are regulated, like the awards themselves, by statute (*Cadbury Ltd v Doddington* [1977] ICR 982).

In summary, the basic award may be reduced where: **12.02**

(a) the employment tribunal considers it just and equitable to reduce the award because of the conduct of the employee before the dismissal (Employment Rights Act 1996 [ERA 1996], s 122(2)); or

(b) the employee unreasonably refuses an offer of reinstatement (ERA 1996, s 122(1)).

In addition, any redundancy payment made to the employee, whether under the **12.03** statutory scheme or otherwise, is set off against the employer's liability to pay the basic award (ERA 1996, s 122(4)).

12.04 The compensatory award may be reduced where:

(a) the tribunal finds that the conduct of the employee caused or contributed to the dismissal (ERA 1996, s 123(6));

(b) the employee is shown to have failed to mitigate his or her loss (ERA 1996, s 123(4));

(c) the tribunal considers it just and equitable to limit its award for some other reason (ERA 1996, s 123(1)); or

(d) the employee unreasonably fails to comply with the Advisory, Conciliation, and Arbitration Service (ACAS) 2009 Code of Practice on disciplinary and grievance procedures, pursuant to s 207A(3) of the Trade Union and Labour Relations (Consolidation) Act 1992 (TULR(C)A 1992).

12.05 Moreover, if the employee has received a redundancy payment, any part of it that has not been set off against the basic award will be set off against the compensatory award (ERA 1996, s 123(3)).

12.06 This chapter considers the circumstances in which it may be just and equitable to limit the compensatory award under ERA 1996, s 123(1). Chapters 13–16 look at the other factors that may give rise to a reduction in compensation.

B. Limiting the Compensatory Award

12.07 The statutory provisions recognize that a compensatory award will be made only where it is 'just and equitable' to do so. The breadth of discretion conferred on tribunals by this provision was recognized by the House of Lords in *W Devis & Sons Ltd v Atkins* [1977] IRLR 314, in which Viscount Dilhorne noted that the relevant provision (now ERA 1996, s 123(1)):

> does not . . . provide that regard should be had only to the loss resulting from the dismissal being unfair. Regard must be had to that, but the award must be just and equitable in all the circumstances, and it cannot be just and equitable that a sum should be awarded in compensation when in fact the employee has suffered no injustice by being dismissed.

This principle has become particularly important since the House of Lords' ruling in *Polkey v AE Dayton Services Ltd* [1987] IRLR 503, in which their Lordships approved the ruling of Browne-Wilkinson J in *Sillifant v Powell Duffryn Timber Ltd* [1983] IRLR 91 to the effect that, although the so-called 'any difference' rule did not apply in determining liability for unfair dismissal, the degree of injustice suffered by the applicant was relevant to the issue of compensation. It has therefore been accepted that there may be circumstances in which it is just and equitable to make no award at all or to limit the compensatory award to a specific period of time.

C. General Principles

No injustice, no award

In *Tele-Trading Ltd v Jenkins* [1990] IRLR 430, the Court of Appeal stated that   **12.08**
the authorities established that it may be just and equitable to make no award
where:

(a) at the time of the application to the industrial tribunal, the employer can show
    that the employee is, in fact, guilty of the misconduct alleged against him or her,
    or some other serious misconduct (see *Polkey v AE Dayton Services Ltd* [1987]
    IRLR 503, 506–508, *per* Lord Mackay); or
(b) the employer would, or might, have fairly dismissed the employee if a thorough
    and just investigation had been conducted prior to the dismissal, whether or
    not the employee is in fact guilty of the alleged misconduct (ibid, *per* Lord
    Bridge).

Category (a)

The facts in *W Devis & Sons Ltd v Atkins* [1977] IRLR 314 are a classic illustration   **12.09**
of a case falling within category (a). Mr Atkins was the manager of Devis & Sons'
abattoir in Preston. He was dismissed for his persistent refusal to obey directions
from his employer in relation to the purchase of livestock. After his dismissal, information came to light that showed that, during his employment, Mr Atkins had been
involved in dishonest dealing in live animals. The House of Lords remitted the case
to the industrial tribunal to consider whether any compensation should be awarded
in the light of Mr Atkin's gross misconduct that, had it in fact been known at the
time of his dismissal, would have been a fair ground for dismissal in the first place.

Category (b)

The decision of the EAT in *Parker v D & J Tullis Ltd* EAT 306/91 illustrates the   **12.10**
kind of case that falls within category (b). Mr Parker was dismissed for allegedly
stealing scrap metal. The main evidence against him was from two other employees
who had witnessed the incident. However, the names of the witnesses were not
disclosed to Mr Parker in the course of the disciplinary proceedings and the
industrial tribunal held that his dismissal was unfair for this reason. Nevertheless,
a majority of the tribunal considered that it was not just and equitable to make a
compensatory award because the employers would have been entitled to prefer
the evidence of the two witnesses to that of Mr Parker, and therefore Mr Parker
suffered no injustice as a result of the procedural irregularity. The industrial tribunal's
decision was upheld by the EAT (see also *Martin v British Railways Board* [1989]
ICR 198). It follows that, although a procedural irregularity will normally lead to
the dismissal being held unfair, it is open to tribunals to award no compensation

where employers can show that they would have been justified in dismissing the employee had they followed a fair procedure.

12.11 However, a category (b) argument will not succeed if the employer is unable to show that the dismissal would have been fair had a fair procedure been followed. In *Panama v London Borough of Hackney* [2003] IRLR 278, the employment tribunal upheld the dismissal on procedural grounds, but refused to award compensation on the basis that, if the disciplinary proceedings against Ms Panama had taken place, she would have been found guilty of gross misconduct and dismissed. Allowing the appeal, the Court of Appeal ruled that the employment tribunal had erred because it had failed to consider whether the dismissal would have been fair had such a hearing taken place. The Court ruled that it would not, because although the employer genuinely believed Ms Panama to be guilty and hence met the first of the *Burchell* [1978] IRLR 379 requirements, the second and third requirements of the *Burchell* test—namely, that it had reasonable grounds for that belief and had carried out a reasonable investigation—were not established by the evidence. There was insufficient evidence of fraud and obvious questions that should have been asked in the course of the disciplinary process had not been so asked. Furthermore, there was no reason to believe that those questions would have been asked if the disciplinary process had been completed.

Insufficient evidence of an employee's guilt

12.12 This argument will not be successful if the employer is unable to satisfy the tribunal that there is sufficient evidence that the employee was in fact guilty of the alleged misconduct. For example, in *Tele-Trading Ltd v Jenkins* [1990] IRLR 430, the company was unable to satisfy the tribunal that it had reasonable grounds for suspecting Mr Jenkins of dishonesty. At the hearing on compensation, it sought to rely on police evidence that was not available at the time of dismissal, but the tribunal considered that this evidence was inconclusive and accordingly made a full award of compensation. The Court of Appeal upheld the employment tribunal's ruling on the grounds that the tribunal was entitled to conclude on the evidence before it that the employer did not have reasonable grounds for its belief in the applicant's guilt and therefore the tribunal was justified in making a full award.

Distinction between procedure and substance?

12.13 It is clear that it will be easier for employers to show that a particular defect made no difference to the decision where the defect is characterized as purely procedural— for example, where redundancy was inevitable despite a failure to consult. Conversely, it will be more difficult for employers to show that a particular defect made no difference to the decision where the defect was one of substance—for example, where the employer applied the wrong redundancy selection procedure. However, in *Steel Stockholders (Birmingham) Ltd v Kirkwood* [1993] IRLR 515, the EAT went further than this and suggested that, as a matter of law, it would not be 'just and equitable' to limit compensation in cases in which the defect in procedure related to the 'substance of the decision'. So, for example, in the *Kirkwood* case, it was not open to the employers to argue that Mr Kirkwood would have been selected for redundancy if the employers had used the correct pool for redundancy selection purposes, because this related to the substance of the decision and was not a matter of mere procedure.

It must be doubted, however, whether the House of Lords in *Polkey* (and Lord   **12.14**
Bridge's judgment in particular) intended to limit its decision to procedural defects alone, and there is nothing to support such a distinction in the statute itself. Moreover, as the EAT recognized, in both *Boulton & Paul Ltd v Arnold* [1994] IRLR 532 (another redundancy selection case involving the misapplication of redundancy selection criteria) and *Highfield Gears Ltd v James* EAT 702/93 (a misconduct case involving a number of procedural errors), the distinction suggested by the EAT in *Kirkwood* is often very difficult to apply in practice. Similarly, in *O'Dea v ISC Chemicals Ltd* [1995] IRLR 599, Peter Gibson LJ, giving the judgment of the Court of Appeal, said that he did not regard it as 'helpful to characterize the defect as procedural or substantive', nor, in his view, 'should the industrial tribunal be expected to do so'.

The position was clarified by the Court of Session's ruling in *King v Eaton Ltd*   **12.15**
(*No 2*) [1998] IRLR 686. In that case, the Court stated that the distinction between 'procedural' and 'substantive' errors may be of some practical use in deciding whether it is realistic, or practicable, or just and equitable to embark upon an attempt to reconstruct a hypothesis to assess what would have happened had the error not occurred. As the Court points out, where the lapse is procedural, 'it may be relatively straightforward to envisage what would have been if procedures had stayed on track'. On the other hand, if what went wrong was more fundamental (or 'substantive'), 'it may be more difficult to envisage what track one would be on, in the hypothetical situation of the unfairness not having occurred'. If, in a particular case (such as *O'Dea*), it is possible to say that the claimant would have been made redundant or dismissed for some other reason in any event, or the tribunal is able with a degree of certainty to reach such a conclusion on a percentage chance basis, then there is no reason why the *Polkey* principle should be limited to procedural errors alone. However, where (to follow the analogy in *King*) the process had been completely derailed, an employment tribunal will not necessarily be required to speculate on the outcome because, as the Court recognized in *King*, this would involve embarking 'upon a sea of speculation where the opinions of witnesses could have no reliable factual starting point'. For this reason, the Court of Session upheld the tribunal's conclusion that it would not allow the employer to call evidence speculating on what the outcome would have been had there been meaningful consultation over the redundancy selection criteria. The Court of Session's approach to this question was approved by the Court of Appeal in *Lambe v 186K Ltd* [2004] EWCA Civ 1045 (in which there was a failure to offer alternative

employment that was regarded as a substantive failure). The Court restated the point that the distinction between procedural and substantive defects was not helpful, because the real issue is whether it is possible for the tribunal to reach a reasoned conclusion on this issue.

12.16 It would therefore seem that the EAT's ruling in *Kirkwood* is incorrect in so far as it purports to establish a general principle that awards cannot be limited where the defect is regarded as one of substance as opposed to procedure. It follows that it is still open to a tribunal to limit its awards where the defect is one of substance if it considers this to be just and equitable in the particular circumstances. On the other hand, it may refuse to limit its award in such cases in which the process has been completely derailed and the outcome would be too speculative.

Is dismissal inevitable?

12.17 A tribunal must be satisfied that dismissal was inevitable or at least 'likely' on a balance of probabilities—that is, the employer must satisfy the 'any difference' test that the procedural omission made no difference to the decision to dismiss and that an employer would have been reasonable in so concluding. For example, in *Townson v The Northgate Group* [1981] IRLR 382, the EAT held that a tribunal was wrong to limit compensation to four weeks' loss of pay since it thought that Mr Townson's attendance might have improved if he had been given a warning, so dismissal was not inevitable. On the other hand, in *Highfield Gears Ltd v James* EAT 702/93, the EAT held that the tribunal should have considered whether Mr James would (or might) have been dismissed if the employers had conducted a proper investigation and had not taken into account a spent disciplinary warning.

12.18 Moreover, it is open to the tribunal to conclude that, although the procedural omission made no difference to the substantive decision, it did make a difference to its timing. In such circumstances, the award of compensation may be limited to the period between the actual dismissal and the time at which a fair decision to dismiss could have been taken. This principle is particularly important in redundancy dismissals where there has been a failure to consult (see below).

Degrees of injustice: Limiting the award

12.19 In other cases, tribunals may be required to weigh up the degree of injustice suffered by the applicant (*Townson v The Northgate Group Ltd* [1981] IRLR 382). This may involve considering the likelihood of dismissal and limiting compensation accordingly. This principle is again particularly important in redundancy and ill health cases in which it may be necessary to consider whether the employee would, in fact, have been made redundant if consultation had taken place (see *Airscrew Howden Ltd v Jacobs* EAT 773/82 and the other cases referred to in **12.23–12.28** below), and, as noted by the Court of Session in *King v Eaton Ltd (No 2)* (**12.15** above), it is open to tribunals to approach this issue on a percentage chance basis.

Unlike its role in determining the reasonableness of dismissal, a tribunal is under a **12.20** duty to consider for itself whether or not to reduce or limit its award in accordance with these principles based on the evidence presented to it (*Fisher v California Cake & Cookie Ltd* [1997] IRLR 212). Failure to do so may be grounds for appeal even if the issue is not raised by the parties (*Hepworth Refractories Ltd v Lingard* EAT 555/90, but see *Wolesley Centres Ltd v Simmons* [1994] ICR 503). If the employer seeks to contend that the award should be limited for one or more of these reasons, the employer should call evidence in support of this contention, although the tribunal should have regard to all of the evidence when making its assessment, including any evidence given by the employee (*Software 2000 Ltd v Andrews* [2007] IRLR 568). The parties should also be given an opportunity to make representation to the tribunal on the nature and extent of the *Polkey* percentage reduction. A tribunal's failure to do this will amount to an error of law (*Market Force (UK) Ltd v Hunt* [2002] IRLR 863), but the tribunal will not be required to speculate as to the possible outcome if evidence is not placed before it (*Boulton & Paul Ltd v Arnold* [1994] IRLR 532).

The reduction should be made after the claimant's loss has been calculated (see *Cox* **12.21** *v London Borough of Camden* [1996] IRLR 389 and *Digital Equipment Co Ltd v Clements (No 2)* [1997] IRLR 140).

Limiting loss: Options

The options open to tribunals in category (b) cases are as follows: **12.22**

(a) to make no award;
(b) to limit the award to a particular period of time;
(c) to make an assessment of the outcome on a percentage chance basis; or
(d) to refuse to speculate on the outcome and to make a full award.

(See *Software 2000 Ltd v Andrews* [2007] IRLR 568, in which the principles are summarized, but some of the points are no longer valid in the light of the repeal of the statutory disputes procedure.)

D. Illustrations of the Principles

Redundancy dismissals

The application of these principles is particularly relevant to the assessment of **12.23** compensation in redundancy dismissals where the dismissal itself is held unfair on the grounds that the employers should have warned or consulted the employee prior to dismissal. A tribunal will have to weigh the consequences of the failure to consult or give prior notice of redundancy in the particular circumstances of the case.

Procedural defects

12.24 Provided that a meeting is held in accordance with the statutory requirements, it is open to a tribunal to conclude that further consultation would have been 'futile' or utterly useless (*Polkey v A E Dayton Services Ltd* [1987] IRLR 503). But an employment tribunal is more likely to hold that the dismissal was unfair and that, at the very least, consultation would have led to the dismissal being postponed for a short period of time (*Abbotts v Wesson Glynwed-Steels Ltd* [1982] IRLR 51).

12.25 Normally, the award is limited to the period of time that it would have taken for the employer to go through the process of consultation (*Mining Supplies (Longwall) Ltd v Baker* [1988] IRLR 417). The award for a failure to consult where dismissal is inevitable is therefore normally between 14 days (*Abotts*) and one month (*Castleman & Patterson v A & P Appledore (Aberdeen) Ltd* EAT(S) 478/90, a case that involved a failure to consult in the context of a business transfer). A similar period may be appropriate if the tribunal is satisfied that the employee would have rejected an offer of alternative employment had it been made (*Lambe v 186K Ltd* [2004] EWCA Civ 1045). A period of six weeks was considered excessive by the EAT in *Mining Supplies (Longwall) Ltd v Baker*, but in *Gover v Propertycare Ltd* [2006] EWCA Civ 286—a non-redundancy case— the Court of Appeal upheld an employment tribunal's assessment that it would have taken the employer four months to consult over a variation in contractual commission.

12.26 However, there is no rigid rule that compensation should be limited to assessing how long the consultation period should have lasted and limiting the award accordingly. For example, in *Elkouil v Coney Island Ltd* [2002] IRLR 174, the EAT held that the employment tribunal had erred in limiting the compensatory award to two weeks' pay where the employer had been aware of the redundancy situation some ten weeks before the dismissal and, had the claimant been warned of his impending redundancy earlier, he would have had a longer period to find himself a new job. In these circumstances, it was just and equitable to award compensation for a ten-week period.

12.27 On the other hand, a full award of compensation should be made where it is clear that the employee would have been retained had proper consultation taken place— for example, where the failure to consult has led to the wrong employee being selected for redundancy or where consultation would have resulted in the employee being offered alternative employment (see *Guest v A & P Appledore (Aberdeen) Ltd and Hall Russell Ltd* EAT(S) 503/90).

12.28 The position becomes more complicated where dismissal would have been a possible, but not inevitable, outcome—for example, where the employee might have come up with an alternative proposal to avoid the redundancy or where the employee might have been offered suitable alternative employment. In such circumstances, tribunals will consider the likelihood of redundancy and limit their awards accordingly. For example, in *Hough v Leyland DAF Ltd* [1991] IRLR 194, the EAT upheld an industrial tribunal's ruling that compensation should be reduced by 50 per cent to take account of the chances of the employees being retained had the employers consulted them prior to making them redundant. Similarly, in *Moran v A D Hamilton* EAT 509/89, the EAT held that, if there had been consultation, the applicant might have been offered alternative employment with an associated company. Unlike the tribunal, it considered that there was a 50 per cent chance of this happening because the applicant would have been willing to accept a drop in salary. It accordingly limited the award to 50 per cent of the full award. (See also *Airscrew Howden Ltd v Jacobs* EAT 773/82, in which the EAT remitted the case to the tribunal to 'attempt the assessment, difficult though it may be', of deciding the chances of Mr Jacobs getting another job within the group; *Rao v Civil Aviation Authority* [1992] IRLR 203—at **12.40** below—in which the Court of Appeal made a similar assessment in the context of an ill health dismissal; and *O'Dea v ISC Chemicals Ltd* [1995] IRLR 599, in which the Court of Appeal upheld an industrial tribunal ruling that the applicant would have had a one in five chance of not being selected for redundancy had he been given the opportunity of being considered for a new post, and accordingly reduced his award of compensation by 80 per cent.) Where a tribunal concludes that the applicant would or might have been offered alternative employment, compensation for loss of earnings should be assessed on the earnings that the employee would have received in that new job (*Red Bank Manufacturing v Meadows* [1992] IRLR 209). So, for example, if an employee would have been earning £200 a week in the new job instead of £250 in the old job and there is an even chance of the employee getting the job, the award of compensation for continuing loss of earnings should be assessed at £100 a week—that is, that there was a 50:50 chance of the employee being offered the alternative job (see *Weston v Metzler (UK) Ltd* EAT 303 and 304/91).

12.29 A tribunal will err in law if it fails to assess the chances of success in accordance with the principles outlined above (see *GEC Energy Systems Ltd v Gufferty* EAT 590/87, in which the tribunal failed to assess the chances of alternative employment).

12.30 This is a discrete legal issue and the parties should be given an opportunity to make representations to the tribunal on the nature and extent of the *Polkey* percentage reduction. A tribunal's failure to do this will amount to an error of law (*Market Force (UK) Ltd v Hunt* [2002] IRLR 863). Furthermore, a tribunal must give sufficient reasons for the parties to know why a *Polkey* reduction has or has not been made (*Market Force UK Ltd v Hunt* and *D36 Ltd v Castro* EAT 0853/03).

Example

Limits on full compensation

Mrs James, a school cleaner, is found to have been unfairly dismissed. However, the industrial tribunal accepts the employer's evidence that it is going to privatize the school cleaning service in three months. The hearing is held three months after dismissal.

(a) Assuming that Mrs James could not have been redeployed, compensation is limited to six months' loss of earnings.
(b) Assuming that Mrs James could have been redeployed and would have accepted the job, she is entitled to *full* compensation; if she would have rejected the job, the tribunal may refuse to make an award for future loss, or limit its award, on the ground that she would have failed to mitigate her loss.

Substantive defects

12.31 The position may be even more complicated where the defect is regarded as substantive rather than procedural. For example, in *Steel Stockholders (Birmingham) Ltd v Kirkwood* [1993] IRLR 515, the EAT ruled that an industrial tribunal had not erred in refusing to assess the chance that Mr Kirkwood would still have been dismissed if the employers had identified the correct pool of employees for redundancy selection purposes. Similarly, in *Boulton & Paul Ltd v Arnold* [1994] IRLR 532, the EAT ruled that the industrial tribunal had not erred in law in failing to raise and consider the question of whether the employee's compensation should be reduced to reflect the possibility that she would have been made redundant if the employers had correctly applied the agreed redundancy selection criteria. The EAT stressed that the onus of adducing such evidence is on the employer and the tribunal was not obliged to raise the issue itself.

12.32 Similarly, in *Eaton v King (No 2)* [1998] IRLR 686, the Court of Session ruled that an employment tribunal was entitled to refuse to allow the employer to call evidence as to what the outcome would have been if different criteria had been used, because this went to the 'heart of the matter' and, as stated above, would have involved an unreasonable degree of speculation. However, in *Lambe v 186K Ltd* [2004] EWCA Civ 1045, the Court of Appeal endorsed the view in *O'Dea and Eaton v King (No 2)* that the distinction between the procedural and substantive errors was not helpful, and that the real issue is whether it is possible for the tribunal to reach a conclusion as to what the outcome would have been if the correct approach had been followed.

Future risk of redundancy

12.33 Compensation may also be limited where the tribunal finds that the employee's job was insecure because of impending redundancy. Thus, in *Youngs of Gosport Ltd v*

Kendell [1977] IRLR 433, the EAT reduced the amount of the compensatory award from 12 months to nine months because it found that Mr Kendell was likely to be made redundant in nine months' time.

However, employers wishing to pursue this line of argument must show that the **12.34** employee would have been made redundant, or at least was among the group of employees who could reasonably have been selected for redundancy. It is not enough to show that the employee might have been made redundant if other factors had remained the same. An interesting application of this principle arose in *Gilham v Kent County Council* [1986] IRLR 56. The council argued that compensation should be limited to one year because, if the vast majority of staff employed in the school dinner service had not agreed to new terms of employment, it would have had to close the service within a year, thereby making all of the employees redundant (including those who claimed that their dismissals were unfair). The EAT rejected this argument, saying that the tribunal should have assessed compensation on the basis of what actually happened. Thus, because the service had not closed, the employees were entitled to full compensation.

Capability

Capability dismissals generally fall into two categories. The first concerns cases in **12.35** which employees are to blame for their lack of ability (which may be viewed as a dismissal for 'misconduct'), and the second, cases in which they are not to blame— that is, in which the dismissal flows from an innate lack of ability due to ill health or some other reason beyond their control.

In most cases, tribunals will be required to consider whether the employee should **12.36** have been given an opportunity to improve and, if so, whether any improvement was likely (*Winterhalter Gastronom Ltd v Webb* [1973] IRLR 120). If the tribunal concludes that the warning would or may have resulted in an improvement, the loss flowing from the dismissal is substantial, since it would not accord with justice and equity to limit the compensatory award.

On the other hand, if the tribunal finds that an improvement is unlikely, it may **12.37** hold that dismissal was in all probability inevitable and limit compensation accordingly. For example, in *Mansfield Hosiery Mills Ltd v Bromley* [1977] IRLR 301, an industrial tribunal found that Mr Bromley's dismissal was unfair because of inadequate warnings and lack of supervision. However, it also found that he would probably not have come up to scratch even if he had been given a further opportunity to improve and he was therefore awarded limited compensation on the ground that he would have been fairly dismissed a short time later. The EAT upheld the decision. Similarly, in *Webb*, the NIRC ruled that Mr Webb's compensation should be limited to three months because it was by no means certain that, 'even if Mr Webb had received a warning, he would have been able to hold down the job in future'. See also *Plumley v A D International Ltd* EAT 591/82, in which compensation was limited to two months' loss of earnings because Ms Plumley was 'constitutionally unable to rectify her conduct'. The EAT observed that 'had she been given the necessary warnings, it would not have been long before her employment would have been terminated'.

12.38 Where the tribunal concludes that the dismissal was inevitable, it may award no compensation at all (see **12.17** above).

Ill-health dismissals

12.39 The principles set out above in relation to redundancy dismissals also apply in ill health dismissals. Thus, a tribunal may decline to make a compensatory award where medical evidence obtained after the dismissal shows that the employee was incapable of doing the job and therefore dismissal was inevitable (*Slaughter v C Brewer & Sons Ltd* [1990] IRLR 426; *Gowland v BAT (Export) Ltd* IRLIB 269; and *Gourley v Kerr* EAT 692/81). But, as in cases of redundancy, it will normally be appropriate to make some award to reflect the length of time that it would have taken to obtain a medical report and therefore to consult the employee in accordance with the 'guidelines' established for ill health dismissals (*East Lindsey District Council v Daubney* [1977] IRLR 181). A full compensatory award is likely where the employee should have been offered suitable alternative employment or retained for some other reason.

12.40 In some cases, however, the position may not be so clear-cut and it will be necessary for a tribunal to assess, in percentage terms, the chances of the applicant being retained. For example, in *Rao v Civil Aviation Authority* [1992] IRLR 203, the EAT and the Court of Appeal ([1994] IRLR 240) upheld an industrial tribunal's ruling that there was only a 20 per cent chance that Mr Rao would have kept his job if the employer had postponed its decision on his future pending the outcome of further treatment for a recurring back problem, and accordingly reduced the award by 80 per cent.

12.41 However, as stated above, the *Polkey* principle assumes that, had a fair procedure been followed, the decision to dismiss would have been a fair one. Compensation will not be limited where the dismissal would have been unfair. In *Edwards v Governors of Hanson School* [2001] IRLR 733, the EAT ruled, in the context of an ill health dismissal, that it was open to the tribunal not to limit its award of compensation where the employer has intentionally caused the illness that led to the dismissal. So, for example, in cases of bullying and harassment, it may be open to the tribunal to make a full award even though the employer is able to show that the employee would have been dismissed even if a fair procedure had been followed. The EAT's reasoning was thought to be open to doubt on the basis that it was inconsistent with the EAT's earlier ruling, in *London Fire and Civil Defence Authority v Betty* [1994] IRLR 384, that it was inappropriate for the tribunal to consider the cause of the illness in judging the reasonableness of the dismissal even though the

EAT itself sought to distinguish between issues of liability and compensation. However, the EAT's ruling in *Betty* was not followed by the EAT in *Frewin v Consignia plc* EAT 0981/02, and therefore it is likely that the EAT's ruling in *Edwards* will now be followed in an appropriate case.

Breach of disciplinary procedures

Similar considerations apply in considering whether the compensatory award **12.42** should be limited as a result of a failure to follow a disciplinary procedure. For example, it may be necessary to decide whether, as a matter of justice and equity, the employee should have been given a warning and, if so, whether compensation should be limited in the light of its likely effect.

As noted at **12.08** above, it is open to tribunals to award no compensation at all **12.43** where the employee's dismissal is held unfair on procedural grounds, but the employee suffers no injustice as a result. Moreover, in *Mining Supplies (Longwall) Ltd v Baker* [1988] IRLR 417, the EAT indicated that the argument that compensation should be awarded for the period during which it would have taken to handle the matter fairly will not apply where there is an internal appeal, because this will have already been taken into account. The EAT, however, appeared to overlook the fact that the employee will often not be paid in the intervening period.

Alternative reason for dismissal

In a number of cases, it has been suggested that it is 'unjust' to award compensation **12.44** where an employer can show that the employee who was unfairly dismissed for one reason could have been fairly dismissed for another reason, which existed at the time of dismissal. In support of this argument it is said that if employers are entitled to rely on information that comes to light after a dismissal that would have justified dismissal, as in *W Devis & Sons Ltd v Atkins*, why should they not be entitled to rely on another reason that existed at the time of dismissal and which, if relied on, would have amounted to a fair dismissal?

This argument appears to have been accepted by the EAT in *McNee v Charles Tenant &* **12.45** *Co Ltd* EAT 338/90, in which an industrial tribunal, having held that a dismissal on health grounds was unfair, refused to make a compensatory award on the ground that the employee could have been fairly dismissed on the ground of his unsatisfactory attendance record. The industrial tribunal's decision was upheld by the EAT.

However, in the earlier case of *Trico-Folberth Ltd v Devonshire* [1989] IRLR 396, on **12.46** almost identical facts to those in *McNee*, the Court of Appeal rejected this argument. May LJ considered that it was nonetheless 'just and equitable to award the employee compensation since, put simply, she no longer had the job that she would have had but for the dismissal which the industrial tribunal had held to be unfair'. Nourse LJ had different reasons. He said: '[I]t cannot be just and equitable for an employee to be deprived of the compensation to which she would otherwise be entitled if the employers themselves would not have relied on that other ground.'

12.47　This leaves open the possibility that compensation may be so reduced where, as a matter of evidence, employers can persuade the tribunal that they would have dismissed on the alternative ground. They were unable to do this on the particular facts of *Devonshire*; indeed, the evidence was to the contrary. The Court of Appeal's decision does not appear to have been cited in *McNee* and, in the face of conflict, its ruling is likely to prevail at least in England and Wales. (See also the more recent EAT decision in *Melia v Magna Kansei Ltd* [2005] IRLR 449, in which the appeal against the tribunal's decision to limit the award in such circumstances was dismissed.)

E. Other Reasons for Limiting Compensation

12.48　It may be just and equitable to limit the compensatory award in a number of other situations.

Risk of future dismissal

12.49　Tribunals may limit the loss where it is proved, on a balance of probabilities, that the claimant would have been fairly dismissed at some definite point in the future. In *O'Donoghue v Redcar & Cleveland Borough Council* [2001] IRLR 615, the Court of Appeal upheld an employment tribunal's decision to award six months' salary to the claimant on the basis that she would have been fairly dismissed after her actual dismissal because of her divisive and antagonistic approach to her colleagues. Dismissing the appeal, the Court of Appeal accepted that the employment tribunal was entitled to reach such a conclusion if the evidence shows that 'the applicant would have been bound soon thereafter to have been dismissed fairly by reason of some course of conduct or characteristic attitude which the employer reasonably regards as unacceptable and the employee will not moderate' (although the Court recognized that the evidence in that case was somewhat exceptional). The Court did not rule out the possibility that the risk of future dismissal could be assessed in percentage terms rather than in absolute terms as the tribunal did in *O'Donoghue*.

12.50　Similarly, in *Scope v Thornett* [2007] IRLR 155, an employment tribunal limited its award to six months' loss of earnings because it considered that this was a reasonable period for resolving a conflict between two employees. The EAT overturned the tribunal's judgment on the basis that its decision was too speculative, but, in allowing the appeal and remitting the case to the tribunal for further consideration, the Court of Appeal ruled that any assessment of future loss inevitably involved 'a speculative element' and that the tribunal was bound to consider 'various uncertainties'. The evidence suggested that there was a risk that the employment would not have continued indefinitely, but the Court concluded that the tribunal's reasons lacked sufficient clarity. There is no report of the final outcome, but this is the sort of case that would lend itself to an assessment on a percentage chance basis referred to above.

Alternatively, it is open to tribunals to take this factor into account in determining their award for future loss (see **7.62**).   **12.51**

Loss of secondary employment

In *Bakr v Sade Bros Ltd* EAT 470/83, the EAT upheld a tribunal's decision to limit to six weeks the amount of compensation received by an employee for the loss of his second job. Mr Bakr was unfairly dismissed from his part-time job as assistant chef in a restaurant that he held in addition to a full-time job in a hotel. The tribunal held that compensation should be limited to six weeks' loss of earnings. He appealed on the ground that the tribunal should have awarded him 11 months' loss of earnings because he had not been able to find himself a new secondary job. The EAT, dismissing the appeal, said that the decision lay within the discretion of the tribunal and that it was entitled to conclude that Mr Bakr could reasonably have been expected to find himself a new job within the six-week period.   **12.52**

It may be queried whether the EAT in *Bakr* confused the power to reduce compensation on the grounds of 'justice and equity' with the employee's duty to mitigate (see Chapter 13), and *Bakr* would appear to be inconsistent with the EAT's decision in *Soros and Soros v Davison and Davison* [1994] IRLR 264 (see **12.57**).   **12.53**

Dismissal during notice period

In certain circumstances, it may be just and equitable to limit the amount of the compensatory award to the unexpired period of notice due under the contract—for example, where the employer commits a fundamental breach of contract in the notice period after an employee has handed in his or her resignation. In such circumstances, the employee could claim constructive dismissal, but it would be unjust to award compensation beyond the expiry of the notice period (see *Ford v Milthorn Toleman Ltd* [1980] IRLR 30).   **12.54**

Other inequitable conduct

It would appear that the compensatory award may also be limited where an industrial tribunal is critical of other 'inequitable' conduct on the part of the employee. For example, in *Cullen v Kwik Fit Euro Ltd* EAT 483/83, the EAT upheld an employment tribunal's decision not to make a compensatory award to an employee who failed to answer an allegation that he had been involved in 'private trading'. The tribunal considered that the resultant dismissal was attributable to the employee's   **12.55** own action. Subsequently, in *Onions v Apollo Design and Construction (Scotland) Ltd* EAT 156/88, the EAT upheld an industrial tribunal's decision that compensation should be reduced by 50 per cent under s 74(1) of the Employment Protection (Consolidation) Act 1978 (now ERA 1996, s 123(1)) on account of the employee's 'obstructive' conduct in response to his employer's decision to impose a pay cut. It is submitted that, in both of these circumstances, a tribunal could have made a reduction for contributory fault and that, unless such conduct merits a reduction for contributory fault (see Chapter 14), it should not be open to a tribunal to make a reduction under ERA 1996, s 123(1). For this reason, the correctness of these decisions is open to doubt.

Onus on employers

12.56 The onus is on the employer to satisfy the tribunal that compensation should be limited to a certain period, although in practice some tribunals will bring the question to the employer's attention at the hearing (*Boulton & Paul Ltd v Arnold* [1993] IRLR 532).

Post-dismissal conduct

12.57 The power to limit compensation under ERA 1996, s 123(1) cannot be relied on where the employee's conduct takes place after dismissal. So, for example, in *Soros and Soros v Davison and Davison* [1994] IRLR 264, the EAT held that the industrial tribunal was correct in refusing to limit its award on account of the fact that the applicants had sold allegedly confidential information about their employment to national newspapers after their dismissal.

F. Power to Reduce the Compensatory Award

12.58 Previously, the compensatory award could be reduced where an employee failed to comply with the statutory disputes resolution procedure set out in EA 2002, Sch 2. These provisions continue to apply to dismissals that took place on or before 5 April 2009 (see **10.11** above).

12.59 EA 2008, s 3 inserted what was then a new s 207A into the TULR(C)A 1992. This empowers tribunals to reduce the compensatory award by such amount as they consider just and equitable, up to a maximum of 25 per cent, where an employee 'unreasonably' fails to comply with the ACAS 2009 Code of Practice on disciplinary and grievance procedures. ERA 1996, s 124(a) provides that the reduction takes place before any reduction is made for contributory fault under ERA 1996, s 123(6), or the payment of an enhanced redundancy payment under ERA 1996, s 123(7).

At the time of writing, there are no reported decisions at an appellate level on the **12.60** operation of this provision, but claimants would be at risk of such a reduction in the two examples cited below.

Example: Failure to appeal

An employee is dismissed for failing to comply with the employer's absence control policy. The dismissal is found to be unfair because the policy was not clearly communicated to staff. The employer has an appeal procedure that is clearly stated in the company handbook, but the employee refuses to appeal for reasons that the tribunal considers to be unreasonable.

In the circumstances of the above example, it would be open to the tribunal to **12.61** reduce its award by up to 25 per cent, but we would suggest the amount of the reduction is likely to depend on the degree of culpability of the employee.

Under the old rules, it was a statutory requirement for an employee to raise a griev- **12.62** ance before bringing a constructive dismissal complaint. The ACAS Code recommends that employees should aim to settle grievances informally with their line manager or, if this is unsuccessful, pursue a formal internal grievance.

Example: Constructive dismissal

Despite this recommendation, the claimant who is the victim of an abusive comment by her line manager, resigns and successfully complains of constructive dismissal without first raising an internal grievance. The employment tribunal upholds the constructive dismissal complaint on the basis that the abusive comment was in breach of the implied duty of mutual respect, but finds that the claimant acted unreasonably in failing to pursue the matter as an internal grievance.

In the circumstances of the above example, it would be open to the tribunal to **12.63** reduce its award by as much as 25 per cent, but again we would suggest that the extent of the reduction will depend on the culpability of the employee.

For the power to increase the compensatory award, see **10.11**. **12.64**

13

MITIGATION OF LOSS

A. Introduction

13.01 This chapter looks at the circumstances in which compensation may be reduced as a result of an employee's failure to mitigate the loss caused by the dismissal.

Statutory provisions

13.02 In determining the loss suffered by the employee, a tribunal is under a duty to 'apply the same rule concerning the duty of a person to mitigate his loss as applies to damages recoverable under the common law of England and Wales or (as the case may be) Scotland' (Employment Rights Act 1996 [ERA 1996], s 123(4)). The intention of the statutory wording is that the common law rules on mitigation should apply to unfair dismissal (*Fyfe v Scientific Furnishings Ltd* [1989] IRLR 331).

13.03 The common law duty to mitigate actually embodies two ideas. The first is that a claimant should not recover damages for any loss that could reasonably have been avoided. The second is that a claimant must give credit for benefits received in consequence of the defendant's breach. Sometimes, the first duty is described as the 'duty to mitigate in law' and the second as 'the duty to mitigate in fact', but not too much importance should be attached to this terminology, because it does not affect the basic principles outlined above. The distinction is used here purely as a matter of convenience.

In the context of unfair dismissal law, the first duty requires an employee to take **13.04** reasonable steps to minimize the loss by, for example, finding a new job. The first part of this chapter looks at what steps claimants are expected to take in this respect. The second aspect of the duty requires employees to bring into account the benefits that they have received since dismissal, thereby reducing the overall loss. This respect, which has already been discussed in detail in Chapter 7, is briefly summarized at the end of this chapter.

B. Defining the Duty to Mitigate in Unfair Dismissal Cases

In *Archbold Freightage Ltd v Wilson* [1974] IRLR 10, Sir John Donaldson gave the **13.05** following description of the duty to mitigate: 'It is the duty of an employee who had been dismissed to act as a reasonable man would do if he had no hope of receiving compensation from his previous employer.' But in *Fyfe v Scientific Furnishings Ltd* [1989] IRLR 331, Wood J suggested that the standard of reasonableness is not appropriate, because it is the respondent employer who is the wrongdoer. Moreover, in *Johnson v The Hobart Manufacturing Co Ltd* EAT 210/90, the Employment Appeal Tribunal (EAT) held that the test is a subjective one rather than an objective one—that is, has the particular applicant taken reasonable steps to mitigate his or her loss? However, it would appear that these statements are inconsistent with the Court of Appeal's ruling in *Wilding v British Telecommunications plc* [2002] IRLR 524 (referred to below), which established that the steps taken by the employee must be reasonable and that a claimant cannot recover compensation for any loss that he or she could have avoided by taking reasonable steps to do so. This may be particularly important when considering whether an employee acted reasonably in turning down an offer of reinstatement or re-engagement.

Overall approach

In *Savage v Saxena* [1998] IRLR 182, the EAT ruled that an employment tribunal **13.06** should ask itself the following questions in relation to mitigation of loss: first, it should identify the steps that the claimant should have taken to mitigate his or her loss; second, it should make an assessment of the date on which such steps would have produced an alternative income and thereafter reduce the award accordingly.

Question of fact or law?

13.07 Despite some differences over the precise formulation of the duty itself, the essence of the duty is clear—namely that an employment tribunal will need to be satisfied that the applicant has taken positive steps to minimize the loss caused by the dismissal. In most cases, this will involve taking reasonable steps to find a new job, but in some cases, employees may be penalized if they unreasonably turn down an offer of re-employment from their former employer (see **13.11** below).

13.08 The question 'what is reasonable' is essentially one of fact and one pre-eminently to be decided by employment tribunals as industrial juries. The tribunal's decision will only be overturned on appeal if it is shown that it misdirected itself in law (that is, by failing to consider the question at all) or the decision is perverse in the sense that it is one to which no reasonable tribunal could have come. The citation of authority in this context in particular is principally of illustrative value (*Yetton v Eastwoods Froy Ltd* [1966] 3 All ER 353 and *Bessenden Properties Ltd v Corness* [1974] IRLR 338).

13.09 A failure to consider the issue of mitigation will amount to an error of law and will be grounds for appeal (*Morganite Electrical Carbon Ltd v Donne* [1987] IRLR 363).

C. Re-employment Orders

13.10 Where an industrial tribunal orders reinstatement or re-engagement and an employee unreasonably prevents such an order from being complied with, the employee's conduct may be failure to mitigate for the purpose of assessing the compensatory award (ERA 1996, s 117(8)).

D. Offers of Re-employment

13.11 The idea that employees might be under a duty to accept an offer of re-employment in mitigation of their loss is well established at common law and was held by the EAT to apply to cases of unfair dismissal in *Martin v Yeomen Aggregates Ltd* [1983] IRLR 49, *Sweetlove v Redbridge and Waltham Forest Area Health Authority* [1979] IRLR 195, and *Fyfe v Scientific Furnishings Ltd* [1989] IRLR 331.

Reasonableness test

13.12 The test under ERA 1996, s 123(4) is whether the employee acted reasonably in turning down the employer's offer. Thus an offer of re-employment may be considered reasonable even though it does not amount to full reinstatement. For example, in *Smith v NE Transport & Plant Hire (Broughty Ferry) Ltd* EAT 402/83, the EAT held that Mr Smith was unreasonable to turn down a job as a DAF lorry driver when he had previously been employed as a heavy goods vehicle (HGV) driver. The EAT said that Mr Smith had acted unreasonably even though he was not being offered his old job back. (Contrast this decision with the EAT's ruling in *Artisan Press Ltd v Srawley and Parker* [1986] IRLR 126.)

The reasonableness of the offer appears to be judged subjectively: the fact that 'a **13.13** particular job is satisfactory for nine men out of ten' does not necessarily mean a failure to mitigate if it is 'unsuitable for the man in question' (*per* Ian Kennedy J in *Johnson v The Hobart Manufacturing Co Ltd* EAT 210/89). Indeed, in *Wilding v British Telecommunications plc* [2002] IRLR 524, a disability discrimination case, Sedley LJ suggested that the question that a tribunal should consider was whether the refusal by the former employee to accept the job offer was within the range of reasonable responses open to a reasonable employee. It is therefore necessary for a tribunal to consider both the reasonableness of the offer itself and of the reasons for the employee's refusal.

General principles

In *Wilding*, the Court of Appeal ruled that the following general principles apply in **13.14** determining whether a dismissed employee who has refused employment has breached the duty to mitigate:

(a) it is the duty of the employee to act as a reasonable person unaffected by the prospect of compensation from his or her former employer;

(b) the onus is on the former employer as wrongdoer to show that the employee has failed to mitigate by unreasonably refusing the job offer;

(c) the test of reasonableness is an objective one based on the totality of the evidence;

(d) in applying that test, the circumstances in which the offer was made and refused, the attitude of the former employer, the way in which the employee had been treated, and all of the surrounding circumstances, including the employee's state of mind, should be taken into account; and

(e) the tribunal must not be too stringent in its expectations of the injured party (that is, the employee).

Reasonableness of the employer's offer

Where the employer offers re-engagement, as opposed to reinstatement, the tribunal **13.15** will normally first consider the reasonableness of the employer's offer. The test applied by tribunals is not dissimilar from that used to determine whether alternative employment is suitable in redundancy dismissals. Thus tribunals will look at the terms of the offer, such as pay, hours of work, status, responsibility, location, etc and decide whether it is suitable for the employee, in the light of his or her training and other qualifications.

Reasonableness of the employee's refusal

13.16   If the employer's offer is considered reasonable, tribunals must then go on to consider the reasons for the employee's refusal of the employer's offer. These may relate to the terms of the offer (as in **13.15** above) or the idea of being re-employed by the employer in the light of the circumstances surrounding the dismissal. Where the claimant gives detailed reasons for turning down the job offer, the ultimate question for the tribunal is whether the claimant acted unreasonably in turning down the job offer, taking into account the history and all of the circumstances of the case, including the claimant's state of mind, the burden of proof, and that the standard of reasonableness to be applied is not high (*Wilding v British Telecommunications plc* [2002] IRLR 524). As a rule of thumb, claimants will not normally be penalized for turning down an offer of re-employment if it involves significant changes in the terms of employment. However, where the job is virtually the same, the burden will be very much on the applicant to show why it was reasonable to turn it down.

13.17   In determining 'reasonableness', tribunals take account of the following factors.

(a) *Timing of the offer*   An employee is more likely to be found to have acted reasonably if the offer is made at the '11th hour'—that is, just before the hearing—than if it is made shortly after the dismissal, since in the latter situation, the employee might be found to have 'closed his mind' to the employer's offer (*per* Kilner Brown J in *Martin v Yeomen Aggregates Ltd* [1983] IRLR 49). Nonetheless, as a matter of law, in exceptional circumstances, an offer will not necessarily be unreasonable even if it is made after the tribunal hearing, particularly if this is requested by the employee (see *Wilding v British Telecommunications plc* [2002] IRLR 542, in which the claimant was anxious to return to work and his solicitor requested that his client should return on a part-time basis, as a result of which the employer offered the claimant part-time work, but by the time the offer was made, the claimant had changed his mind and rejected the offer; contrast *HM Prison Service v Beart* [2005] IRLR 171, in which an offer made shortly before the hearing was considered too late).

(b) *Clarity of the offer*   An employee might not be unreasonable in rejecting an offer that is vague or unclear as to its terms (*John Crowther & Sons (Milnsbridge) Ltd v Livesey* EAT 272/84).

(c) *Reason for dismissal*   The grounds of dismissal may justify the employee's rejection of the offer—for example, where the employer makes an unjustified allegation of dishonesty.

(d) *Reasonableness of the dismissal*   The manner of dismissal may justify the employee's refusal of an offer—as in *Livesey*, for example, in which the employee was held to have acted reasonably because he had lost his confidence and trust in management as a result of the manner of dismissal.

In the following instances, the employee was held to have acted reasonably in refusing a re-employment offer: **13.18**

(a) the employee failed to ask for reinstatement following an industrial dispute (*Courtaulds Northern Spinning Ltd v Moosa* [1974] IRLR 101);

(b) the employer was trying to ascertain whether police were still considering prosecuting the employee for a till offence (*How v Tesco Stores Ltd* [1974] IRLR 194);

(c) the employee feared that there would be a bad atmosphere at work if he were to return (*Dobson, Bryant, Heather v KP Morritt Ltd* [1979] IRLR 101);

(d) the manner of dismissal had been humiliating or there had been other humiliating treatment of the employee at the hands of the employer (*Simmonds v Merton, Sutton and Wandsworth Area Health Authority* EAT 789/77; *Farrell v Exports International Ltd* EAT 569/89; *Fyfe v Scientific Furnishings Ltd* [1989] IRLR 331); and

(e) the employee had found a new job (*Yetton v Eastwoods Froy Ltd* [1966] 3 All ER 353).

However, much will depend on the particular circumstances of the case. For example, in *Gallear v JF Watson and Son Ltd* [1979] IRLR 306, the EAT held that Mr Gallear had acted unreasonably in turning down two offers of re-employment even though they were made after he presented his originating application and the dismissal had been handled in a manner that contravened the ACAS Code. Similarly, in *Wilding v British Telecommunications plc* [2002] IRLR 542, the Court of Appeal upheld the employment tribunal's conclusion that it was unreasonable for the claimant to turn down the offer of re-engagement in the circumstances referred to in **13.17** above. **13.19**

Offers of alternative employment

In principle, it is open to an employer to argue that there has been a failure to mitigate loss where the applicant turns down an offer of alternative employment. As above, this argument is more likely to succeed where the terms of employment on offer are similar to the original terms than where the new job involves a substantial deterioration in the terms and conditions of employment. **13.20**

In *Baillie Brothers v Pritchard* EAT 59/89, an employee was held to have acted reasonably in turning down an offer of alternative employment made to him some months after the dismissal where the new job involved a reduction in pay of £13 a week, and the loss of a van that he had previously used for travelling to and from work. On the other hand, in *Plewinski v McDermott Engineering London* EAT 465/88, an employee was held to have acted unreasonably in choosing to become self-employed for a short time, rather than accepting a cut in overtime in his old job. **13.21**

An employee may be held to have acted unreasonably in turning down the same job in a different location (see *Pearson v Leeds Polytechnic Students Union* EAT 182/84), **13.22** but, in judging reasonableness, tribunals will take account of the amount of travelling involved and the personal circumstances of the employee.

13.23 Tribunals may take a more lenient view if the employee has already found another job (*How v Tesco Ltd* [1974] IRLR 194). Consideration will also be given to other reasons why the applicant turned down the job offer and whether he or she was reasonable to do so (see **13.17** above).

Offers of early retirement

13.24 In principle, it is open to employers to argue that employees who unreasonably turn down an offer of early retirement on generous terms in redundancy or ill health cases have failed to mitigate their loss by so doing. But employees will not necessarily act unreasonably in turning down such an offer.

13.25 For example, in *Fyfe v Scientific Furnishing Ltd* [1989] IRLR 331, the employer failed to show that the applicant had failed to mitigate his loss when he turned down an offer of early retirement made shortly after his dismissal for redundancy. The early retirement package, on its face, appeared to be extremely generous when compared to the redundancy payment to which the applicant was entitled. The tribunal found that Mr Fyfe was unreasonable in turning down the offer and held that he had failed to mitigate his loss. But the EAT, allowing the appeal, held that Mr Fyfe had not acted unreasonably because his employer had failed to set out the full implications of its offer and had failed to give Mr Fyfe more time in which to make up his mind. The employers had therefore failed to discharge the burden of proving that Mr Fyfe had failed to mitigate his loss.

E. Duty to find Employment

13.26 Offers of re-employment are comparatively uncommon. Normally, the duty to mitigate will require the employee to look for a new job. 'Signing on' is not normally enough (*Burns v Boyd Engineering Ltd* EAT 458/84), but two visits a week to the local jobcentre were considered reasonable in *British Garages Ltd v Lowen* [1979] IRLR 86.

13.27 Many tribunals, however, expect claimants to cast their net more widely than the vacancies advertised at the jobcentre. Claimants may be asked if they have looked at adverts in the trade press or local newspapers. For example, in one case, an employee was held not to have mitigated his because he had sought employment from only one agency rather than approaching other agencies that might have had appropriate vacancies on their books. The employee was also criticized for not having taken up a reference that had been promised by his old employers (*Field v Leslie & Godwin Ltd* [1972] IRLR 12).

State of the labour market

Tribunals will take their knowledge of the local labour market into account in **13.28** deciding whether the employee has made reasonable efforts to find a new job. Tribunals are also influenced by the current levels of unemployment. For example, in one case, a London tribunal regarded 30 weeks' loss of earnings as 'a medium period' (*Plessey Military Communications Ltd v Bough* IDS 310) and, in *Scottish & Newcastle Breweries plc v Halliday* [1986] IRLR 29, the EAT suggested that, 'with mass unemployment', it is frequently 12 months or even more. However, this may no longer be true with lower levels of unemployment and skill shortages in some parts of the labour market. Nonetheless, even the most work-shy claimant will be given some period of grace in which to find a new job. So, for example, in *Savage v Saxena* [1998] IRLR 182, the employment tribunal was found to have erred in law when it awarded no compensation to a claimant on the basis that he had made no serious attempt to find work. Allowing the appeal, the EAT ruled that, in effect, the tribunal was penalizing him rather than applying the rules on mitigation in a proper manner.

Personal characteristics of the applicant

Tribunals will also take account of any personal characteristics of the employee that **13.29** put him or her at a disadvantage in the labour market. For example, an employee who is elderly or in poor health may experience particular difficulty in finding a new job. In *Bennett v Tippins* EAT 361/89, the EAT recognized the difficulties that pregnant women have in finding employment and a similar principle may well apply to mothers with childcare responsibilities.

Reasonable offers of employment

A further aspect of the duty to mitigate is that employees should not turn down a **13.30** reasonable offer of employment. Thus, as Sir John Donaldson said in *Archbold Freightage Ltd v Wilson* [1974] IRLR 10, a claimant should 'accept alternative employment if, taking account of the pay and other conditions of that employment, it is reasonable to do so'.

However, this does not mean that employees have to accept the first job that is **13.31** offered to them. As the National Industrial Relations Court (NIRC) said in *AG Bracey Ltd v Iles* [1973] IRLR 210:

> It may not be reasonable to take the first job that comes along. It may be much more reasonable, in the interests of the employee and of the employer who has to pay compensation, that he should wait a little time. He must, of course, use the time well and seek a better paid job which will reduce his overall loss and the amount of compensation that the previous employer ultimately has to pay.

It should be observed that this statement was made at a time when unemployment **13.32** was relatively low and it is possible that tribunals may react less favourably if an employee turns down a comparable job in a time or area of high unemployment. In general, tribunals are likely to be sympathetic to employees who, in the short term, turn down jobs that are lower paid or offer other less favourable terms and conditions of employment.

Flexibility

13.33 However, applicants who have been out of work for some time may be required to accept lower-paid jobs in mitigation of their loss. In extreme cases, applicants have been penalized for turning down jobs where the pay offered in the new job was less than the amount that they were receiving as unemployment benefits, although the EAT has warned tribunals that they should be 'slow' to reach this conclusion (*Daley v A E Dorsett (Almar Dolls) Ltd* [1981] IRLR 385).

13.34 Flexibility may also be required in relation to other conditions of employment. Thus, in *Lloyd v The Standard Pulverized Fuel Co Ltd* [1976] IRLR 115, it was held that an employee who had previously worked during the day was unreasonable to turn down night work. Similarly, employees may be expected to be prepared to move to a new location where suitable work is available. Thus, in *Collen v Lewis* IDS 390, an industrial tribunal held that a language teacher who had previously been employed in London should have accepted a job in Wales even though the job offer involved a reduction in pay and the loss of a London weighting allowance. The tribunal awarded the net difference in earnings between the two jobs for one year (see also *O'Reilly v Welwyn and Hatfield District Council* [1975] IRLR 334). But, in other cases, tribunals have been reluctant to penalize employees who refuse to move away from their home town, particularly where this involves moving home and uprooting their family (see *Ramsay v WB Anderson & Sons Ltd* [1974] IRLR 164).

13.35 Some applicants may be required to accept temporary work or part-time work by tribunals for giving up a temporary job when there is no prospect of finding a more permanent one (*Hardwick v Leeds Area Health Authority* [1975] IRLR 319). But tribunals may take a more lenient view if there are good reasons for so doing (see *Dundee Plant Co Ltd v Riddler* EAT 377/88, in which the applicant gave up a permanent job for another permanent, but less well-paid, job, because the first job involved too much travelling, and *Wilson v Gleneagles Bakery Ltd* EAT 40/88, in which the EAT held that an applicant had not acted unreasonably when she gave up her new job on the ground that she could not cope with her new responsibilities).

Setting up business

13.36 If there is no suitable alternative employment available, it is possible to mitigate loss by setting up a business or becoming self-employed, but it is for the tribunal to decide whether an applicant was reasonable in doing this rather than looking for employment elsewhere.

In the past, tribunals tended to regard self-employment as an unreasonable way of **13.37** mitigating loss due to the length of time that it normally takes for a business to become profitable. However, high levels of unemployment led to a more sympathetic response from tribunals, particularly in cases in which the applicant was at a disadvantage in the labour market because of age or the limited employment opportunities available to someone with the applicant's particular skills.

The leading case on this point, *Gardiner-Hill v Roland Berger Technics Ltd* [1982] **13.38** IRLR 498, is a good illustration of the sort of situation in which setting up a business in mitigation may be considered reasonable. Mr Gardiner-Hill was dismissed from his post as managing director of a consultancy service at the age of 55 after 16 years of employment. He decided to set up his own business. In the six-and-a-half months between his dismissal and the tribunal hearing, he had spent some 80–90 per cent of his time starting up and running the business, but had received only £1,500 from his new employment. His former employers argued that this had prevented him from looking for alternative employment and that he had therefore failed to mitigate his loss. The EAT disagreed. It held that Mr Gardiner-Hill had acted reasonably because it was 'at least as prudent of him to seek to exploit his own expertise by conducting his own business and gaining an income from his own business to replace the income that he had previously received from his employment'. The EAT also permitted him to recover £500 for the expenses that he incurred in setting up the business (see *Glen Henderson Ltd v Nisbet* EAT 34/90 for another illustration).

Furthermore, provided that the decision to set up the business was a reasonable **13.39** one, the employee will not be penalized if the business subsequently fails (see *Blick Vessels & Pipework Ltd v Sharpe* EAT/681/84).

Retraining as mitigation

Another possible way of mitigating loss is for the applicant to undergo a period of **13.40** training, thereby increasing the chances of finding alternative employment.

For example, in *Sealy v Avon Aluminium Co Ltd* EAT 516/78, the EAT rejected the **13.41** argument that the applicant had failed to mitigate his loss by attending a college course for part of the time covered by the compensatory award, and, in *Glen Henderson Ltd v Nisbet* EAT 34/90, the EAT held that the applicant had not failed to mitigate her loss by attending a business enterprise course for five weeks before starting up her own business. In more unusual circumstances, tribunals have accepted that it was reasonable for claimants to attend a specialist course. For example, in *Khanum v IBC Vehicles* EAT 785/98, the tribunal found that it was reasonable for the claimant to have taken up a place at Luton University to study for a computer systems degree because she realized that it would be difficult to find employment without it. The EAT, dismissing the appeal, noted that there were special factors present, such as the fact that Ms Khanum had completed an apprenticeship with a view to taking up a specialist job in the motor industry and that her former employer held a dominant position in that industry.

13.42   Here, again, in determining the question of reasonableness, tribunals are likely to be influenced by levels of unemployment and the state of the labour market in the locality (see *Larkin v Korean Airlines Ltd* EAT 1241/98, in which the state of the labour market was an important consideration in support of the conclusion that it was reasonable for the claimant to train for a new career). There is also some evidence that tribunals take a more sympathetic attitude to short-term vocational courses than longer academic ones (see *Holroyd v Gravure Cylinders Ltd* [1984] IRLR 259, but compare *Orthet Ltd v Vince-Cain* [2004] IRLR 857, a sex discrimination case, in which the tribunal was held not to have erred in awarding compensation for loss of earnings during a four-year period when the claimant was attending a university course to become a dietician).

'Signing on' for sickness benefits as mitigation

13.43   A similar problem may arise where an employee who is unfairly dismissed on health grounds elects to receive sickness/invalidity benefits rather than to look for alternative employment. Depending on the circumstances, it may not be unreasonable for an employee to 'sign on' sick if the employee reasonably believes that this is the best way of securing an income. In *Wilson v (1) Glenrose (Fishmerchants) Ltd and (2) Chapman and others* EAT 444/91, an industrial tribunal ruled that it was not just and equitable to award compensation in such circumstances because the applicant had voluntarily taken himself out of the labour market. Allowing the appeal, the EAT held that the crucial issue was whether the applicant had acted unreasonably in signing on sick rather than waiting for a job to turn up. This involved considering the reasonableness of his conduct at the time that he signed on (including the fact that his previous applications for employment had all been unsuccessful), and whether it was reasonable for him to continue to receive benefit rather than look for work at any time during the period for which he received benefit. However, it should be noted that, in this case, the applicant was fit enough to carry out duties that he had been required to do prior to his dismissal and there was a clear finding that the applicant would have been likely to continue in his employment until his retirement but for his dismissal. Both of these factors are critical if the applicant is to have a claim for loss of earnings in the first place.

Pregnancy dismissals

13.44   The duty to mitigate applies where a dismissal is found to be automatically unfair under ERA 1996, s 104 for pregnancy or pregnancy-related reasons. However, in *MOD v Sullivan* [1994] ICR 193, a sex discrimination claim brought under the Equal Treatment Directive (76/207/EEC), the EAT ruled that a woman could not reasonably be expected to mitigate loss in the period immediately after childbirth, and that the duty would not arise until her physiological and mental functions had returned to normal. The EAT also held that an employee who was dismissed in such circumstances was entitled to compensation for loss of earnings for a period of up to six months whilst she decided whether or not to return to work.

F. Limits to the Duty to Mitigate

The duty imposed on employees by statutory provisions is simply to take reason- **13.45** able steps to lessen their loss. Ultimately, it is up to the tribunal to decide whether the employee's efforts in this respect are sufficient. However, in the following circumstances, employees will not be held to be in breach of the statutory duty as a matter of law.

Duty arises after dismissal

The duty to mitigate arises only after the dismissal. This means that an offer of **13.46** re-employment made by employers before the employee is dismissed cannot be relied on as evidence of a failure to mitigate. For example, in *Gilham v Kent County Council* [1986] IRLR 56, the council argued that the applicants should have lessened their loss by accepting the new terms that the council were offering to its dinner ladies. The industrial tribunal, following *Trimble v Supertravel Ltd* [1982] IRLR 451, ruled that, because the employer's offer was made before the dismissal, it could not be said that the employees had failed to mitigate their loss. Similarly, in *McAndrew v Prestwick Circuits Ltd* [1988] IRLR 514, the applicant was held not to have failed to mitigate his loss when he turned down an offer to work in a nearby factory because the offer was made prior to his dismissal. The lesson for employers is that an offer made before dismissal should be renewed after the dismissal.

Failure to use grievance procedure

It follows that, in constructive dismissal cases, employees will not be penalized if **13.47** they fail to pursue a grievance under their employer's grievance procedure before they resign (*Seligman & Latz Ltd v McHugh* [1979] IRLR 130), although this may amount to contributory conduct (see Chapter 14).

Internal appeals

In law, an internal appeal normally takes place after the date of dismissal (*J Sainsbury* **13.48** *Ltd v Savage* [1981] ICR 1); therefore, in principle, it should be open to employers to argue that there is a failure to mitigate when an employee fails to appeal against dismissal where the appeal would have been successful and the employee would have been reinstated or re-engaged.

13.49 This view was supported by the EAT in *Hoover Ltd v Forde* [1980] ICR 239, in which the EAT ruled that a failure to appeal may be a breach of the employee's duty to mitigate loss for the reason given above and reduced compensation by 50 per cent. The decision in *Forde* was followed in *Ever Ready v Foster* EAT 310/81, in which the employer persuaded the EAT that the appeal would almost certainly have been successful. However, in *William Muir (Bond 9) Ltd v Lamb* [1985] IRLR 95, the EAT considered that a failure to appeal could not be regarded as a failure to mitigate because there were too many 'imponderable factors' and therefore an employee who failed to appeal could not be regarded as having acted unreasonably. The EAT's decision in *Lamb* was followed and approved of by the EAT in *Lock v Connell Estate Agents Ltd* [1994] IRLR 444. Overturning its earlier ruling in *Hoover Ltd v Forde* , the EAT stated:

> [I]t is one thing to say that a plaintiff is required in certain circumstances to consider an offer by a wrongdoer; it is quite another to say that if no such offer is made, then the plaintiff is under a duty to solicit the wrongdoer to change his mind.

13.50 At the time of writing, the position is that employees will not be in breach of the duty to mitigate if they fail to pursue an internal appeal. On the other hand, it would appear that a claimant who unsuccessfully pursues an internal appeal will not be held to have acted unreasonably in not looking for alternative employment until the appeal has been determined (*Williams v Lloyds Retailers Ltd* [1973] IRLR 262). It will be interesting to see what effect, if any, the introduction of the statutory dispute procedures (and the consequential amendments to the time limits for presenting employment tribunal complaints) have on the application of the duty to mitigate, because it is at least arguable that an employee who is (in good faith) pursuing an internal resolution of his or her grievance, or an appeal against dismissal, may act reasonably in not looking for alternative work until the grievance or the dispute is resolved.

Compensation negotiations

13.51 Employees will not normally be penalized for dragging their feet, or being inefficient or muddled in compensation negotiations, because this will not in itself have caused the loss (*Blick Vessels & Pipework v Sharpe* IRLIB 274, February 1985). Negotiations conducted on a 'without prejudice' basis are inadmissible in any event.

G. Onus of Proof

13.52 In *Fyfe v Scientific Furnishings Ltd* [1989] IRLR 331, the EAT confirmed that the burden of proving that the employee has failed to lessen the loss flowing from the dismissal is on the party alleging it—that is, the employer. This is the same as the rule that exists at common law (*per* Roskill LJ in *Bessenden Properties Ltd v J K Corness* [1974] IRLR 338 and *per* Browne Wilkinson J in *Daley v A E Dorsett (Almar Dolls) Ltd* [1981] IRLR 385).

Strictly speaking, this means that an employee should not be held to be in **13.53** breach of the duty to mitigate unless the issue is both raised by the employer and some evidence to that effect is produced by the employer. However, in practice, tribunals tend to disregard the technicalities of the legal burden of proof and raise the issue of mitigation themselves. This means that applicants should come to the tribunal prepared to show what steps they have taken since dismissal to mitigate, and they should be ready to offer copies of adverts, job applications, replies, etc and to give reasons for not applying for vacancies. This also applies to applicants who wish to argue that it was reasonable for them to set up a business, since they must still show that they acted reasonably in mitigating their loss in this way.

From the employer's point of view, it is important to find out before the hearing **13.54** what steps the former employee has taken to lessen his or her loss. This can be achieved by asking the applicant to disclose information as to the steps that he or she has taken to find a new job prior to the hearing. The request for information may be made in the form suggested below. If the applicant refuses to supply the information voluntarily, the employer may apply to the tribunal for an order to compel disclosure (Employment Tribunals (Constitution and Rules of Procedure) Regulations 2004, SI 2004/1861, r 10(2)). Doubt has been cast on the employer's right to obtain such an order before the issue of liability has been determined as a result of the EAT's decision in *Colonial Mutual Life Assurance Society Ltd v Clinch* [1981] ICR 752. The EAT reasoning, which assumes that the information can be obtained before the hearing through a conciliation officer, is open to question and would probably not preclude an order from being made after liability had been established. Employers who wish to challenge the reasonableness of the employee's action may produce evidence of their own—for example, details of local vacancies and advertisements in the press. This evidence should normally be disclosed to the employee before the hearing.

The burden of proof is likely to come into play only in borderline cases in which the **13.55** applicant's evidence is either unchallenged or unsuccessfully challenged, or in which the employer is shown to have acted unreasonably in some other way, as in *Fyfe* itself (see **13.05** above).

Mitigation of loss: Discovery

The following letter may act as a precedent when acting for an employer which is **13.56** seeking information regarding the steps that a dismissed employee is taking to find a new job.

> **Example**
>
> Dear Mr Brown
>
> Re: *Brown v Discoveror Ltd*
>
> Would you please send me details of any steps that you have taken since your dismissal to find a new job, including:
>
> (a) a list of all job applications that you have made;
> (b) any job offers that have been made to you; and
> (c) any jobs that you have rejected?
>
> If you fail to send me these particulars within 14 days, I will apply to the tribunal for an order to compel disclosure under rule 10(2) of the Employment Tribunals (Constitution and Rules of Procedure) Regulations 2004.
>
> Yours sincerely
> cc ROIT

These particulars may be requested at the same time as making an application for disclosure of documents relating to liability.

H. Assessing the Deduction

13.57   There is no specific statutory guidance on how the deduction for failure to mitigate is to be calculated. The normal approach is to decide when the employee would have found other work or set up a reasonably secure business and limit the compensatory award accordingly. This is similar to the principle applied in wrongful dismissal cases (*Savage v Saxena* [1998] IRLR 182).

13.58   The approach that tribunals ought to apply was described by the EAT in *Ladbroke Racing Ltd v Connolly* EAT 160/83. The EAT said that tribunals should forecast the date on which the employee would have been re-employed, and award the net loss of earnings between the date of dismissal and the date on which the employee ought, in the tribunal's view, to have found a new job (*Savage v Saxena* [1998] IRLR 182).

13.59   If the tribunal concludes that the new job would be less well paid, this will be reflected in its award for continuing loss (*Smith , Kline & French Laboratories Ltd v Coates* [1977] IRLR 276; *Peara v Enderlin Ltd* [1979] ICR 804). Tribunals should not, however, reduce the compensatory award on a percentage basis as they do in assessing contributory fault.

Where an employment tribunal concludes that it is reasonable for the claimant to set **13.60** up a business in mitigation of loss, the conventional way of assessing compensation requires the tribunal, first, to calculate what sum represents loss of remuneration, then to add any reasonable costs in setting up the business (that fall to be included in the assessment of overall loss), and then to deduct the earnings from the new business (*Aon Training Ltd v Dore* [2005] IRLR 891).

I. Mitigation in Fact

The second aspect of the duty to mitigate requires employees to give credit for any **13.61** income received since dismissal, including income from self-employment (but excluding unemployment benefits and other state benefits that are dealt with separately by the regulations providing for recoupment—see Chapter 16). These amounts may therefore be set off against the loss suffered by the employee between the dismissal and the date of the hearing.

J. Practical Tips

As stated above, the burden of proving that the claimant has failed to mitigate his **13.62** or her loss is on the employer. This is easily overlooked when preparing for a tribunal hearing. A tribunal is likely to be fairly sympathetic to a claimant who can show that he or she has applied for jobs on a regular basis in the absence of evidence of vacancies for which he or she could have applied, but did not.

Tips for claimants

From a claimant's point of view, **13.63**

(a) it is important to keep a record of all vacancies applied for, all interviews attended, and any letters of rejection; and
(b) if the claimant has registered with an employment agency or other job search recruitment company, evidence should be retained of any jobs for which the claimant was considered and the outcome of any interviews.

It is also important to demonstrate the necessary flexibility in job search. For example, **13.64** consideration should be given to working part-time or on a temporary basis in appropriate cases and the evidence should demonstrate that, after reasonable period of, say, six months, the claimant has applied for reasonable alternatives (even if these involve reduced pay or status).

Evidence of lack of opportunities in the labour market will be particularly impor- **13.65** tant where the claimant wishes to argue that it was reasonable to undergo a period of training or set up their own business.

Tips for respondents

13.66 From a respondent's point of view, it is important to be in a position to challenge the claimant's assertion that he or she took reasonable steps to mitigate his or her loss by, for example, collecting evidence of vacancies either in trade journals or newspapers for which the claimant was qualified.

13.67 It is prudent to collect this information as early as possible rather than to leave it to the last minute. Such evidence will be particularly important where the claimant undergoes a period of training and, as a result, is seeking substantial compensation from the respondent or is in the process of setting up a business. As regards the latter, it is useful to obtain evidence to show how much the claimant is earning from the business, bearing in mind that the annual accounts (whilst entirely proper for tax purposes) may give a misleading impression of the receipts of the business. Employers have also been known to hire private detectives where there is a genuine suspicion that the claimant has been working.

14

CONTRIBUTORY FAULT

A. Introduction

All awards of unfair dismissal compensation except the additional award (*City and* **14.01**
Hackney Health Authority v Crisp [1990] IRLR 47) may be reduced for contributory
fault by such amount as the industrial tribunal considers just and equitable in the
circumstances. This chapter looks at the circumstances in which an award may be
reduced.

In relation to the compensatory award, it is provided that, where the tribunal finds **14.02**
that the dismissal was to any extent caused or contributed to by any action of the
claimant, it shall reduce the amount of the compensatory award by such proportion
as it considers just and equitable having regard to that finding (Employment Rights
Act 1996 [ERA 1996], s 123(6)).

Originally, the wording of the statutory provisions relating to the basic award was **14.03**
identical to that of the compensatory award, but it was changed following the House
of Lords' ruling in *W Devis & Sons Ltd v Atkins* [1977] IRLR 314 that a reduction
in accordance with these provisions would be justified only where the conduct relied
on was known to the employer at the time of dismissal. It is now provided that the

basic and awards may be reduced for any conduct of the claimant before dismissal irrespective of whether this conduct is known or unknown to the employer at the time of dismissal. This means that the basic and award can be reduced where, for example, an employee has been stealing money from his or her employers, although this was not known to the employer at the time of dismissal, whereas the compensatory award cannot be reduced for contributory fault in such circumstances. However, the practical effect of the difference in wording is very much reduced as a result of the House of Lords' acceptance in *W Devis & Sons Ltd v Atkins* that, in such circumstances, it is possible for an employment tribunal to make no compensatory award at all on the alternative basis that, under the Employment Protection Act 1975 [EPA 1975], s 74(1) (previously the Trade Union and Labour Relations Act 1974, s 6(8); now see ERA 1996, s 123(1)), it was not just and equitable to do so.

14.04 A possible consequence of the difference in the wording of the statutory provisions arises in relation to the nature of the conduct that can be taken into account by an employment tribunal. Thus, it could be argued that the wider wording in relation to the basic employment award would entitle a tribunal to reduce these awards on account of any conduct on the part of the employee throughout the duration of the employment and that the conduct in question need not be causally linked to the dismissal (see *Optikinectics Ltd v Whooley* EAT 1275/95), whereas, in relation to the compensatory award, a reduction is justified only if the conduct complained of causes or contributes to the dismissal. There is some support for this view in the Court of Appeal's decision in *Parker Foundry Ltd v Slack* [1992] IRLR 11, the decision of the Northern Ireland Court of Appeal (NICA) in *Morrison v Amalgamated Transport and General Workers' Union* [1989] IRLR 361, and the Employment Appeal Tribunal (EAT) in *Polentarutti v AutoKraft Ltd* [1991] IRLR 457 and *Optikinectics Ltd v Whooley* EAT 1275/95 (see also ERA 1996, s 122(2)). But the distinction may not matter much in practice because a tribunal is unlikely to consider it just and equitable to reduce the award if the conduct in question is only remotely connected with the events that led to the dismissal.

14.05 It should be noted that, although the same general principles apply to both the basic and the compensatory awards, special statutory provisions apply where dismissals are found to be unfair for trade union reasons.

B. General Principles

14.06 Three conditions must be met before a reduction for contributory fault is justified:

(a) there must be culpable or blameworthy conduct on the part of the employee;

(b) subject to the point made above in relation to the basic award, the conduct complained of must have caused or contributed to the dismissal; and

(c) it must be just and equitable to reduce the award.

Whether each of these conditions is met is essentially a question of fact to be determined **14.07**
by the employment tribunal. As such, it lies very much at the heart of the fact-
finding role of an employment tribunal, the decision of which will not be overturned
unless the tribunal misdirects itself in law or reaches a perverse decision on the
facts—that is, a decision to which no reasonable tribunal could have come (*Hollier
v Plysu Ltd* [1983] IRLR 260). It follows that the EAT is extremely reluctant to
overturn an employment tribunal's decision provided that the relevant principles of
law have been taken into account.

What conduct is considered culpable or blameworthy?

The requirement that the employee's conduct must be blameworthy was established **14.08**
by the Court of Appeal in *Nelson v BBC (No 2)* [1979] IRLR 346, in which it was
held that this requirement was implicit in the provision that the conduct itself
should have caused or contributed to the dismissal. Alternatively, the Court considered
that it would not be just and equitable to make a reduction unless the employee's
conduct were shown to be blameworthy.

In *Nelson*, Brandon LJ sought to describe the sort of conduct that could be regarded **14.09**
as blameworthy:

> The concept does not, in my view, necessarily involve any conduct of the complainant
> amounting to a breach of contract or a tort. It includes, no doubt, conduct of that kind.
> But it also includes conduct which, while not amounting to a breach of contract or a
> tort, is nevertheless perverse or foolish, or, if I may use the colloquialism, bloody
> minded. It may also include action which, though not meriting any of those more
> perjorative epithets, is nevertheless unreasonable in all the circumstances. I should
> not, however, go as far as to say that all unreasonable conduct is necessarily culpable
> or blameworthy; it must depend on the degree of unreasonableness involved.

Most, if not all, misconduct would therefore be regarded as blameworthy conduct. **14.10**
The following have all been so regarded: dishonesty (*Gaskin v MSW Business Systems
Ltd* IDS 309); breach of company rules (*McNicholas v AR Engineering* IDS 309);
going on holiday or returning late from holiday without permission (*Allen v
N E Lancashire Dairies Ltd* EAT 230/83 and *Hall v Vincemark Ltd* COIT 2029/54);
soliciting customers for a rival business or working for a rival outside normal
working hours (*Baxter v Wreyfield* EAT 9/82 and *Fraser v Tullos Business Services*
EAT 655/87); setting up a rival business (*Connor v Comet Radiovision Services Ltd*
EAT 650/81); poor attendance record (*McNicholas*); conduct setting back recovery
from an illness (*Patterson v Bracketts* EAT 486/76); failing to reply to a letter
requiring an employee to attend a disciplinary interview or to undergo a medical
examination (*Slaughter v C Brewer & Sons Ltd* [1990] IRLR 426); and negligence
(*Coalter v Walter Craven Ltd* [1980] IRLR 262). Employees have also been penalized for other unreasonable conduct, such as a refusal to disclose the names of
employees who had been involved in acts of misconduct (*Simpson v British Steel
Corporation* EAT 594/83), a failure to use an internal grievance procedure to resolve

a pay dispute (*Walls v Brookside Metal Co Ltd* EAT 579/89), and a failure to abide by an agreement with the company regarding time spent on union duties (*Dundon v GPT Ltd* [1995] IRLR 403).

14.11 On the other hand, compensation will not be reduced for contributory fault if the employee's conduct is not regarded as blameworthy in the sense described by the Court of Appeal in *Nelson*. For example, a refusal to obey an instruction to falsify records (*Morrish v Henlys (Folkestone) Ltd* [1973] IRLR 6), a refusal to disclose a criminal conviction that is spent under the Rehabilitation of Offenders Act 1974 (*Property Guards Ltd v Taylor* [1982] IRLR 175), and a failure to call a witness at a disciplinary hearing (*British Steel Corporation v Williams* EAT 776/82) have all been held not to justify a reduction in compensation.

14.12 Moreover, a reduction will not be justified if there is insufficient evidence of such conduct before the tribunal. For example, in *Tele-Trading Ltd v Jenkins* [1990] IRLR 430, the Court of Appeal upheld a tribunal's refusal to make a reduction for contributory fault where the tribunal was not satisfied that there were reasonable grounds for believing that the employee was guilty of the conduct alleged by the employers either at the time of dismissal or at the hearing itself. It is also doubtful whether every breach of contract would justify a reduction for contributory fault, since liability for breach of contract can arise without any fault on the part of the employee and a reduction in such circumstances would be contrary to the underlying principle that the conduct in question must be of a blameworthy nature.

Industrial action and contributory fault

14.13 Following a series of conflicting EAT decisions, the Court of Appeal and the House of Lords, in *Crosville Wales Ltd v Tracey and others* [1996] IRLR 91 and [1997] IRLR 691, respectively, confirmed that tribunals should not reduce compensation for contributory fault where an employee is dismissed for taking part in industrial action and the dismissal is found to be unfair under s 238 of the Trade Union and Labour Relations (Consolidation) Act 1992 (TULR(C)A 1992), which deals with the discriminatory re-engagement of strikers. In support of its decision, the Court endorsed the views expressed by the EAT in *Courtaulds Northern Spinning Ltd v Moosa* [1984] IRLR 43, that the general immunity from claims in such circumstances is an indication of Parliament's intention that tribunals should not seek to weigh up the rights and wrongs of a particular industrial dispute, and that therefore mere participation in industrial action could not be regarded as blameworthy conduct justifying a reduction in compensation for contributory fault. However, the Court said that a reduction for contributory fault might be justified if the employee went beyond mere participation by, for example, acting over-hastily or in an inflammatory manner. The same may also apply if strikers behave in an intimidatory manner.

14.14 Similar principles would probably also apply where employees were unfairly dismissed for threatening industrial action. For example, in *Adapters and Eliminators v Paterson*

EAT 801/82, the EAT doubted whether a threat of industrial action by itself amounted to blameworthy conduct.

Contributory fault and dismissals for incapability

In general, compensation will be reduced in capability dismissals only if the employee **14.15** is to blame for the actions that led to the dismissal, but should not be reduced where the employee's lack of ability cannot be regarded as blameworthy conduct.

The distinction between these two types of capability dismissal was considered by the **14.16** EAT in *Kraft Foods Ltd v Fox* [1977] IRLR 43. Mr Fox was dismissed from his job as a sales manager after he had failed to meet the high standards set by his predecessor. The employment tribunal held that the dismissal was unfair, but reduced the award by 50 per cent on the grounds of contributory fault. The EAT allowed the employer's appeal against the tribunal's finding that the dismissal was unfair, but it also held that the tribunal had erred in law on the issue of contributory fault because Mr Fox was not to blame for lacking the ability of his predecessor. The EAT said that:

> If an employee is incompetent or incapable and cannot, with the best will in the world, measure up to the job, it seems to us to be wrong to say that that condition of incapacity is a contributory factor to his dismissal.

It drew a distinction between actions over which an employee has control and those **14.17** outside his or her control. In the former situation, the employee is guilty of misconduct and compensation may be reduced, but in the latter situation, the employee cannot be blamed and therefore compensation should not be reduced.

However, some doubt was cast on this principle in the subsequent case of *Moncur v* **14.18** *International Paint Co Ltd* [1978] IRLR 223. Here again, Mr Moncur's dismissal arose as a result of his lack of managerial ability. In particular, it was alleged that he was not good at getting on with his superiors and fell short of the required standards of administrative control. The employment tribunal, having found the dismissal unfair, reduced compensation by 40 per cent. The EAT, upholding this decision, said that the tribunal had not erred in law and that it was entitled on the facts to make such a reduction. The decision in *Moncur* was followed by the EAT in *Finnie v Top Hat Frozen Foods Ltd* [1985] IRLR 365. However, the EAT's approach in *Fox* appears to be more consistent with the underlying principle that compensation should not be reduced unless the employee's conduct is shown to be blameworthy.

This, of course, does not mean that a reduction in capability dismissals will never be **14.19** justified. For example, in *Sutton & Gates (Luton) Ltd v Boxall* [1978] IRLR 486, the EAT said that an employment tribunal was wrong to refuse to reduce the award where an electrician was dismissed for poor performance. The EAT said that the ruling in *Fox* applied only to what it called 'true' capability dismissals—that is, cases in which the employee's dismissal was due to a lack of ability beyond his or her control. It did not apply to cases in which the dismissal was brought about by the employee's laziness, idleness, or negligence, because these were matters that lay within the employee's control and therefore were matters that could justify a reduction for contributory fault.

Contributory fault and ill health dismissals

14.20 Compensation should not be reduced for contributory fault in ill health dismissals unless the applicant is shown to be guilty of blameworthy conduct. This principle was reaffirmed by the EAT in *Slaughter v C Brewer & Sons Ltd* [1990] IRLR 426, when it overturned an employment tribunal's decision to reduce its award by 80 per cent because of the applicant's incapacity for work at the time of his dismissal. However, the EAT recognized that there may be circumstances in which a reduction for contributory fault would be appropriate—for example, where an employee refused to obtain a medical report or to attend a medical examination. A reduction may also be justified if an employee acted in a manner that was detrimental to his or her recovery (*A Links Ltd v Rose* [1991] IRLR 353).

Conduct judged objectively

14.21 The test for determining whether or not the conduct is blameworthy is objective. It is an issue to be determined by the employment tribunal on the evidence and it is better practice in an unfair dismissal case for a tribunal to keep its findings on the unfair dismissal issue separate from its findings on disputes facts that are relevant only to issues such as contributory fault (*London Ambulance Service NHS Trust v Small* [2009] IRLR 563).

14.22 It is irrelevant, for the purpose of determining blameworthiness, for the tribunal to consider whether the employee knew that the conduct complained of was wrong. (See *Ladbroke Racing Ltd v Mason* [1978] ICR 49, in which two employees' involvement in negotiations for their employer's betting shops was held to be a gross breach of trust even though the employees did not know that their conduct was wrong.)

14.23 Nevertheless, an employee's state of mind may be relevant for the purpose of determining the degree of blameworthiness since, once it has been established that blameworthiness exists, the extent of the deduction may be determined by reference to the employee's knowledge of the wrongfulness of the action. Thus, where an employee knew that the conduct was wrong, the deduction may be larger than would otherwise be the case to reflect this knowledge (see *Washbrook v Podger* EAT 123/85, in which the employee's contribution was increased from 40 per cent to 80 per cent because he knew that he was acting contrary to his employer's instructions).

Conduct of agents

14.24 Employees may be responsible for the actions of those acting on their behalf if the agent's conduct causes or contributes to the dismissal. Similarly, it is no defence for employees to say that their act was based on advice from a third party if that advice is negligent or unreasonable (see *Allen v Hammett* [1982] IRLR 89, in which the applicant was held responsible for the negligent advice given to him by his solicitor).

Employee's conduct alone relevant

Tribunals may take into account only the conduct of the employee (or the employee's **14.25** agents) in deciding whether or not to make a reduction for contributory fault and are not entitled to consider how the employer treated others involved in the same incident (*Allders International Ltd v Parkins* [1981] IRLR 68). This principle was confirmed by the Court of Appeal in *Parker Foundry Ltd v Slack* [1992] IRLR 11, in which the Court upheld an employment tribunal's decision to reduce compensation by 50 per cent for contributory fault where the applicant had been dismissed for fighting. The Court rejected the argument that the tribunal should have taken account of the fact that the other employee who had been involved in the fight had only been suspended without pay for two weeks, ruling that the statutory provisions are concerned only with the conduct of the applicant and not the conduct of others. However, it is submitted that a tribunal is entitled to consider the conduct of others in order to determine the extent to which the applicant was to blame for the dismissal—for example, in *Slack*, it is clear that the tribunal did have regard to the extent to which Mr Slack was to blame for the fight.

Conduct linked to the dismissal

As far as the compensatory award is concerned, the statutory provisions make it clear **14.26** that compensation may be reduced only where the conduct genuinely causes or contributes to the dismissal. For example, in *Smith & Smith v McPhee and Stewart* EAT 338/339/89, the EAT held that an employment tribunal was correct not to make a reduction for contributory fault where it was found that the cause of the dismissal was that the employer was trying to save face over an embarrassing incident for which it was partly responsible. In these circumstances, the applicants' carelessness had not itself caused or contributed to the dismissal. Similarly, in *Hutchinson v Enfield Rolling Mills* [1981] IRLR 318, the EAT held that the employment tribunal had erred in law when it took into account the unrelated factors, such as the employee's political views or its adverse view of him as a troublemaker. The EAT said that the only relevant matters were those that led to the dismissal and that all other factors should be ignored. Tribunals should not therefore 'simply point to some bad behaviour of employees and say that by reason of that matter they are going to reduce compensation' (*Steer v Messrs Primlock Ltd* EAT 687/85). The principle was reiterated by the EAT in *Lindsay v General Contracting Ltd t/a Pik a Pak Home Electrical* EAT 1096/00 and 1126/000, in which the claimant was found to have been unfairly dismissed for union membership reasons, but the tribunal had reduced the award for unrelated conduct that was not sufficiently serious in any event.

On the other hand, employers are not confined to relying on the conduct that con- **14.27** stitutes their principal reason for dismissal; they can also rely on other subsidiary reasons for dismissal provided that those reasons contribute to the decision to dismiss (*Robert Whiting Designs Ltd v Lamb* [1978] ICR 89). For example, in *McNicholas v AR Engineering* IDS 309, a tribunal thought that Mr McNicholas' poor record for absence and time-keeping contributed to his dismissal.

14.28 As noted in **14.03** above, the power to reduce the basic award is somewhat wider than the power to reduce the compensatory award, since tribunals may take account of 'any conduct' of the claimant. Some tribunals have held that this includes conduct that is unrelated to the employer's reasons for dismissal. For example, in *Artisan Press Ltd v Srawley and Parker* [1986] IRLR 126, an employment tribunal reduced Mr Parker's special award by 10 per cent because of his persistent lateness, even though this had nothing to do with the reason for dismissal, as found by the tribunal. However, it must be doubted whether the amendment made by s 9(2) of the Employment Act 1980 (EA 1980) was intended to change the test of causation. The better view is that it is not just and equitable to reduce the basic award unless there is some link between the employee's conduct and the dismissal.

Conduct in the notice period

14.29 Employment tribunals have no power to reduce compensation for contributory fault if the misconduct occurs during the notice period. Thus, in *Bell v Service Engines (Newcastle) Ltd* IDS 309, an employment tribunal held that it was not entitled to reduce the basic award where thefts occurred during the employee's notice period.

14.30 In relation to the compensatory award, compensation may be limited on the alternative ground of 'justice and equity' under ERA 1996, s 123(1) (see Chapter 12). Thus, in *Bell* above, the tribunal held that it was inequitable to make a compensatory award in the light of the employee's conduct during the notice period.

Internal appeals

14.31 An employee's failure to lodge an internal appeal does not justify compensation being reduced for contributory fault. An internal appeal is an event after the dismissal takes effect, so the employee's failure to appeal does not contribute to the dismissal and does not justify a reduction in either the basic award (ERA 1996, s 122(1)) or the compensatory award (ERA 1996, s 123(6)) (see *Hoover Ltd v Forde* [1980] ICR 239 and *Ever Ready Co (GB) Ltd v Foster* EAT 310/81). However, a reduction for contributory fault may be justified for failing to use the grievance procedure prior to dismissal. The position in relation to the duty to mitigate is discussed at **13.47**. It should be noted, however, that a failure to appeal may well lead to a reduction in the award by up to 25 per cent under TULR(C)A 1992, s 207A(3) (see **12.59** above) where the former employee's failure to appeal is found to be contrary to the Advisory, Conciliation, and Arbitration Service (ACAS) 2009 Code of Practice on disciplinary and grievance procedures or unreasonable, and where it is considered just and equitable to make such a reduction.

Constructive dismissals and contributory fault

The same general principles apply irrespective of whether the dismissal is direct or **14.32**
constructive. So, provided that the employee's conduct is blameworthy in the sense
described by Brandon LJ in *Nelson v BBC (No 2)* [1979] IRLR 346 (see **14.09**
above) and can be said to have caused or contributed to the dismissal, there is no
reason in principle why a reduction for contributory fault should not be made
simply because the dismissal is constructive rather than direct (see *Garner v Grange
Furnishing Ltd* [1977] IRLR 206).

In *Holroyd v Gravure Cylinders Ltd* [1984] IRLR 259, the EAT ruled that compensa- **14.33**
tion should be reduced for contributory fault in constructive dismissals only in
'exceptional circumstances', by which the EAT appears to have meant cases involving
a variation in contract. The EAT's ruling was subsequently given a wider interpretation that suggested that a reduction for contributory fault should not be made in
'constructive dismissal' cases. However, in *Morrison v Amalgamated Transport and
General Workers Union* [1989] IRLR 361, the NICA ruled that, in so far as *Holroyd*
purported to lay down a rule of law, it was wrongly decided and that it was not necessary to show 'exceptional' circumstances before a reduction for contributory fault
would be justified in constructive dismissal cases. This decision has now been
followed and approved by the EAT in *Polentarutti v Autokraft Ltd* [1991] IRLR 457.

Tribunals have also been encouraged to take a 'broad common sense' approach to **14.34**
issues of causation in constructive dismissal cases. So, although the immediate cause
of the dismissal is the employer's repudiatory conduct, tribunals are entitled to consider the extent to which the employee's own behaviour caused or contributed to the
situation that led to the constructive dismissal. For example, in *Morrison*, the NICA
held that a tribunal was entitled to consider the reason why the applicant had been
suspended without pay, which resulted in her being constructively dismissed. (See
also *Polentarutti*, in which the EAT said that the tribunal was entitled to take into
account the applicant's bad workmanship that led to his constructive dismissal.)

Relationship with power to limit compensation

In principle, it is open to tribunals both to limit the period over which compensa- **14.35**
tion is awarded (see Chapter 6) and to reduce the award for contributory fault. For
example, where the principal reason for dismissal is ill health, a tribunal might
conclude that dismissal would have been fair within a month and therefore limit
the award to a month's compensation. It may also reduce the award for contributory
fault on the grounds that the employee had retarded recovery by gardening or playing
a sport (see *Rao v Civil Aviation Authority* [1994] IRLR 240).

However, if the reason for limiting the compensatory award is not related to the **14.36**
fault of the employee, there will be no further reduction under ERA 1996, s 123(6).
For example, in redundancy dismissals, although compensation may be limited to
the period that it would have taken the employers to consult the employees, a

further reduction for contributory fault would not normally be justified (see *Abbotts v Wesson-Glynwed Steel Ltd* [1982] IRLR 52). The same applies to capability dismissals where the employee is not to blame for the dismissal (see **14.15** above). Moreover, some tribunals are unwilling both to limit compensation and reduce the award for contributory fault if this means penalizing the employee twice for the same conduct. For example, in *Vildung v Ocean Electronics Ltd* EAT 295/79, a case of gross negligence, the EAT thought that both to limit and to reduce the award was 'unjust and the application of a double penalty'.

C. Amount of Reduction

14.37 Once the employee's conduct is shown to be blameworthy, the tribunal has to go on to decide whether it is just and equitable to reduce the award, and, if so, by how much.

14.38 In *Hollier v Plysu Ltd* [1983] IRLR 260, the Court of Appeal gave some guidance to employment tribunals on how they should approach the issue of apportioning blame for the dismissal. As a rule of thumb, the EAT suggested that there were four types of casem as follows:

(a) the employee is wholly to blame for the dismissal and compensation could be reduced by 100 per cent;
(b) the employee is largely to blame and nobody would quarrel with a reduction of 75 per cent;
(c) both parties are equally to blame and compensation should be reduced by 50 per cent; or
(d) the employee is slightly to blame and compensation should be reduced by 25 per cent.

14.39 In *York v Brown* EAT 262/84, the EAT added a fifth category—namely, cases in which the employee's degree of blame is so small that it would not be worth making a reduction at all. The EAT suggested that this would apply to reductions of 10 per cent or less.

14.40 Although subsequently endorsed by the Court of Appeal in the same case, these 'guidelines' should be treated with some caution since the Court stressed that the question of apportionment is a matter for the tribunal, which should adopt 'a broad commonsense view of the situation'. It follows that a failure to apply the guidelines is not in itself sufficient grounds for appeal unless it can also be shown that the tribunal made an error of law—that is, misunderstood or misconstrued its statutory powers, or came to a decision that no reasonable tribunal could have reached.

14.41 Thus, sometimes, tribunals reduce awards by less than the recommended 25 per cent. For example, in *Artisan Press Ltd v Srawley and Parker* [1986] IRLR 126, the tribunal reduced Mr Parker's award by 10 per cent because of the persistent lateness.

At the other end of the spectrum, tribunals have been known to reduce compensation by 90 per cent. For example, in *Gibson and others v British Transport Docks Board* [1982] IRLR 228, a case in which nine employees were dismissed for allegedly intimidating two colleagues, the EAT substituted a reduction of 90 per cent for 100 per cent because 'the overwhelming blame for the dismissal lies in this case at the door of these applicants'. For a further example, see *Thompson v Imperial College of Science and Technology* IDS 309.

No reduction

In the overwhelming majority of cases, the tribunal will make some reduction if it **14.42** finds the employee to blame for the dismissal. However, it is open to a tribunal not to reduce compensation at all where it regards the employee's conduct as falling within the *de minimis* principle, as suggested by the EAT in *York v Brown* EAT 262/84 (see **14.39** above), or where it considers that it would not be just and equitable to make a reduction (see *Central Nottinghamshire Health Authority v Shine* EAT 562/82).

Full (100 per cent) reduction

At one time, it was thought that it was wrong in principle for a tribunal to hold a **14.43** dismissal unfair and reduce compensation by 100 per cent. However, in *W Devis & Sons Ltd v Atkins* [1977] IRLR 314, the House of Lords approved earlier EAT decisions to the effect that such a reduction is possible where the employee's conduct was the sole cause of the dismissal (see also *Kelly Madden v Manor Surgery* [2007] IRLR 17, in which the principle was confirmed).

An illustration of such a case is *Maris v Rotherham Borough Council* [1974] IRLR 147. **14.44** Mr Maris, who worked in the council's cleaning department, was dismissed as a result of being convicted of submitting fraudulent expenses. The decision to dismiss was finally taken after industrial pressure from the workforce and the dismissal was found to be unfair for this reason. However, the employment tribunal awarded no compensation because it thought that such an award was not just and equitable in the circumstances. The NIRC affirmed this decision on different grounds. It said that no award should be made to Mr Maris because he was the sole author of his own misfortune.

The right to make a 100 per cent reduction for contributory fault in appropriate **14.45** cases was confirmed by the EAT in *Chaplin v Rawlinson* [1991] ICR 553, in which the dismissal was held unfair on procedural grounds, but a 100 per cent reduction was justified, because the employee had been dismissed for urinating on a consignment of wheat before delivering it to a customer. Other cases in which 100 per cent reductions have been upheld include *Baxter v Wreyfield* EAT 9/82 (soliciting customers for a rival company) and *Allen v NE Lancashire Dairies Ltd* EAT 230/83 (going on holiday without permission).

14.46 However, as Chadwick LJ pointed out in *Friend v Civil Aviation Authority* [2001] IRLR 819, assuming that the loss caused by the dismissal is attributable to the employer under ERA 1996, s 123(1), a 100 per cent reduction in the award is appropriate only in exceptional circumstances. Before reducing compensation by 100 per cent, a tribunal must be satisfied that the employee was wholly to blame for the dismissal, and that such a reduction is just and equitable in the circumstances. Thus, in *Trend v Chiltern Hunt Ltd* [1977] IRLR 66, the EAT said that it thought that a 100 per cent reduction would be appropriate only where 'a dismissal has been found to be unfair on technical grounds or where later ascertained facts had they been known at the date of the hearing would have amply justified it' (see **14.51** below). But a 100 per cent reduction should not be made where the employer's conduct is also blameworthy (*Kelly Madden v Manor Surgery* [2007] IRLR 17). So, in *Gibson v British Transport Docks Board* [1982] IRLR 228, the EAT held that a reduction of 100 per cent was inconsistent with the tribunal's ruling that the employer was at fault for not investigating the circumstances of Mr Gibson's particular case. It therefore said that a 90 per cent reduction was appropriate (see also *Thomas v Gauges North West* (*Scientific Instruments*) IRLIB 277, March 1985).

Industrial pressure and contributory fault

14.47 Tribunals must ignore industrial pressure in deciding whether the dismissal is fair or unfair (ERA 1996, s 107). Similarly, once a dismissal is held to be unfair, in assessing compensation, no account is taken of industrial pressure (ERA 1996, s 123(5)—see **14.13** above).

14.48 This rule does not prevent tribunals from reducing the award for contributory fault where the employee was to blame for the actions that led to the industrial pressure to dismiss. For example, in *Colwyn Borough Council v Dutton* [1980] IRLR 420, Mr Dutton's colleagues in the refuse collection service refused to work with him because his driving was so bad. The EAT held that Mr Dutton's conduct contributed to the dismissal. In some cases, such as *Maris v Rotherham Borough Council* [1974] IRLR 147, a reduction of 100 per cent may be justified where it is shown that the employee was wholly to blame for the dismissal.

Reduction not proportional to employer's loss

14.49 The amount of the reduction need not be proportional to the loss to the employer caused by the employee's conduct. For example, in *Acorn Shipyard Ltd v Warren* EAT 20/81, the company lost £8,500 as a result of Mr Warren's underestimation of the length of time and the cost of building a ship. It was argued that the reduction in the award should reflect the loss suffered by the company. The EAT, however, refused to interfere with employment tribunal's decision that compensation should only be reduced by 25 per cent. It said that the tribunal had taken this factor into account in making its assessment and concluded that the error was not entirely

Mr Warren's responsibility. Further, the reduction in the award should be proportional to the financial loss suffered by the company.

D. Consistent Reductions of Awards

The general rule is that both the basic and compensatory awards should be reduced **14.50** by the same amount. Thus, in *GM McFall & Co Ltd v Curran* [1981] IRLR 455, the NICA overturned a tribunal's decision to reduce the compensatory award by 40 per cent and not to reduce the basic award at all. The Court said that both awards should be reduced by the same amount (see also *RSPCA v Cruden* [1986] IRLR 83).

However, in exceptional circumstances, the EAT has upheld decisions to reduce the **14.51** awards by different amounts. For example, in *Les Ambassadeurs Club v Bainda* [1982] IRLR 5, the EAT upheld a tribunal's decision to reduce the compensatory award by 70 per cent, but not to reduce the basic award at all. Similarly, in *Thompson v Woodland Designs Ltd* [1980] IRLR 423, the EAT upheld a decision to reduce the basic award by 85 per cent and the compensatory award by 100 per cent.

Another situation in which it might be considered just and equitable to reduce **14.52** the awards by different amounts is where the tribunal has limited the compensation award under ERA 1996, s 123(1) and also decided to reduce the award for contributory fault (see **14.35** above). In such a case, a tribunal might decide that it is just and equitable to reduce the compensatory award by a lower or higher amount than the basic award (*Rao v Civil Aviation Authority* [1994] IRLR 240 and *Charles Robertson (Developments) Ltd v White and another* [1995] ICR 349).

It is also possible that an inconsistent reduction could be applied on the grounds **14.53** that the power to reduce the basic award is wider than the power to reduce the compensatory award (see **14.03** above).

The reduction for contributory fault is made after the applicant's loss has been **14.54** quantified (and after the award is reduced or increased pursuant to ERA 1996, s 124A(1)(b), but before applying the statutory ceiling on the compensatory award (*Walter Braund (London) Ltd v Murray* [1991] IRLR 100). (See also **15.17** below as to the treatment of *ex gratia* payments.)

E. New Evidence after the Hearing

A further reduction in compensation may be made if new evidence of misconduct **14.55** comes to light after the hearing. This arose in *Ladup Ltd v Barnes* [1982] IRLR 8. Mr Barnes was dismissed after being charged with growing and possessing cannabis. His dismissal was found to be unfair on the grounds that the company had failed to carry out an independent investigation into the allegation. The tribunal refused to reduce the award of compensation because it considered that Mr Barnes was not to blame for the dismissal. About a month after the hearing, Mr Barnes was convicted of possessing cannabis and the company applied to the tribunal for a review. Its request was turned down by the tribunal, but the tribunal's decision was overturned by the EAT on appeal. The EAT said that the tribunal's refusal to reduce the award in the first instance was correct, but that the position had changed in the light of Mr Barnes' conviction. This new evidence meant that the decision should be reviewed in the interests of justice and that compensation should be reduced by 100 per cent.

14.56   The EAT's decision in *Ladup Ltd v Barnes* is open to doubt for two reasons. First, it would appear to conflict with the principle in *W Devis & Sons Ltd v Atkins* [1977] IRLR 314 that information coming to light after the dismissal is not relevant to the issue of contributory fault. (The same objection would seem to apply to reducing the basic award in such circumstances even though statutory powers to reduce such an award for contributory fault are wider.) Second, the decision is open to the more general criticism that, by allowing the award to be reviewed outside the 14-day period provided for by the tribunal rules, the EAT has created a degree of uncertainty in an area in which finality should be the guiding principle. On the other hand, if *Ladup Ltd v Barnes* is correct, the same principle should apply to an employee who is subsequently acquitted or whose conviction is quashed on appeal (Employment Tribunals (Constitution and Rules of Procedure) Regulations 2004, SI 2004/1861, r 34(3)(e)).

14.57   Where there is a split hearing, the chairman should make it clear to the parties whether the issue of contributory fault is to be dealt with at the hearing on liability or at the remedies hearing (*Dundon v GPT* [1995] IRLR 403).

F. Key Points

14.58   In *Optikinectics Ltd v Whooley* EAT 1275/97, the EAT helpfully summarized the principles regarding the circumstances in which the compensatory award may be reduced for contributory fault as follows:

- The Claimant must be found to have acted in a culpable, blameworthy, or wholly unreasonable manner. The tribunal's enquiry in this regard should be directed solely at the conduct of the Claimant, not the employer or others.
- The conduct must be known to the employer prior to the dismissal and have been the cause of it.
- Once blameworthy conduct is established, a tribunal is bound to reduce the award by such amount as it considers just and equitable, although the tribunal retains a complete discretion over the amount of the reduction and may in some circumstances conclude that the behaviour was too trivial to justify any reduction

(see *Lindsay v General Contracting Ltd t/a Pik a Pak Home Electrical* EAT 1096/00 and 1126/00).

- It is open to a tribunal to reduce the basic and compensatory awards by different amounts.
- Appellate courts will rarely interfere with an Employment Tribunal's assessment of the reduction for contributory fault.

15

EX GRATIA PAYMENTS AND OTHER DEDUCTIONS

15.01 Redundancy and *ex gratia* payments are liable to be deducted from an award of unfair dismissal compensation. This chapter looks at the circumstances in which such payments are deducted.

A. Deducting Redundancy Payments from Unfair Dismissal Compensation

15.02 The primary purpose of the statutory provisions is to prevent employees from receiving both a basic award and a redundancy payment. However, where an employee receives an enhanced redundancy payment—that is, a payment over and above the statutory maximum—this may be set off against the compensatory award, but this applies only where redundancy is found to be the true reason for dismissal (*Boorman v Allmakes Ltd* [1995] IRLR 553). The relevant statutory provisions are examined in greater detail below.

Statutory redundancy pay and the basic award

15.03 It is provided that, where an employee receives a redundancy payment, 'The amount of the basic award shall be reduced or further reduced by the amount of . . . any redundancy payment' (Employment Rights Act 1996 [ERA 1996], s 122(4)).

This provision applies irrespective of whether the payment is made by the employer **15.04** or awarded by the tribunal.

Example

An employee aged 28, who earns £120 a week, with four years' service, is made redundant. The employer gives him a redundancy payment of £360. The dismissal is found to be unfair.

The employee would be entitled to a basic award of £480, but he has already received £360, so the balance payable is £120.

Enhanced redundancy payments and the compensatory award

It is provided that if the amount of any payment made by an employer on the **15.05** ground that the dismissal was by reason of redundancy exceeds the amount of the basic award that would be payable but for ERA 1996, s 122(4), the excess shall go to reduce the amount of the compensatory award (ERA 1996, s 123(7)). This provision may be relied on by employers where the basic award is reduced for contributory fault (a redundancy payment being irreducible), and where the redundancy payment exceeds the minimum payment provided for under the statutory redundancy payment scheme. So, if the facts in the example given above were varied so that a payment of £800 were made under a company redundancy scheme, there would be a reduction in the compensatory award of £320.

Relationship with compensation claim for enhanced payment

ERA 1996, s 123(3) allows an employee to recover compensation for the loss of **15.06** an enhanced redundancy payment as part of the compensatory award (see 7.25 above). It is unclear whether any sum awarded by the tribunal under s 123(3) should then be set off against the rest of the award of compensation, thereby putting an employee in the position in which he or she would have been had the employer made the payment at the time of dismissal, or whether it should only be set off where the payment is made by the employer. It would seem from the wording of s 123(7) that it is intended to apply only in this latter situation. If this interpretation is correct, s 123(7) will not apply where the compensation for the loss of an enhanced redundancy payment is awarded by the tribunal as part of the compensatory award, with the result that employees who receive their redundancy payments from their employers at the time of dismissal will be worse off than those who recover such payments as part of their claim for unfair dismissal compensation.

These provisions apply only where the dismissal is both 'by reason of redundancy' **15.07** and unfair. Thus they will not affect employees who claim compensation for the loss of an enhanced redundancy payment in a non-redundancy dismissal (see *Addison v Babcock FATA Ltd* [1986] IRLR 388).

Order of reductions in redundancy cases

15.08 An issue has arisen as to order in which the reductions should be made where an employee receives an enhanced redundancy payment prior to termination. The issue was resolved in *Digital Equipment Co Ltd v Clements (No 2)* [1998] IRLR 134, in which the Court of Appeal ruled that a redundancy payment in excess of a statutory redundancy payment should be deducted in full from the compensatory award itself and not merely taken into account in calculating the loss on which the compensatory award is based. The correct procedure following the *Digital Equipment* case is therefore:

(a) calculate the loss suffered by the claimant;

(b) give full credit for any payments received by the claimant including any payments made by the former employer to the claimant, such as a payment in lieu of notice (*Heggie v Uniroyal Englebert Tyres Ltd* [1999] IRLR 802) and any payments received from third parties in mitigation (such as payments received from the new employer);

(c) make a *Polkey* reduction (where appropriate);

(d) reduce the award for contributory fault;

(e) set off any payment that the employee has received from the former employer by way of enhanced redundancy payment.

15.09 This means that the former employer gets full credit for any enhanced redundancy payment made at the time of termination of employment and would appear to cover enhanced redundancy payments whether or not they are contractual or *ex gratia*.

B. *Ex Gratia* Payments

15.10 It is not uncommon for employers to make an *ex gratia* payment in addition to any payment that an employee is entitled to receive on dismissal, such as a payment in lieu of notice. For this purpose, an *ex gratia* payment may be defined as any sum paid to an employee without any legal liability to do so.

C. *Ex Gratia* Payment as a Defence

15.11 In *Chelsea Football Club & Athletic Co Ltd v Heath* [1981] IRLR 73, the Employment Appeal Tribunal (EAT) ruled that, in principle, there was no objection to employers relying on an *ex gratia* payment as a defence to the statutory liability to pay compensation.

Example

Mr Heath was dismissed from his job as Chelsea Football Club's chief talent scout as a result of the appointment of a new manager. After his dismissal, he was sent a cheque for £7,500 by the club. Mr Heath subsequently successfully claimed that he had been unfairly dismissed. When it came to assessing compensation, the club argued that the tribunal should take the *ex gratia* payment into account. The industrial tribunal accepted this argument and declined to make a compensatory award, although it did make a basic award of £1,920.

On appeal, the club argued that because the *ex gratia* payment exceeded the statutory maximum (which, at that time, was £5,200), the balance should be set off against the basic award. The EAT agreed, saying that, although the payment did not specifically refer to the basic award, there was a presumption that the club was really offering to pay the full statutory compensation 'without prejudice' to the issue of liability.

In *Horizon Holidays Ltd v Grassi* [1987] IRLR 371, it was held that, following the **15.12** Court of Appeal's decision in *Babcock FATA Ltd v Addison* [1987] IRLR 173, an *ex gratia* payment should normally be deducted from an award of unfair dismissal compensation. But the circumstances in which it is paid may be important in deciding at what stage of the calculation it is brought into account. For example, in *Rushton v Harcross Timber & Building Supplies Ltd* [1993] IRLR 254, in which the EAT appears to have treated an *ex gratia* payment made to the employee at the time of his redundancy as an enhanced redundancy payment falling within Employment Protection (Consolidation) Act 1978 (EP(C)A 1978), s 74(7) (now ERA 1996, s 123(7)), which, as such, would be deducted at the end of the process (see *Digital Equipment Co Ltd v Clements (No 2)* [1998] IRLR 134). By contrast, in *Boorman v Allmakes* [1995] IRLR 553, Lord Justice Evans suggested that, where an enhanced redundancy payment is paid by mistake, the payment can be deducted from the compensatory award (in such circumstances, the payment is likely to be treated as an 'ordinary' *ex gratia* payment and ERA 1996, s 123(7) may well not apply).

Payments that count

Following the Court of Appeal's ruling in *Babcock FATA Ltd v Addison* [1987] **15.13** IRLR 371, and the EAT and Court of Appeal's ruling in *Digital Equipment Ltd v Clements (No 2)* [1998] IRLR 134, all post-dismissal payments are taken into account in determining a claimant's loss under ERA 1996, s 123(1). The previous distinction between a payment in lieu of notice that fell to be included in the assessment of loss under s 123(1) and an *ex gratia* payment that did not, but nonetheless was taken into account in the overall assessment of the compensatory award, is no longer good law.

15.14 The current position is that the claimant must give credit for all post-dismissal payments, including any payments such as a payment in lieu of notice (*Heggie v Uniroyal Ltd* [1999] IRLR 802) or an *ex gratia* payment, and any payments received from third parties such as a new employer or the state (other than to the extent that the latter payments are covered by the Employment Protection (Recoupment of Jobseeker's Allowance and Income Support) Regulations 1996, SI 1996/2349 [the Recoupment Regulations]), in calculating an employee's loss under ERA 1996, s 123(1). Furthermore, where an employer fails to comply with a re-employment order, account may be taken of any back pay received by the claimant (*Butler v British Railways Board* EAT 510/89).

15.15 The only exception is if it can be shown that the *ex gratia* payment would have been made to the employee in any event, in which case it does not fall to be deducted. For example, in *Addison v Babcock FATA Ltd* [1987] IRLR 173, the applicant recovered compensation for the loss of any *ex gratia* payment that he would have received had he been dismissed at the same time as his colleagues some 15 months later when the employer's business was closed. Similarly, in *Roadchef Ltd v Hastings* [1988] IRLR 142, the EAT held that the tribunal was correct not to deduct an *ex gratia* payment that the employee would have received even if he had not been dismissed. The same reasoning was held to apply to the non-deduction of a bonus payment that an employee would have received had he remained in employment during the period covered by the award in *Quiring v Hill House International School* EAT 500/88. However, somewhat surprisingly, in *DCM Optical Clinic plc v Strark* EAT 0124/04, the EAT ruled that a retention payment paid to secure the employee's services during his three-month redundancy notice period did fall to be deducted when he received part of that enhanced pay as an *ex gratia* payment representing two months' gross pay. The EAT, relying on *MBS v Calo* [1983] IRLR 189, considered that an employee was bound to give credit for enhanced notice pay irrespective of whether he or she was entitled to it or whether it was paid on an *ex gratia* basis. The EAT rejected the argument that this was a payment to which the claimant was entitled in any event on the basis that ERA 1996, s 123(1) requires 'an account to be taken of what he would have received, but for the unfair dismissal and what he in fact received'. However, the EAT appears to have overlooked the nature of the payment, which was arguably collateral and unrelated to the claimant's unfair dismissal.

15.16 Doubt has been cast on the correctness of these decisions by the EAT in *Rushton v Harcross Timber & Building Supplies Ltd* [1993] IRLR 254, in which the EAT declined to follow its earlier ruling in *Hastings* and ruled that an employer always should be given credit for an *ex gratia* payment made to a redundant employee, adding that such a payment should always be set off against an employer's liability to make a compensatory payment. In support of its decision, the EAT relied on the 'meaning and intent of [EP(C)A 1978] s 74(7)' (now ERA 1996, s 123(7))—that is, that, in the calculation of a compensatory award, an employer should receive credit for any redundancy payment that it makes since 'the manifest purpose of that subsection was to encourage employers who find it necessary to dismiss for redundancy to be generous in making *ex gratia* payments'. However, the EAT appears to have misunderstood Mr Rushton's argument—namely, that he would have received such a payment in any event—although no evidence in support of this argument was placed before the tribunal. The EAT also appears to have failed to distinguish between an '*ex gratia*' payment and a payment under ERA 1996, s 123(7), because such payments may be made for different reasons. The decision therefore may be open to doubt.

Example

Wording

The following wording in a letter enclosing an *ex gratia* payment is likely to have the effect that the payment is deducted from any entitlement to compensation that the recipient may have: 'We are making the above payment in discharge of any liability to pay compensation under current employment legislation.'

Deduction from total loss or final award

Assuming that the *ex gratia* payment is deductible, the next question is whether it should be included in the assessment of overall loss under ERA 1996, s 123(1) or whether it should be deducted from the final award. The point is important, because, if the former approach is correct, the *ex gratia* payment will be brought into the assessment before compensation is reduced for contributory fault, whereas, if the latter approach is correct, the payment will be deducted from the final award. Prior to the EAT's ruling in *Digital Equipment Ltd v Clements (No 2)* [1997] IRLR 140, there was a conflict of authority on this point. **15.17**

In *UBAF Bank Ltd v Davis* [1978] IRLR 442, Mr Davis was given the sum of £3,156 on dismissal from his job at the bank. This was equivalent to six months' pay even though he was entitled to only three months' notice. The tribunal held that the correct approach was to deduct the *ex gratia* payment from its assessment of Mr Davis' loss and then reduce the award for contributory fault, which it found to be 50 per cent. On appeal, the bank argued that this was wrong and that the tribunal should have first given credit for the part of the payment that was referable to the notice period and included that in the overall assessment of loss; it should then have reduced the award by 50 per cent, and finally deducted the balance of the *ex gratia* payment from the final award. Rejecting the argument, the EAT said that the tribunal's approach was correct on the ground that the employee could not be said to have suffered loss during a period for which compensation had been paid. **15.18**

However, in *Clement-Clarke International Ltd v Manley* [1979] ICR 74 (a case decided a few days after *Davis*, but before it was reported), the EAT came to the **15.19** opposite conclusion and held that an *ex gratia* payment should be deducted from the final award, because otherwise employers would not be given the full credit for the payment that they had made. In another case, *Parker & Farr Ltd v Shelvey* [1979] IRLR 434, the EAT followed *Davis*, although it reached the rather surprising conclusion that there was no conflict between the two decisions.

15.20   In *Derwent Coachworks v Kirby* [1994] IRLR 639, the EAT came down firmly in favour of the approach taken in *Clement Clarke International Ltd v Manley*, arguing that justice and equity required the award to be reduced for contributory conduct before any payments made by the employer are deducted (although it should be noted that the *Kirby* case involved a payment in lieu; the reasoning would apply more strongly to an *ex gratia* payment). The significance of the point is illustrated by the examples given below.

Examples

Example 1

Applying *Davis*, the calculation is as follows.

An employment tribunal assesses compensation at £3,500, but says that the award should be reduced by 50 per cent for contributory fault. In addition, the employer has made an *ex gratia* payment of £1,500.

	£
Award of compensation	3,500
Less ex gratia payment	1,500
Balance:	2,000
Less 50% reduction for contributory fault	1,000
Total award	£1,000

Example 2

Applying *Kirby*, the calculation is as follows.

	£
Award of compensation	3,500
Less 50% reduction for contributory fault	1,750
Balance:	1,750
Less ex gratia payment	1,500
Total award	£250

15.21   The EAT in *Digital Equipment Co Ltd v Clements (No 2)* [1997] IRLR 140 has now endorsed the approach in *Davis* and *Shelvey* (Example 1), confirming that the reduction for a failure to mitigate and for contributory fault should be made *after* taking into account any payments made by the employer, thereby overturning its earlier rulings in *Kirby* and *Manley* (Example 2).

The EAT's reasoning applies to all post-termination payments received by the **15.22** employee, with the exception of an enhanced redundancy payment (see **15.08** above). However, it is possible that a further exception may apply where, as in *Chelsea Football Club Atheltic Co Ltd v Heath* [1981] IRLR 73, the payment is made on account of statutory liability. In such circumstances, it may be argued that the payment should be taken into account at the very end of the process, as in *Kirby* and *Manley*, and that the employer should receive full credit for the payment made. Much will depend on the intention and the timing of the payment. For example, if the letter enclosing payment stated 'we are making the following payment in discharge of any liability to pay compensation under current employment legislation', it may be argued that such a payment should be set off against the final award rather than in the assessment of loss under ERA 1996, s 123(1). Nevertheless, in practice, it will often be difficult to distinguish between a payment made on this basis and an ordinary *ex gratia* payment.

(a) Summary: Order of deduction in ordinary cases

(a) Ascertain the loss sustained by the claimant.   **15.23**

(b) Give credit for all payments received on or since dismissal.

(c) Make a *Polkey* reduction, if appropriate.

(d) Increase or reduce the award if appropriate (see **10.12** and **12.58** above).

(e) Reduce the award for contributory fault.

Example

Where there is an uplift pursuant to ERA 1996, s 124A

Where an award is increased pursuant to s 207A of the Trade Union and Labour Relations (Consolidation) Act 1992 (TULR(C)A 1992), ERA 1996, s 124A provides that the adjustment in the amount award shall be applied immediately before any reduction under ERA 1996, s 123(6) or (7). The correct order is therefore as follows.

(a) Loss £15,000.

(b) Credit for £5,000

(c) *Polkey* reduction £5,000

(d) Uplift, say, 25% = £1,250

(e) Reduce the award for contributory fault

Award = £6,250

Ex gratia **payments and the statutory maximum**

15.24   A related issue is whether an employer is given credit for an *ex gratia* payment before or after the statutory maximum is applied. On this point, the statutory provisions give a clear answer. ERA 1996, s 124(5) provides as follows:

> (5)   The limit imposed by this section applies to the amount which the industrial tribunal would, apart from this section, award in respect of the subject matter of the complaint after taking into account—
>
> (a)   any payment made by the respondent to the complainant in respect of that matter, and
>
> (b)   any reduction in the amount of the award required by any enactment or rule of law.

15.25   The effect of this provision was considered by the EAT in *McCarthy v British Insulated Callenders Cables plc* [1985] IRLR 94. In that case, the tribunal assessed the total compensatable loss at £15,820. It then applied the statutory maximum (which, at that time, was £7,000) and deducted an *ex gratia* payment received by Mr McCarthy from the maximum, leaving a balance of £5,726.

15.26   On appeal, the EAT said that this was wrong—the employment tribunal should have first assessed the loss, then deducted the *ex gratia* payment, and then applied the statutory maximum. This meant that, although the *ex gratia* payment was taken into account in working out Mr McCarthy's overall loss, it had no impact on the final award, because his loss, even allowing for the payment, far exceeded the statutory maximum.

15.27   The decision in *McCarthy* was followed by the EAT in *Milnbank Housing Association v Murphy* EAT 281/85 and was confirmed by the EAT in *Walter Braund (London) Ltd v Murray* [1991] IRLR 100, in which it held that, for the same reason, the statutory maximum should be applied after making the deduction for contributory fault.

15.28   Thus employers will only obtain a financial advantage by making an *ex gratia* payment in discharge of their statutory liability to pay the compensatory award if that liability—that is, the total loss suffered by the employee as a result of the dismissal (as determined by the tribunal)—is likely to be less than the maximum that a tribunal may award as a compensatory award.

Example

The employee's loss is £70,000 and it is thought that the tribunal is likely to reduce compensation by 25 per cent.

As the law stands, if an employer were to make an *ex gratia* payment of £5,000, the award would be calculated as follows.

	£
Total loss	70,000
Less ex gratia payment	5,000
Balance	65,000
Less 25% reduction for contributory fault	16,050
Tribunal award	£48,750

It is impossible for employers to overcome the problem raised in *McCarthy*, because **15.29** the deduction in relation to the compensatory award is governed by the express wording of the statutory provisions. However, there is no equivalent provision in relation to the basic award. It is therefore possible that, if the *ex gratia* payment were made in discharge of the liability to pay the basic award, it would count. However, to do this, it would be necessary to link the payment expressly to the basic award by stating that 'the above payment is made in discharge of any liability to pay a basic award under current employment protection legislation'.

D. Accelerated Payment

In addition to deducting any redundancy payment or *ex gratia* payment, a deduction **15.30** should be made for the accelerated receipt of any payment covered in the award. Allowance for accelerated receipt should be made in the award for future loss of earnings and benefits, and falls to be assessed in the calculation of the claimant's loss under (a) and (b) above.

The reason for this deduction is that the claimant should not be put in a better **15.31** position than that in which he or she would have been had the payments been received as and when they fell due (that is, week by week, or month by month). The claimant will have the use of the money in the interim period, and will be in a position either to invest the money and have the benefit of capital growth or to receive interest on the money.

The need to take account of this factor in calculating the award was first recognized **15.32** by the National Industrial Relations Court (NIRC) in *York Trailer Co Ltd v Sparkes* [1973] IRLR 348, although such a reduction may not be necessary if the period of future loss is relatively small (*Les Ambassadeurs Club v Bainda* [1982] IRLR 5). The position is different where a substantial award is made for future loss of earnings or pensions or both.

There is no established method of calculating the reduction. In *Les Ambassadeurs* **15.33** *Club v Bainda*, the EAT suggested that the calculation should be as simple as possible and, prior to the Court of Appeal's ruling in *Bentwood Bros (Manchester) Ltd v Shepherd* [2003] IRLR 364, it was not uncommon for tribunals simply to reduce the overall award for future loss by the prevailing discount rate in personal injury cases (currently, 2.5 per cent).

15.34 In *Page v Sheerness Steel plc* [1996] PIQR Q26, in determining a discount rate for a lump-sum payment of damages for personal injury (which included pension loss), Dyson J applied a rate of 3 per cent, being the rate of return on index-linked gilt securities. More recently, in the case of *Benchmark Dental Laboratories Group Ltd v Perfitt* EAT 0304/04, an employment tribunal made a one-off reduction of 2.5 per cent for accelerated receipt of an award for loss of earnings for a period of loss of eight years and two months. The EAT commented on the practice in personal injury cases. It noted that the discount for accelerated payment should reflect the fact that the employee would be able to invest the sum and that, without a discount, the claimant would be overcompensated. The employment tribunal's discount of 2.5 per cent was wrong. This did not recognize that the amount to meet the loss in the eighth year would be available for the claimant to invest for seven years before it was required, and so on. The EAT noted that if the claimant's loss accrues in a straight line, rateably over the whole period, receipt of this sum is, overall, accelerated for approximately half the period and so the discount rate should apply to the whole sum for approximately half the period. On that basis, the EAT decided that it would expect a discount of 10 per cent, but the parties were invited to refer the employment tribunal to 'an appropriate table' (see **15.37** below).

15.35 In *Shepherd*, the employment tribunal awarded the claimant £195,000 as compensation for sex discrimination and unfair dismissal. The award included compensation for two-and-a-half years' loss of future earnings and ten years' loss of pension rights. From the total award for future loss, the tribunal made a single deduction of 5 per cent to take account of the fact of accelerated payment. The Court of Appeal ruled that the employment tribunal had erred in discounting the award by only 5 per cent, notwithstanding that the award covered future loss of earnings for two-and-a-half years and future loss of pension for ten years, pointing out that the conventional discount of 5 per cent reflects an annual yield rather than a cumulative yield.

15.36 The Court of Appeal stated that it was open to tribunals to factor accelerated payment into the award in more than one way, provided that proper allowance is made for this factor on an annual basis.

15.37 One option—particularly where the award for future loss is for a long period—is to use the figures for accelerated receipt in the Ogden tables.

16

RECOUPMENT REGULATIONS, TAX, AND MISCELLANEOUS MATTERS

A. Recoupment of Benefits from Tribunal Awards

The amount of unemployment benefits or income support received by employees **16.01** between the date of dismissal and the hearing is disregarded for the purpose of assessing the compensatory award. However, such payments are deducted by the employer from the final award and must be paid directly to the Secretary of State under the Employment Protection (Recoupment of Jobseeker's Allowance and Income Support) Regulations 1996, SI 1996/2349—the 'Recoupment Regulations'), made pursuant to the Employment Tribunals Act 1996 (ETA 1996), ss 16 and 17.

The Recoupment Regulations preserve the fundamental principle that an **16.02** employee should recover compensation only for the loss suffered as a result of the dismissal, whilst at the same time ensuring that the state and not the employer is the beneficiary from the operation of this principle. The Regulations apply only where the employee has been in receipt of one or more of the recoupable benefits since dismissal (reg 4(8)).

B. The Monetary Award

In assessing a monetary award of compensation, a tribunal must disregard any **16.03** amount of Jobseeker's Allowance (JSA) or income support that may have been paid to or claimed by the employee (reg 4(1)). The tribunal must state the amount of the award to which the Recoupment Regulations apply. This is known as 'the prescribed element'. In relation to awards of unfair dismissal compensation, the prescribed element is based on the employee's past loss of earnings between the date of dismissal and either the date on which the employee has, or should have, found an equivalent job, or (if the employee is still out of work) the date of the hearing. So, for example, if an employment tribunal awards six months' loss of earnings between the date of dismissal and the date of the hearing, which takes place ten months later, the prescribed element should be based on the six-month period (*Homan v A1 Bacon Ltd* [1996] ICR 721). It does not cover sums awarded for loss of future earnings or loss of fringe benefits (reg 3 and Sch, para 7).

16.04 If the monetary award is reduced for contributory fault or on account of a statutory limit to the amount of the award, the prescribed element is reduced proportionately (reg 2). In *Tipton v West Midlands Co-operative Society* (*No 2*) EAT 859/86, the Employment Appeal Tribunal (EAT) held that the correct procedure is for an employment tribunal first to assess the compensatory award, then to reduce it to the statutory maximum, and finally to reduce the prescribed element by the same proportion as it has reduced the overall award to bring it down to the statutory maximum (see also *Mason v* (*1*) *Wimpey Waste Management Ltd and* (*2*) *Secretary of State for Employment* [1982] IRLR 454, which is to the same effect).

Particulars of award

16.05 The tribunal's decision must contain certain particulars and must inform the parties about the effect of regs 7 and 8 (see **16.07** below), unless the tribunal is satisfied that the employee did not receive or claim JSA or income support during the period to which the claim relates. In addition to stating the monetary award, the particulars must state:

(a) the amount of the prescribed element;
(b) the dates of the period to which the prescribed element relates; and
(c) the amount, if any, by which the monetary award exceeds the prescribed element.

16.06 Similar particulars must be sent by the Secretary of Tribunals to the Secretary of State (reg 4(3)).

16.07 To effectuate this procedure, the applicant must, within certain time limits, give the tribunal clerk the address of the local benefits office from which the benefits were received. The employer also has to provide certain information to the Department for Work and Pensions (DWP) directly. This is explained in the 'annex' that is attached to the tribunal's decision when it is sent to the parties.

C. Recoupment Procedure

The payment of the prescribed element is stayed until the Secretary of State either **16.08** serves a recoupment notice on the employer or notifies the employer that he or she does not intend to serve a notice (reg 7(2) and (3)). The notice must be served on the employer within 21 days of either the announcement or notification of a decision to make a monetary award, or 'as soon as practicable thereafter'. Where judgment is reserved, the 21-day period will run from the date on which the decision is sent to the parties (reg 8(6)(a) and (b)).

A copy of the notice must be sent to the employee and, if requested, to the Secretary **16.09** of Tribunals (reg 8(4)).

The notice operates as an instruction to the employer to deduct from the award the **16.10** amount claimed by the Secretary of State. This is deemed to be a complete discharge of the employer's duty to pay the amount to the employee, although the employee may challenge the amount of benefit recouped by the Secretary of State (reg 8(10)).

The maximum recoupable amount is the total benefit received in the period **16.11** covered by the award for loss of pay. In cases in which this is less than the prescribed element, the balance is paid to the employee (reg 8(2) and (3)).

Challenging the determination

An employee who feels that the amount of benefit recouped is incorrect has a right **16.12** of appeal to the First-tier Tribunal (Social Security and Child Support). In order to appeal, the employee must give notice in writing to the Secretary of State within 21 days of receiving a copy of the recoupment notice. If the Tribunal decides that the Secretary of State has recouped more benefit than the employee received, the excess must be repaid to the employee (reg 10).

Balance of the monetary award

The amount awarded over and above the prescribed element is not affected by the **16.13** Recoupment Regulations and is payable immediately. This covers compensation for future loss. In theory, those employees whose unfair dismissal compensation includes an award for future loss are ineligible for JSA during the period covered by the award, but how the relevant statutory regulation operates in practice is uncertain.

D. Effect of the Recoupment Regulations

The Recoupment Regulations apply only to awards of compensation made by the **16.14** tribunal. This does not normally include settlements, although it has been suggested that they may apply where the terms of the settlement are recorded in full as an award of the tribunal (see Clayton, 'Practice and procedure in industrial tribunals', *Legal Action*, March 1986). Normally, it will be impracticable to apply the Regulations in such circumstances because, in general, the parties do not break down the settlement into its constituent parts—that is, the settlement does not state the proportion of the payment relating to past loss of earnings—so, in practice, the Regulations are not enforced. This gives employees a strong incentive to settle their claims and the effect of the Regulations should always be borne in mind in settlement negotiations.

16.15 The Regulations do not apply to compensation awarded under discrimination legislation (see Chapter 18), but the Regulations do apply to other awards, such as an application for interim relief or an award of remuneration as a protective award made pursuant to s 192(1) of the Trade Union and Labour Relations (Consolidation) Act 1992 (TULR(C)A 1992).

Example

An employment tribunal makes an award of £15,000, £9,000 of which is for loss of earnings to the date of the hearing. This represents the prescribed element. The claimant has received income support of £3,000 to the date of the hearing. The respondent should therefore immediately pay the claimant the sum of £6,000. The balance of £3,000 should be retained pending receipt of information from the DWP. If the Department notifies the employer that it does wish to recoup against the sum retained, then the £3,000 should paid to the Department and the balance of £6,000 should be paid to the employee. The Recoupment Regulations do not apply to settlements.

E. Tax

16.16 The maximum award for unfair dismissal now exceeds the tax threshold for lump-sum payments (currently £30,000) under the Income Tax (Earning and Pensions) Act 2003 (IT(EP)A 2003), ss 401, 403, and 404.

Grossing up

16.17 This means that, in accordance with the principle in *Shove v Downs Surgical plc* [1984] 1 All ER 7, an employment tribunal must gross up any award for unfair dismissal that it makes over £30,000, including any compensation for pension loss (*Yorkshire Housing Ltd v Cuerden* EAT/0397/09), to ensure that, after tax, the claimant receives the net award made by the employment tribunal (see **2.02** for current rates).

Example

An employment tribunal makes an award of £34,000. The first £30,000 is tax-free. Tax is payable at a rate of 40 per cent on £4,000.00. Therefore the award should be 'grossed up' to £35,600 to allow for the tax that will be payable on the award.

This example does not take account of any personal allowance that may have an impact on taxable earnings for the purpose of applying the threshold in IT(EP)A 2003, ss 403 and 404, or the lower rate of tax (*Yorkshire Housing Ltd v Cuerden* EAT/0397/09). The higher rate of tax will not apply in unfair dismissal claims because of the statutory cap. Furthermore, 'grossing up' will not be necessary if the claimant is not a UK resident for tax purposes unless the claimant will be required to pay tax on the lump sum under local tax rules, in which case, it will then be necessary to gross up the payment in accordance with those rules (see, for example, *Bhatia v Sterlite Industries Ltd* unreported 2204571/2000, in which the award was grossed up in accordance with US tax rates).

Relationship with statutory maximum

In some cases, the grossed-up award will exceed the statutory maximum prescribed by ERA 1996, s 124(5)—currently £68,400.

16.18

An issue has arisen as to whether the tribunal has jurisdiction to award a sum in excess of the statutory maximum where the net amount, after tax, is equal to or less than the statutory maximum. This is a matter that still has to be determined by the EAT.

16.19

It is reported that, in one case—*Barton v Sheffield City Council* (2800284/2000) (ELA Briefing, November 2004)—an employment tribunal grossed up the net award even though the final sum was in excess of the statutory maximum, but gave no reasons for adopting this approach. An argument in favour of this approach is that the statutory maximum only applies after 'a reduction in the amount of the award required by any enactment or rule of law' (ERA 1996, s 124(5)(b)), and that, clearly, after tax had been deducted, the award fell within the employment tribunal's jurisdiction. Alternatively, it has been suggested that it might be open to a claimant to apply to the tribunal for the judgment to be reviewed under r 34(3)(e) of the Employment Tribunals (Constitution and Rules of Procedure) Regulations 2004, SI 2004/1861, once the tax assessment has been made, and that the employment tribunal would be empowered in such circumstances to increase the award to the statutory maximum. This also some support for this view in *Williams v Ferosan Ltd* [2004] IRLR 607 (see **7.93** above).

16.20

F. Interest

16.21 The payment of interest on industrial tribunal awards is governed by the Employment Tribunals (Interest) Order 1990, SI 1990/479, which came into force on 1 April 1990. This provides that interest is payable on any industrial tribunal award that is unpaid 42 days after the judgment is sent to the parties—that is, after the time for appealing against the decision has expired.

16.22 Tribunals are required to notify the parties of the relevant rate of interest (that is, the rate specified by s 17 of the Judgments Act 1838—currently 8 per cent) and the date from which it accrues.

16.23 Interest is not payable on:

(a) sums representing costs and expenses; or

(b) any sum that is payable to the Secretary of State under the Recoupment Regulations (see **16.01** above); or

(c) any sum that is payable to HM Revenue and Customs (HMRC) or the DWP.

16.24 An important point to bear in mind is that interest will accrue after the 42-day period even if there is a review or appeal. So, where an appeal is partly successful, interest will still be payable on the original award as varied (reg 7). However, where the 'relevant decision' is reviewed by the EAT, the relevant decision day is the date on which the order reviewed was promulgated (that is, the date of the EAT's decision) (reg 10). On the other hand, perhaps surprisingly, where the appeal is successful and the case is remitted to the First-tier Tribunal for reassessment of the sum of money payable, the relevant decision day is either the date of the previous decision or the date on which the appellate tribunal promulgated its decision (reg 6). This means that interest will be awarded retrospectively to either the date of the original award or the date on which the appeal decision was promulgated. Unlike discrimination cases, there is no power to vary these periods.

16.25 A power to vary the current rules on the award of interest is to be found in ETA 1996, s 14.

Part III

REDUNDANCY

17

CALCULATING REDUNDANCY PAYMENTS

A. Introduction

The statutory rules relating to the right to a redundancy payment are now set out in **17.01** Pt XI of the Employment Rights Act 1996 (ERA 1996). A detailed account of the law relating to redundancy is outside the scope of this book, but the rules relating to the calculation of a redundancy payment are set out below.

Preconditions for payment

Entitlement to a redundancy payment is subject to the following qualifying **17.02** conditions:

(a) the claimant must be an employee;

(b) the claimant must have been continuously employed for two years or more ending with the relevant date (ERA 1996, s 155); and

(c) the claimant must have been dismissed by reason of redundancy (ERA 1996, ss 136 and 139).

261

Relevant date

17.03 Entitlement to a redundancy payment depends on the period of continuous employment on the 'relevant date'. This is defined in ERA 1996, s 145 as:

(a) the date on which notice expires, where the employee is given notice (ERA 1996, s 145(2)(a));

(b) the date of dismissal, where the employee is summarily dismissed (ERA 1996, s 145(2)(b));

(c) the date on which a fixed-term contract (referred to as a 'limited contract') takes effect by virtue of the limiting event without being renewed (ERA 1996, s 145(2)(c)).

The relevant date is extended by the statutory period of notice in cases in which the employee would have been entitled to such notice pursuant to ERA 1996, s 86 (ERA 1996, s 145(5) and (6)).

17.04 Special statutory rules apply if the employment terminates during a trial period (ERA 1996, s 145(3) and (4)).

Trial periods and other situations of non-dismissal

17.05 In certain circumstances, an employee is deemed by the statutory provisions not to have been dismissed even though a dismissal has taken place.

17.06 In cases of renewal and re-engagement, where an employee's contract is renewed or the employee is re-engaged under a new contract of employment and:

(a) the offer, whether in writing or not, is made before the end of the existing contract; and

(b) it is to take effect either immediately on the ending of the original contract of employment or within a period of not more than four weeks thereafter,

no dismissal will be deemed to have taken place in respect of the termination of the original contract (ERA 1996, s 141(1)).

17.07 Other situations of non-dismissal include cases in which an employee is offered work in the circumstances set out in **17.06** above by an associated company (ERA 1996, s 146(1)). In addition, there will be no dismissal in some circumstances in which an employee volunteers for redundancy (see *Birch v University of Liverpool* [1985] IRLR 165).

Definition of redundancy

17.08 A claim for a redundancy payment will lie only where the employee is 'redundant', as defined by ERA 1996, s 139(1). This provides that a dismissal is by reason of redundancy if it is:

wholly or mainly attributable to:

(a) the fact that his employer has ceased or intends to cease to carry out the business for the purpose of which the employee was employed by him, or has ceased or intends to cease, to carry on that business in the place where the employee was so employed, or

(b) the fact that the requirements of that business for employees to carry out work of a particular kind or for employees to carry out work of a particular kind in the place where he was so employed, have ceased or diminished, or are expected to cease or diminish.

This definition covers the obvious redundancy situations, such as those in which **17.09** the employer is forced to close down the business or reduce the size of the workforce. However, the application of this definition has led to some difficulties where an employer reorganizes the business without wishing to cut down on the workforce. Problems have also arisen in relation to these provisions in cases in which there is a reduction in demand for one type of work that an employee can be required to do, but the employer's demands are unchanged for other types of work that fall within the scope of the contract (see *Nelson v BBC (No 2)* [1979] IRLR 346; *Cowen v Haden Carrier Ltd* [1982] IRLR 225; *Murray v Foyle Meats Ltd* [1999] IRLR 562). (See also *Harvey on Industrial Relations and Employment Law* for a more detailed analysis of these provisions.)

Lay-offs and short-time working

Special provisions apply to lay-offs and short-time working. An employee who is **17.10** laid off—that is, is not entitled to wages due to lack of work—or is put on short time—that is, is entitled to less than half a week's pay for four consecutive weeks, or six or more weeks in a continuous period of 13 weeks (three of that must have been consecutive), because of a shortage of work—may claim a redundancy payment on his or her own initiative without waiting to be dismissed by the employer (ERA 1996, s 148).

In order to claim redundancy in these circumstances, a special statutory procedure **17.11** must be followed: the claim must be made in writing by sending the employer a notice of termination and liability may be contested where the employer believes that normal working is likely to resume within four weeks (ERA 1996, s 149).

Exclusions of the right to a redundancy payment

Some categories of employee are excluded from the right to a redundancy payment. **17.12** These include:

(a) employees over the age of 65 (ERA 1996, s 156);
(b) share fishermen (ERA 1996, s 199(2));
(c) civil servants and public employees (ERA 1996, ss 159 and 191(6));

(d) domestic servants of any close relative (ERA 1996, s 161);

(e) those in overseas government employment (ERA 1996, s 160); and

(f) employees who are covered by an exemption order (ERA 1996, s 157).

Loss of right to redundancy payment

17.13 The right to a redundancy payment may be lost where:

(a) an employee unreasonably refuses an offer of suitable alternative employment (ERA 1996, s 139(6)) either with or without a trial period (ERA 1996, s 141(4)); or

(b) the employee fails to make a claim within the time limit prescribed by the statutory provisions (referred to below).

B. Calculation of a Redundancy Payment

17.14 Broadly speaking, the rules governing the calculation of a redundancy payment are the same as those used to calculate the basic award.

Calculating a redundancy payment

17.15 The amount of a redundancy payment depends on the length of the employee's period of continuous employment, the amount of a week's pay at the calculation date, and the employee's age at the relevant date (ERA 1996, s 162(1)). The payment itself is then worked out by counting backwards from the relevant date to calculate the number of years of employment, allowing (ERA 1996, s 162(2)):

(a) one-and-a-half week's pay for each year of employment in which the employee was not below the age of 41;

(b) one week's pay for each year of employment in which the employee was not below the age of 22;

(c) half a week's pay for each year of employment in which the employee was not within paragraph (a) or (b).

17.16 The maximum number of 'reckonable years' of employment is 20 (ERA 1996, s 162(3)).

17.17 Table 17.1 is a ready reckoner for the calculation of a redundancy payment. It shows the number of weeks' pay to which an employee is entitled in view of his or her age and the number of complete years of service.

Statutory extension of the relevant date

17.18 The statutory definition of relevant date is considered at **17.03** above. That date may be extended in certain circumstances in order to calculate a redundancy payment. Thus, if an employee is dismissed without being given the required period

Table 17.1 Ready reckoner for calculating the number of weeks' pay due

Age (years)	Service (years)																		
	2	3	4	5	6	7	8	9	10	11	12	13	14	15	16	17	18	19	20
18	1	1½	2																
19	1	1½	2	2½															
20	1	1½	2	2½	3														
21	1	1½	2	2½	3	3½													
22	1	1½	2	2½	3	3½	4												
23	1½	2	2½	3	3½	4	4½	5											
24	2	2½	3	3½	4	4½	5	5½	6										
25	2	3	3½	4	4½	5	5½	6	6½	7									
26	2	3	4	4½	5	5½	6	6½	7	7½	8								
27	2	3	4	5	5½	6	6½	7	7½	8	8½	9							
28	2	3	4	5	6	6½	7	7½	8	8½	9	9½	10						
29	2	3	4	5	6	7	7½	8	8½	9	9½	10	10½	11					
30	2	3	4	5	6	7	8	8½	9	9½	10	10½	11	11½	12				
31	2	3	4	5	6	7	8	9	9½	10	10½	11	11½	12	12½	13			
32	2	3	4	5	6	7	8	9	10	10½	11	11½	12	12½	13	13½	14		
33	2	3	4	5	6	7	8	9	10	11	11½	12	12½	13	13½	14	14½	15	
34	2	3	4	5	6	7	8	9	10	11	12	12½	13	13½	14	14½	15	15½	16
35	2	3	4	5	6	7	8	9	10	11	12	13	13½	14	14½	15	15½	16	16½
36	2	3	4	5	6	7	8	9	10	11	12	13	14	14½	15	15½	16	16½	17
37	2	3	4	5	6	7	8	9	10	11	12	13	14	15	15½	16	16½	17	17½
38	2	3	4	5	6	7	8	9	10	11	12	13	14	15	16	16½	17	17½	18

(*Continued*)

Table 17.1 (*Continued*)

Age (years)	\ Service (years)																		
	2	3	4	5	6	7	8	9	10	11	12	13	14	15	16	17	18	19	20
39	2	3	4	5	6	7	8	9	10	11	12	13	14	15	16	17	17½	18	18½
40	2	3	4	5	6	7	8	9	10	11	12	13	14	15	16	17	18	18½	19
41	2	3	4	5	6	7	8	9	10	11	12	13	14	15	16	17	18	19	19½
42	2½	3½	4½	5½	6½	7½	8½	9½	10½	11½	12½	13½	14½	15½	16½	17½	18½	19½	20½
43	3	4	5	6	7	8	9	10	11	12	13	14	15	16	17	18	19	20	21
44	3	4½	5½	6½	7½	8½	9½	10½	11½	12½	13½	14½	15½	16½	17½	18½	19½	20½	21½
45	3	4½	6	7	8	9	10	11	12	13	14	15	16	17	18	19	20	21	22
46	3	4½	6	7½	8½	9½	10½	11½	12½	13½	14½	15½	16½	17½	18½	19½	20½	21½	22½
47	3	4½	6	7½	9	10	11	12	13	14	15	16	17	18	19	20	21	22	23
48	3	4½	6	7½	9	10½	11½	12½	13½	14½	15½	16½	17½	18½	19½	20½	21½	22½	23½
49	3	4½	6	7½	9	10½	12	13	14	15	16	17	18	19	20	21	22	23	24
50	3	4½	6	7½	9	10½	12	13½	14½	15½	16½	17½	18½	19½	20½	21½	22½	23½	24½
51	3	4½	6	7½	9	10½	12	13½	15	16	17	18	19	20	21	22	23	24	25
52	3	4½	6	7½	9	10½	12	13½	15	16½	17½	18½	19½	20½	21½	22½	23½	24½	25½
53	3	4½	6	7½	9	10½	12	13½	15	16½	18	19	20	21	22	23	24	25	26
54	3	4½	6	7½	9	10½	12	13½	15	16½	18	19½	20½	21½	22½	23½	24½	25½	26½
55	3	4½	6	7½	9	10½	12	13½	15	16½	18	19½	21	22	23	24	25	26	27
56	3	4½	6	7½	9	10½	12	13½	15	16½	18	19½	21	22½	23½	24½	25½	26½	27½
57	3	4½	6	7½	9	10½	12	13½	15	16½	18	19½	21	22½	24	25	26	27	28
58	3	4½	6	7½	9	10½	12	13½	15	16½	18	19½	21	22½	24	25½	26½	27½	28½
59	3	4½	6	7½	9	10½	12	13½	15	16½	18	19½	21	22½	24	25½	27	28	29
60	3	4½	6	7½	9	10½	12	13½	15	16½	18	19½	21	22½	24	25½	27	28½	29½
61*	3	4½	6	7½	9	10½	12	13½	15	16½	18	19½	21	22½	24	25½	27	28½	30

* The same figures should be used when calculating the redundancy payment for a person aged 61 and above.

of statutory notice, the 'relevant date' is that date on which that notice would have expired (ERA 1996, s 145(2)(a) and (5)).

Where the contractual notice exceeds the employee's statutory entitlement, the **17.19** relevant date is the date on which the notice expires (ERA 1996, s 145(2)(a)).

Finally, where the contract is for a fixed term (what the statutory provisions refer to **17.20** as a 'limited-term contract'), the relevant date is the date on which the term expires without being renewed under the same contract (ERA 1996, s 145(2)(c)).

Upper age limit

The upper age limit for a redundancy was removed by the Employment Equality **17.21** (Age) Regulations 2006, SI 2006/103 (see **4.09** and **4.10**), as were the previous provisions that required the payment to be scaled down by 1/12th for each whole month between the relevant date and the 64th birthday (ERA 1996, s 162(4),(5)), but the payment is still subject to a cap of 20 years' reckonable employment (ERA 1996, s 162(3)).

A week's pay

The rules governing the statutory calculation of a week's pay are considered in **17.22** Chapter 5. The following is a summary of the main points.

(a) For most employees, a week's pay is the amount that they earn in the course of their normal hours.

(b) Normal working hours are the minimum number of hours for which employees may be required to work under their contract of employment. Thus overtime hours are not included in an employee's normal working hours unless overtime is guaranteed by the employer (*Brownson v Hire Shops Ltd* [1978] IRLR 73).

(c) Not all payments received by employees in their pay packet count. Most 'contractual payments' are included in the calculation of a week's pay. For example, wages, salary, shift bonuses, and productivity bonuses are all included. Other regular payments may also count (see *A & B Marcusfield Ltd v Melhuish* [1977] IRLR 484), but tips and some other discretionary payments or *ex gratia* payments do not count.

(d) Benefits in kind, such as the provision of a company car, do not form part of a week's pay.

(e) A week's pay is based on an employee's gross earnings—that is, earnings before tax.

(f) The amount of pay that qualifies as a week's pay is subject to a statutory ceiling fixed by the Secretary of State and is varied annually in line with the increase in the retail price index. The new rate takes effect from 1 February (ERA 1996, s 227(1)(c)). The current maximum is £400 (Employment Rights (Increase of Limits) Order 2010 SI 2010 No 2926).

Statutory maximum

17.23   The statutory maximum is fixed at 30 weeks' pay. The current statutory maximum is therefore £8,400. Those who are aged between 61 and 64, and have worked for the same (or an associated) employer for more than 20 years, qualify for the statutory maximum.

The calculation date

17.24   The calculation date for redundancy dismissals is either (ERA 1996, s 225(5)):

(a) the date x weeks before the date on which the employment ends, where x is the minimum period of notice required by ERA 1996, s 86(1); or

(b) the date on which the employment ended if the employee was dismissed with no notice, or with less notice than required by ERA 1996, s 86(1).

Dismissal with minimum period of notice required by statute

17.25   An employee with five years' service is dismissed with the statutory minimum period of notice—that is, five weeks. The calculation date is five weeks before the last day of employment.

Summary dismissal

17.26   An employee with five years' service is summarily dismissed. The 'calculation date' is the last day of employment.

Dismissal with less than the statutory minimum period of notice

17.27   An employee with five years' service is dismissed and given three weeks' notice. The calculation date is the date on which notice expires.

C.   Reducing Redundancy Payments

17.28   Apart from the scaling-down provisions (considered above), redundancy payments may be reduced where:

(a) an employee commits an act of misconduct during the notice period;

(b) an employee leaves work before the redundancy notice period has expired without the employer's consent; or

(c) an employee fails to comply with a notice of extension served by the employer after taking part in a strike in the obligatory period.

Misconduct

17.29   The general rule is that employees who are dismissed for misconduct are not entitled to a redundancy payment at all (ERA 1996, s 140(1)). However, in certain circumstances, the employment tribunal is given a discretion to award a proportion of the redundancy payment if it considers this to be just and equitable (ERA 1996, s 140(3)). These provisions do not apply where the employee is dismissed for taking part in a strike.

Entitlement excluded

There will be no entitlement to a redundancy payment where an employer is **17.30** entitled to dismiss the employee by reason of the employee's conduct and the employer terminates the contract:

(a) without notice; or
(b) by giving shorter notice than that required by either the contract or by the statutory provisions; or
(c) by giving the full entitlement to notice accompanied by a statement in writing to the effect that, by reason of the employee's conduct, the employer would have been entitled to terminate the contract without notice (ERA 1996, s 140(1)).

This covers the normal situation in which the employer dismisses for misconduct **17.31** and/or redundancy. It would also apply to a case in which the employee was found to have been guilty of misconduct before being given notice, although this was unknown to the employer at the time that the notice was given, because the ERA 1996 preserves the common law rule that an employer is entitled to rely on misconduct, which is unknown at the time of dismissal, which would have merited dismissal (see *Boston Deep Sea Fishing and Ice Co v Ansell* (1888) 39 Ch D 339). The test for determining whether the employee is guilty of the alleged misconduct is an objective one. It is not sufficient for the employer to show a reasonable belief in the employee's guilt (*Bonner v H Gilbert & Co* [1989] IRLR 475).

Entitlement reduced at the tribunal's discretion

Special provisions apply where the employee, having been given notice of redun- **17.32** dancy, commits an act of misconduct during the notice period that would entitle the employer to terminate the contract without notice. In such circumstances, if the employer does nothing, the employee's entitlement to the full redundancy payment is preserved. However, if the employer dismisses the employee immediately, or shortens the notice period, or allows the employee to continue to work out the notice period as before, but serves a notice in writing to the effect that the employer would have been entitled to terminate without notice, the tribunal is given a discretion to reduce the redundancy payment in such a way as it considers just and equitable in the circumstances (ERA 1996, s 140(3)).

Examples of operation of the statutory provisions

In *Simmons v Hoover* [1976] IRLR 266, the EAT gave the following examples of the **17.33** operation of this provision. In each example, it is assumed that the contract may be terminated by giving the employee three months' notice.

(a) An employee is given two months' redundancy notice when it was known or subsequently discovered that he had stolen from the employers. Redundancy payment is lost under ERA 1996, s 140 for the reason given above and is not saved by s 140(3) because there is only one dismissal.

(b) An employee is given three months' notice, but is dismissed without notice one month later after he is discovered to have been stealing from the employers. Redundancy payment is not lost, but may be reduced in whole or in part as the tribunal thinks fit (ERA 1996, s 140(3)).

(c) An employee is given six months' notice. During the last three months, the employee is caught stealing and is dismissed immediately. The dismissal is still covered by ERA 1996, s 140(3), and the tribunal may award such proportion of the redundancy as it considers just and equitable.

Guidelines on the exercise of the statutory discretion

17.34   In cases in which ERA 1996, s 140(3) applies, it is for the tribunal to determine the proportion of the payment due to the employee. Although there have not been many reported cases involving these provisions, it is likely that the following factors would influence employment tribunals in their judgments:

(a) the gravity of the misconduct;

(b) the employee's length of service; and

(c) other penalties imposed on the employee, such as the loss of notice pay and other benefits.

17.35   In common with other areas in which the tribunal is given discretion of this nature, the EAT will not overrule the tribunal unless it has erred in law or reached a decision to which no reasonable tribunal could have come. For example, in *Lignacite Products Ltd v Krollman* [1979] IRLR 22, Mr Krollman was summarily dismissed for stealing shortly before the end of his redundancy notice period. The employment tribunal awarded 60 per cent of his redundancy pay. On appeal, the EAT said that it was surprised that the tribunal had not reduced the award by more, but refused to interfere on the ground that the reduction lay within the tribunal's discretion.

Early leavers

17.36   The statutory provisions lay down a strict procedure that has to be followed by employees who wish to leave their job before their notice period has ended. Failure to follow this procedure may result in the employee's redundancy payment being reduced or lost altogether.

17.37   The statutory procedure is as follows: once the employer has given the employee notice, the employee may give a written notice of an intention to leave before the expiry of the employer's notice. However, this notice must be given within 'the obligatory notice period'—that is, the minimum period of notice that an employer is required to give the employee by law (ERA 1996, s 86(1)), and must indicate when the employee intends to leave (ERA 1996, ss 136(3) and 142).

Faced with such a notice, the employer may either agree to the employee's request, **17.38** in which case the employee is entitled to the full amount of the redundancy payment, or serve on the employee a counter-notice requiring the employee to withdraw his or her notice of termination and to continue in the employment until the employer's notice expires. In addition, the counter-notice must state that, if the employee fails to comply with the request, the employer will contest liability to pay the redundancy payment (ERA 1996, s 142(2)).

If the employee still leaves, the matter will have to be determined by the employ- **17.39** ment tribunal, which, having regard to the reasons why the employee wishes to leave early and the reason why the employer wants the employee to stay, must decide whether it is just and equitable for the employee to receive a redundancy payment and, if so, how much (ERA 1996, s 142(3)).

Where the employee's contractual notice is longer than the statutory minimum, the **17.40** statutory procedure does not commence until the start of the period equivalent to the statutory notice period. Thus an employee, who is given eight weeks' notice having worked for the employer for four years, will be entitled only to serve his or her notice of intention at the start of the last four weeks of the eight-week period. In some cases, the EAT has overcome this technical difficulty by finding a mutually agreed variation in the date of expiry of the employer's notice (see *Tunnel Holdings Ltd v Woolf* [1976] IRLR 387), but the provisions still pose a potential trap for the unwary employee.

Strike dismissals

The provisions in ERA 1996, s 140(1) do not apply where the employee takes part **17.41** in a strike during the notice period. In such circumstances, the right to a redundancy payment is preserved by s 140(2) provided that the dismissal occurs during the obligatory period. It would appear that, where the dismissal occurs during the contractual notice period, the right to a redundancy payment is lost, although the point remains open to further argument.

However, where a strike takes place during the notice period, the redundancy **17.42** payment may be reduced in whole or in part if the employee fails to comply with a notice of extension served by the employer in the form prescribed by statute (ERA 1996, s 143).

Notice of extension

A notice of extension is a notice in writing that requests the employee to extend the **17.43** contract of employment beyond the time of expiry by a period comprising the days lost as a result of a strike (referred to as the 'period of extension'). The notice must refer to the reason why the employer is making the request and must state that the employer will contest liability to make the redundancy payment unless the employee either complies with the request, or the employer is satisfied that the employee is unable to comply as a result of sickness or injury, or that it is reasonable for the employee not to comply for some other reason. An employee complies with the provision either by agreeing to the request or by being available for work within the proposed period of extension (ERA 1996, s 143(2)). It is also open to an employer to agree with the employee to make the redundancy payment even though the employee has failed to comply with the notice (ERA 1996, s 143(3)). However, in the absence of agreement, if the employee fails to comply, the employee is not entitled to a redundancy payment unless the employment tribunal considers that it was reasonable for the employee not to comply (ERA 1996, s 143(5)) and orders the employer to pay an 'appropriate payment', as determined by ERA 1996, s 143(6). An appropriate payment is either the whole of the payment to which the employee would have been entitled or such amount of that payment as the tribunal considers fit.

17.44 These provisions only apply if the employee takes part in a strike after he or she has been given his or her redundancy notice. In cases in which the workers are on strike before the redundancy notice is issued, the employer will normally be entitled to terminate their employment summarily as a result of the strike itself, with the result that they will be disqualified from redundancy pay (see *Simmons v Hoover* [1976] IRLR 266).

D. Tax Liability

17.45 A statutory redundancy payment is exempt from income tax by IT(EP)A 2003, s 309(1), as is an approved contractual payment that is less than £30,000. An approved contractual payment is defined under s 309(5) as 'a payment to a person on the termination of the person's employment under an agreement in respect of which an order is in force under section 157 of the ERA 1996 or Article 192 of ER(NI)O 1996 [the Employment Rights (Northern Ireland) Order 1996, SI 1996/1919]'. Any payment over the £30,000 threshold is taxable under IT(EP)A 2003, s 403. Payment for this purpose includes the aggregate of all payments made on termination in respect of the same employment (IT(EP)A 2003, s 404(1)).

E. Claiming a Redundancy Payment

17.46 An employment tribunal has exclusive jurisdiction to determine any question arising out of the statutory provisions as to the right of an employee to a redundancy payment or the amount of such a payment (ERA 1996, s 163(1)).

Entitlement to a redundancy payment will be lost unless one of the following occurs **17.47** before the end of the period of six months beginning with the relevant date:

(a) the payment is agreed and paid (ERA 1996, s 164(1)(a));
(b) the employee has made a written claim for a redundancy payment to the employer (ERA 1996, s 164(1)(b))
(c) the question has been referred to an employment tribunal (ERA 1996, s 164(1)(c)); or
(d) the employee has presented a complaint of unfair dismissal to an employment tribunal (ERA 1996, s 164(1)(d)).

The 'relevant date' is usually the date on which the employment ends. For example, **17.48** if an employee exercises the right to leave the job before the notice has expired in accordance with ERA 1996, s 136, the relevant date is the date on which the employee leaves the job. The same applies if the employee leaves the job during the trial period—that is, the relevant date is not postponed as it is for some other purposes.

Failure to make a claim for a redundancy payment within six months (or the **17.49** extended period) is not fatal, beccause the tribunal has discretion to allow claims to be made within a year of the relevant date if the employee has:

(a) made a written request for a redundancy payment to the employer; or
(b) referred the question to an employment tribunal; or
(c) made a complaint of unfair dismissal,

and the employment tribunal considers it just and equitable that the employee should receive a redundancy payment having regard to the reason for not taking action in the first six months and to all other relevant circumstances.

PART IV

COMPENSATION IN DISCRIMINATION CASES

18

COMPENSATION IN DISCRIMINATION CASES: GENERAL PRINCIPLES

A. Introduction

Introduction

This part examines the rules and principles governing compensation under all **18.01** strands of unlawful discrimination. It also considers the difficult area of the interrelationship with unfair dismissal compensation under the Employment Rights Act 1996 (ERA 1996), s 123.

According to the latest Equal Opportunities Review (EOR) annual survey of compensation awards (No 201, June 2010), compensation totalling over £8m with **18.02** interest was awarded by employment tribunals in 375 discrimination cases in 2009. A quarter of that amount was for injury to feelings (including aggravated damages).

18.03 The survey of 2009 awards made three key findings, as follows.

(a) The overall average award for total compensation in 2009 is the highest yet recorded, at £20,910. The median total award has decreased to its 2007 level, at £7,806.

(b) There were a record number of awards over £100,000 in 2009, with 14 such awards across all jurisdictions—double the 2008 level and more than three times the 2007 level.

(c) The average and median awards for injury to feelings (including aggravated damages) have both decreased compared to 2008, with two-thirds of 2009 awards falling within the low band of *Vento v Chief Constable of West Yorkshire Police* (*No 2*) [2003] ICR 318; [2003] IRLR 102, CA.

The statutory torts

18.04 Compensation for discrimination was originally recoverable under the following legislation:

(a) the Equal Pay Act 1970 (EqPA 1970);

(b) the Sex Discrimination Act 1975 (SDA 1975);

(c) the Race Relations Act 1976 (RRA 1976);

(d) the Disability Discrimination Act 1995 (DDA 1995);

(e) the Part-time Workers (Prevention of Less Favourable Treatment) Regulations 2000, SI 2000/1551 (PTWR 2000) as from 1 July 2000;

(f) the Fixed-term Employees (Prevention of Less Favourable Treatment) Regulations 2002, SI 2002/2034 (FTER 2002) as from 1 October 2002;

(g) the Employment Equality (Sexual Orientation) Regulations 2003, SI 2003/1661 (SOR 2003) as from 1 December 2003;

(h) the Employment Equality (Religion or Belief) Regulations 2003, SI 2003/1660 (RBR 2003) as from 2 December 2003; and

(i) the Employment Equality (Age) Regulations 2006, SI 2006/1031 (EEAR 2006), as from 1 October 2006.

18.05 The many and disparate pieces of anti-discrimination legislation have now (with the exception of the PTWR 2000 and the FTER 2002) largely been repealed and consolidated in the more accessible and coherent form that is the Equality Act 2010 (EqA 2010), most of which will be in force from 1 October 2010.

18.06 The EqA 2010 therefore covers the nine protected characteristics of age, disability, gender reassignment, marriage and civil partnership, pregnancy and maternity, race, religion or belief, sex, and sexual orientation (EqA 2010, s 4).

18.07 Conduct that is prohibited in respect of the protected characteristics is governed by EqA 2010, Pt 2, ch 2. In general, there are five principal ways in which a person may discriminate against another:

(a) direct discrimination (s 13);

(b) dual direct discrimination (s 14—in force from 1 April 2011);

(c) indirect discrimination (s 19);

(d) harassment (s 26); and

(e) victimization (s 27).

Enforcement

Under EqA 2010, s 120, an employment tribunal has jurisdiction to determine a **18.08** complaint relating to a contravention of Pt 5 (work) and a contravention of ss 108 (relationship that has come to an end), 111 (instructing, causing, and inducing contraventions), or 112 (aiding contraventions) that relates to Pt 5. Enforcement in armed forces cases is made subject to the provisions of s 121. An employment tribunal also has jurisdiction to determine various applications and questions relating to occupational pension schemes (EqA 2010, s 120(2)–(5)).

Consistency in interpretation between protected characteristics

Discrimination cases such as *Vento v Chief Constable of West Yorkshire Police (No 2)* **18.09** [2003] ICR 318, [2003] IRLR 102, CA, and *Rhys-Harper v Relaxion Group plc; D'Souza v London Borough of Lambeth; Jones v 3M Healthcare Ltd* [2003] IRLR 484, HL, make it clear that there should be no significant distinction in relation to compensation awarded in respect of different protected characteristics. With effect from 2006, the implementation of the Employment Directive (2000/78/EC) has required common standards in relation to outlawing discrimination on the grounds of sexual orientation, religion or belief, disability, and age. The consolidating effect of the EqA 2010 should largely help to achieve this.

It is clear, however, that different principles will continue to apply to the recovery **18.10** of compensation in cases of equal pay, part-time workers, and fixed-term employees. These discrimination claims are dealt with separately below.

B. General Principles

'Just and equitable' discretion to award any remedy

Where an employment tribunal finds that a complaint of unlawful discrimination **18.11** presented to it is well founded, it may, if it considers it just and equitable to do so, make one or more of the following orders (EqA 2010, s 124(2)):

(a) make a declaration as to the rights of the claimant and the respondent in rela-
    tion to the matters to which the proceedings relate;

(b) order the respondent to pay compensation to the claimant; or

(c) make an appropriate recommendation.

It should not be assumed that, if unlawful discrimination is established, a remedy **18.12** will be automatically awarded. Although the discriminator's motives and intentions are irrelevant to the issue of liability for unlawful discrimination, nevertheless, those considerations might be relevant to the issue of remedy, and it is for the tribunal to decide, having regard to all of the circumstances of the case, whether it is just and equitable to award any of the available remedies to the claimant (*obiter, per* Mummery J in *O'Neill v Governors of St Thomas More Roman Catholic Voluntarily Aided Upper School* [1997] ICR 33, 43, EAT).

18.13 In *Chief Constable of Manchester v Hope* [1999] ICR 338, EAT, the claimant, a police sergeant, had been charged with allegations that, as a consequence of forming a brief sexual relationship with a 17-year-old female civilian trainee, he may have compromised his authority as a serving police officer. During a police disciplinary interview into these allegations, a chief inspector put to the claimant that the position was more serious because he was white and the community of Asian origin to which the girl belonged would not approve of a white sergeant forming a relationship with an Asian girl from its community. At the time of this interview, there were four other separate allegations of sexual and racial misconduct towards young policewomen outstanding against the claimant. The tribunal upheld the complaint and awarded compensation of £750 for injury to feelings. Allowing the appeal, a majority of the Employment Appeal Tribunal (EAT) comprising the two lay members (Judge Peter Clark dissenting) held that the tribunal had misdirected itself in law by ruling out, as a matter of principle, the option not to make any award of compensation, or, alternatively, had reached a perverse decision in awarding compensation, and that the proper course was to exercise the powers of the tribunal and to hold, on the facts found, that it was not just and equitable to make an award of compensation. The majority considered that, whilst justification (that is, the community reaction) for the line of questioning cannot be a defence to a claim of direct discrimination, it may be considered relevant to the issue of remedies for that discrimination and that, in the absence of an intention to discriminate, the tribunal should have made a nil award of compensation. In the light of Judge Peter Clark's dissenting judgment, the majority decision may be open to doubt.

Tortious measure of damages

18.14 Once a tribunal has decided that it is 'just and equitable' to make an order for compensation, the amount of compensation must correspond to 'the amount which could be awarded by a county court or the sheriff under section 119' (EqA 2010, s 124(6). Under EqA 2010, s 119, 'the county court has power to grant any remedy which could be granted by the High Court—(a) in proceedings in tort . . .', which would include damages for breach of the statutory tort of discrimination.

18.15 The amount is not to be assessed on the basis of what the tribunal considers to be just and equitable in the particular circumstances of the case (*Hurley v Mustoe (No 2)* [1983] ICR 422, EAT). This means that, unlike the calculation of a compensatory award in unfair dismissal cases under ERA 1996, s 123(1), in discrimination cases, there is no discretion to decide what amount is 'just and equitable'.

Instead, the general principle in assessing compensation is that, as far as possible, **18.16** claimants should be put in the same position in which they would have been but for the unlawful act (*Ministry of Defence v Wheeler* [1998] IRLR 23, CA).

Compensation must be adequate and full

Tribunals must keep in mind the *dicta* in *Marshall v Southampton and South-West* **18.17** *Hampshire Area Health Authority* (*No 2*) C–281/91 [1993] ICR 893, [1993] IRLR 445, ECJ, that financial compensation must be adequate, in the sense of allowing the loss and damage actually sustained as a result of the discrimination to be made good in full in accordance with the applicable national rules.

Following the decision of the European Court of Justice (ECJ) in *Marshall* (*No 2*), **18.18** the statutory cap on compensatory awards in sex discrimination cases was removed by the Sex Discrimination and Equal Pay (Remedies) Regulations 1993, SI 1993/2798, from 22 November 1993. These Regulations had retrospective effect (*Harvey v The Institute of the Motor Industry* (*No 2*) [1995] IRLR 416). The Regulations have since been replaced by the Employment Tribunals (Interest on Awards in Discrimination Cases) Regulations 1996, SI 1996/2803.

From 3 July 1994, the statutory limit on compensation was removed in race discrimi- **18.19** nation cases by virtue of the Race Relations (Remedies) Act 1994.

For all other kinds of unlawful discrimination, there has never been a statutory cap. **18.20**

Causation and remoteness of damage

The discriminator must take his or her victim as he or she finds him or her (the **18.21** 'eggshell skull' principle). This means that a discriminator runs the risk that his or her victim may be very much affected by an act of discrimination, for example, by reason of the victim's character and psychological temperament.

The tortious measure of loss is subject to the important qualification that (contrary **18.22** to the normal rule on remoteness of damage in tort) the damage does not need to be of a type that was reasonably foreseeable; it is enough that the damage was caused by the unlawful act of discrimination (*Essa v Laing Ltd* [2004] ICR 746; [2004] IRLR 313, CA). In this regard, the majority view in *Essa* (Pill and Clarke LJJ) preferred the *obiter dictum* in *Sheriff v Klyne Tugs Ltd* (*Lowestoft*) [1999] ICR 1170; [1999] IRLR 481, CA to the *obiter* comments in *Coleman v Skyrail Oceanic Ltd* [1981] IRLR 398, CA. The Court of Appeal was, however, careful to limit its findings by reference to the particular facts of the case, which concerned psychological injury resulting from direct and intentional racial abuse. It would appear to be open to a tribunal to find that, in an appropriate case involving a more subtle form of discrimination causing serious personal injury, it would be necessary for the claimant to show that the type of damage suffered was a reasonably foreseeable consequence of the unlawful act.

18.23 The loss must be attributable to the specific acts that have been held by the tribunal to constitute unlawful discrimination, and not to other discriminatory acts that have not been properly presented in the claim form, or which were relied upon by the claimant as merely background to specific substantive complaints, or which were not found to have been unlawful. This is so even if the tribunal finds that such discriminatory acts occurred and, in fact, caused the loss. Such findings should not be used to increase awards for minor substantiated claims giving rise to a small award. For example, in *Thaine v London School of Economics* UKEAT/0144/10/SM, [2010] All ER (D) 105 (Sep), Keith J held, at [17], that the test for causation when more than one event caused the harm was to ask:

(1) Did the conduct for which an employer was liable materially contribute to the harm?

(2) If so, to what extent should liability for that harm fairly be attributd to the respondent?

It might be difficult to quantify the extent of the contribution, but the tribunal would be required to undertake that task. On the facts, the tribunal had found that the employer had materially contributed to the harm. It also found that the unlawful discrimination to which she was subjected at work was 40 per cent responsible for her ill health. The tribunal found that a number of other factors had contributed to her ill health, including, inter alia, her obsessive–compulsive disorder, depression, the break-up of her relationship with her boyfriend, and concern over her mother's health. The tribunal had been correct to reduce the award by 60 per cent (see [23] of the judgment).

18.24 Interestingly, in *Alexander v Home Office* [1988] ICR 685; [1988] IRLR 190, CA, the Court of Appeal in giving guidance on the assessment of the compensatory award, amongst other things, observed (at 695E) that the amount of the award may be affected by the conduct of both the respondent and the claimant; bad behaviour by a claimant may thus have an effect similar to that of contributory negligence in a negligence action.

18.25 In *Way and another v Crouch* [2005] IRLR 603, [11], EAT, HHJ Birtles held that, as a matter of law, an award of compensation in a sex discrimination case (and by analogy in other discrimination claims) is subject to the Law Reform (Contributory Negligence) Act 1945, which allows for reduction in compensation in tortious claims where the claimant's conduct itself amounts to negligence or breach of a legal duty and contributed to the damage.

18.26 Notably, the 1945 Act is restricted to where there is 'negligence or breach of a legal duty' by the claimant. Arguably, whilst there is no express statutory duty placed on employees not to discriminate, employees are liable for knowingly aiding the vicariously liable breaches of the employer's duty not to discriminate.

Awards against individual respondents

18.27 Where discriminators have been named as individual respondents, it is open to the tribunal to make an order for compensation against them also (*Gbaja-Biamila v DHL International (UK) Ltd* [2000] ICR 730, EAT).

18.28 By way of example, in *Armitage, Marsden and HM Prison Service v Johnson* [1997] ICR 275, [1997] IRLR 162, EAT two fellow respondent employees were ordered to pay £500. And in *HM Prison Service v Salmon* [2001] IRLR 425, EAT, £1,000 was ordered to be paid by the discriminating officer.

Joint and several liability between separately named respondents

18.29 Does the tribunal have power to apportion compensation between named respondents? There is no express provision in the anti-discrimination statutes nor in the tribunal rules providing for such a discretion. In *Armitage, Marsden and HM Prison Service v Johnson* [1997] ICR 275, [1997] IRLR 162, EAT, Smith J stated that whether or not to make a separate award of compensation against individual employees named as respondents is for the discretion of the tribunal. It was also said that *Deane v London Borough of Ealing* [1993] IRLR 209 was not authority for the general proposition that, wherever it is possible to order the employer to pay by finding him or her vicariously liable for the employee's act, that should be done.

18.30 In *Way and another v Crouch* [2005] IRLR 603, EAT, the tribunal made a sex discrimination award against both the claimant's former employer and its managing director after she was dismissed because she refused to carry on a personal relationship with the managing director. Rather than apportion liability as between the company and its employee, the tribunal made a joint and several award that was 100 per cent against each co-respondent. That would have allowed the claimant to enforce the award against either or both respondents, allowing recovery against the individual discriminator if the employer were to become insolvent. The EAT held (at [23]) that this was permissible in principle, even though it will usually be unnecessary in practice. It is not open to the tribunal to make a joint and several award of compensation because of the relative financial resources of the respondent. Indeed, in applying this aspect of the decision in *Way*, the EAT held, in *Rooproy v Rollins Elliott and another* [2005] All ER (D) 27 (Jul), EAT, that a tribunal was wrong to award compensation against a limited company that had no legal existence at the time of making a joint and several liability award against an individual respondent and the company. The EAT held that the tribunal had power to apportion an award. It was wrong to make the award joint and several because one of the respondents was insolvent. Financial ability to pay is an irrelevant consideration in such awards. However, the EAT in *Way* also held that, having regard to s 2(1) of the Civil Liability (Contribution) Act 1978, such an award must have regard to the relative responsibility of each wrongdoer for the unlawful act. The EAT in *Munchkins Restaurant Ltd v Karmazyn and ors* UKEAT/0359/09/LA, [2010] All ER (D) 76 (Jun), *per* Langstaff J at [32]–[34], had 'very considerable doubts' about this part of the decision in *Way*. Langstaff J held, at [33]:

> where there is an award of joint and several liability the Respondents or any one of them is liable for the full extent of the damages to the Claimant. As between the Respondents a Respondent may have a right to seek contribution from a co-Respondent, depending upon the relative contribution and responsibility of each of the Respondents to the wrong which has been done, but we do not see how that affects the position of the Claimant, who is entitled, if the award is joint and several, to receive the full extent of his award from any such of the Respondents as he chooses.

It follows that the assessment of the percentage of liability between co-respondents may be a factor when deciding whether to make an award jointly and severally, but it should not impact on the enforceability of such an award once it is made.

18.31 Ordinarily, each employee is deemed to have aided the employer to do what he himself or she herself did, and so to be personally liable for it, but he or she is not deemed to have aided the employer to do what fellow employees did. However, an individual manager can be jointly and severally liable to pay compensation not only for acts of discrimination and harassment that he himself or she herself commits, but also for 'aiding' acts of discrimination carried out by his or her fellow employees, in circumstances in which he or she consciously encouraged the others to discriminate (*Gilbank v Miles* [2006] EWCA Civ 543, [2006] IRLR 538, CA, in which G, a salon manager, knowingly fostered and encouraged a sustained campaign of bullying and discrimination by her other staff against M, a pregnant employee).

Dismissals that are both discriminatory and unfair

18.32 Where a dismissal is both unlawful discrimination and unfair, ERA 1996, s 126 prevents double recovery of any head of loss that has already been taken into account in awarding compensation under other Acts or regulations.

18.33 Where the claim is for a discriminatory unfair dismissal, tribunals should order compensation under the discrimination legislation (rather than the unfair dismissal provisions of the ERA 1996, s 123) in order to give the employee full compensation (*D'Souza v London Borough of Lambeth* [1997] IRLR 677, EAT). This is important not only because there is no upper limit on compensation, but also because there is no general power to decide the amount of an award on the basis of what is 'just and equitable', and because the recoupment provisions do not apply where the award is made under the anti-discrimination statutes. However, the advantage of the unfair dismissal provisions is that they allow the tribunal to order that the respondent reinstate or re-engage the claimant, and that if the respondent fails to comply with such a re-employment order, then an additional award can be made.

18.34 Importantly, there is a potential pitfall here for practitioners to avoid. If, at the first remedies hearing, a tribunal orders re-employment and compensation for injury to feelings, there is a real risk that it will be taken to have made a final order on compensation for discrimination, such that it would be unable to make any further award for discrimination if the respondent were not to comply with the re-employment order, as occurred in *London Borough of Lambeth v D'Souza* [1999] IRLR 240, CA. This is because a re-employment order is a provisional order in respect of remedy for unfair dismissal and not discrimination. Practitioners who wish to keep alive the possibility of seeking further discrimination compensation should seek to ensure that the tribunal's award for discrimination made at the same time as a reinstatement order is itself expressed as provisional or conditional and not as a final order on the matter.

If the dismissal is discriminatory but fair, the claimant will be able to recover only **18.35** an injury to feelings award (*Lisk-Carew v Birmingham City Council* [2004] EWCA Civ 565, [2004] All ER (D) 215 (Apr), CA).

For the effect on future loss of earnings where there is an unlawful discriminatory **18.36** act followed by a subsequent fair dismissal, see *O'Donoghue v Redcar and Cleveland Borough Council* [2001] IRLR 615, CA; *Chagger v Abbey National plc* [2009] EWCA Civ 1202, [2010] IRLR 47 CA (see **19.58**); for subsequent unfair dismissal, see *HM Prison Service v Beart* (*No 2*) [2005] EWCA Civ 467, [2005 ICR 1206, CA (see **19.59–19.60**).

C. Compensation for Indirect Discrimination

Because of the impact of the EqA 2010 on this aspect of compensation (see below), **18.37** it will be helpful to set out the pre-existing position.

Unintentional indirect sex discrimination

Since 25 March 1996, tribunals have had the power to award compensation for **18.38** unintentional indirect discrimination in cases of sex discrimination and equal pay (see SDA 1975, s 65(1A) and (1B), inserted by the Sex Discrimination and Equal Pay (Miscellaneous Amendments) Regulations 1996, SI 1996/438).

In so far as a claim of indirect discrimination that was made under the SDA 1975, **18.39** s 1(1)(b) was concerned (that is, condition or requirement cases), an award of compensation for indirect discrimination could be made either where the indirect discrimination was intentional (SDA 1975, s 66(3)) or where it would not have been just and equitable merely to make a declaration and/or a recommendation (SDA 1975, s 65(1A)).

It should be noted that there is a conflict of case law as to whether or not indirect **18.40** discrimination can be intentional (see *Enderby v Frenchay Health Authority and Secretary of State for Health* [1991] IRLR 44, in which this was rejected, and *London Underground Ltd v Edwards* [1995] IRLR 355, in which it was accepted). For the meaning of 'intention' for this purpose, see *JH Walker Ltd v Hussain* [1996] IRLR 11, considered at **18.45**.

18.41 Where a complaint was made under the SDA 1975, s1(2)(b), an order for compensation could be made where the 'provision, criterion or practice' in question was not applied with the intention of treating the claimant unfavourably on the ground of sex or marital status, but only if the tribunal would have made the same declaration and/or recommendation if it had no power to order compensation and, having made such a declaration and/or recommendation, it considered it just and equitable to order the respondent to pay the claimant damages (SDA 1975, s 65(1B)). There have been no reported cases on this provision.

Unintentional indirect sexual orientation, and religion or belief, discrimination

18.42 There were provisions similar to the above in cases of unintentional indirect sexual orientation or religion or belief discrimination (SOR 2003, reg 30(2); RBR 2003, reg 30(2)).

Unintentional indirect race discrimination

18.43 As far as race discrimination cases were concerned, the RRA 1976, s 57(3) provided that compensation may not be awarded in cases of indirect discrimination unless it was shown that a discriminatory requirement or condition was applied with the intention of treating the claimant less favourably on racial grounds.

18.44 Where such an intention is established, the award could include compensation for injury to feelings (see also *Orphanos v Queen Mary's College* [1985] AC 761, [1985] IRLR 349, HL).

18.45 However, such an intention might have been inferred where it was established that the employer deliberately took steps or applied requirements knowing the discriminatory effect that they would have (*JH Walker Ltd v Hussain* [1996] ICR 291, [1996] IRLR 11, EAT). Mr Hussain's employer refused to grant his employees time off work to celebrate Eid (a Muslim feast day). This was held to be indirect race discrimination and an award of £1,000 was made to Mr Hussain. In upholding the tribunal's decision, Mummery J held that intention was established where an employer knew that certain consequences would follow from its acts, and it wanted those consequences to follow. The employer's motive (to promote business efficiency) did not mean that it had not intended to treat the claimant unfavourably on unlawful grounds. The result is that compensation for indirect race discrimination may be awarded where the employer knows that the requirement or condition has an indirectly discriminatory effect, but still seeks to enforce it by dismissing an employee who refuses to accept that condition.

No provision was made where the complaint was brought under the RRA 1976, **18.46** s 1(1A)—that is, where the complaint related to a 'provision, criterion or practice'.

Impact of the Equality Act 2010

From 1 October 2010, the EqA 2010, s 124(4) and (5) extended the pre-existing **18.47** approach to compensation for indirect discrimination under the SDA 1975, the SOR 2003, and the RBR 2003 to all nine protected characteristics. Accordingly, under EqA 2010, s 124(4), if the tribunal finds unlawful indirect discrimination under EqA 2010, s 19, but is satisfied that the provision, criterion, or practice was not applied with the intention of discriminating against the claimant, then the tribunal may make an order for compensation, but it must first consider whether to make a declaration and/or an appropriate recommendation before doing so.

D. Recommendation

Appropriate recommendations

Where a tribunal considers it just and equitable to do so, it may make an appropriate **18.48** recommendation (EqA 2010, s 124(2)(c)), which is defined as a recommendation that, within a specified period, the respondent takes specified steps for the purpose of obviating or reducing the adverse effect of any matter to which the proceedings relate on the claimant and on any other person (EqA 2010, s 124(3)). The tribunal's power to make recommendations was extended under the EqA 2010, so that recommendations can be made that will benefit the wider workforce and help to prevent future discrimination (s 124(3)(b)), but this does not apply to claims in respect of equality of terms (s 113(6)). This statutory provision gives the tribunal an extremely wide discretion (*Vento v Chief Constable of West Yorkshire Police (No 2)* [2002] IRLR 177, EAT). Importantly, the removal of the reference to the step or steps being 'practicable', and the new power to recommend steps affecting 'any other person' may cast doubt on the continuing applicability of the following authorities, which were decided under: SDA 1975, s 65(1)(c); RRA 1976, s 56(1)(c); DDA 1995, s 17A(2)(c); SOR 2003, reg 30(1)((c); RBR 2003, reg 30(1)(c); EEAR 2006, reg 38(1)(c).

Tribunals have no power to order an employer to discontinue a discriminatory prac- **18.49** tice (*Ministry of Defence v Jeremiah* [1978] IRLR 402, EAT). However, as explained above, the tribunal may now be empowered to make such a recommendation.

Financial compensation is governed by the compensatory award, so that a tribunal **18.50** should not make a recommendation that the employer increase a woman's wages (*Irvine v Prestcold Ltd* [1981] IRLR 281, CA). The wider powers to make a recommendation introduced by the EqA 2010, s 124(c), may now allow for such a recommendation as rejected in *Irvine*.

18.51 In *Bayoomi v British Railways Board* [1981] IRLR 431, the tribunal reminded itself that, although it thought that British Rail should generally introduce a proper training scheme, it could only make recommendations that would obviate or reduce the adverse effect of the discrimination on Mr Bayoomi himself and not on any other person (a situation now covered by EqA 2010, s 124(3)(b)). Mr Bayoomi had, by then, left the job and was not likely to return. The tribunal therefore recommended that a note be placed on his personal file to the effect that he had been dismissed in circumstances that amounted to racial discrimination. That way, prospective employers might be prevented from drawing an adverse inference from his dismissal, should they seek a reference.

18.52 Where statutory rules govern an appointment, a tribunal cannot recommend a claimant's appointment. It can merely recommend that the appointing body be made aware of the need to comply with the RRA 1976 and be informed that the claimant's previous application had failed because of racial discrimination (*North West Thames Regional Health Authority v Noone (No 2)* [1988] ICR 813, [1988] IRLR 530, CA). Likewise, there is no power to recommend that a victim of discrimination be promoted automatically to the next open post without consideration of merit (*British Gas plc v Sharma* [1991] ICR 19, [1991] IRLR 101, EAT). This, said the EAT, would be an impermissible act of positive discrimination.

18.53 The EAT in *Vento (No 2)* upheld a recommendation under SDA 1975, s 65(1)(c) that the deputy chief constable should interview named police officers, and discuss with them relevant parts of the decisions of the employment tribunal and the EAT on liability. In holding that the recommendation was appropriate, the EAT held that it is good practice that any employer, faced with findings such as those made in the present case, should consider its behaviour and discuss the findings of the tribunal with those concerned. The tribunal had found 'institutional denial' and that finding needed to be addressed. The knowledge that it was being addressed fell, on the facts of the present case, within SDA 1975, s 65(1)(c). To know that the wrongdoers have been confronted with the findings could plainly reduce injury to feelings. However, the EAT did overrule the tribunal's further recommendation that each of the officers should be invited to apologize in writing to the claimant, and that the deputy chief constable should report in writing as to whether or not the invitation to apologize was accepted in each case. The claimant had already received an apology from the police force. The officers in question had not had an opportunity to make their position clear to the tribunal; nor was there any means of enforcing the recommendations against them and, even if apologies were forthcoming, they would be unlikely to be perceived as being sincere. Again, in view of the wider power given to tribunals by the EqA 2010 to make recommendations, it may now be open to tribunals to make a recommendation in the form of the apology rejected by the EAT in *Vento (No 2)*.

18.54 In *Atos Origin IT Services UK Ltd v Haddock* [2005] IRLR 20, EAT (see above for facts), as an alternative remedy to compensation for future loss, the EAT observed (at [33]), *obiter*, that the tribunal has the power to recommend that the employer continues to employ the claimant until his or her normal retirement age and to pay him or her 100 per cent of the salary, and to provide all of the contractual benefits that he or she would have enjoyed but for his or her disability, on the condition that he or she continues to comply with all reasonable requirements of his or her employer and/or the insurance company, to submit to medical examinations so as to ensure continued payment of the benefits under the insurance scheme by the insurance company to the employer.

There is no tribunal power to enforce a recommendation. Instead, if without **18.55** reasonable excuse (see *Nelson v Tyne and Wear Passenger Transport Executive* [1978] ICR 1183, EAT) the respondent fails to comply with an appropriate recommendation in so far as it relates to the claimant, then (EqA 2010, s 124(7)):

(a) the tribunal may increase the amount of compensation to be paid; or
(b) if no such order for compensation was made, make one.

19

COMPENSATION IN DISCRIMINATION CASES: LOSS AND INTEREST

A. Non-financial Loss

Injury to feelings

19.01 Compensation in respect of an unlawful act of discrimination may include compensation for injured feelings whether or not it includes compensation on any other basis: Equality Act 2010 [EqA 2010], s 119(4).

19.02 An award for injury to feelings will not automatically be made when unlawful discrimination is established. The claimant must still show that anger, distress, and affront have been caused by the unlawful act of discrimination, although it will often be easy to prove (*Ministry of Defence v Cannock* [1994] ICR 918, [1994] IRLR 509, EAT). In an earlier decision, the Employment Appeal Tribunal (EAT) held that an injury to feelings claim is so fundamental to a sex discrimination case that it is almost inevitable. All that is required is that the matter of hurt feelings be simply stated. It is then for the tribunal to consider the extent of hurt feelings suffered and to make an award accordingly (*Murray v Powertech (Scotland) Ltd* [1992] IRLR 257, EAT). In *Assoukou v Select Services Partners Ltd* [2006] EWCA Civ 1442, [2006] All ER (D) 122 (Oct), the Court of Appeal ruled that a tribunal erred in law by not making an award for injured feelings where the claimant was merely angry and frustrated by the discrimination. In *Abegaze v Shrewsbury College of Arts & Technology* [2009] EWCA Civ 96, [2010] IRLR 238, the Court of Appeal held that whilst it is correct to say that there must be evidence of injury to feelings, a tribunal could readily conclude that there had been some injury necessarily flowing from an unlawful discriminatory act, even if it rejected the extent of the claim. At the very least, it might reasonably be anticipated that the claimant would recover a sum at the lower end of the scale.

In *Taylor v XLN Telecom Ltd* [2010] IRLR 499, EAT, Underhill P held (distinguish- **19.03** ing *Skyrail Oceanic Ltd v Coleman* [1981] ICR 864, CA, and explaining *Alexander v Home Office* [1988] ICR 685, [1988] IRLR 190, CA, as *obiter* on the point) that, in a discrimination claim, a claimant is entitled to recover for any injury to feelings and psychiatric injury attributable to the act complained of, irrespective of his or her knowledge or otherwise of the discriminatory motivation of the employer. There is nothing in the statutory provisions to suggest that it should be governed by any special principles. Distress and humiliation may be caused by conduct that is not overtly discriminatory, and if such conduct is, in fact, on the grounds of, or by reason of, the relevant protected characteristic or protected act, it would seem artificial and arbitrary to withhold compensation for it, even though the victim may not at the time have known of, or indeed even suspected, the employer's discriminatory motivation. It is still an injury attributable to the discriminatory conduct.

The Court of Appeal in *Vento v Chief Constable of West Yorkshire Police (No 2)* [2003] **19.04** ICR 318, [2003] IRLR 102, observed that subjective feelings of upset, frustration, worry, anxiety, mental distress, fear, grief, anguish, humiliation, stress, depression, etc and the degree of their intensity are incapable of objective proof or of measurement in monetary terms. Translating hurt feelings into hard currency is bound to be an artificial exercise. Nevertheless, employment tribunals have to do the best that they can on the basis of the available material to make a sensible assessment. In carrying out this exercise, they should have in mind the summary of the general principles on compensation for non-pecuniary loss by Smith J in *Armitage, Marsden and HM Prison Service v Johnson* [1997] ICR 275, [1997] IRLR 162, EAT:

(1) Awards for injury to feelings are compensatory. They should be just to both parties. They should compensate fully without punishing the tortfeasor. Feelings of indignation at the tortfeasor's conduct should not be allowed to inflate the award.

(2) Awards should not be too low, as that would diminish respect for the policy of the anti-discrimination legislation. Society has condemned discrimination and awards must ensure that it is seen to be wrong. On the other hand, awards should be restrained, as excessive awards could, to use Lord Bingham's phrase [in the libel case *Elton John v MGN* [1996] 3 WLR 593], be seen as the way to untaxed riches.

(3) Awards should bear some broad general similarity to the range of awards in personal injury cases. We do not think this should be done by reference to any particular type of personal injury awards; rather to the whole range of such awards.

(4) In exercising their discretion in assessing a sum, tribunals should remind themselves of the value in everyday life of the sum they have in mind. This may be done by reference to purchasing power or by reference to earnings.

(5) Finally, tribunals should bear in mind Lord Bingham's reference to the need for public respect for the level of awards made.

19.05 The Court of Appeal in *Vento v Chief Constable of West Yorkshire Police (No 2)* [2003] ICR 318, [2003] IRLR 102 (a sex discrimination case in which an award of £50,000 for injury to feelings was reduced to £18,000 on appeal) identified three broad bands for assessing injury to feelings awards, as follows.

(a) An award of £500–£5,000 is appropriate for 'less serious' cases in which the unlawful act is an 'isolated' or 'one-off' incident. Awards of less than £500 should be 'avoided altogether'. Indeed, in *Doshoki v Draeger Ltd* [2002] IRLR 340, EAT (a race discrimination case), it was held that awards of less than £750 are unlikely to be made.

(b) An award of £5,000–£15,000 is for 'serious cases that do not merit an award in the highest band'.

(c) Awards of £15,000–£25,000 are for the 'most serious' cases—for example, where there has been a 'lengthy campaign of discriminatory harassment'. Awards of more than £25,000 should be made in only the 'most exceptional' cases.

19.06 In *Da'Bell v National Society for the Prevention of Cruelty to Children* [2010] IRLR 19, the EAT formally uprated these bands by 20 per cent to take account of inflation.

(a) the higher band for the most serious cases is now £18,000–£30,000;
(b) the middle band is from £6,000–£18,000; and
(c) the lower band is now up to £6,000.

19.07 The Court of Appeal in *Vento (No 2)* suggested that the Judicial Studies Board (JSB) *Guidelines for the Assessment of General Damages in Personal Injury Cases* (in which awards are routinely uprated) should be read alongside its own guidance. Indeed, in *Ministry of Defence v Cannock* [1994] ICR 918, [1994] IRLR 509, the EAT observed that although awards for injury to feelings have increased both due to inflation, and due to greater appreciation of the distress and hurt that discrimination may cause, a tribunal should always award the going rate for compensation, even if it is more in real terms than it would have been at the date of the injury complained of.

Practitioners should always take care to bring up to date any particular awards made in past cases that are sought to be relied upon.

However, tribunals must guard against the risk of double compensation where **19.08** injury to mental health is claimed alongside injury to feelings, since it is not always clear at what point serious injury to feelings stops and mental illness begins (see *HM Prison Service v Salmon* [2001] IRLR 425, EAT).

The latest Equal Opportunities Review survey of awards, *Compensation Awards* **19.09** *2009* (No 201, June 2010), points to the average award for injury to feelings (including aggravated damages) in 2009 as being £5,849 (which was lower than the 2008 level of £6,612 and 2007 level of £6,016). Meanwhile, the median award in 2009 was £4,500 (lower than the 2008 level of £4,800 and the same as the 2007 level).

Of course, out-of-court settlements can, and often do, result in the payment of **19.10** larger sums, especially when the kind of publicity associated with alleged discrimination is seen as damaging to a respondent's business interests.

In *Coleman v Skyrail Oceanic Ltd* [1981] IRLR 398, the Court of Appeal ruled that **19.11** injury to feelings not caused by the unlawful discrimination is not properly attributable to an unlawful act and therefore must be disregarded in the assessment of compensation.

In *Voith Turbo Ltd v Stowe* [2005] IRLR 228, EAT, HHJ McMullen QC observed **19.12** (at [7]–[8]) that dismissal on racial grounds is a very serious incident and cannot be described as 'one-off' or 'isolated'. The tribunal in that case was therefore right to assess compensation for injury to feelings in accordance with the middle band in *Vento (No 2)*.

Injury to feelings awards are compensatory and not punitive. It is wrong for awards **19.13** for injury to feelings to be used as a means of punishing or deterring employers from particular courses of conduct (*Ministry of Defence v Cannock* [1994] ICR 918, [1994] IRLR 509, 524, EAT).

Where there is more than one unlawful act of discrimination, a global approach to **19.14** assessing injury to feelings is preferable to making separate awards for each act, since it would be unrealistic to seek to ascribe to each discriminatory act a proportion of the overall injury to feelings suffered (*ICTS (UK) Ltd v Tchoula* [2000] ICR 1191, [2000] IRLR 643, EAT). However, in *Al Jumard v Clywd Leisure Ltd* [2008] IRLR 345, the EAT held that a more nuanced approach was necessary. The losses flowing from the two forms of race and disability discrimination—at least where they did not arise out of the same facts—should have been separately considered and the tribunal should have identified whether any separate loss was to be awarded for victimization.

In assessing injury to feelings, the relevant circumstances to which a tribunal may **19.15** have regard include the nature of the lost employment. In *Orlando v Didcot Power*

Station Sports and Social Club [1996] IRLR 262, the EAT held that the tribunal had not erred in having regard to the fact that the claimant's position was part-time in making its award for injury to feelings. Although a tribunal should be cautious about making generalized assumptions and a wrongdoer must take the victim as he or she is, 'a person who unlawfully loses an evening job may be expected to be less hurt and humiliated by the discriminatory treatment than a person who loses their entire professional career'.

19.16 Also in *Orlando*, the Court of Appeal held that, in assessing injury to feelings, the willingness of the employer to admit that it has acted in breach of the discrimination legislation may help to reduce the hurt that is felt, where it can spare the claimant the indignity and further hurt of having to rehearse the nature of his or her treatment.

19.17 The fact that the claimant would have been lawfully dismissed at a later date in any event is not a ground for reducing the award for injury to feelings (*O'Donoghue v Redcar and Cleveland Borough Council* [2001] IRLR 615, CA). The claimant remains entitled to this head of loss in full without any *Polkey*-type reduction.

19.18 In assessing how much to award for injury to feelings, the tribunal should ignore the fact that the claimant will receive interest on the sum (*Ministry of Defence v Cannock* [1994] ICR 918, [1994] IRLR 509, EAT).

19.19 Awards for injury to feelings should be made without regard to tax implications of the award and therefore should not be grossed up (*Orthet Ltd v Vince-Cain* [2004] IRLR 857, EAT).

19.20 In *Gilbank v Miles* [2006] EWCA Civ 543, [2006] ICR 1297, [2006] IRLR 538, in which G, a salon manager, knowingly fostered and encouraged a sustained campaign of bullying and discrimination by her other staff against M, a pregnant employee, the Court of Appeal upheld an award of £25,000, pointing out that if the discrimination involved the well-being of the unborn child, then this increased the degree of seriousness.

Loss of congenial employment

19.21 There is sufficient overlap between compensation for injury to feelings and loss of congenial employment due to discrimination for tribunals to confine themselves to making an award for injury to feelings, where such has been proved, which will include compensation for the hurt caused by the loss of a chosen career that gave job satisfaction (*Ministry of Defence v Cannock* [1994] ICR 918, [1994] IRLR 509, EAT).

Aggravated damages

19.22 Aggravated damages are recoverable where the respondent has behaved in a high-handed, malicious, insulting, or oppressive manner in committing the act of discrimination (*Alexander v Home Office* [1988] ICR 685, [1988] IRLR 190, CA). The discriminatory acts may be sufficiently intentional as to enable the claimant to rely upon malice or the respondent's manner of committing the tort or other conduct as aggravating the injury to feelings (*Armitage, Marsden and HM Prison Service v Johnson* [1997] ICR 275, [1997] IRLR 162, EAT).

In *MOD v Fletcher* [2010] IRLR 25, the EAT held that, in assessing the amount **19.23** of the award, regard should be had to the overall sum awarded in respect of non-pecuniary loss. Double recovery should be avoided by taking appropriate account of the overlap between the individual heads of damage. Awards should bear some broad general similarity to the range of awards in personal injury cases. If the manner of or malice in committing the acts of discrimination are not fully reflected in an award for injury to feelings, it is not an error of law for a tribunal to make an award of aggravated damages in respect of those acts. In doing so, a tribunal would still be taking appropriate account of the overlap between individual heads of damage. It is not, however, necessary to establish that the conduct is malicious, although malicious conduct may attract aggravated damages.

The claimant must show that he or she had knowledge or suspicion of the aggra- **19.24** vating conduct or motive and that such knowledge caused his or her hurt feelings to be aggravated (*Ministry of Defence v Meredith* [1995] IRLR 539, EAT).

In *Scott v Commissioners of the Inland Revenue* [2004] IRLR 713, the Court of **19.25** Appeal ruled that aggravated damages are intended to deal with cases in which the injury was inflicted by conduct that was high-handed, malicious, insulting, or oppressive. Therefore, it should not be aggregated with and treated as part of the damages for injury to feelings (this decision overrules in practice at least one EAT decision on this point—*ICTS (UK) Ltd v Tchoula* [2000] IRLR 643, EAT). Furthermore, the EAT, in *Crofton v Yeboah* EAT 475/00, interpreted the *Vento (No 2)* guidance as meaning that the brackets of awards exclude any award for aggravated damages made up as part of the injury to feelings award.

Each case will necessarily turn on its own facts. However, examples of circum- **19.26** stances in which aggravated damages are recoverable include:

(a) where an employer has failed to investigate complaints of racial discrimination and failed to apologize (*Armitage, Marsden and HM Prison Service v Johnson* [1997] ICR 275, [1997] IRLR 162, EAT, in which £7,500 was awarded and in which case the EAT held that the greatest mitigation would have been an apology, which was never offered);

(b) where the respondent has attempted to cover up and trivialize acts of discrimination (*HM Prison Service v Salmon* [2001] IRLR 425, EAT, in which £5,000 was awarded);

(c) where the respondent's conduct in defending the tribunal proceedings is inappropriate and intimidatory (*Zaiwalla & Co v Walia* [2002] IRLR 697,

EAT, in which £7,500 was awarded; see also *MOD v Fletcher* [2010] IRLR 25, EAT, in which an award of £20,000 was reduced to £8,000 on appeal);

(d) where the respondent's answers to a statutory discrimination questionnaire were unsatisfactory (*City of Bradford Metropolitan Council v Arora* [1989] IRLR 442, EAT); and

(e) where the discriminator was not punished and remained in post, and was then promoted, even though the charges against him had not been determined (*BT plc v Reid* [2004] IRLR 327, CA, in which £2,000 was awarded). Although there is no principle that an employer cannot promote an employee whilst disciplinary proceedings are hanging over his or her head, on the particular facts and circumstances of a particular case, it can be a material factor demonstrating the high-handedness of the employer.

Exemplary damages

19.27 Following the Court of Appeal decision in *AB v South Western Water Services Ltd* [1993] QB 507, [1993] PIQR P167, exemplary damages could only be awarded for torts for which exemplary damages had been awarded prior to the House of Lords' decision in *Rookes v Barnard* [1964] AC 1129. Accordingly, in *Deane v London Borough of Ealing* [1993] ICR 329, [1993] IRLR 209, EAT, it was held that exemplary damages were not recoverable in race (and by analogy all) discrimination cases. Further, the EAT, in *Ministry of Defence v Meredith* [1995] IRLR 539, ruled that exemplary damages were not recoverable for breach of the Equal Treatment Directive (76/207/EEC).

19.28 However, following *Kuddus v Chief Constable of Leicestershire Constabulary* [2002] 2 AC 122, HL (a case involving misfeasance in public office), exemplary damages are now recoverable, but only:

(a) if compensation is insufficient to punish the wrongdoer; and
(b) if the conduct is either:
  (i) oppressive, arbitrary, or unconstitutional action by the agents of government; or
  (ii) where the respondent's conduct has been calculated by him or her to make a profit that may well exceed the compensation payable to the claimant.

19.29 In *MOD v Fletcher* [2010] IRLR 25, EAT (exemplary damages of £50,000 set aside), Slade J held that certain 'ordinary' employment law functions performed under statute by an official of a public body of sufficient seniority may, subject to other conditions, be capable of supporting an award of exemplary damages. In particular, the exercise by those of sufficient seniority within the army of its functions under statutory procedures for the redress of complaints is capable of falling within the scope of that category. The wrongdoing must, however, be conscious and contumelious. Exemplary damages are reserved for the very worst cases of oppressive use of power by public authorities. The EAT further ruled that such damages are punitive, not compensatory, and intended to deter. Overlap or double recovery is to be avoided. On the facts, the EAT held that the army's failure to provide or operate procedures for the redress of Ms Fletcher's complaints, deplorable as it was, did not cross the high threshold warranting an award of exemplary damages. It ruled that even if exemplary damages could have been awarded, the sum of £50,000 was too high. That sum was the absolute maximum to be awarded in cases of wrongful arrest and false imprisonment. If an award of exemplary damages had been warranted, it should have been at the lower end of the scale: no more than £7,500. There was no authority for the approach of the tribunal that the amount of exemplary damages should match the aggregate amount of the sums awarded for injury to feelings and aggravated damages. Such an approach would be likely to lead to double counting. Because the damages would have been met from the public purse, the amount of such damages might therefore be of less significance to the perpetrator of the misconduct than the fact that its conduct had been subject to public criticism.

19.30 Notably, exemplary damages are not recoverable in equal pay cases brought under the equality of terms provisions in the EqA 2010 because such claims are, by definition, contractual and not tortious.

Physical and psychiatric injury

19.31 In *Sheriff v Klyne Tugs (Lowestoft) Ltd* [1999] ICR 1170, [1999] IRLR 481, the Court of Appeal confirmed that claimants can recover general damages for personal injury caused by unlawful discrimination.

19.32 Damages for personal injury are recoverable where they are caused by the discriminatory act and claimants are not additionally required to show that injury to health was a reasonably foreseeable type of damage (*Essa v Laing Ltd* [2004] ICR 746, [2004] IRLR 313, CA). This principle may be limited to cases of intentional and direct abuse, and may not apply to other more subtle forms of discrimination.

19.33 In principle, injury to feelings and psychiatric injury are distinct heads of loss. In practice, however, it is often not easy to identify where injury to feelings ends and injury to mental health (such as depression) begins, and so there is a risk of double recovery.

(a) In *HM Prison Service v Salmon* [2001] IRLR 425, the EAT upheld the making of a separate award for personal injury, but suggested that tribunals were permitted to make a single award to include both injury to feelings, and stress and depression. The EAT emphasized that injury to feelings can cover a very wide range. At the lower end are comparatively minor instances of upset or distress, typically caused by one-off acts or episodes of discrimination. At the upper end, the victim is likely to be suffering from serious and prolonged feelings of humiliation, low self-esteem, and depression; in the latter scenario, it may be fairly arbitrary whether the symptoms are put before the tribunal as a psychiatric illness, supported by a formal diagnosis and/or expert evidence.

(b) In *Essa v Laing Ltd* [2004] IRLR 313, [42], CA, Pill LJ said that 'while there may be a difference between "injury to health or personal injury" and "injury to feelings", the two are not inconsistent, may overlap and injury to feelings may contribute to injury to health'.

19.34 General damages for pain and suffering and loss of amenities are usually assessed in accordance with the JSB *Guidelines for the Assessment of General Damages in Personal Injury Cases* (10th edn, 2010). The most common form of personal injury claim in discrimination cases involves psychiatric damage.

19.35 According to the JSB Guidelines, the factors to be taken into account in valuing claims of psychiatric damage generally are as follows:

(a) the injured person's ability to cope with life and work;
(b) the effect on the injured person's relationships with family, friends, and those with whom he comes into contact;
(c) the extent to which treatment would be successful;
(d) future vulnerability;
(e) prognosis;
(f) whether medical help has been sought;
(g) whether the injury results from sexual and/or physical abuse and/or breach of trust; and, if so, the nature of the relationship between victim and abuser, the nature of the abuse, its duration, and the symptoms caused by it.

19.36 There are four categories of award, as follows.

(a) *Severe (£36,000–£76,000)* This is the appropriate bracket where the claimant has serious problems in relation to factors (a)–(d) set out above and the prognosis is very poor.

(b) *Moderately severe (£12,500–£36,000)* Into this bracket fall cases in which there are significant problems associated with the above factors (a)–(d), but in which the prognosis is much more optimistic than in **19.36(a)**. The Guidelines state: 'Cases of work-related stress resulting in a permanent or long-standing disability preventing a return to comparable employment would appear to come within this category.'

(c) *Moderate (£3,875–£12,500)* This applies to cases in which, while there may have been the sort of problems associated with factors (a)–(d) above, there has been significant improvement by the date of the remedies hearing and in which the prognosis is good.

(d) *Minor (£1,000–£3,875)* This will be appropriate to cases involving symptoms of limited duration that have adversely affected daily activities and sleep. Temporary 'anxiety' sometimes attracts awards below this bracket.

19.37 Where part of the psychiatric injury includes post-traumatic stress disorder (PTSD), any award will tend towards the upper end of the above brackets. Cases in which PTSD is the sole psychiatric condition are covered by a separate set of

Guideline brackets. The Guidelines also separately deal with chronic pain conditions, which almost invariably include an element of psychological damage.

Once the tribunal has decided which of the JSB brackets is most appropriate to **19.38** the claimant's condition, it will need to assess the extent to which the unlawful discriminatory acts actually contributed to the relevant injury. So, for example, in *Salmon*, compensation for psychiatric injury was reduced by 25 per cent on the basis that the depressive illness was only caused to the extent of 75 per cent by the acts of discrimination found to be unlawful by the tribunal.

B. Financial Loss

Loss of financial benefits and expenses

The financial losses that a claimant may sustain as a result of unlawful discrimination **19.39** may take the form of:

(a) loss of financial benefits (principally loss of earnings) of which he or she is or may be deprived because of the unlawful act; and/or
(b) out-of-pocket expenses to which he or she is put.

Loss of earnings should be calculated on the basis of the claimant's net, rather than **19.40** gross, income (*Visa International Service Association v Paul* [2004] IRLR 42, EAT).

In relation to each type of financial loss, damages are recoverable where the claimant **19.41** can show that they are caused by the unlawful discriminatory act, and claimants do not also have to prove (at least in cases of intentional and direct abuse) that the particular loss in question was a reasonably foreseeable type of damage (*Essa v Laing Ltd* [2004] ICR 746, [2004] IRLR 313, CA).

Loss of financial benefits that, but for the unlawful act, the claimant would have **19.42** received may include any of the following:

(a) net loss of earnings including salary increases, overtime, tips, commission, bonuses, and profit-related pay;
(b) attendance or Christmas bonuses;
(c) holiday pay;
(d) notice pay;
(e) pension;
(f) share schemes;
(g) private health care;
(h) loss of use of company car, plus free fuel, servicing, insurance, road tax, etc;
(i) travel concessions;
(j) cheap loan facilities;
(k) clothing allowances or free goods;

    (l) club memberships;

    (m) expense accounts;

    (n) free accommodation, plus household bills;

    (o) subsidized meals;

    (p) free telephone; and

    (q) childcare benefits.

19.43 Expenses may include the cost of items such as:

    (a) looking for alternative work;

    (b) retraining, or starting up a business;

    (c) medical expenses;

    (d) paid or unpaid care;

    (e) equipment or special aids and appliances;

    (f) transport;

    (g) accommodation (either because of a necessary move or because of adaptations or alterations);

    (h) domestic help;

    (i) additional holiday expenses;

    (j) divorce; and

    (k) administering the claimant's affairs.

19.44 If, for example, an intentional act of discrimination were to cause the claimant to suffer severe depression, which in turn caused him or her to divorce his or her spouse, assuming that there was no intervening act, it would appear that a claimant should be able to recover the reasonably incurred costs of the divorce. In the case of unintentional acts of discrimination causing such loss, the claimant might additionally be required to show that the type of loss was reasonably foreseeable. This issue was left for a future appellate court to decide following the majority decision in *Essa v Laing Ltd* [2004] ICR 746, [2004] IRLR 313, CA.

19.45 It is important to distinguish between past and future loss. The quantification of past loss is essentially an arithmetical exercise. The tribunal will consider the expenses that have, in fact, been reasonably incurred up to the date of the remedies hearing.

19.46 Unlike past financial loss, future financial loss is not certain, in that it is impossible to say definitely at the time that the assessment is made that a certain type of loss will be sustained or the precise amount of it—for example, what income will be earned, for how long, what the claimant would have earned but for the discriminatory act, and how long he or she would have continued to earn those wages, and whether medical treatment will be required, and for how long and how much it will cost.

19.47 Tribunals should normally calculate damages for future loss of earnings by using the usual multiplicand and multiplier method adopted by the courts (*Ministry of*

Defence v Cannock [1994] ICR 918, [1994] IRLR 509, [142], EAT). In the joined cases *Kingston upon Hull City Council v Dunnachie (No3)*; *HSBC Bank plc v Drage* [2003] IRLR 843, the EAT discouraged the use of multipliers based on Ogden tables (which are published by the Government Actuary's Department [GAD] as an aid to the calculation of damages in personal injury cases) in order to calculate unfair dismissal compensation for future loss of earnings (and, presumably, for future loss of earnings in discrimination cases), but not when calculating pension loss. The EAT held that Ogden tables should be used only where the claimant has established a prima facie claim that his or her loss will last for the rest of his or her career.

In *Abbey National plc v Chagger* [2009] ICR 624, [2009] IRLR 86, the EAT, in **19.48** assessing the compensation payable to Mr Chagger, took into consideration the risk that future potential employers might decline to employ Mr Chagger because he had brought tribunal proceedings against a past employer. The tribunal found that Mr Chagger should be compensated for the loss of his earnings for the rest of his working life in 'equivalent or better paid employment'. It adopted a multiplier/multiplicand approach in assessing that loss. In selecting a multiplier of 16, it used the Ogden tables. Underhill P observed (at [114]) that 'even in a case where it is appropriate to use the Ogden Tables, it will never be right to use the multiplier taken from the main tables without considering the contingencies which those tables do not reflect'. (See also 7.84–7.89.)

In the joined appeals *Sheffield Forgemasters International Ltd v Fox*; *Telindus Ltd v* **19.49** *Brading* [2009] IRLR 192, the EAT held that receipt of Incapacity Benefit did not preclude the claimants from obtaining compensation for loss of earnings during the same period. Being eligible for incapacity benefits does not mean that the individual could not obtain paid work during that period. It is important for the employment tribunal to consider all of the evidence (including, if the information is available, the basis of any application made by a claimant for Incapacity Benefit) before deciding if he or she would have earned any money in a period for which compensation is being claimed.

Discount for accelerated receipt

Where a claimant receives a sum in respect of future loss, a discount should be made **19.50** for accelerated receipt unless the sums concerned are so small as to make it an unnecessary complication (*Bentwood Bros (Manchester) Ltd v Shepherd* [2003] ICR 1000, [2003] IRLR 364, CA). The Court of Appeal held that tribunals should take into account the fact that an employee receiving compensation has the benefit of receiving immediately what he or she would otherwise have had to wait to receive in instalments over a period of loss. This should be done on the basis of an appropriate percentage year on year and not via a single deduction. In this case, the tribunal erred in discounting the employee's total award for future loss by a single deduction of 5 per cent to take account of accelerated payment, even though the loss in question covered two-and-a-half years' future earnings and ten years' pension contributions. However, the Court of Appeal questioned whether the 5 per cent discount rate normally applied by employment tribunals remains appropriate, given that the discount applied by statute in personal injury cases was 2.5 per cent (see also **15.30–15.37**).

Loss of a chance

19.51 Tribunals often have to address the question, but for the discrimination, what was the chance that the claimant would have remained in the original job for the period of the compensation claim? This will involve assessing whether the claimant would have left voluntarily or involuntarily by some future date, or would have remained in the job until the birth of a child or retirement.

19.52 If there is a chance of loss, the claimant is entitled to be compensated in respect of the risk. The tribunal has to value the percentage chance of loss occurring.

(a) In *Ministry of Defence v Cannock* [1994] ICR 918, [1994] IRLR 509, 523, EAT, Morison J observed that it was wrong to assess loss in a situation in which there had been a dismissal on grounds of pregnancy on the basis of what would have happened (based on a balance of probabilities) to the woman in her job had she not been discriminated against. Instead, the calculation of loss should be dealt with as the evaluation of the loss of a chance. This approach was subsequently endorsed by the Court of Appeal in *Vento v Chief Constable of West Yorkshire Police (No 2)* [2003] ICR 318, [2003] IRLR 102, [32], Mummery LJ. In so doing, Mummery LJ commented:

> As Morison J pointed out, this hypothetical question requires careful thought before it is answered. It is a difficult area of the law. It is not like an issue of primary fact, as when a court has to decide which of two differing recollections of past events is the more reliable. The question requires a forecast to be made about the course of future events. It has to be answered on the basis of the best assessment that can be made on the relevant material available to the court. That includes statistical material, such as that produced to the tribunal showing the percentage of women who have in the past continued to serve in the police force until the age of retirement.

(b) It is not necessarily perverse for the tribunal to conclude that there is a 100 per cent chance (that is, certainty) that, but for the discrimination, a relevant event would have occurred (*Ministry of Defence v Hunt* [1996] ICR 544, EAT).

(c) Where there are a number of contingent possibilities, the correct approach is to cumulate the percentage chances of each event occurring (*Ministry of Defence v Hunt* [1996] ICR 544, EAT). But for her dismissal, there was a 75 per cent chance that Mrs Hunt would have returned to work following the birth of her child. Had she returned to work, there was then a 50 per cent chance of her having a pay rise. The loss of a chance of her earning the higher rate of pay was therefore 75 per cent × 50 per cent.

(d) If a tribunal regards certain contingencies as too remote or unlikely to arise during the period for which the claimant is to be compensated, then it is not required to take them into account (*Mayor and Burgesses of the London Borough of Tower Hamlets v Wooster* [2009] IRLR 980, EAT).

(e) In assessing the percentage loss of a chance event occurring, the tribunal is no more than encouraged to rely upon statistical evidence. However, statistical evidence is simply one relevant factor. Hence, in *Vento v Chief Constable of West Yorkshire Police (No 2)* [2003] ICR 318, [2003] IRLR 102, CA, the tribunal was entitled to conclude that, but for the discriminatory dismissal, there was a 75 per cent chance that the claimant probationary police constable would have remained in the police force until retirement at the age of 55 (a period of 21 years of service), despite statistical evidence tending to show that only 9 per cent of female officers leaving the respondent police authority had served for more than 18 years. The claimant could not have any more children and the reason why most women left the force was to have children. Also, the statistics related to past practice and 'family-friendly policies' indicated that these would make it more likely that women would stay on. Accordingly, the award could not be said to be perverse.

(f) Where a respondent has made an *ex gratia* payment to the claimant or the claimant has partially mitigated the loss, then such sums must be deducted before applying the percentage chance (*Ministry of Defence v Hunt* [1996] ICR 544, EAT; *Ministry of Defence v Wheeler* [1998] ICR 242, [1998] IRLR 23, CA; *Digital Equipment Ltd v Clements (No 2)* [1998] IRLR 134, CA).

Chance of future fair dismissal

A particular factor that the tribunal may have to consider is whether, but for the **19.53** discrimination, the claimant would in any event have actually been dismissed lawfully or 'fairly' at a later date.

(a) The Court of Appeal in *O'Donoghue v Redcar and Cleveland Borough Council* [2001] EWCA Civ 701, [2001] IRLR 615, held that the tribunal was entitled to find that although the claimant had been unfairly dismissed and victimized on grounds of sex because she had embarrassed council members by raising in her previous tribunal proceedings sexist remarks that those members had made, her divisive and antagonistic approach to her colleagues was such that it would inevitably have led to her fair dismissal within a further period of six months. The tribunal was entitled, therefore, to regard the date six months after the date of termination as a cut-off point for the purposes of compensation. Where the tribunal was satisfied that the claimant was on an inevitable course towards dismissal, it was legitimate to avoid the complicated problem of some sliding scale percentage estimate of her chances of dismissal as time progressed (for example, a 20 per cent chance of dismissal in six months, but a 30 per cent chance in a year), by assessing a safe date by which the tribunal was certain that dismissal would have taken place and making an award of full compensation in respect of the period before that date.

(b) Whilst, in *O'Donoghue*, the Court of Appeal rejected the percentage chance approach because of the certainty of a future event happening, in most other cases in which the tribunal is not so certain, the percentage chance approach has been preferred.

(c) In *Brash-Hall v Getty Images Ltd* [2006] EWCA Civ 531, (2006) 811 IDS Brief 5, the Court of Appeal held that, where an employee had been constructively dismissed whilst on maternity leave in both an unfair and discriminatory manner, and the tribunal had found that she would have been fairly dismissed for redundancy anyway, and where payment of enhanced redundancy pay was conditional upon signing a standard severance agreement, her compensation could only include contractual enhanced severance pay if she proved that she would have signed the severance agreement.

19.54 Notably, there is an important difference of approach compared with unfair dismissal cases. In unfair dismissal cases, the tribunal asks whether a hypothetical reasonable employer would have fairly dismissed in any event. In discrimination cases, however, the tribunal asks whether the actual respondent would have fairly dismissed the claimant (*Abbey National plc v Formoso* [1999] ICR 222, [1999] IRLR 222, EAT).

19.55 In *Chagger v Abbey National plc* [2010] EWCA Civ 1202, [2010] IRLR 47, CA, Mr Chagger was selected for compulsory redundancy from a pool of two. The tribunal found that he had been selected for redundancy dismissal on racial grounds. It did not consider whether Mr Chagger would have been dismissed in any event on legitimate grounds. The tribunal accepted that his difficulties in getting a job in the finance industry were partly due to the stigma of having brought proceedings against a past employer. It found that he should be compensated for the loss of his earnings for the rest of his working life in 'equivalent or better paid employment'.

19.56 Should compensation be reduced to reflect the chance that Mr Chagger would have been dismissed for redundancy in any event?

(a) The Court of Appeal held that there was a genuine redundancy situation and that there were two candidates from which one would be selected. On the evidence, there was plainly a realistic prospect that Mr Chagger would have been dismissed even if the selection had been on a non-discriminatory basis, and the tribunal had to assess that prospect.

(b) Since the unlawful act is the discriminatory ground for dismissal, not the dismissal itself, the question is whether the dismissal would have occurred on non-discriminatory grounds. Elias LJ (at [57]) confirmed:

> It is necessary to ask what would have occurred had there been no unlawful discrimination. If there were a chance that dismissal would have occurred in any event, even had there been no discrimination, then in the normal way that must be factored into the calculation of loss.

(c) Elias LJ further held (at [62]) that: 'The gravity of the alleged discrimination is irrelevant to the question what would have happened had there been no discrimination.'

Should future compensation be limited to the period during which Mr Chagger **19.57** would have remained in employment with Abbey? In saying 'no', the Court of Appeal (at [65]–[75]) gave the following helpful guidance:

66. ... in many cases, the starting point in the case of a discriminatory dismissal will be the period when the employee would have been employed by the discriminating employer. For example, if the employer can show that the dismissal would have occurred in any event after a specific period of time, for example because of redundancies or the closing down of the business, then this will normally set the limit to the compensation payable. If there is a chance as opposed to a certainty of this occurring, that should be assessed and factored into the calculation of future loss as the answer to the first question indicates. In such a case, the employee would have been on the labour market in any event once the employment had ceased, and the usual effect of the discriminatory dismissal would simply have been to put him on the labour market earlier than would otherwise have been the case.

67. Similarly, there may be circumstances—although in practice they will be rare— where the evidence is that the employee would voluntarily have left in the near future in any event, whether or not he had another job to go to. This could occur, for example, if the employee is dismissed shortly before he was due to retire, or if he had already given notice of resignation when the discriminatory dismissal occurred. It would be wrong to award compensation beyond the point when he would have left because there would be no loss with respect to any subsequent period of employment.

69. ... The task is to put the employee in the position he would have been in had there been no discrimination; that is not necessarily the same as asking what would have happened to the particular employment relationship had there been no discrimination. The reason is that the features of the labour market are not necessarily equivalent in the two cases. The fact that there has been a discriminatory dismissal means that the employee is on the labour market at a time and in circumstances which are not of his own choosing. It does not follow therefore that his prospects of obtaining a new job are the same as they would have been had he stayed at Abbey. For a start, it is generally easier to obtain employment from a current job than from the status of being unemployed. Further, it may be that the labour market is more difficult in one case compared with another. For example, jobs may be particularly difficult to obtain at the time of dismissal and yet by the time they become more plentiful, when in the usual course of events Mr Chagger might have been expected to have changed jobs had he remained with Abbey, he will have been out of a job and out of the industry for such a period that potential employers will be reluctant to employ him. In addition, he may have been stigmatised by taking proceedings, and that may have some effect on his chances of obtaining future employment.

70. The result of these factors is that the discriminatory dismissal does not only shorten what would otherwise have been Mr Chagger's period of employment with Abbey; it also alters the subsequent career path that might otherwise have been pursued.

On the facts of *Chagger*, the period during which Mr Chagger would have remained **19.58** in employment with Abbey had there been no discrimination was irrelevant, given that it was a case in which he would leave only for another job that was at least as favourable. The proper assessment of loss was therefore to be determined by asking when Mr Chagger might expect to obtain another job on an equivalent salary. Whether that was shorter than the period for which he would have served with Abbey, or whether it was longer and included time when, but for the discriminatory dismissal, he would have been employed elsewhere was immaterial. The best evidence to answer that question was provided by the efforts that Mr Chagger had made to obtain employment. On the evidence, the approach adopted by the tribunal—namely, assessing compensation as though Mr Chagger would have remained with Abbey throughout his career in financial services—was justified.

Impact on compensation of a future unfair dismissal

19.59　It is not entirely clear what bearing a future unfair dismissal has on an award of compensation for unlawful discrimination. In *HM Prison Service v Beart (No 2)* [2005] IRLR 171, the EAT, relying on the principle that a tortfeasor may not benefit from his or her wrong, concluded that a subsequent unfair dismissal does not break the chain of causation and that the claimant is entitled to recover full compensation for unlawful discrimination in these circumstances. The Court of Appeal upheld the EAT's ruling ([2005] EWCA Civ 467, [2005] ICR 1206, [2005] IRLR 568) on the basis that, in the particular circumstances of that case, the 'second wrong' (namely, the unfair dismissal) did not break the chain of causation. Rix LJ pointed out that all that happened was that the employer had committed two discrete wrongs in respect of which the statute provided a cap for one, but not the other. Critically, in *Beart*, the employment tribunal had found in relation to her discrimination claim that if the claimant had been redeployed (as recommended by an internal report), she would 'probably still have been employed' by the employer (that is, there was a continuing loss) and that, in relation to her unfair dismissal claim, the tribunal had found that the allegations of misconduct were unproven (that is, there was no valid reason for dismissal).

19.60　However, the Court of Appeal recognized that the position may be different if the employee 'commits a repudiatory breach of his own contract'—that is, if there is a 'new intervening act' (either before or after the unlawful discriminatory act). In such circumstances, a subsequent dismissal for a valid and lawful reason may well break the chain of causation. It follows that, in such a situation, the award should be limited to the current maximum for unfair dismissal even if it is held unfair for procedural reasons.

Pension loss

19.61　Guidance in relation to the calculation of pension loss is provided by Employment Tribunal Guidelines, *Compensation for Loss of Pension Rights* (3rd edn, 2003).

19.62　Tribunals can be reluctant to hear complicated expert actuarial evidence on pension loss. Unsurprisingly, therefore, it is not uncommon to adopt the simpler, but less accurate, method of awarding a sum equivalent to the employer's contributions into the pension scheme. In *London Borough of Lambeth v D'Souza* [1999] IRLR 240, CA, the respondent did not have to make pension contributions during the relevant period. The EAT held that an employer's contributions holiday should not result in the claimant's pension loss being reduced. In such a case, it was inappropriate to apply the loss of contributions method.

In *Orthet Ltd v Vince-Cain* [2004] IRLR 857, the EAT held that, in a case in which   **19.63** the period of loss is likely to be more than two years, the correct method of calculating future pension loss is the 'substantial loss approach', as suggested in the guidelines to employment judges on *Compensation for Loss of Pension Rights*.

However, in the unfair dismissal case of *Port of Tilbury (London) Ltd v Birch* [2005]   **19.64** IRLR 92, the EAT (in setting aside a tribunal decision rejecting the evidence and submissions of both parties solely because neither approach was one suggested in the tribunal's guidance booklet) held that there is no duty on a tribunal to follow the pension guidelines. The tribunal's first duty is to consider any credible evidence and submissions put forward by the parties in order to ascertain whether a fair and equitable assessment of the loss of pension rights can be worked out on that basis. Where there is little forthcoming from the parties, the booklet may assist the tribunal in making its assessment.

In *Greenhoff v Barnsley Metropolitan Borough Council* [2006] ICR 514, EAT, Silber J   **19.65** ruled (at [17]–[19]) that, when calculating compensation for loss of pension rights, it is important for an employment tribunal to explain not only what approach it adopted, but also the reasons as to why it adopted that approach and rejected other approaches, especially those set out in the booklet *Compensation for Loss of Pension Rights*. Tribunals should approach such cases in general by:

(a) identifying all possible benefits that the employee could obtain under the pension scheme;
(b) setting out the terms of the pension relevant to each possible benefit;
(c) considering in respect of each such possible benefit the advantages and disadvantages of applying the 'simplified approach' or the 'substantial loss approach' (identified in the booklet), and also any other approach that might be considered appropriate by the tribunal or by the parties;
(d) explaining why it has adopted a particular approach and rejected any other possible approach; and
(e) setting out its conclusions and explaining the compensation at which it has arrived in respect of each head of claim so that the parties and the appeal tribunal can ascertain if it has made an error.

Future handicap on the labour market (loss of earning capacity)

Loss of earning capacity is concerned with the position in which either the claim-   **19.66** ant has no continuing loss of earnings or salary at the date of the remedies hearing, or he or she has a continuing loss fixed at a particular level; in either event, the effects of his or her injuries are such that, if he or she were ever to lose his or her current employment, he or she would have difficulty obtaining employment at all or he or she would only be able to obtain less well-paid employment. It is often referred to as a '*Smith v Manchester* award', after the case of *Smith v Manchester Corp* (1974) 17 KIR 1.

19.67   The tribunal has to quantify the present value of the risk that the claimant would at some future time suffer financial damage because of his or her disadvantages in the labour market. In *Moeliker v Reyrolle & Co Ltd* [1976] ICR 253, CA, the Court of Appeal indicated a two-stage approach to be adopted in assessing damages under this head, as follows.

(a) Where the claimant is in work at the date of the remedies hearing, the first question is, is there a 'substantial' or 'real' risk that a claimant will lose his or her present job at some time before the estimated end of his or her working life?

(b) If the answer is 'yes' (but not otherwise), the tribunal must assess and quantify the present value of the risk of the financial damage that the claimant will suffer if that risk materializes, having regard to the degree of the risk, the time at which it may materialize, and the factors, both favourable and unfavourable, that in a particular case will, or may, affect the claimant's chances of getting a job at all, or an equally well-paid job.

Loss of career prospects

19.68   There is no separate head of damage for loss of career prospects. The financial consequences of being deprived of the opportunity of promotion should be compensated for under damages for loss of earnings (*Ministry of Defence v Cannock* [1994] ICR 918, [1994] IRLR 509, EAT).

Stigma damages

19.69   In *Chagger v Abbey National plc* [2010] EWCA Civ 1202, [2010] IRLR 47 CA (a case in which the claimant unsuccessfully applied for 111 jobs), Elias LJ held (at [85]–[99]) that an employer who has been found to have unlawfully discriminated in dismissing an employee can be liable for compensation reflecting the stigma that results from the employee having taken discrimination proceedings against the former employer, where there is evidence that other employers have been unwilling to employ the dismissed employee for this reason.

(a) The original employer must remain liable for so-called stigma loss. The mere fact that third party employers contribute to, or are the immediate cause of, the loss resulting from their refusal to employ does not, of itself, break the chain of causation. If those employers could lawfully refuse to employ on the grounds that they did not want to risk recruiting someone who had sued his or her employer and whom they perceived to be a potential troublemaker, there is no reason why that would not be a loss flowing directly from the original unlawful act. It is already firmly established that if a stigma attaches to employees from the unlawful way in which their employer runs its business, then the employer will be liable for losses that may result from the fact that other employers will not want to recruit employees because of their link with the business. The decision not to recruit does not break the chain of causation, nor does the action of the employee in taking proceedings.

(b) The position is not altered by the fact that the actions of the third-party employers are unlawful. It can be very difficult for an employee to make good his or her suspicions that he or she is subject to unlawful victimization discrimination, and he or she ought not to be criticized for being reluctant or unwilling to devote the time, money, and stress necessary to advance that claim. It is doubtful whether Parliament, in passing the victimization provisions, intended to weaken the extent of protection that the discriminated victim would have against his or her own employer. Moreover, an employee who has taken proceedings for unfair dismissal could be stigmatized in that way quite lawfully. It would be unsatisfactory and somewhat artificial if tribunals were obliged to discount stigma loss in the context of discrimination law, but not in other contexts.

(c) Once it is accepted that stigma loss is, in principle, recoverable, in most cases, it need not be considered as a separate head of loss at all. There will be evidence about the steps that have been taken by the employee to mitigate loss and this will, in practice, guide the tribunal to reach a view on the likely period of unemployment. The stigma problem will simply be one of the features relevant to the question of how long it will be before a job can be found.

(d) This will not lead to unrealistically high awards by tribunals. It is far from common experience that those taking proceedings against their employer thereafter become virtually unemployable in their chosen field. The fact that, in a discrimination context, it is unlawful to refuse employment for that reason should further reduce the likelihood of employees being adversely affected in this way. Its impact is likely to be small when compared to other factors, such as opportunities generally in the labour market for jobs of that kind.

(e) A tribunal should take a sensible and robust approach to the question of compensation. Plainly, it would be wrong to infer that the employee will, in future, suffer from widespread stigma simply from his or her assertion to that effect, or because he or she is suspicious that this might be the case. If he or she is unwilling to make good his or her suspicious by taking proceedings against the alleged wrongdoing employers, notwithstanding that it may be understandable why he or she is reluctant to do so, he or she cannot expect the tribunal to put much weight on what is little more than conjecture. This is particularly so given that it will, in practice, be impossible for the employer effectively to counter that evidence. However, where there is very extensive evidence of attempted mitigation failing to result in a job, a tribunal is entitled to conclude that, whatever the reason, the employee is unlikely to obtain future employment in the industry.

(f) There is one exceptional case in which it could be necessary for a tribunal to award compensation specifically by reference to the impact of stigma on future job prospects. This is where this is the only head of future loss. An example would be where tribunal has found that the claimant would definitely have been dismissed even had there been no discrimination. He or she would be on the labour market at exactly the same time and in the same circumstances as if he or she had been dismissed lawfully. Accordingly, the damage to his or her employment prospects from the stigma of taking proceedings would be the only potentially recoverable head of future loss.

(g) Here, however, the employee would be asserting that this is a head of loss, and the onus would be on him or her to prove it. In practice, this would be a difficult task. If he or she does establish such a loss, the tribunal will then be faced with the almost impossible task of having to assess it. The tribunal would have to determine how far difficulties in obtaining employment result from general market considerations and how far from the stigma. In the unlikely event that the evidence of the stigma difficulties is sufficiently strong, it would be open to the tribunal to make an award of future loss for a specific period. But, in the more likely scenario that the evidence showed that stigma was only one of the claimant's difficulties, it may be that a modest lump sum would be appropriate to compensate him or her for the stigma element in his or her employment difficulties. This approach would be analogous to the lump sum awards sometimes made in personal injury cases to compensate an injured claimant for the risks of future disadvantage on the labour market. Even then, however, this should not be an automatic payment; there should be some evidence from which the tribunal can infer that stigma is likely to be playing a part in the difficulties facing the employee who seeks fresh employment.

19.70   On the facts of *Chagger*, the employment tribunal had adopted the correct approach to the evidence of stigma, by treating it as a part of the evidence relating to Mr Chagger's attempts to mitigate his loss, so that it was both undesirable and unnecessary for the tribunal to reach a concluded view on the particular contribution that the stigma factor might have played in the difficulties that Mr Chagger faced in obtaining fresh employment. It was sufficient for it to conclude that he was unlikely to obtain employment in the finance industry.

Childcare costs

19.71   Childcare costs that notionally would have had to be incurred to enable a claimant to return to work should be set off in full against his or her damages for loss of earnings. Whether or not some of the costs would have been borne by a third party is not a matter that should be taken into account (*Ministry of Defence v Cannock*

[1994] ICR 918, [1994] IRLR 509, EAT; see also the unfair dismissal case of *Visa International Ltd v Paul* [2004] IRLR 42 considered at **8.40**).

C. Mitigation

Duty to mitigate loss generally

Normal common law principles of mitigation apply. Claimants are under a duty to   **19.72** mitigate each and every head of loss. They cannot sit back and relax and expect to profit from the unlawful discrimination. Whether the claimant has embarked on a reasonable course of conduct will depend on the facts of each case.

In *Ministry of Defence v Hunt* [1996] IRLR 139, EAT, it was emphasized that the   **19.73** burden of proving a failure to mitigate loss is on the person who asserts it. If a tribunal is to decide whether or not there has been a failure to mitigate or, if there has been such a failure, the amount of any reduction in the claim, then it is for the respondent to adduce evidence either arising from cross-examination or from evidence called. It is not the job of the tribunal, as an industrial jury, to fill an evidential vacuum.

Refusing offers of re-employment

In *Wilding v BT plc* [2002] IRLR 524, the Court of Appeal upheld a tribunal's find-   **19.74** ing that a disabled claimant had acted unreasonably in refusing the employer's offer of re-employment and had therefore failed to mitigate his loss. Potter LJ ruled that the following principles apply as to whether a dismissed employee who has refused an offer of re-employment has failed in his or her duty to mitigate his or her loss:

(a) It is the duty of the employee to act as a reasonable person unaffected by the prospect of compensation from his or her former employer.
(b) The onus is on the former employer as the wrongdoer to show that the employee had failed in his or her duty to mitigate his or her loss by unreasonably refusing an offer of re-employment.
(c) The test of reasonableness is an objective one based on the totality of the evidence.
(d) In applying that test, the circumstances in which the offer was made and refused, the attitude of the former employer, the way in which the employee had been treated, and all of the surrounding circumstances, including the employee's state of mind, should be taken into account.
(e) The court or tribunal must not be too stringent in its expectations of the injured party.

Potter LJ pointed out that reference to objectivity does no more than emphasize   **19.75** that the duty of the claimant is to act reasonably. At the same time, the tribunal must consider 'all of the circumstances'. These must inevitably be related to the individual conduct and circumstances of the particular claimant when faced with a choice whether or not to accept an offer of re-employment. If an offer is made that is, on the face of it, suitable to a claimant who has expressed himself or herself anxious to return to work as a means of mitigating his or her loss, and the offer is then rejected for reasons peculiar to the particular claimant, that is bound to involve investigation by the tribunal of whether, in the context of the claimant's circumstances and abilities, his or her refusal of that offer was reasonable or unreasonable. To this extent, the subjective reasons of the claimant in refusing the offer will fall to be examined in the light of the explanations that he or she gives. In an appropriate case, they may critically affect the reasonableness or unreasonableness of his or her decision. Where a claimant has given a clear account of his or her reasons for turning down an offer of re-employment, the ultimate question for the employment tribunal is whether it has been shown that he or she did act unreasonably in turning down the offer, taking into account the history and all of the circumstances of the case, including his or her state of mind, bearing in mind that the burden of proof is on the employer and that the standard of reasonableness to be applied is not high.

19.76　In *Wilding*, Sedley LJ added that it is not enough for the wrongdoer to show that it would have been reasonable to take the steps that he has proposed. He must show that it was unreasonable of the innocent party not to take them. This is an important legal distinction. It reflects the fact that if there is more than one reasonable response open to the wronged party, the wrongdoer has no right to determine his or her choice. It is only where the wrongdoer can show affirmatively that the other party acted unreasonably in relation to his or her duty to mitigate that the defence will succeed. Indeed, Sedley LJ suggested that the 'range of reasonable responses' approach should be applied to the question of whether an employee mitigated reasonably.

19.77　It should be noted that, at the time of writing, the question of the correct approach as to whether a claimant has discharged his or her duty to mitigate is indeed the 'range of reasonable responses' test as suggested by Sedley LJ is currently the subject of an appeal in *DeBique v MOD* EAT/1098/2010.

Seeking alternative employment

19.78　Remaining unemployed unnecessarily or accepting low-paid work when higher-paid work is available will often amount to a failure to mitigate unless difficulties in securing a suitable job exist.

Becoming self-employed

19.79　Dismissed employees may reasonably mitigate their loss of earnings by setting up in self-employment, especially where the individual is not young, or is in a specialized trade in which job opportunities are few and far between. In such cases, profits may not be immediately forthcoming, so that post-dismissal loss of earnings tend to be higher than where the claimant simply seeks out another employed job.

For example, in *Gardiner-Hill v Roland Berger Technics Ltd* [1982] IRLR 498, EAT, **19.80** a 55-year-old managing director with 16 years' experience in a specialist business was held to have acted prudently in spending 80 per cent of his time seeking to market his expertise and experience in his own business.

Further, it may be possible to recover expenses in setting up the business (*United* **19.81** *Freight Distribution Ltd v McDougall* EAT 218/94).

In *Aon Training Ltd v Dore* [2005] IRLR 835, the Court of Appeal held that the **19.82** employment tribunal wrongly limited Mr Dore's loss to the interest on loans taken out by him to set up in business. The Court held that where a dismissed employee attempts to mitigate his or her loss by setting up his or her own business, and the tribunal is satisfied that mitigation in that way was reasonable in the circumstances, the conventional way to assess compensation, under both the Employment Rights Act 1996 (ERA 1996) and the Disability Discrimination Act 1995 (DDA 1995) (and, by analogy, the other anti-discrimination statutes), requires the tribunal:

(i) First to calculate what sum represents loss of remuneration;
(ii) It should then consider the costs incurred in mitigating loss and such a sum, if reasonably incurred, should be added to the loss;
(iii) From that sum should be deducted the earnings from the new business.

Seeking retraining

It is possible for a dismissed employee reasonably to mitigate his or her loss by **19.83** retraining at the ex-employer's expense.

In *ICTS (UK) Ltd v Tchoula* [2000] ICR 1191, [2000] IRLR 643, the EAT ruled **19.84** that the tribunal was entitled to find that the claimant had not failed to mitigate his loss after he was dismissed from his job as a security officer by retraining in a different field, notwithstanding that this resulted in his being compensated for being out of employment for over two years. The tribunal was entitled to accept the claimant's evidence that he did not pursue work in the security field because he needed a clean record and that his dismissal meant that his record was not clean. In those circumstances, it was open to the tribunal to find that it was reasonable for the claimant to retrain and that it was 'reasonably foreseeable' that this would be necessary as a result of his unlawful dismissal by the respondent. However, following *Essa v Laing Ltd* [2004] ICR 746, [2004] IRLR 313, CA, there may be an issue as to whether reasonable foreseeability has any part to play in the assessment of compensation. Certainly, in cases of intentional discrimination, the claimant, it would appear, need show only that such loss was caused by the unlawful act. It is arguable that, unlike in unfair dismissal cases, loss during retraining will only be recoverable where a tribunal is satisfied that it is still attributable to the employer's unlawful act.

In unfair dismissal cases, the Court of Appeal has ruled that compensation in these circumstances depends on what is just and equitable (see *Dench v Flynn & Partners* [1998] IRLR 653).

19.85 In *Orthet Ltd v Vince-Cain* [2004] IRLR 857, EAT, HHJ McMullen QC held that the tribunal did not err in awarding compensation to the claimant for loss of earnings during a four-year period when she was, or was to be, a university student retraining. The tribunal did not err in finding that the claimant had not failed to mitigate her loss. It was entitled to find that the decision by the claimant to change careers was a reasonable step, in circumstances in which the employer was unable to prove that there was suitable work that the claimant could and should have taken, and the tribunal found that, if such work were to become available, the claimant would abandon her course.

Loss that will be avoided

19.86 A claimant cannot recover damages for loss that will be avoided, other than collateral payments such as payments from benevolent third parties and from an insurance policy for which the claimant has paid or contributed to the premiums. In *Atos Origin IT Services UK Ltd v Haddock* [2005] IRLR 20, EAT, the claimant suffered disability discrimination and developed a depressive illness. He was unable to return to work although he remained an employee of the company. He was covered by a permanent health insurance (PHI) scheme underwritten by an insurance company. The scheme provided that, in the event of permanent incapacity for work, the employer could recoup up to 75 per cent of the employee's salary from the insurer provided that he remained an employee of the company, continued to be permanently incapacitated, and had not reached normal retirement age. The insurer accepted the employer's claim in relation to Mr Haddock. Accordingly, he continued to receive 100 per cent of his salary from his employer, but it recovered 75 per cent of that amount from the insurers. The EAT held (at [28]–[30]) that, just as in personal injury cases, payments made by the underwriters of an accident or a health insurance policy for which the premiums were paid by the tortfeasor employer, without contribution from the claimant employee, should be deducted when calculating an award for financial loss. The effect of DDA 1995, s 8(3) (now EqA 2010, s 17A(3)) is that the same deductions must be made from an award of compensation to victims of disability discrimination as would be made in the case of claimants to whom an award of damages for personal injury was made.

19.87 The EAT stated that, in principle, it makes no difference that the payments under the PHI scheme will be made in the future. As in the case of any assessment of future loss, contingencies and chances must be allowed for. A contractual entitlement to a payment may make it more certain that a loss will be mitigated than a mere expectation that a discretion will be favourably exercised or that the employers would continue to employ the employee. The obligations of underwriters may also need to be considered and, if they have a discretion to exercise, so may the chances of their doing so in a way favourable to a beneficiary. The tribunal must undertake this exercise even though it may be difficult and unlikely to produce a figure that is precisely right.

Any figures deducted by way of mitigation or failure to mitigate should be applied **19.88** before the application of the multiplier or the percentage loss of a chance figure (*Ministry of Defence v Hunt* [1996] IRLR 139, EAT).

Example

If the claimant earns £750 a week and finds a new job in which the earnings are £500 a week, the net loss is £250 and the percentage chance is applied to that figure.

Hence, in *Ministry of Defence v Wheeler* [1998] IRLR 23, the Court of Appeal held that the correct approach in calculating the compensation due to the claimant ex-servicewomen dismissed on grounds of pregnancy was to take the sum that they would have earned had they remained in the forces, deduct from that sum the amount that they had, or should have, earned elsewhere, and then discount the net loss by a percentage to reflect the chance that they might have left the armed forces in any event.

Deduction of state benefits

Invalidity Benefit (now Incapacity Benefit) is to be deducted from the compensa- **19.89** tory award (*Chan v Hackney London Borough Council* [1997] ICR 1014, EAT). This is because Incapacity Benefit is paid only because of inability to earn an income, and thus credit should not be given for this as well as for the lost earnings themselves. (Incapacity Benefit was introduced on 13 April 1995 to replace, inter alia, Invalidity Benefit.)

Incapacity Benefit falls to be deducted in full (*Morgans v Alpha Plus Security Ltd* **19.90** [2005] IRLR 234, EAT, an unfair dismissal case following the approach in *Puglia v C James & Sons* [1996] IRLR 70, EAT).

D. Compliance with Statutory Codes

Failure to comply with the ACAS Code of Practice

With effect from 6 April 2009, the Employment Act 2008 (EA 2008), s 1 repealed **19.91** the statutory dispute resolution procedures that had been introduced in October 2004 under the Employment Act 2002 (EA 2002), ss 29–33 and Schs 2–4, and the

Employment Act 2002 (Dispute Resolution) Regulations 2004 (DRR 2004), SI 2004/752.

19.92 Meanwhile, EA 2008, s 3 inserted a new s 207A and Sch A2 into the Trade Union and Labour Relations (Consolidation) Act 1992 (TULR(C)A 1992), which provides a new, more flexible and less prescriptive regime based on a revised Advisory, Conciliation, and Arbitration Service (ACAS) Code of Practice on Disciplinary and Grievance Procedures that is more 'principles-based'.

19.93 As a result, in the case of any proceedings to which TULR(C)A 1992, s 207A applies (this includes discrimination claims, because they are listed in Sch A2), if it appears to the employment tribunal, that:

(a) the claim to which the proceedings relate concerns a matter to which a relevant Code of Practice applies;

(b) the employer or employee has failed to comply with that Code in relation to that matter; and

(c) that failure was unreasonable,

the employment tribunal may, if it considers it just and equitable in all of the circumstances to do so, increase or decrease any award that it makes to the employee by no more than 25 per cent. It is important to note that this power to adjust awards only applies to a breach of the ACAS Code of Practice on Disciplinary and Grievances Procedures, and not to a breach of any of the equality codes of practice.

19.94 The TULR(C)A 1992, s 207A adjustment in the compensatory award is made after deductions for *ex gratia* payments and mitigation.

19.95 Any adjustment of award under s 207A must be made prior to any adjustment to be made under EA 2002, s 38 (which prescribes minimum awards where there has been a failure to give a statement of employment particulars).

E. Interest

Interest on awards

19.96 At the same time as removing the statutory limit on compensation in cases of unlawful discrimination, provision was also made for the award of interest in discrimination cases. Awards of interest are currently governed by the Employment Tribunals (Interest on Awards in Discrimination Cases) Regulations 1996, SI 1996/2803 (the Interest Regulations). However, EqA 2010, s 139(1) provides for further regulations to be made governing interest on awards.

19.97 Where a tribunal makes an award of compensation for unlawful discrimination, it may include interest on the sums awarded and it shall consider whether to do so without the need for any application by a party in the proceedings (reg 2(1)). Alternatively, the tribunal may award interest on terms that have been agreed between the parties (reg 2(2)).

Rate of interest

Interest is calculated as simple interest, which accrues from day to day (reg 3(1)). **19.98** Under reg 3(2), the rate of interest to be applied in England and Wales is that pre- scribed for the special investment account under r 27(1) of the Court Funds Rules 1987, SI 1887/821. The rate of interest currently prescribed for England and Wales is 6 per cent (as from 1 March 2002). The previous rate was 7 per cent (as from 1 August 1999). In Scotland, the rate is that fixed for the time being by the Act of Sederunt (Interest on Sheriff Court Decrees or Extracts) 1975, SI 1975/948. Where the rate has varied over the relevant period, the tribunal may, in the inter- ests of simplicity, apply such median or average of those rates as seems to it appropriate (reg 3(3)).

Interest on injury to feelings

Interest on injury to feelings awards runs from the date of the contravention or act **19.99** of discrimination complained of to the day of calculation (reg 6(1)(a)). It is clear that Parliament intended that, unlike interest on other awards where the mid-point was to be taken, interest on an award for injury to feelings should normally be from the date of the discriminatory act. That must be taken to allow for the fact that injury to feelings is not a one-off event, but something that will often persist over a period of time (*Derby Specialist Fabrication Ltd v Burton* [2001] IRLR 69, EAT).

Interest on financial loss

For all heads of loss other than injury to feelings, interest is calculated for the period **19.100** from the mid-point date to the day of calculation (reg 6(1)(b)). The mid-point date is the halfway point between the date of the act of discrimination complained of and the date on which interest is being calculated (reg 4).

Interest on early payment of compensation

If a respondent has made a payment to the claimant before the day of calculation, **19.101** the date of payment is treated as if it were the day of calculation for the purposes of calculating the interest to be awarded (reg 6(2)).

Exceptional circumstances

Where, having regard to the circumstances of the case as a whole or to a particular **19.102** sum in the award, the tribunal considers that serious injustice would be caused if interest were to be awarded in respect of the ordinary periods set out above, it may calculate interest by reference to different periods or use different periods for different sums in the award (reg 6(3)). In *Ministry of Defence v Cannock* [1994] ICR 918, [1994] IRLR 509, the EAT held that the tribunal is entitled to exercise its powers under the then reg 7(3) of the Sex Discrimination and Equal Pay (Remedies) Regulations 1993, SI 1993/2798, to depart from the normal procedure of awarding interest from the mid-point date between the act of discrimination and the date of the tribunal hearing, and to award interest over a different and longer period by reason of the fact that the whole of the loss was incurred many years ago. The statutory provisions expressly cater for the exceptional case and what is exceptional is a matter for the tribunal.

No interest on future loss

19.103   *Cannock* is also authority for the proposition that a tribunal is not entitled to award interest in respect of future loss of pension. This is because what is now reg 5 of the Interest Regulations precludes interest 'in respect of a sum awarded for a loss or matter which will occur after the day of calculation'.

Interest on aggravated damages

19.104   Interest on aggravated damages for conduct in resisting a claim subsequent to termination of employment should not be based on the whole period since the discriminatory act (*Zaiwalla & Co v Walia* [2002] IRLR 697, EAT).

Interest on net loss

19.105   The function of an award of interest is to compensate the party to whom it is awarded for being kept out of the money that he or she should have had in their pocket at an earlier date. There is no logical basis for awarding interest on sums that the employee would never have received. Therefore, interest should be awarded on the claimant's net loss (that is, after deductions for income tax and National Insurance contributions [NICs]) and not on the gross loss (*Bentwood Bros (Manchester) Ltd v Shepherd* [2003] ICR 1000, [2003] IRLR 364, CA).

Late payment of compensation

19.106   If payment of the full amount of the award (including any interest under reg 2 of the Interest Regulations is not made within 14 days after the relevant decision day, then the Employment Tribunals (Interest) Order 1990, SI 1990/479, applies to awards under the discrimination legislation, so that interest on the tribunal award accrues from the day immediately following the relevant decision day (see reg 8(1) of the Interest Regulations).

20

COMPENSATION IN DISCRIMINATION
CASES: OTHER EQUALITY CLAIMS

A. Compensation for Unequal Contract Terms (Including Pay)

Sex equality clause

The Equality Act 2010 (EqA 2010), s 66 provides that a sex equality clause operates **20.01** so as to modify the terms of a contract to include such a term where there is no such term or where that term is less favourable to the corresponding term of the contract of a comparator who is employed on equal work.

The tribunal has jurisdiction to hear four types of case: **20.02**

(a) a claim by an employee for breach of an equality clause or rule (EqA 2010, s 127(2));

(b) an application by a responsible person for a declaration as to the rights of that person and a worker in relation to a dispute about the effect of an equality clause or rule (s 127(3));

(c) an application by the trustees or managers of an occupational pension scheme for a declaration as to their rights and those of a member in relation to a dispute about the effect of an equality rule (s 127(4)); and

(d) if, in proceedings before a court, a question arises about an equality clause or rule, the court may (whether or not on an application by a party to the proceedings) refer the question, or direct that it be referred by a party to the proceedings, to an employment tribunal for determination, and stay or assist the proceedings in the meantime (s 127(5)).

Remedy

20.03　The remedies available to the employee are the same as those in any claim for breach of contract. Normally, this will involve a claim for a declaration, damages for breach of contract, and possibly an injunction (although this remedy is not available in the employment tribunal). Where the sex equality clause has the effect of modifying any of the terms that relate to wages within the meaning of Pt 2 of the Employment Rights Act 1996 (ERA 1996), s 27(1), a claim may be brought under those provisions for the recovery or non-payment of such wages.

20.04　A claim under the Equal Pay Act 1970 (EqPA 1970) (now EqA 2010, Pt V, ch 3) is a financial claim only. Compensation cannot be recovered for non-economic loss such as injury to feelings, aggravated damages, and/or exemplary damages (*Council of City of Newcastle upon Tyne v Allen and others* [2005] IRLR 504, EAT).

Arrears day

20.05　The normal period for a 'standard case' for which arrears of remuneration or damages may be claimed is six years before the day on which proceedings were instituted (EqA 2010, s 132(4)).

20.06　However, in a 'concealment case' or an 'incapacity case' (or a case that is both), the arrears day is the day on which the breach first occurred (EqA 2010, s 132(4)).

Awards of interest in equality of terms cases

20.07　Under the Employment Tribunals (Interest on Awards in Discrimination Cases) Regulations 1996, SI 1996/2803, in relation to a loss that extended over a period, the calculation of interest should start at the beginning of the period, and be taken up to the date of calculation. Interest at the full rate should then be applied to half of that period.

20.08　Regulation 4(3) provides that the relevant period 'is the period beginning on the date, in the case of an award under the 1970 Act [now EqA 2010], of the contravention and, in other cases, of the act of discrimination complained of, and ending on the day of calculation'. Although, on a literal construction, it is possible to argue that the contravention there referred to occurs week by week, or day by day, so that the mid-point should be taken day by day, or week by week, between each contravention and the date of calculation, there is no sensible reason for drawing a distinction between cases in which an employee is dismissed and cases in which the employee remains employed. Such a bizarre result can be avoided by a sensible reading of reg 4(3), aided by the Interpretation Act 1978, so that it reads as follows (*Redcar and Cleveland Borough Council v Degnan* [2005] IRLR 179, EAT): 'The period referred

to in para (2) is the period beginning on the date, in the case of an award under the 1970 Act, of the beginning of the contraventions and ending on the day of calculation.'
Degnan was, at the time of writing, on appeal to the Court of Appeal.

B. Compensation for Part-time Workers and Fixed-term Employees

Less favourable treatment against part-time workers and fixed-term employees

Where a tribunal finds that a complaint presented to it under the Part-time Workers **20.09** (Prevention of Less Favourable Treatment) Regulations 2000, SI 2000/1551 (PTWR 2000), or the Fixed-term Employees (Prevention of Less Favourable Treatment) Regulations 2002, SI 2002/2034 (FTER 2002), is well founded, it has the power to take any of the following steps that it considers just and equitable:

(a) to make a declaration as to the rights of the claimant and the employer in relation to the matters to which the complaint relates;

(b) to order the employer to pay compensation to the claimant; or

(c) to recommend that the employer take, within a specified period, action appearing to the tribunal to be reasonable, in all of the circumstances of the case, for the purposes of obviating or reducing the adverse effect on the claimant of any matter to which the complaint relates (PTWR 2000, reg 8(7); FTER 2002, reg 7(7)).

In contrast with the position under the main anti-discrimination statutes, the **20.10** amount of compensation to be awarded will be such as the tribunal considers just and equitable in all of the circumstances, having regard to:

(a) the infringement to which the complaint relates; and

(b) any loss that is attributable to the infringement, having regard, in the case of an infringement of the right conferred by PTWR 2000, reg 5, to the pro rata principle except where it is inappropriate to do so (PTWR 2000, reg 8(9); FTER 2002, reg 7(8)).

That loss will include any reasonable expenses and any benefit the claimant might **20.11** reasonably be expected to have had but for the infringement (PTWR 2000, reg 8(10); FTER 2002, reg 7(9)).

There is no statutory cap on the amount of compensation that can be awarded, but **20.12** the claimant is under the usual common law duty to mitigate loss (PTWR 2000, reg 8(12); FTER 2002, reg 7(11)).

By further contrast with the main anti-discrimination statutes, injury to feelings **20.13** cannot be awarded for less favourable treatment (PTWR 2000, reg 8(11); FTER 2002, reg 7(10)).

20.14 Also, the principle of contributory conduct applies so that, where the tribunal finds that the act, or failure to act, to which the complaint relates was to any extent caused or contributed to by action of the claimant, it shall reduce the amount of the compensation by such proportion as it considers just and equitable having regard to that finding (PTWR 2000, reg 8(13); FTER 2002, reg 7(12)).

20.15 Where an employer fails, without reasonable justification, to comply with a recommendation, the tribunal may, if it thinks it just and equitable to do so, increase the amount of compensation ordered or, if no compensation order has been made, make such an order (PTWR 2000, reg 8(14); FTER 2002, reg 7(13)).

C. Occupational Pension Schemes

20.16 The Employment Equality (Sexual Orientation) Regulations 2003, SI 2003/1661 (SOR 2003), and the Employment Equality (Religion or Belief) Regulations 2003, SI 2003/1660 (RBR 2003), contained specific provisions outlawing discrimination or harassment involving pensions schemes. The EqA 2010, s 126 provides similar remedies, but in respect of all nine protected characteristics, if an employment tribunal finds that there has been a contravention of a provision referred to in s 120(1) in relation to either:

(a) the terms on which persons become members of an occupational pension scheme; or

(b) the terms on which members of an occupational pension scheme are treated,

then, in addition to the remedies available under s 124(2), the tribunal may also by order declare:

(c) if the complaint relates to the terms on which persons become members of a scheme, that the complainant has a right to be admitted to the scheme; or

(b) if the complaint relates to the terms on which members of the scheme are treated, that the complainant has a right to membership of the scheme without discrimination.

20.17 An order made under s 124(2):

(a) may make provision as to the terms on which, or the capacity in which, the claimant is to enjoy the admission or membership; and

(b) may have effect in relation to a period before the order is made.

20.18 A tribunal may only make an order to pay compensation for injury to feelings or under s 124(7) for failure, without reasonable excuse, to comply with an appropriate recommendation.

Part V

COMPENSATION FOR OTHER EMPLOYMENT TRIBUNAL CLAIMS

21

COMPENSATION FOR CLAIMS ARISING DURING EMPLOYMENT

A. Introduction

21.01 In addition to claims for breach of contract, unfair dismissal, redundancy pay, and discrimination, employment tribunals have power to award compensation in a wide variety of other jurisdictions.

21.02 Foremost amongst these in statistical terms are disputes over payment of wages (Pt II of the Employment Rights Act 1996 [ERA 1996]).

21.03 This section of the book covers the remedies available in employment tribunals for claims arising during the period of employment and not necessarily upon its termination.

21.04 The ERA 1996 gives employment tribunals jurisdiction to determine complaints relating to:

(a) the failure to provide written particulars (ERA 1996, Pt I);
(b) the non-payment of wages (ERA 1996, Pt II);
(c) the non-payment of guarantee payments (ERA 1996, Pt III);
(d) a breach of the rules on Sunday working for shop and betting workers (ERA 1966, Pt IV);
(e) detriment suffered in employment (ERA 1996, Pt V);
(f) a breach of the statutory rights to time off work (ERA 1996, Pt VI);
(g) suspension from work on medical or maternity grounds (ERA 1996, Pt VII); and
(h) maternity, adoption, parental, paternity leave, and flexible working (ERA 1996, Pt VIII).

21.05 In addition, tribunals have jurisdiction to determine disputes relating to the special protection that is conferred on trade union representatives and trade union members in Pt III of the Trade Unions and Labour Relations (Consolidation) Act 1992 (TULR(C)A 1992) and disputes relating to the right to be accompanied to a disciplinary or grievance hearing pursuant to ss 10 and 11 of the Employment Relations Act 1999 (as amended) (ERelA 1999), and the right to written reasons for dismissal.

B. Written Particulars

21.06 The right to written particulars of employment is set out in ERA 1996, Pt I.

Statement of employment particulars

21.07 In essence, an employee has the right to be given a complete statement of particulars of the various matters referred to in the statutory provisions 'not later than two months after the beginning of employment' (ERA 1996, s 1(2)), although some of the statutory particulars may be given by instalments within that period. The statement must accurately state the particulars at a specified date not more than seven days before the statement or instalment was given to the employee.

In general, the statement must itself set out the relevant particulars (ERA 1996, **21.08** s 2(4)), but special provision is made for particulars relating to sick pay, pensions, disciplinary and grievance procedure, and collective agreements that allow the employer to refer in the statement to some other document, provided that this is reasonably accessible to the employee (ERA 1996, ss 2(2) and (3), and 3(1)(aa)). A document is treated as 'reasonably accessible' if it is one that the employee has a reasonable opportunity of reading in the course of employment or if it is made reasonably accessible in some other way (ERA 1996, s 6).

Apart from this, the other statutory particulars required by ERA 1996, s 1(4)(a)–(k) **21.09** may now be given in a number of ways—that is, in a contract of employment or a letter of engagement (ERA 1996, s 7A(1) and (2)). These documents may also incorporate the requirements under ERA 1996, s 3. Furthermore, where such a document is given before the commencement of employment, it is treated as having been given when the employment begins (ERA 1996, s 7B).

Right to itemized pay statements

Also included in ERA 1996, Pt I is the right to an itemized pay statement (ERA **21.10** 1996, s 6). Such a statement should contain particulars of the gross amount of wages or salary, the amount of any variable and fixed deductions, the net amount of wages or salary, and, where those amounts are paid in different ways, the amount and method of each part-payment.

Remedy

The remedy for a failure to comply with the statutory requirement to provide a **21.11** written statement of particulars of employment or failure to provide an itemized pay statement is set out in ERA 1996, ss 11–12.

Where an employer does not give an employee a statement in accordance with the **21.12** statutory provisions (either because no statement is given or because the statement does not comply with what is required), the employee may require that a reference be made to an employment tribunal to determine what particulars ought to have been given to comply with the statutory provisions.

In essence, the employment tribunal may grant a declaration confirming the particulars **21.13** that should have been included, amending those particulars, or substituting other particulars (ERA 1996, s 12(2)) or, in the case of itemized wage statements, simply make a declaration to the effect (ERA 1996, s 12(3)). Furthermore, where the tribunal finds that un-notified deductions have been made from the pay of an employee during the period of 13 weeks prior to the date of the application for reference, the tribunal may order the employer to pay the employee a sum not exceeding the aggregate of the un-notified deductions (ERA 1996, s 12(4)).

21.14 Until the Employment Act 2002 (EA 2002) came into force on 1 October 2004, there was no power to order compensation or award any other financial penalty where an employer failed to supply written particulars or supplied written particulars that failed to comply with the statutory requirements. However, since 1 October 2004, a financial penalty is available where:

(a) a complaint is made in relation to one or more of the matters specified in EA 2002, Sch 5;

(b) the employment tribunal finds in favour of the employee in relation to one or more of those matters, but makes no award to the employee in relation to those claims; and

(c) it is shown that the employer is in breach of the statutory duty to provide particulars.

21.15 In such circumstances, the tribunal must make an award of two weeks' pay and may, if it considers it just and equitable, award up to four weeks' pay (EA 2002, s 38(1)–(4)). This duty does not apply if there are exceptional circumstances that would make such an award unjust or inequitable (EA 2002, s 38 (5)).

21.16 Claims within the scope of EA 2002, Sch 5 include complaints of unfair dismissal, detriment in employment, discrimination, redundancy payment, and unlawful deduction from wages.

21.17 A week's pay for this purpose is the amount prescribed by the Secretary of State pursuant to ERA 1996, s 227 (from 1 February 2010, this was £380).

21.18 Such a claim must be brought within three months beginning with the date on which employment ceases, or, where this is not reasonably practicable, within such further period as the employment tribunal considers reasonable (ERA 1996, s 11(4)).

C. Payment of Wages

21.19 The right to complain to an employment tribunal regarding unauthorized deductions from wages is set out in ERA 1996, Pt II (previously the Wages Act 1986). The substantive provisions are summarized below, as a more detailed consideration of these provisions lies outside the scope of this book.

Right not to suffer unauthorized deduction

21.20 In essence, the statutory provisions protect an employee against any deduction from 'wages' that has not been authorized by:

(a) a statutory provision;

(b) a relevant provision of the worker's contract; or

(c) some other written agreement under which the worker has previously given his or her consent to the deduction being made (ERA 1996, s 13(1)–(2)).

Such an agreement must be made before the circumstances arose that led to the deduction in question (see ERA 1996, s 13(5) and *Discount Tobacco & Confectionary v Williamson* [1993] IRLR 327).

21.21 An amount is treated as a 'deduction' where the total amount of wages paid on any occasion by an employer to a worker employed by it is less than the total amount of the wages 'properly payable' to the worker. This covers both a reduced payment, as well as a non-payment of wages (*Delaney v Staples* [1991] IRLR 112), but does not apply where the error is simply one of computation (ERA 1996, s 13(4)).

21.22 Wages are 'properly payable' to a worker when they fall due. In relation to contractual payments, this will depend on the terms of the contract. For example, in *Brand v Compro Computer Services Ltd* [2005] IRLR 196, the Court of Appeal ruled that a commission payment payable to a recruitment consultant was earned when the employer was in possession of signed time sheets from its clients (the calculation being done at the end of each month even though the payment was not made until the end of the following month) and that the sum was payable even though the claimant had been summarily dismissed before the payment had been made. In relation to non-contractual payments, the entitlement will depend either on the words of the statute or, in the case of non-contractual bonuses, when the payment is declared (*Farrell Matthews & Weir v Hansen* [2005] IRLR 160).

Exceptions

21.23 The statutory provisions do not apply to a deduction from a worker's wages where the purpose of the deduction is reimbursement of the employer in respect of:

(a) an overpayment of wages (ERA 1996, s 14(1)(a));

(b) an overpayment of expenses incurred by the worker in carrying out his or her employment (ERA 1996, s 14(1)(b));

(c) where the deduction is made in consequence of any disciplinary proceedings if those proceedings were held by virtue of a statutory provision (ERA 1996, s 14(2));

(d) where the deduction is made in pursuance of a statutory requirement (ERA 1996, s 14(3));

(e) where the employee has consented or agreed either by way of a provision in the contract or by agreement to payments being made to a third party (ERA 1966, s 14(4));

(f) where the worker has taken part in a strike or other industrial actions and the deduction is made on account of the worker so taking part (ERA 1996, s 14(5)); or

(g) where the employee has consented or agreed to payments being made in satisfaction of a court order or tribunal requiring payment of an amount by the worker to the employer (ERA 1996, s 14(6)).

21.24 Nonetheless, an employment tribunal has jurisdiction to determine whether the deduction under these exceptions is properly made (*Gill v Ford Motor Co Ltd* [2004] IRLR 840). Special rules apply to cash shortages and stock deficiencies (ERA 1996, ss 17–22).

Meaning of wages

21.25 Wages are defined by ERA 1996, s 27 as 'any sums payable to the employee in connection with his employment', including (ERA 1996, s 27(1)):

(a) any fee, bonus, commission, holiday pay, or other emolument referable to his or her employment, whether payable under his or her contract or otherwise—which is restricted to a claim for contractual holiday pay, not statutory holiday pay, where the claim must be brought under the Working Time Regulations 1998, SI 1998/1833 (WTR 1998), reg 30 (see *Commissioners of the Inland Revenue v Ainsworth* [2005] EWCA Civ 441, overturning *List Design Group Ltd v Douglas and Catley* [2003] IRLR 14);

(b) statutory sick pay under Pt XI of the Social Security Contributions and Benefits Act 1992 (SSCBA 1992);

(c) statutory maternity pay under SSCBA 1992, Pt XII;

(ca) statutory paternity pay payable under SSCBA 1992, Pt 12ZA;

(cb) statutory adoption pay under SSCBA 1992, Pt 12ZB;

(d) guarantee pay under ERA 1996, s 28;

(e) payments for time off under ERA 1996, Pt IV, or TULR(C)A 1992, s 169, or the other statutory provisions referred to below (see **21.131**);

(f) remuneration for suspension on medical and maternity grounds;

(fa) remuneration on ending the supply of an agency worker on maternity grounds under ERA 1996, s 68C;

(g) any sum payable in pursuance of an order for reinstatement or reinstatement under ERA 1996, s 113;

(h) any sum payable under an order for interim relief under ERA 1996, s 130, or TULR(C)A 1992, s 164; or

(i) remuneration under a protective award payable under TULR(C)A 1992, s 189.

21.26 The following payments do not count as wages (ERA 1996, s 27(2)):

(a) any payment by way of an advance under an agreement for a loan or by way of an advance of wages (but without prejudice to the application of s 13 to any deduction made from the worker's wages in respect of such advances);

(b) any payment of expenses in the course of employment;

(c) any payment by way of a pension, allowance, or gratuity in connection with a worker's retirement or as compensation for loss of office;

(d) any payment referable to redundancy; and

(e) any payment made to a worker other than in his or her capacity as a worker.

It should also be noted that other non-financial benefits, such as a company car, **21.27** received by a worker in connection with his or her employment do not qualify as 'wages'. Loss of such benefits, or a failure to pay any of the excluded payment, can be recovered in an action for breach of contract, but not as an unlawful deduction.

Contractual right or otherwise

The definition in ERA 1996, s 27(1)(a) covers any payment that is referable to **21.28** employment, 'whether payable under his contract or otherwise'. This has been held to cover payments that arise as a result of statutory entitlement such as a payment of wages under the National Minimum Wage Act 1998. It has also been held to cover a non-contractual bonus (*Farrell Mathews & Weir v Hansen* [2005] IRLR 100). ERA 1996, s 27(3) specifically provides that where a payment in the nature of a non-contractual bonus is (for any reason) made to a worker, 'the amount of the payment shall . . . be treated as wages . . . payable . . . on the day when the payment is made'.

Can a claim be based on a reasonable expectation of payment?

In *Kent Management Services v Butterfield* [1992] ICR 272, the Employment Appeal **21.29** Tribunal (EAT) ruled that a bonus payment was recoverable under ERA 1996, Pt II where there was a reasonable expectation of such a payment or if it was within the reasonable contemplation of the parties. However, this interpretation was rejected by the Court of Appeal in *New Century Cleaning Ltd v Church* [2000] IRLR 27, in which the Court ruled that wages only fell within the scope of ERA 1996, s 27(1) where there was a contractual or some other legal entitlement.

In *Church*, the claimant (and his fellow window cleaners) were paid on a piecework **21.30** system. Each team had a leading hand and he or she would agree with the other members of the team how the amount that was payable for each job was to be divided between them. The leading hand then submitted a weekly wage summary to the employer, showing how each week's total for all jobs would be split among members of the team, and the employer would prepare each worker's wages on that basis. The dispute arose after the price charged was reduced by 10 per cent as a result of falling profits. The claimants alleged that this amounted to an unlawful deduction, but the Court of Appeal ruled that there was nothing in the contract that entitled either the claimant or his team to do the same jobs each week for the same price. Furthermore, there was no basis for implying a term that the employer was obliged to maintain the rate at which a job was offered or was not entitled unilaterally to reduce that rate. The entitlement to a particular rate only arose once the wage summary had been completed by the leading hand and handed to the employer for payment. It followed that the reduction in the job price was not a reduction from the wage that was properly payable, but a change in one of the components necessary for its calculation.

Whilst this interpretation would appear to be correct on the particular facts in **21.31** *Church*, the extent to which a claim to a contractual bonus may now be based on the reasonable expectation of the parties needs to be seen in the context of more recent legal developments concerning the exercise of contractual discretion and, in particular, the Court of Appeal's ruling in *Horkulak v Cantor Fitzgerald Ltd* [2004] IRLR 924 (see **1.51–1.53**), in which it was emphasized that such contractual discretion should be exercised in a rational manner and that there was an expectation that it would not be exercised 'willy nilly'.

Payments made after termination

21.32 In *Robertson v Blackstone Franks Investment Ltd* [1998] IRLR 376, the Court of Appeal ruled that a claim could be brought in respect of commission on orders placed prior to termination even though the payment itself was not due until after termination of employment. The Court reasoned that the payment related to work done prior to termination and did not lose its character simply because the payment was not due until after termination (see also *Brand v Compro Computer Services Ltd* [2005] IRLR 196).

Payments in lieu of notice

21.33 In *Delaney v Staples* [1992] IRLR 191, the House of Lords ruled that a payment in lieu of notice in the technical sense—that is, a payment of damages for wrongful dismissal—does not qualify as wages within the meaning of ERA 1996, s 27(1). But, as Lord Browne-Wilkinson pointed out in that case, the phrase 'payment in lieu' is used 'to describe many types of payment the legal analysis of which differs'. For example, the phrase may be used to describe payments made to an employee on garden leave that clearly would qualify as wages within the meaning of s 27(1). Similarly, payments made in Lord Browne-Wilkinson's second category—namely, where the contract gives the employer the right to terminate by making a payment in lieu of notice—have been held to be wages (*Jenkins v City Index* ELA Briefing, July/August 2000), and, in principle, the same reasoning should apply to agreed termination payments (*Richardson* (*HM Tax Inspector*) *v Delaney* [2001] IRLR 663), although there is no direct authority on the point under ERA 1996, Pt II.

Disputes over state benefits

21.34 Although various payments referred to above under the provisions of the SSCBA 1992 fall within the statutory definition of 'wages', in *Taylor Gordon & Company Ltd v Stuart Timmons* EAT 0159/03, the EAT held that a tribunal did not have jurisdiction to determine whether Statutory Sick Pay (SSP) was 'properly payable'. The EAT reasoned that such decisions regarding the entitlement to SSP are dealt with by the relevant Board of HM Revenue and Customs (HMRC) rather than by employment tribunals and that a decision to the contrary could lead to inconsistent decisions. The EAT recognized that its reasoning would also apply to other statutory payments such as Statutory Maternity Pay (SMP), Statutory Paternity Pay (SPP), and Statutory Adoption Pay (SAP).

Whilst the EAT's decision makes a certain amount of common sense, it does beg **21.35** the question as to why such payments are included in the definition of wages in ERA 1996, s 27(1), and why the reference to what is properly payable in ERA 1996, s 13 does not appear to be limited to contractual disputes. The decision means that tribunals will have jurisdiction only over such statutory payments for which the payment is admitted by the employer or for which the determination by the relevant statutory authority has taken place by the time of the hearing.

The EAT's reasoning would not necessarily apply where the employer pays more **21.36** than the statutory minimum—for example, contractual maternity pay.

Remedy

A worker has the right to complain to an employment tribunal where there has been **21.37** an unauthorized deduction from his or her wages or a breach of any of the other rights conferred by ERA 1996, Pt II (ERA 1996, s 23).

The orders that can be made on such a complaint under this section are set out in **21.38** ERA 1996, s 24. Where a tribunal upholds such a complaint, it is required to make a declaration to that effect and shall order the employer to pay to the worker the amount of any deduction made in contravention of ERA 1996, ss 13 or 15 or any unlawful deductions made under the special provisions that protect shopworkers in cases of cash shortages or stock deficiencies. Section 24(2) was added by s 7(1) of the Employment Act 2008 (EA 2008) as from 6 April 2009, empowering the tribunal to:

> order the employer to pay to the worker (in addition to any amount ordered to be paid under [s 24(1)]) such amount as the tribunal considers appropriate in all the circumstances to compensate the worker for any financial loss sustained by him which is attributable to the matter complained of.

Where such a declaration (and order for repayment) is made, an employer cannot **21.39** recover the sum that was unlawfully deducted by any other means—that is, in an action for breach of contract or tort (*Delaney v Staples* [1991] IRLR 112 and *Potter v Hunt Contracts Ltd* [1992] IRLR 108, 119). However, an employer must not be ordered to repay to the worker any amount of a deduction or payment (or combination of the two) that appears to the tribunal to have already been paid or repaid. So, for example, where a worker receives an advance, the tribunal will be entitled to take this into account in determining the sums due to the worker (*Robertson v Blackstone Funds Investment Management Ltd* [1998] IRLR 381).

There is no limit on the amount that can be awarded where an employer is found to **21.40** be in breach of the statutory provisions. So, for example, in *Jowitt v Pioneer Technology Ltd* [2002] IRLR 790, a claim was made under ERA 1996, Pt II to recover payments that the claimant said were due to him under a permanent health insurance (PHI) scheme; the same would apply to claims for bonus payments. The principal advantage of bringing such a claim before an employment tribunal is that the costs regime is more liberal. A further possible perceived advantage is that the claim may be determined by a panel including lay members rather than a judge sitting alone. However, as the *Jowitt* case illustrates, the issues involved are sometimes highly technical and it is perhaps for this reason that claims of this nature are normally brought in the High Court.

21.41 It should be noted that claims under ERA 1996, Pt II may be brought by workers as well as employees. It thus applies to those who work either under a contract of employment or under any other contract, whether express or implied, whereby the individual under-takes to do or perform personally any work or services for another party to the contract whose status is not by virtue of the contract that of a client or customer of any profession or business undertaking carried out by the individual (ERA 1996, s 230(3)).

21.42 A complaint under these provisions may be made in relation to unpaid statutory holiday pay under the WTR 1998, even though these Regulations have their own means of recovery in reg 30 (*Revenue and Customs v Stringer* [2009] UKHL 31, [2009] IRLR 677, [2009] ICR 985, HL). This might be significant because the provision on time limits in ERA 1996, s 230(3) is more generous (in relation to a continuing failure to pay) than reg 30.

21.43 Such a claim must normally be brought within three months of the deduction taking place—or, in the case of a payment received by the employer, the date on which the payment was received by the employer (ERA 1996, s 23(2)—unless it was not reasonably practicable to bring such a complaint within the statutory time limit, in which case the tribunal may consider the complaint if it is presented within such period as the tribunal considers reasonable (ERA 1996, s 23(4)). There is one exception to the statutory time limit: where the complaint relates to a 'series of deductions' within the meaning of ERA 1996, s 23(3), where the three months' time runs from the last deduction in the series.

D. National Minimum Wage

21.44 The National Minimum Wage Act 1998 (NMWA 1998) gives every worker the right to a specified minimum wage.

Scope

21.45 The statutory provisions relating to the national minimum wage are set out in the NMWA 1998 and the National Minimum Wage Regulations 1999, SI 1999/584 (NMWR 1999). A detailed consideration of those Regulations lies outside the scope of this book, but the basic principle is that a 'person who qualifies for the national minimum wage shall be remunerated by his employer in respect of his work in any pay reference period at a rate that is not less than the national minimum wage' (NMWA 1998, s 1(1)).

A person qualifies for the national minimum wage if he or she is an individual who **21.46** is a worker who ordinarily works in the UK under his or her contract and has ceased to be of compulsory school age (NMWA 1998, s 1(2)). Special provision is made for agency workers (NMWA 1998, s 34(2)) and home workers (NMWA 1998, s 54(3)). in so far as these groups do not fall within the definition of 'worker'.

Certain workers are excluded from protection, such as share fisherman (NMWA **21.47** 1998, s 43), voluntary workers (NMWA 1998, s 44), prisoners working under prison rules (NMWA 1998, s 45), and certain religious communities. Other exclusions have been created by the definition of 'work' under the NMWR 1999.

The rate of the national minimum wage is set and revised by the Secretary of State **21.48** by means of regulation (NMWA 1998, s 2). For workers aged 22 and over:

(a) from 1 April 1999, the rate was originally set at £3.60;
(b) from 1 October 2000, the rate was £3.70;
(c) from 1 October 2001, the rate was £4.10;
(d) from 1 October 2002, the rate was £4.20;
(e) from 1 October 2003, the rate was £4.50;
(f) from 1 October 2004, the rate was £4.85;
(g) from 1 October 2005, the rate was £5.05;
(h) from 1 October 2006, the rate was £5.35;
(i) from 1 October 2007, the rate was £5.52;
(j) from 1 October 2008, the rate was £5.73;
(k) from 1 October 2009, the rate was £5.80; and
(l) from 1 October 2010, the rate was £5.93.

The rate is set as an hourly rate. The rate is the gross rate before the deduction of tax **21.49** and National Insurance contributions (NICs). The latest guidance and code of practice on the minimum wage can be found online at <http://www.bis.gov.uk/policies/employment-matters/rights/nmw>.

Calculation of the hourly rate

NMWR 1999, reg 14 deals with the method of determining whether the national **21.50** minimum wage has been paid.

This states: **21.51**

(1) The hourly rate paid to a worker in a pay reference period shall be determined by dividing the total calculated in accordance with paragraph (2) by the number of hours specified in paragraph (3).
(2) The total referred to in paragraph (1) shall be calculated by subtracting from the total remuneration in the pay reference period determined under regulation 30, the total reduction determined under regulations 31 to 37.
(3) The hours referred to in paragraph (1) are the total number of hours of time work, salaried hours work, output work and unmeasured work worked by the worker in

the pay reference period that have been ascertained in accordance with regulations 20 to 29A.

21.52 There are therefore a number of key concepts that need to be considered in order to determine whether the national minimum wage has, in fact, been paid.

21.53 The pay reference period is defined as a month, or, where the worker is paid by reference to a shorter period such as a week, that period (NMWR 1999, reg 10(1)). Special rules apply if the employment contract terminated inside the pay reference period.

21.54 Having determined the pay reference period, it is then necessary to consider what counts as pay for this purpose. The Regulations make clear that this, like a 'week's pay', is based on the concept of remuneration. So all money payments count as pay for this purpose (NMWR 1999, regs 14(2) and 30), but benefits in kind are not included (reg 9) and special provision is made for the treatment of accommodation within the meaning of reg 30(d). Furthermore, certain elements are excluded from being treated as payments. These include an advance of wages or a loan (reg 8(a)), any pension payments (reg 8(b)), payment of an award made by a court or tribunal or a similar settlement other than a payment due under the worker's contract (reg 8(c)), any payment referable to redundancy (reg 8(d)), and any payment by way of a reward under a suggestion scheme (reg 8(e)).

21.55 The next step under the statutory formula is to subtract the total reductions under NMWR 1999, regs 31–37. These include payments made in respect of periods during which the worker is absent from work or taking part in industrial action (reg 31(1)(b)), and overtime and shift premiums (reg 31(1)(c)). Tips and gratuities are also excluded (reg 31(1)(e)), as are allowances paid by the employer (other than allowances that are attributable to the performance of the worker in carrying out the work) (reg 31(1)(d)). In addition, any payments or deduction made to cover payments made by the worker in the course of work are excluded subject to the detailed requirements in NMWR, regs 31, 32, and 34.

21.56 The next stage in the process is to identify the working time for which the national minimum wage is payable in order to determine whether the appropriate rate has been paid. This is far from straightforward, because the Regulations identify four different patterns of work, each with their own rules on working time. The four types of work are defined in NMWR 1999, Pt III as 'time work', 'salaried hours', 'output work', and 'unmeasured work'.

21.57 The detailed rules on 'time work' are set out in NMWR 1999, regs 3 and 15. In essence, time work is work that is paid for according to set or varying hours or period of time and that are not salaried hours. A detailed consideration of these provisions lies outside the scope of this book.

21.58 The detailed rules on 'salaried work' are set out in NMWR 1999, regs 4, 16, and 21–23. In essence, salaried work is work done under a contract to do salaried hours' work under which the worker receives a fixed annual salary (other than a bonus) for an ascertainable number of basis hours in respect of which the worker is entitled to an annual salary by either weekly or monthly instalments regardless of how many hours the individual works in that period. A detailed consideration of these provisions lies outside the scope of this book.

The detailed rules on 'output work' are set out in NMWR 1999, regs 5, 17, 24, **21.59** and 25. In essence, output work is work that is not time work and is work for which the worker is paid by reference to output, such as piece work or payment by commission. A detailed consideration of these provisions lies outside the scope of this book.

The detailed rules on the residual category of 'unmeasured work' are set out in **21.60** NMWR 1999, regs 6, 18, 27, and 28. In essence, unmeasured work is defined as any work that does not fall within one of the other three types of work—that is, work for which there are no specific hours, and where the worker is required to work when needed or when work is available. In common parlance, this is likely to cover so-called 'zero-hours contracts'. A detailed consideration of these provisions lies outside the scope of this book.

Remedy

If a worker who qualifies for the national minimum wage is remunerated for any **21.61** pay reference period by his or her employer at a rate that is less than the national minimum wage, the worker shall be taken to be entitled under his or her contract to be paid, as additional remuneration in respect of that period, the amount set out in NMWA 1998, s 17(2) (NMWA 1998, s 17(1)).

That amount is essentially the difference between the payment that the employee **21.62** actually receives in the pay reference period and the amount that the worker should have received under NMWA 1998, s 2.

Such a claim can be brought in the employment tribunal as a claim for breach of **21.63** contract in accordance with the Employment Tribunals (Extension of Jurisdiction) Order 1994, SI 1994/1623. Indeed, this was regarded by the EAT in *Walton v Independent Living Ltd* [2002] ICR 1406 as the 'preferable' course, although it is arguable that, if the worker qualifies as a worker within the meaning of ERA 1996, Pt II, such a claim can be brought as an unlawful deduction (NMWA 1998, s 18(1) (a)), since this provision expressly provides that the national minimum wage is to be regarded as an entitlement under those statutory provisions, and the statutory definition of 'wages' covers any sums payable in connection with employment whether payable under contract or otherwise (ERA 1996, s 27(1)(a)). This would appear to be broad enough to cover wages payable under the NMWA 1998.

In *Blue Chip Trading Ltd v Helbawi* [2009] IRLR 128, EAT, the claimant was a **21.64** foreign student, who was subject to immigration restrictions on working in the UK that precluded him from working more than 20 hours a week during term-time, but allowed him to work full-time during vacations. In some weeks during term-time, he knowingly unlawfully worked more than 20 hours. When he brought a claim for non-payment of the national minimum wage, the preliminary issue arose as to whether the contract of employment was tainted by illegality and therefore unenforceable. The employment judge noted that there were times when the claimant was working legally and concluded that the whole contract should not be treated as illegal. Allowing an appeal in part, Mr Justice Elias (P) held that public policy would not 'be properly served by allowing the claimant to recover for any of the work done in term when he was knowingly acting in breach of the licence conditions'. However, Elias P went on to hold that the right solution was to sever the unlawful elements of performance and allow the claimant to recover the minimum wage in respect of those periods, such as vacations, during which there were no hours' limitations at all.

21.65 The statutory regime is also enforceable by state officials. A new regime of enforcement notices was introduced by the EA 2008, s 9 as from 6 April 2009, which substituted new ss 19–19H (for ss 19–22F). The detailed powers of the employment tribunal in these circumstances lie outside the scope of this work.

E. Guarantee Payments

21.66 The right to complain to an employment tribunal regarding the non-payment of a guarantee payment is set out in ERA 1996, Pt III. The right to a guarantee payment is considered in outline only, because a more detailed analysis of the statutory provisions lies outside the scope of this book. Readers who require such an analysis are referred to specialist texts on the topic.

Right to guarantee payment

21.67 In essence, an employee is entitled to a guarantee payment for any day (referred to as a 'workless day') on which the employee is not provided with work by his or her employer as a result of a diminution in the requirements of the employer's business for work of the particular kind that the employee is employed to do or any other occurrence affecting the normal working of the employer's business in relation to work of the kind that the employee is employed to do (ERA 1996, s 28(1)).

21.68 The entitlement is to five days' pay in any three-month period (ERA 1996, s 31(2)–(3)).

21.69 The rules on calculating a day's pay are set out in ERA 1996, s 30, but it is not normally necessary to consider the application of those rules, because the maximum daily rate is prescribed by statute (ERA 1996, s 31(1)). The current maximum is £21.20 (as from 1 February 2010). The maximum is increased or decreased by the Secretary of State in line with changes to the retail price index. The new rate, subject to the approval of Parliament, takes effect from 1 February.

It is common for employers to pay a higher daily rate and, to that extent, the specific **21.70** statutory rules may be relevant. Such a contractual payment goes towards discharging the statutory liability (ERA 1996, s 32).

Exclusions

The right to a guarantee payment is conditional on the employee having continuously **21.71** worked for the employer for at least one month ending with the day before that in respect of which the payment is claimed (ERA 1996, s 29(1)).

The entitlement is excluded where the workless day occurs in consequence of a **21.72** strike, or a lockout, or other industrial action involving the employer or an associated employer (ERA 1966, s 29(3)).

The entitlement is also excluded where an employee unreasonably turns down an **21.73** offer of suitable alternative work (ERA 1996, s 29(3)) or where the employee has no normal hours of work (ERA 1996, s 30(1)).

Remedy

An employee may present a complaint to an employment tribunal that his or her **21.74** employer has failed to pay the whole or any part of a guarantee payment (ERA 1996, s 34). Such a payment also qualifies as wages for the purpose of ERA 1996, Pt II (ERA 1996, s 27(1)(d)).

A complaint to an employment tribunal must be made within three months of the **21.75** workless day in question or, where this is not reasonably practicable, within such further period as the tribunal considers reasonable (ERA 1996, s 34(2)).

Where the tribunal upholds the complaint, it is empowered to order the employer **21.76** to pay to the employee the amount of the guarantee payment due to him or her (ERA 1996, s 32(4)).

F. Statutory Rights to Time Off Work

In broad terms, statutory rights to time off work fall into three categories: **21.77**

(a) rights in connection with the performance of public duties;
(b) rights in connection with duties of a collective nature; and
(c) specific individual rights.

There are some significant variations in the statutory provisions—for example, **21.78** some rights are paid, whereas other rights are unpaid. A breach of some of the statutory provisions may result in an award of compensation; a breach of others may result in a punitive award of pay for the time off that was unreasonably refused; in relation to others, neither remedy is available. Nonetheless, all of the rights set out below are enforceable by way of a complaint to an employment tribunal.

21.79 In this section, the various rights to time off are considered in outline only, although the remedies available for a contravention of those rights will be considered in greater detail. Readers who require a more detailed analysis of these rights are referred to specialist texts on the topic.

Right to time off for public duties

21.80 The right to time off for public duties is set out in ERA 1996, Pt VI. There are also special statutory provisions that deal with the rights of army reservists and those in the territorial army that are not covered in this book.

The right

21.81 There is a statutory right to unpaid time off during working hours to carry out the duties of the office of a Justice of the Peace (ERA 1996, s 50(1)).

21.82 In addition, there is a statutory right to unpaid time off during working hours for any employee who is a member of (ERA 1996, s 50(2)):

(a) a local authority;

(b) a statutory tribunal;

(c) a police authority;

(d) the service authority for the National Criminal Intelligence Service or the service authority for the National Crime Squad;

(e) an independent monitoring board for a prison or a prison visiting committee;

(f) a relevant health authority;

(g) a relevant education body;

(h) the Environment Agency or Scottish Environment Protection Agency; or

(i) Scottish Water or a water customer consultation panel.

21.83 The right is for the purpose of attendance at a meeting of the body or any of its committees, and the doing of any other thing approved by the body or anything of a class so approved for the purpose of the discharge of the function of the body or any of its committees or subcommittees, and, in the case of local authorities operating executive arrangements, attendance at the meeting of the executive or committee of that executive and the doing of any other thing of that executive for the purpose of the discharge of any function that is to any extent the responsibility of that executive (ERA 996, s 50(3)).

21.84 The right to time off is qualified by ERA 1996, s 50(4). This provides that the amount of time off that an employee is to be permitted to take under this provision, and the occasions on which and any condition subject to which such time off is to be taken, are those that are reasonable in the circumstances having regard to how much time off is necessary for the proper performance of the duties of the office in question and any particular duties carried out by the claimant, how much time off the claimant has already had in relation to other duties covered by the section or trade union duties and activities, and the circumstances of the employer's business and the effect that the employee's absence has on the running of the business.

Remedy

Employees who allege that their rights under this provision have been infringed **21.85** may complain to an employment tribunal.

Where the employment tribunal upholds the complaint, it shall make a declaration **21.86** to the effect and may make an award of compensation to be paid by the employer to the employee (ERA 1996, s 51(3)).

The award of compensation shall be such as the tribunal considers just and equitable **21.87** having regard to the employer's default in failing to permit the time off to be taken, and the loss sustained by the employee that is attributable to the matters to which the complaint relates (ERA 1996, s 51(4)). The wording of s 51(4) is not materially different from that of TULR(C)A 1992, s 172(2), which has been held to be wide enough to include the concept of a cash reparation to the claimant having regard to the employer's default without the need to prove any loss (*Skiggs v South West Trains Ltd* [2005] IRLR 459, EAT; see also **21.95** below). It is arguable that an award for injury to feelings or emotional upset could be made where an employer contravenes this provision. The amount of the award is not subject to a statutory maximum (ERA 1996, s 51).

The complaint should be presented to a tribunal within three months of the date on **21.88** which the failure to permit time off took place unless it was not reasonably practicable to bring the complaint within this period, in which case, the complaint should be brought within such period as the employment tribunal considers reasonable (ERA 1996, s 51(2)).

Rights of a collective nature

The rights to time off of a collective nature are largely to be found in TULR(C)A **21.89** 1992, Pt III, although, for the sake of convenience, the right to time off for pension fund trustees and employee representatives that are found in ERA 1996, Pt VI will also be covered in this section.

Time off for trade union duties

Under TULR(C)A 1992, s 168, officials of an independent trade union recognized **21.90** by their employer have a statutory right to reasonable paid time off during work hours for the purpose of carrying out any duties as such an official concerned with:

(a) negotiations with the employer related to, or concerned with, collective bargaining;
(b) the performance on behalf of employees of the employer of functions related to, or concerned with, matters of a collective bargaining nature that the employer has agreed may be performed by the trade union;
(c) the receipt of information from the employer and consultation by the employer under TULR(C)A 1992, s 188, or under the Transfer of Undertakings (Protection of Employment) Regulations 2006, SI 2006/246 (TUPE 2006);

(d) negotiations with a view to entering into an agreement under TUPE 2006, reg 9, which applies to employees of the employer; or

(e) the performance on behalf of employees of the employer of functions related to, or connected with, the making of an agreement under that regulation.

21.91 The employer is also required to permit such an official to take time off for the purpose of undergoing training relevant to carrying out such duties as approved by the Trades Union Congress (TUC) or an independent union.

21.92 The amount of time off that an employee is permitted to take is such amount as is reasonable in the circumstances, having regard to the Advisory, Conciliation, and Arbitration Service (ACAS) Code of Practice 3, *Time Off for Trade Union Duties and Activities* (2010).

21.93 A trade union official who is denied his or her statutory right to time off or is refused payment for such time off may complain to an employment tribunal (TULR(C)A 1992, ss 168(4) and 169).

21.94 As far as payment is concerned, the union official is entitled to receive the normal rate of pay that he or she would have received had he or she worked during the relevant period. But where the rate of remuneration varies with the amount of work done, the employee is entitled to an amount based on his or her average hourly earnings or the average hourly earnings for that work either of the employee concerned or of an employee in comparable employment, or, if there are no employees in comparable position, a figure that is reasonable in the circumstances (TULR(C)A 1992, s 169(2)–(4)). The tribunal is empowered to order the employer to pay the employee any sums due (TULR(C)A 1992, s 172(3)), although any payment made by the employer goes towards discharging the statutory liability (TULR(C)A 1992, s 169(4)).

21.95 In addition to any such payment, if it upholds the complaint, the tribunal is required to make a declaration to that effect, and may make an award of compensation to the employee of such amount as the tribunal considers just and equitable having regard to the employer's default and any loss suffered by the employee (TULR(C)A 1992, s 172(1)–(2)). In *Skiggs v South West Trains Ltd* [2005] IRLR 459, the EAT held that s 172(2) is wide enough to include the concept of a cash reparation to the claimant for the fact that a wrong has been done to him or her, independently of any special consequential loss, financial or other, that he or she can prove to have also suffered. An employment tribunal can properly consider whether it is just and equitable to make some reasonable and proportionate award by way of reparation to a union official for the wrong done to him or her without infringing the principle that the purpose must be compensation to the claimant, not the imposition of any form of fine or collective punishment on the respondent employer. It is arguable that an award for injury to feelings or emotional upset could be made where an employer contravenes this provision. The award of compensation is not subject to any statutory maximum (TULR(C)A 1992, s 172).

The complaint should be presented to the tribunal within three months of the date **21.96** on which the failure took place unless it is not reasonably practicable to do so, in which case, the complaint should be presented within such period as the tribunal considers reasonable (TULR(C)A 1992, s 171).

Time off for union learning representatives

A learning representative of an independent trade union recognized by the employer **21.97** is entitled to paid time off for the purpose of carrying on the following activities in relation to qualifying members of a trade union: analysing learning or training needs; providing information and advice about learning or training matters; arranging learning or training; and promoting the value of learning or training (or consulting with the employer in relation to any of these matters or preparing for any of these matters) (TULR(C)A 1992, s 168A(1)–(2)). There is also a statutory right for a union representative to undergo training that is relevant to the functions of a learning representative (TULR(C)A 1992, s 168A(7)).

The amount of time off that an employee is permitted to take is such amount as is **21.98** reasonable in the circumstances, having regard to the ACAS Code of Practice, for any of these purposes (TULR(C)A 1992, s 168A(8)).

A trade union learning representative who is denied his or her statutory right to **21.99** time off or is refused payment for such time off may complain to an employment tribunal (TULR(C)A 1992, ss 168A(9) and 169).

As far as payment is concerned, the union official is entitled to receive the normal **21.100** rate of pay that he or she would have done had he or she worked during the relevant period. But where the rate of remuneration varies with the amount of work done, the employee is entitled to an amount based on his or her average hourly earnings or the average hourly earnings for that work either of the employee concerned, or of an employee in comparable employment, or, if there are no employees in comparable position, a figure that is reasonable in the circumstances (TULR(C)A 1992, s 169(2)–(4)). The tribunal is empowered to order the employer to pay the employee any sums due (TULR(C)A 1992, s 172(3)), although any payment made by the employer goes towards discharging the statutory liability (TULR(C)A 1992, s 169(4)).

In addition to any such payment, the tribunal, if it upholds the complaint, is **21.101** required to make a declaration to that effect, and may make an award of compensation to the employee of such amount as the tribunal considers just and equitable having regard to the employer's default and any loss suffered by the employee (TULR(C)A 1992, s 172(2)–(3); see **21.95** above). It is arguable that this may include an award for injury to feelings.

The complaint should be presented to the tribunal within three months of the date **21.102** on which the failure took place unless it is not reasonably practicable to do so, in which case, the complaint should be presented within such period as the tribunal considers reasonable (TULR(C)A 1992, s 171).

Time off for trade union activities

21.103 Trade union members have a right to unpaid time off for trade union activities in the workplace, including any activities for which the employee is acting as a representative of the union, but excluding any form of industrial action (TULR(C)A 1992, s 170(1)–(2)). This right does not extend to time off for acting as or having access to a learning representative, because this is dealt with separately (TULR(C)A 1992, s 170(2A)–(2C)).

21.104 The amount of time off that an employee is permitted to take is such amount as is reasonable in the circumstances having regard to the ACAS Code of Practice.

21.105 An employee who is denied his or her right to time off under these statutory provisions may complain to an employment tribunal. Such a complaint should be presented within three months of the date on which the failure occurred, or, if this is not reasonably practicable, within such further period as the tribunal considers reasonable (TULR(C)A 1992, ss 170(4) and (5), and 171).

21.106 Where a tribunal upholds such a complaint, it is required to make a declaration to that effect, and may make an award of compensation to be paid by the employer to the employee of such amount as the tribunal considers just and equitable having regard to the employer's default and any loss suffered by the employee (TULR(C)A 1992, s 172(2)–(3); see **21.95** above). It is arguable that this may include an award for injury to feelings. The amount of the award of compensation is not subject to any statutory maximum (TULR(C)A 1992, s 172).

Elected employee representatives

21.107 Elected employee representatives have the right to take a reasonable amount of paid time off during working hours to stand as a candidate for election or to carry out their duties in respect of collective redundancy consultation pursuant to TULR(C)A 1992, Pt IV, ch II, and TUPE 2006 consultation pursuant to regs 9, 13 and 15 (ERA 1996, s 61).

21.108 An employee who is denied his or her statutory right to time off or is refused payment for such time off may complain to an employment tribunal (ERA 1996, s 63).

21.109 As far as payment is concerned, the elected employee representative is entitled to be paid at the appropriate hourly rate (ERA 1996, s 62(1)). The appropriate hourly rate is the amount of one week's pay divided by the number of normal hours in a week for that employee under the contract in force on the day when the time off was taken (ERA 1996, s 62(2)). However, where the number of hours varies from week to week, one week's pay is divided instead by either the average number of working hours, calculated by dividing by 12 the total number of the employee's normal working hours during the period of 12 weeks ending with the last complete week of work before the day on which time off is taken, or (if the employee has been employed for an insufficient period to enable this calculation to be undertaken) a number that fairly represents the number of normal working hours in a week having regard to the factors specified in the ERA 1996, s 62(4) (ERA 1996, s 62(3) (a)–(b)).

The tribunal is empowered to order the employer to pay the employee any sums due **21.110** (ERA 1996, s 63(4)–(5)). Normally, any payment made by the employer goes towards discharging the statutory liability (ERA 1996, s 62(6)) but, where the employer has unreasonably refused to permit the employee to take time off, then the tribunal is required to award the employee a sum that is equivalent to the sum that he or she would have received had he or she not been refused (in other words, a penalty) (ERA 1996, s 63(4)).

In addition to any such payment, if the tribunal upholds the complaint, it is required **21.111** to make a declaration to that effect, but there is no specific power to award compensation (ERA 1996, s 63(3)).

The complaint should be presented to the tribunal within three months of the date **21.112** on which the failure took place unless it is not reasonably practicable to do so, in which case, the complaint should be presented within such period as the tribunal considers reasonable (ERA 1996, s 63(2)).

Occupational pension scheme trustees

Employees (and employee-directors) who act as pension fund trustees are entitled **21.113** to paid time off for the purpose of performing their duties as a trustee and undergoing training to perform such duties (ERA 1996, ss 58(1) and 59(1); see also the Occupational Pension Schemes (Member-Nominated Trustees and Directors) Regulations 2006, SI 2006/714).

An employee is entitled to a reasonable amount of time off for this purpose having **21.114** regard to the factors in the ERA 1996, s 58(2).

An employee who is denied his or her statutory right to time off or is refused payment **21.115** for such time off may complain to an employment tribunal (ERA 1996, s 60).

As far as payment is concerned, where the payment does not vary with the amount **21.116** of work done, the pension fund trustee is entitled to receive the normal rate of pay that he or she would have done had he or she done the work at the relevant time (ERA 1996, s 59(2)), but where the rate of remuneration varies with the amount of work done, the employee is entitled to an amount based on his or her average hourly earnings or the average hourly earnings of an employee in comparable employment or a figure that is reasonable in the circumstances (ERA 1996, s 59(3)–(4)).

Where the employer has failed to pay the employee, the tribunal is empowered to **21.117** order the employer to pay the employee any sums due (ERA 1996, s 60(5)), although any payment made by the employer goes towards discharging the statutory liability (ERA 1996, s 59(6)).

21.118 In addition to any such payment, the tribunal, if it upholds the complaint, is required to make a declaration to that effect, and may make an award of compensation to the employee of such amount as the tribunal considers just and equitable having regard to the employer's default and any loss suffered by the employee (ERA 1996, s 60(3)–(4); see **21.95** above). It is arguable that this may include an award for injury to feelings. The award of compensation is not subject to any statutory maximum (ERA 1996, s 60).

21.119 The complaint should be presented to the tribunal within three months of the date on which the failure took place unless it is not reasonably practicable to do so, in which case, the complaint should be presented within such period as the tribunal considers reasonable (ERA 1996, s 60(2)).

European works councils

21.120 Employees who are elected members of a special negotiating body, a European works council, or an information and consultation representative, or a candidate for election, are entitled to reasonable paid time off to perform their functions as such a member, representative, or candidate (Transnational Information and Consultation of Employees Regulations 1999, SI 1999/3323 [TICER 1999], reg 25).

21.121 An employee who is permitted time off in accordance with this right is entitled to be paid remuneration by his or her employer for the time off, taken at the appropriate hourly rate, which is defined as the amount of one week's pay divided by the number of normal working hours in a week for that employee when employed under the contract of employment in force on the day when the time is taken (TICER 1999, reg 26(1) and (3)). Special provision is made for those whose normal working hours differ from week to week or over a longer period. In such circumstances, the amount of a week's pay is the average number of normal working hours, which is calculated by dividing by 12 the total number of hours of the employee's normal working hours during the period of 12 weeks ending with the last complete week before the day on which the time off is taken, or, where the employee has not been employed for a sufficient period, a number that fairly represents the number of normal working hours in a week having regard to the average number of normal working hours that an employee could be required to work in accordance with the terms of his or her contract and the average number of hours worked by other employees in comparable work with the same employer (TICER 1999, reg 26(4) and (5)).

21.122 Any contractual remuneration paid to an employee in respect of a period of time off under reg 25 goes towards discharging the employer's liability to pay such remuneration (TICER 1999, reg 26(7)).

21.123 An employee who is 'unreasonably' denied his or her right to time off or refused payment under these statutory provisions may complain to an employment tribunal.

Such a complaint should be presented within three months of the date on which the failure occurred, or, if this is not reasonably practicable, within such further period as the tribunal considers reasonable (TICER 1999, reg 27(1) and (2)).

Where a tribunal upholds such a complaint, it is required to make a declaration to **21.124** that effect. If the complaint is that the employer unreasonably refused to permit the employee to take time off, the tribunal is required to make an award of compensation equal to the remuneration that the employee would have received had he or she not been refused time off. If the complaint is that the employer has failed to pay the employee, the tribunal is required to order the employer to pay the amount due to the employee calculated in accordance with the provisions referred to above (TICER 1999, reg 27(4), (5)).

Information and Consultation of Employees Regulations 2004

Employees who are negotiating representatives or an information and consultation **21.125** representatives are entitled to take a reasonable amount of paid time off during their working hours to perform their functions (Information and Consultation of Employees Regulations 2004, SI 2004/3426 (ICE Regulations 2004), reg 27).

An employee who is permitted to take time off in accordance with this right is **21.126** entitled to be paid remuneration by his or her employer for the time off taken at the appropriate hourly rate, which is defined as the amount of one week's pay divided by the number of normal working hours in a week for that employee when employed under the contract of employment in force on the day when the time off is taken (ICE Regulations 2004, reg 28(1), (3)).

Special provision is made for those whose normal working hours differ from week **21.127** to week or over a longer period. In such circumstances, the amount of a week's pay is the average number of normal working hours, which is calculated by dividing by 12 the total number of hours of the employee's normal working hours during the period of 12 weeks ending with the last complete week before the day on which the time off is taken or, where the employee has not been employed for a sufficient period, a number that fairly represents the number of normal working hours in a week, having regard to the average number of normal working hours that an employee could be required to work in accordance with the terms of his or her contract and the average number of hours worked by other employees in comparable work with the same employer (ICE Regulations 2004, reg 28(4)–(5)).

Any contractual remuneration paid to an employee in respect of a period of time **21.128** under reg 27 goes towards discharging the employer's liability to pay such remuneration (ICE Regulations 2004, reg 28(7)).

An employee who is 'unreasonably' denied his or her right to time off or refused **21.129** payments under these provisions may complain to an employment tribunal. Such a complaint should be presented within three months of the date on which the failure occurred, or, if this is not reasonably practicable, within such further period as the tribunal considers reasonable (ICE Regulations 2004, reg 29(1), (2))

21.130 Where a tribunal upholds such a complaint, it is required to make a declaration to that effect. If the complaint is that the employer unreasonably refused to permit the employee to take time off, the tribunal is required to make an award of compensation equal to the remuneration that the employee would have received had he or she not been refused time off. If the complaint is that the employer has failed to pay the employee, the tribunal is required to order the employer to pay the amount due to the employee calculated in accordance with the provisions referred to above (ICE Regulations 2004, reg 29).

Individual rights to time off

21.131 The rights to time off of an individual nature are to be found in ERA 1996, Pt IV.

Right to time off to look for work or arrange training

21.132 An employee who has been given notice of redundancy has the right to take a reasonable amount of paid time off work to look for new employment or make arrangements for future employment (ERA 1996, s 52(1)).

21.133 This right is, however, subject to a two-year service requirement at the date on which such notice is due to expire (ERA 1996, s 52(2))—that is, it only applies to employees who are eligible for a redundancy payment under the statutory scheme.

21.134 An employee who is unreasonably refused his or her right to time off pursuant to these statutory provisions, or who is denied the right to be paid for his or her period of time off, may complain to an employment tribunal (ERA 1996, s 54(1)).

21.135 As far as payment is concerned, an employee is entitled to be paid at the appropriate hourly rate, which is defined as the amount of one week's pay divided by the number of normal working hours in a week for that employee under the contract of employment in force on the day on which the notice of dismissal was given. Where the hours vary from week to week, the amount of one week's pay is arrived at by calculating the average number of working hours, which is calculated by dividing by 12 the total number of working hours during the period of 12 weeks ending with the last complete week before the day on which notice was given (ERA 1996, s 53(1)–(3)). Rather curiously, the total amount is limited to 40 per cent of a week's pay of that employee (ERA 1996, s 53(5)).

21.136 The tribunal is empowered to order the employer to pay the employee any sums due (ERA 1996, s 54(3)(b)), although any payment made by the employer goes towards discharging the statutory liability (ERA 1996, s 53(7)). Furthermore, the amount that may be ordered shall not exceed the 40 per cent limit referred to above (ERA 1996, s 54(4)).

In addition to any such payment, if the tribunal upholds the complaint, it is required **21.137** to make a declaration to that effect, but there is no specific power to award compensation (ERA 1996, s 54(3)(a)).

The complaint should be presented to the tribunal within three months of the date **21.138** on which the failure took place unless it is not reasonably practicable to do so, in which case, the complaint should be presented within such period as the tribunal considers reasonable (ERA 1996, s 64(2)).

Right to time off for study or training

An employee who is aged 16 or 17 and is not receiving full-time secondary or fur- **21.139** ther education, and has not attained the standard of achievement prescribed by the Secretary of State, has the statutory right to take paid time off work in order to undertake study or training leading to a relevant qualification (ERA 1996, s 63A(1)). This right also applies to employees who are aged 18 and who are undertaking such training (ERA 1996, s 63A(4)). The amount of time off is such amount as is reasonable in the circumstances, having regard to the factors set out in the ERA 1996, s 63A(5).

An employee who is unreasonably denied the right to time off pursuant to these **21.140** statutory provisions or who is denied payment may complain to an employment tribunal (ERA 1996, s 63C).

As far as payment is concerned, an employee is entitled to be paid at the appropri- **21.141** ate hourly rate, which is defined as the amount of one week's pay divided by the number of normal working hours in a week for that employee under the contract of employment in force on the day on which the time off is taken (ERA 1996, s 63B(2)). Where the hours vary from week to week, the amount of one week's pay is arrived at by calculating the average number of working hours, which is calculated by dividing by 12 the total number of working hours, during the period of 12 weeks ending with the last complete week before the day on which time off was taken, or, where the employee has not been employed sufficiently long, a number that fairly represents the number of normal working hours in a week as determined by the factors set out in the ERA 1996, s 63B(4) (ERA 1996, s 63B(3)).

The tribunal is empowered to order the employer to pay the employee any sums due **21.142** (ERA 1996, s 63C(4)). Normally, any payment made by the employer goes towards discharging the statutory liability (ERA 1996, s 63(5)), but where the employer has unreasonably refused to permit the employee to take time off, then the tribunal is required to award the employee a sum that is equivalent to the sum that he or she would have received had he or she not been refused (in other words, a penalty).

In addition to any such payment, if the tribunal upholds the complaint, it is **21.143** required to make a declaration to that effect, but there is no specific power to award compensation (ERA 1996, s 63C(3)).

21.144 The complaint should be presented to the tribunal within three months of the date on which the failure took place unless it is not reasonably practicable to do so, in which case, the complaint should be presented within such period as the tribunal considers reasonable (ERA 1996, s 63C(2)).

Right to time off for antenatal care

21.145 An employee, who is pregnant and has, on the advice of a registered medical practitioner, registered midwife, or registered health visitor, made an appointment to attend any place for the purpose of receiving antenatal care, has the right to be permitted to take time off to enable her to keep the appointment (ERA 1996, s 55(1)), although this is subject to certain conditions set out in ERA 1996, s 55(2).

21.146 An employee who meets these conditions has the right to be paid during her period of absence at the appropriate hourly rate (ERA 1996, s 56(2)). For an employee who works fixed hours, the appropriate hourly rate is one week's pay divided by the number of normal working hours in a week for that employee under the contract in force on the day on which the time off is taken. However, where the number of normal working hours varies from week to week, one week's pay is divided instead by either the average number of working hours, calculated by dividing by 12 the total number of the employee's normal working hours during the period of 12 weeks ending with the last complete week of work before the day on which time off is taken, or (if the employee has been employed for an insufficient period to enable this calculation to be undertaken) a number that fairly represents the number of normal working hours in a week having regard to the factors specified in the ERA 1996, s 56(4) (ERA 1996, s 56(3)).

21.147 An employee who is unreasonably refused the right to time off or is denied payment in breach of the statutory provisions may complain to an employment tribunal. The complaint should be presented to the tribunal within three months of the date on which the failure took place unless it is not reasonably practicable to do so, in which case, the complaint should be presented within such period as the tribunal considers reasonable (ERA 1996, s 57(2)).

21.148 Where such a complaint is upheld, the tribunal is required to make a declaration to that effect (ERA 1996, s 57(3)) and may order the employer to pay the whole or part of any amount to which the employee is entitled. Normally, any payment made by the employer goes towards discharging the statutory liability (ERA 1996, s 56(6)), but where the employer has unreasonably refused to permit the employee to take time off, then the tribunal is required to award the employee a sum that is equivalent to the sum that he or she would have received had he or she not been refused (in other words, a penalty) (ERA 1996, s 57(4)).

Right to time off for dependants

21.149 An employee is entitled to take a reasonable amount of time off during working hours in order to take such action as is necessary:

(a) to provide assistance on an occasion when a dependant falls ill, gives birth, or is injured or assaulted;
(b) to make arrangements for the provision of care for a dependant who is ill or injured;
(c) in consequence of the death of a dependant;
(d) because of the unexpected disruption or termination of arrangements for the care of a dependant; or
(e) to deal with an incident that involves a child of the employee and that occurs unexpectedly in a period during which an educational establishment that the child attends is responsible for the child (ERA 1996, s 57A).

The right to 'emergency leave' is unpaid.

The basic definition of a 'dependant' includes a spouse, child, parent, or a person **21.150** who lives in the same household as the dependant other than as an employee, tenant, or lodger, although this definition is extended in relation to some of these rights (ERA 1996, s 57(3)–(5)).

An employee who is unreasonably denied the statutory right to emergency leave **21.151** may complain to an employment tribunal (ERA 1996, s 57B(1)). Such a complaint must be presented to the tribunal within three months of the date on which the failure took place unless it is not reasonably practicable to do so, in which case, the complaint should be presented within such period as the tribunal considers reasonable (ERA 1996, s 57B(2)).

A tribunal that upholds such a complaint is required to make a declaration to **21.152** that effect and may make an award of compensation payable by the employer to the employee (ERA 1996, s 57B(3)). The amount of compensation depends on what the tribunal considers just and equitable in the circumstances, having regard to the employer's default in refusing time off and any loss sustained by the employee (ERA 1996, s 57B(4)). This may cover the cost of emergency care and other associated expenses (see **21.95** above). It is arguable that the tribunal may also award compensation for injury to feelings caused by the employer's default.

Suspension from work (ERA 1996, Pt VII)

The statutory rules on suspension on medical and maternity grounds are set out in **21.153** the ERA 1996, ss 64 and 66.

There is a right of complaint to an employment tribunal where the employer has **21.154** failed to pay the whole or any part of the remuneration to which the employee is entitled pursuant to the ERA 1996, ss 64 and 68 (ERA 1996, s 70(1)). Such a complaint must be presented within three months of the day on which such a payment should have been made or, if this is not reasonably practicable, such further period as the employment tribunal considers reasonable (ERA 1996, s 70(2)).

21.155 Where such a complaint is upheld, the employment tribunal is empowered to order the employer to pay to the employee the amount of remuneration that it finds due (ERA 1996, s 70(3)). Any payments that the employer has made to the employee during the relevant period will be taken into account by the tribunal (ERA 1996, s 69(3)). The maximum amount of remuneration to which the employee is entitled under the ERA 1996, s 64(1) is 26 weeks' pay.

21.156 An employee also has a right to complaint to an employment tribunal where, in contravention of the ERA 1996, s 67, the employer fails to offer her alternative work or has failed to pay the employee during a period of maternity-related suspension (ERA 1996, s 70(4)). The complaint must be presented to the employment tribunal within three months beginning with the first day of suspension, or, if that is not reasonably practicable, such further period as the employment tribunal considers to be reasonable (ERA 1996, s 70(5)). Where the employment tribunal finds such a complaint well founded, the tribunal may award such compensation as it considers just and equitable, having regard to the infringement of the employee's rights under the ERA 1996, s 67 and any loss suffered by the employee that is attributable to that failure (ERA 1996, s 70(7)). It is arguable that this may include compensation for injury to feelings. In the case of suspension pay, this will normally be the amount that should have been paid. There is no statutory limit on the amount payable.

Maternity, adoption, parental, and paternity leave

21.157 The statutory rules on such cases of leave are now to be found in the ERA 1996, Pt VIII, chs 1 (maternity leave), 1A (adoption leave), II (parental leave), and III (paternity leave).

21.158 All employees are protected against detriment and unfair dismissal for asserting these statutory rights, and may also be unfairly dismissed in specified circumstances in which an employer fails to comply with these provisions.

21.159 A detailed consideration of these statutory provisions lies outside the scope of this book, but the normal rules on the calculation of unfair dismissal compensation apply to such dismissals.

G. Flexible Working

21.160 The statutory right to request flexible working was introduced by the EA 2002. A detailed consideration of the statutory right lies outside the scope of this book.

The right

21.161 The right to request flexible working is set out in the EA 2002, s 47 (which inserted Pt 8A and s 80F–80I into the ERA 1996).

In broad terms, the statutory provisions give employees who have children under the age of 17, or 18 in the case of disabled children, the right to request changes in the hours that they are required to work, the times during which they are required to work, their place of work (or such other terms as the Secretary of State may specify). **21.162**

The process by which such an application is made and handled by the employer is set out in ERA 1996, s 80F(2), the Flexible Working (Procedural Requirements) Regulations 2002, SI 2002/3207, and the Flexible Working (Eligibility, Complaints and Remedies) Regulations 2002, SI 2002/ 3236. **21.163**

The grounds on which an employer can decline such a request are set out in ERA 1996, s 80G. **21.164**

The remedy

An employee has the right to complain to an employment tribunal where an employer fails to comply with the statutory rules (ERA 1996, s 80I(1)). If a tribunal finds such a complaint well founded, it shall make a declaration to that effect and make an award of compensation to be paid by the employer to the employee. **21.165**

The maximum amount of compensation is eight weeks' pay (Flexible Working (Eligibility, Complaints and Remedies) Regulations 2002, reg 7). Employees exercising this right are protected against detriment, and other forms of victimization and dismissal (Flexible Working (Procedural Requirements) Regulations 2002, reg 16). The normal employment tribunal limits on compensation apply in the event of unfair dismissal. Importantly, the tribunal does not have power to order the employer to implement the employee's flexible working request. **21.166**

H. Action Short of Dismissal

Statutory right

A worker has the right not to be subjected to any detriment as an individual by any act, or any deliberate failure to act, by his or her employer if the act or failure takes place for the sole or main purpose of (TULR(C)A 1992, s 146(1), as amended by the Employment Relations Act 2004 [ERA 2004], ss 30–31 and the ERelA 1999, s 2, Sch 2, paras 1, and 2(1) and (2)): **21.167**

(a) preventing or deterring him or her from being or seeking to become a member of an independent trade union, or penalizing him or her for doing so;

(b) preventing or deterring him or her from taking part in the activities of an independent trade union at an appropriate time, or penalizing him or her for doing so;

(c) preventing or deterring him or her from making use of trade union services at an appropriate time, or penalizing him or her for doing so; or

(d) compelling him or her to be or become a member of any trade union, or of any particular trade union, or of one of a number of particular trade unions.

21.168 These provisions were extended to cover inducements made to the worker to refrain from becoming a member of an independent trade union (ERA 2004, s 29, which inserted s 145A into TULR(C)A 1992).

21.169 A worker also has the right not to be subjected to any detriment as an individual by any act, or any deliberate failure to act by his or her employer, if the act or failure to act takes place for the sole or main purpose of enforcing a requirement that, in the event that he or she is not a member of a trade union, he or she must make a payment (TULR(C)A 1992, s 146(3), as amended by the ERA 2004, ss 30–31, and the ERelA 1999, s 2, Sch 2, paras 1, and 2(1) and (3)).

Remedy

21.170 An employee whose rights are infringed in contravention of these provisions may complain to an employment tribunal (TULR(C)A 1992, s 146(5)).

21.171 Such a complaint must be presented within three months of the act or failure to act, or if this is not reasonably practicable, such further time as an employment tribunal considers reasonable (TULR(C)A 1992, s 147)).

21.172 If the employment tribunal finds the complaint well founded, it is required to make a declaration to that effect and may make an award of compensation to be paid by the employer to the claimant. The amount of the award is such amount as the tribunal considers just and equitable in the circumstances, having regard to any loss suffered by the claimant that is attributable to the act or failure that infringed the right (see **21.95** above). Loss is taken to include any expenses incurred by the claimant as a consequence of the act or failure and any benefit that the claimant might reasonably have been expected to receive but for the act or failure (TULR(C)A 1992, s 149(1)–(3)).

21.173 Such loss may include compensation for injury to feelings (*Cleveland Ambulance NHS Trust v Blane* [1997] IRLR 332, in which the EAT ruled that an employment tribunal had not erred in law in awarding £1,000 as compensation for injury to feelings to a shop steward who had complained that the employer had taken action short of dismissal against him by not shortlisting him for a management post on the ground of his trade union activities). The EAT's decision was referred to by the EAT in *Dunnachie v Kingston Upon Hull Council* [2003] IRLR 385, 388, without disapproval, and its correctness does not appear to have been affected by the House of Lords' ruling in the *Dunnachie* case, which was solely concerned with the meaning of 'loss' under ERA 1996, s 123(1). It is therefore likely to remain good law.

The normal rules on compensation for injury to feelings apply to such claims. **21.174**
Guidance on how such awards should be approached in relation to claims made
under TULR(C)A 1999, s 146 was given by the EAT in *London Borough of
Hackney v Adams* [2003] IRLR 402, in which Elias J broadly endorsed the principles that have been established in discrimination cases and, in particular, the
guidelines established by the Court of Appeal in *Vento v Chief Constable of West
Yorkshire Police (No 2)* [2003] ICR 318, [2003] IRLR 102. He rejected the
argument that discrimination on trade union grounds of itself justified a lower
award than other types of discrimination. However, the judge added a word of
caution to the effect that:

> it is far from self evident that, for example, someone refused employment on [trade
> union grounds] will necessarily suffer injury to feelings at all. The status of not
> being a trade union member is not likely, at least in most cases, to be an essential
> part of an individual's make up or to be a characteristic which is central to a person's
> self esteem. Making good the financial loss actually suffered may in such a case be
> adequate compensation. Even if there is any injury to feeling, the distress is likely
> to be less severe than with forms of discrimination which engage the core of a
> person's being.

But the judge recognized this does not mean that: **21.175**

> there may not be particular cases when such injury cannot be established, such as a
> non-unionist who suffers harassment in a trade union shop. But it ought not readily
> to be assumed that injury to feelings inevitably flows from each and every unlawful act
> of discrimination. In each case it is a question of considering the facts carefully to
> determine whether the loss has been sustained. Some persons discriminated against
> on trade union grounds may feel deeply hurt by that affront, particularly where union
> membership is an important feature of their lives; other more robust characters may
> consider it a matter of little consequence and suffer little, if any distress. Since the aim
> is to compensate and not to punish, the compensation awarded ought not to be the
> same in each case.

Elias J then went on to apply the *Vento* guidelines and upheld the tribunal award of **21.176**
£5,000, although he thought that it was on the high side. See also *Virgo Fidelis
Senior School v Boyle* [2004] IRLR 268, below, in which the EAT, applying the *Vento*
guidelines, reduced an award for injury to feelings from £42,000 to £25,000 (in the
upper range) in a complaint under the ERA 1996, s 47B (the whistleblowing
provisions).

The common law rules on mitigation apply in ascertaining the loss (TULR(C)A **21.177**
1992, s 149(4)), but the tribunal must ignore any industrial pressure in determining
the award (TULR(C)A 1992, s 149(5)).

The award may be reduced for contributory fault (TULR(C)A 1992, s 149(6)). **21.178**
There is power to join a third party that has been responsible for the detriment
or the pressure that led to the complaint (TULR(C)A 1992, s 150).

There is no statutory maximum on the award of compensation. **21.179**

I. Protection against Detriment

21.180 Apart from trade union cases, there are statutory provisions of a broadly similar nature that protect individuals from suffering a detriment as a result of exercising their statutory rights.

Statutory rights

21.181 The protection from detriment provisions in the ERA 1996, Pt V cover the following areas:

(a) jury service (ERA 1996, s 43M);

(b) health and safety cases (ERA 1996, s 44);

(c) Sunday working for shop and betting workers (ERA 1996, s 45);

(d) working time cases (ERA 1996, s 45A);

(e) trustees of an occupational pension schemes (ERA 1996, s 46);

(f) employee representatives (ERA 1996, s 47);

(g) employees exercising the right to time off work for study or training (ERA 1996, s 47A);

(h) employees in England aged 16 or 17 participating in education or training (ERA 1996, s 47AA);

(i) protected disclosures (ERA 1996, s 47B);

(j) leave for family and domestic reasons (ERA 1996, s 47C);

(k) tax credits (ERA 1996, s 47D);

(l) flexible working (ERA 1996, s 47E);

(m) study and training (ERA 1996, s 47F);

(n) rights in connection with trade union recognition (TULR(C)A 1992, Sch A1, para 156(1) and (2));

(o) the right to be accompanied at disciplinary and grievance hearings (ERELA 1999, s 12);

(p) the NMWA 1998 (NMWA 1998, ss 23–24);

(q) the rights granted to employee representatives in connection with a European works council (TICER 1999, reg 31(1); ICE Regulations 2004, reg 32); and

(r) part-time workers (Part-time Workers (Prevention of Less Favourable Treatment) Regulations 2000, SI 2000/1551 (PTWR 2000), reg 7(2)(3)) and fixed-term employees (Fixed-term Employees (Protection of Less Favourable Treatment) Regulations 2002, SI 2002/2034 (FTWR 2002), reg 6(2) and (3)).

21.182 The extent of the protection will depend on the precise form of each of these substantive rights. A detailed consideration of these rights lies outside the scope of this book, but the statutory remedy is in virtually identical form.

Meaning of detriment

21.183 In each of these situations, it will be necessary for the claimant to show that he or she has suffered a detriment as a result of the exercise of his or her statutory rights.

The word 'detriment' is not defined, but is considered to be a word of wide import **21.184** and it is likely that tribunals will adopt a similar interpretation as in discrimination cases. In both *Shamoon v Chief Constable of the RUC* [2003] IRLR 285 and *London Borough of Ealing v Garry* [2001] IRLR 681, the House of Lords and Court of Appeal, respectively, ruled that a 'detriment' was something that, in the reasonable perception of an employee, would be to his or her disadvantage in the workplace. This would include any financial or physical disadvantage, but does not, other than where specified, include dismissal itself, for which there are separate statutory remedies.

Special rules apply in cases of Sunday working. There are set out in ERA 1996, **21.185** s 45(5).

It is for the claimant to show that he or she has suffered some detriment and that the **21.186** detriment was caused by some act or deliberate failure to act by the employer. This can give rise to difficult questions of causation—that is, there must be a causal connection between the employee's protected act and the employer's act or omission. The employer's motive or intent is irrelevant for this purpose; the question is whether the claimant has been treated differently and whether the reason for that different treatment was the protected act (see *Harvey on Industrial Relations and Employment Law*, Vol 1, Div DII, paras 591–620).

Enforcement

The statutory rights are enforceable in employment tribunals. **21.187**

ERA 1996, s 48(1) provides that an employee who has been subjected to a detriment **21.188** in contravention of the ERA 1996, ss 43M, 44–47, 47A, 47C, or 47E may present a complaint to an employment tribunal. The ERA 1996, s 48(1ZA) and 1(A) provides that a worker who has been subjected to a detriment in contravention of ERA 1996, ss 45A and 47B may present a complaint to an employment tribunal; the ERA 1996, s 48(1B) provides that a person who has been subjected to a detriment in contravention of the ERA 1996, s 47D may present a complaint to an employment tribunal.

There are identical provisions in relation to the other statutory provisions referred **21.189** to above: NMWA 1998, s 24; TULR(C)A, Sch A1, Pt VIII, para 156(5); TICER 1999, reg 31; ICE Regulations 2004, reg 33; PTWR 2000, reg 8; FTER 2002, reg 7; and ERelA 1999, s 11(1).

Remedy

The remedy and limitation period is similar, but not identical in each of the above. **21.190**

In each case, the complaint must be presented within three months of the act or the **21.191** failure to act (or the last in a series of failures taking place), unless this is not reasonably practicable, in which case, the complaint must be presented within such period as the tribunal considers reasonable (ERA 1996, s 48(3) and (4); TULR(C)A, Sch A1, para 157; NMWA 1998, s 24(2); ERelA 1999, s 12(2); PTWR 2000, reg 8(2); FTER 2002, reg 7(2)—but notably, as regards the last of these regulations, there is a 'just and equitable extension').

21.192 If the complaint is proved, the employment tribunal is under an obligation to make a declaration to that effect and may make an award of compensation.

21.193 Subject to certain restrictions, the award of compensation is such amount as the tribunal considers just and equitable in the particular circumstances, having regard to the infringement to which the complaint relates and the loss attributable to the act or failure to act to which the complaint relates (see **21.95** above). Loss includes any expenses reasonably incurred by the claimant and loss of any benefit that the claimant might reasonably be expected to have had but for the act or the failure to act (ERA 1996, s 49(2), which also covers complaints under the ICE Regulations 2004, NMWA 1998, s 24(2), TULR(C)A, Sch A1, para 159(1), PTWR 2000, reg 8(7)(b), FTER 2000, reg 7(7)(b), and ERelA 1999, s 12(2)).

21.194 Subject to two exceptions, loss may include compensation for injury to feelings (*Virgo Fidelis Senior School v Boyle* [2004] IRLR 268). Such loss is calculated in accordance with the ordinary principle of assessment and in accordance with the *Vento* guidelines. In *Boyle*, the EAT, applying those guidelines, reduced an award from £42,000 to £25,000 in a whistleblowing case. It ruled that there was no reason in principle why such complaints of victimization under these statutory provisions should be treated differently from any other discrimination or victimization complaint. Furthermore, in contrast to the comments made by Elias J in *London Borough of Hackney v Adams* [2003] IRLR 402 (quoted above), the EAT considered that detrimental action taken against whistleblowers should always be regarded as a 'very serious breach of discrimination legislation'. The EAT also suggested that, in certain cases, the award could also cover psychiatric injury (that is, injury to health).

21.195 From these cases, it would seem that different public policy considerations may apply to different forms of victimization. Furthermore, the EAT held that, in the particular circumstances of *Boyle*—namely, a case in which disciplinary proceeding were brought against a teacher who raised a number of protected disclosures about the way in which a school was run—the award fell within the highest band of the *Vento* guidelines. The EAT in *Boyle* also awarded £10,000 by way of aggravated damages having regard to the tribunal findings that the employer's conduct amounted to a 'travesty', which was further aggravated by the absence of any apology or mitigation.

21.196 In *Melia v Magna Kansei Ltd* [2006] EWCA Civ 1547, [2006] IRLR 117, the Court of Appeal held that if an employee suffers a detriment due to making a protected disclosure and is then dismissed by the employer, the employee will be entitled to compensation for the detriment under ERA 1996, s 49 right up until the date of dismissal (including an award for injury to feelings). The position is no different in the case of constructive dismissal. Compensation for the detriment should include all of those matters that occur up to the time of the acceptance of the repudiatory breach (or constructive dismissal).

Compensation for injury to feelings, however, is expressly excluded in relation to claims brought by part-time workers (PTWR 2000, reg 8(11)) and fixed-term workers (FTER 2002, reg 7(10)). **21.197**

The assessment of such loss is subject to the common law duty to mitigate (ERA 1996, s 49(4); NMWA 1998, s 24(1); TULR(C)A 1992, Sch A1, para 159(4); ERelA 1999, s 12(1); PTWR 2000, reg 8(12); FTER 2002, reg 7(12)). **21.198**

The award of compensation may be reduced if the claimant has caused or contrib- **21.199**
uted to the act or failure to act to which the complaint relates to the extent that the tribunal considers just and equitable (ERA 1996, s 49(5); NMWA 1999, s 24(2); TULR(C)A 2002, Sch A1, para 159(5); PTWR 2000, reg 8(13); FTER 2000, reg 7(12); ERelA 1999, s 12(1)).

Applying the statutory maximum

In general, there is no statutory maximum limit to the award that can be made by an **21.200**
employment tribunal for complaints of pre-dismissal detriment; however, this is subject to certain exceptions in relation to whistleblowing (ERA 1996, s 49(6)), trade union recognition (TULR(C)A 1992, Sch A1, para 159(6)), working time (ERA 1996, s 49(5A)), national minimum wage (NMWA 1999, s 24(3)), tax credits (ERA 1996, s 48(7)), and disciplinary and grievance hearings (ERelA 1999, s 12(3)–(6)).

The common factor running through these categories is that, under the statutory **21.201**
provisions, complaints of victimization can be brought by workers that relate to the termination of their employment in circumstances in which such a claimant could not currently be able to bring a complaint of unfair dismissal.

ERA 1996, s 49(5A) provides that, in relation to working time cases, the award is **21.202**
subject to the current statutory cap for unfair dismissal. ERA 1996, s 49(7) makes the same provision for tax credit cases. ERA 1996, s 49(6) provides that, in relation to whistleblowing cases, the award is subject to the same statutory cap as for unfair dismissal claims under ERA 1996, s 103A, but the statutory cap for unfair dismissals does not currently apply to such claims.

Claims under NMWA 1998, s 24(3) and (4) and trade union recognition are **21.203**
subject to the statutory cap for unfair dismissal.

As far as ERelA 1999 is concerned, the position is less clear, but it would appear that **21.204**
the normal cap on unfair dismissal compensation applies.

It should be noted that, in claims brought under PTWR 2000, reg 8(7)(c), and the **21.205**
FTWR 2002, reg 7(7)(c), the employment tribunal also has the power to make recommendations.

J. Working Time Regulations 1998

21.206 The WTR 1998 create a number of specific rights that are enforceable in an employment tribunal—apart from the general protection against unfair dismissal (ERA 1996, s 101A) and victimization (ERA 1996, s 45A)—for the assertion of the rights conferred by the Regulations.

Right to complain to employment tribunal

21.207 More specifically, WTR 1998, reg 30 provides that a worker may present a complaint to an employment tribunal that his or her employer:

(a) has refused to permit him or her to exercise any right to:
  (i) daily rest (reg 10(1) or (2)); weekly rest (reg 1(1)–(3)); rest breaks (reg 12(1) and (4)) or holidays (regs 13 or 13A);
  (ii) compensatory rest (reg 24), in so far as it applies to daily or weekly rest or rest breaks;
  (iii) mobile workers (reg 24A), in so far as it applies to daily or weekly rest or rest breaks; or
  (iv) the rights conferred on young workers (regs 25(3), 27A(4)(b) or 27(2));
(b) has failed to pay the worker the whole or any part of any amount due under regs 14(2) or 16(1) (holidays).

Remedy

21.208 Where an employment tribunal finds a complaint under WTR 1998, reg 30(1)(a) well founded, the tribunal shall make a declaration to that effect and may make an award of compensation to be paid by the employer to the employee (WTR 1998, reg 30(3)).

21.209 The amount of compensation shall be such amount as the tribunal considers just and equitable, having regard to the employer's default in failing to permit the worker to exercise his or her right and any loss sustained by the worker that is attributable to the matters complained of (WTR 1998, reg 30(4)).

21.210 Where the complaint is upheld under WTR 1998, reg 30(1)(b)—that is, there is a failure to pay holiday pay—the tribunal is empowered to order the employer to pay to the worker the amount that it finds due (WTR 1998, reg 30(5)).

21.211 Such complaints must be brought before the end of the period of three months (or, in the case of WTR 1998, reg 38(2), six months) from the date on which it is alleged that the exercise of the right should have been permitted (or, in the case of rest breaks or leave, the period on which such rights should have begun) or, as the case may be, the payment should have been made (WTR 1998, reg 30(2)(a)). This, however, is subject to the usual proviso that, where such a complaint is not reasonably practicable within the stated period, the tribunal may extend the time limit by such further period as it considers reasonable (WTR 1998, reg 30(2)(b)). This means that claims for statutory holiday pay must be brought within three months of the time at which it was payable (see *Commissioners of the Inland Revenue v Ainsworth and others* [2005] EWCA Civ 441).

This provision therefore allows workers to recover statutory holiday and other payments due to them under the WTR 1998. **21.212**

K. The Right to be Accompanied

The statutory right to be accompanied was introduced by the ERelA 1999. A detailed consideration of the statutory right lies outside the scope of this book. **21.213**

The right

The ERelA 1999, s 10 gives all workers the right to be accompanied at disciplinary or grievance hearings by a trade union representative or a work colleague if a worker so 'reasonably requests'. Disciplinary hearings cover any meeting in which a disciplinary penalty may be imposed. This extends to an informal warning (*London Underground v Ferenc-Batchelor and Harding* [2003] IRLR 252). The EA 2002 extends this right to any meeting held under the statutory disputes resolution procedure. **21.214**

Remedy

ERelA 1999, s 11 gives a worker who believes that his or her statutory right to be accompanied has been infringed the right to complain to an employment tribunal. **21.215**

Such a complaint must be brought within three months beginning with the date on which the breach of the statutory provisions took place or such further period as the employment tribunal considers reasonable if it was not reasonably practicable to present the complaint within that period (ERelA 1999, s 11(2)). **21.216**

Where such a complaint is upheld, the employment tribunal will order the employer to pay compensation to the worker of an amount not exceeding two weeks' pay. The normal rules on calculating a week's pay apply to this award and it is subject to the statutory maximum in the ERA 1996, s 227(1) (£380 as from 1 February 2010). The current maximum is therefore £760. **21.217**

Both workers and their representatives are protected against unfair dismissal and action short of dismissal for exercising this statutory right (ERelA 1999, s 12). **21.218**

L. Right to Written Reasons for Dismissal

There is a statutory right to request written reasons for dismissal. **21.219**

The right

21.220 ERA 1996, s 92 provides that an employee is entitled to be provided with a written statement giving particulars of the reasons for the employee's dismissal (as defined therein) if the employee request such reasons, and that such written reasons should be provided within 14 days of such a request.

21.221 An employee has an automatic right to receive written reason for dismissal if she is dismissed when she is pregnant, or during a period of ordinary or additional maternity or adoption leave.

21.222 The statutory right to written reasons only applies to those employees who qualify for the right to bring an unfair dismissal claim, except where dismissal takes place in circumstances in which the employee has an automatic right to written reasons (ERA 1996, s 92(4A)).

Remedy

21.223 An employee has a right to complain to an employment tribunal where an employer unreasonably fails to provide written reasons or the reasons given are inadequate or untrue (ERA 1996, s 93(1)).

21.224 Where an employment tribunal finds that such a complaint is well founded, it may make a declaration as to what it finds the employer's reasons were for dismissal and will award the employee an additional two weeks' pay (ERA 1996, s 93(2)).

21.225 The normal rules on calculating a 'week's pay' apply to this calculation, but the statutory maximum does not. The award is therefore based on an employee's actual gross pay.

M. Other Statutory Rights

Insolvency provisions (ERA 1996, Pt XII)

21.226 Under ERA 1996, s 188, the employment tribunal has the power to order the Secretary of State to make the following payments (as from 1 February 2010) to an employee:

(a) arrears of pay for a period of up to eight weeks, up to a statutory maximum of £3,040;

(b) notice pay up to a statutory maximum of £4,560;

(c) holiday pay up to a statutory maximum of £2,280; and

(d) unfair dismissal basic award up to a statutory maximum of £11,400.

Duty to inform and consult

Transfer of Undertakings (Protection of Employment) Regulations 2006

21.227 TUPE 2006 represents the current domestic implementation of Council Directive 2001/23/EC.

Under TUPE 2006, reg 11, the transferor is under a duty to notify the transferee of **21.228** certain information (in writing or in readily accessible form) relating to any person employed by it who is assigned to the activity that is the subject of the relevant transfer. This information is:

(a) the identity and age of the employee;
(b) those particulars of employment that an employer is obliged to give to an employee pursuant to ERA 1996, s 1;
(c) information of any disciplinary procedure taken against an employee or grievance procedure taken by an employee within the previous two years, in circumstances in which a Code of Practice issued under TULR(C)A 1992, Pt IV, which relates exclusively or primarily to the resolution of disputes, applies;
(d) information of any court or tribunal case, claim, or action brought by an employee against the transferor, within the previous two years or that the transferor has reasonable grounds to believe that an employee may bring against the transferee, arising out of the employee's employment with the transferor; and
(e) information of any collective agreement that will have effect after the transfer, in its application in relation to the employee, pursuant to TUPE 2006, reg 5(a).

If the transferor fails to comply with its obligation to provide the transferee with **21.229** employee liability information under TUPE 2006, reg 11, then the transferee may present a complaint to a tribunal. If successful, the tribunal may award such compensation to the transferee as is just and equitable, in particular having regard to any loss sustained by the transferor that is attributable to the breach and the terms of any contract between the transferor and transferee, which provide for the payment of such a sum in any event. The minimum award is £500 per employer, which may be lowered if the tribunal considers it just and equitable.

Under TUPE 2006, reg 13, long enough before a relevant transfer to enable the **21.230** employer of any affected employees to consult the appropriate representatives of any affected representatives, the employer (be it transferor or transferee) must inform those representatives of:

(a) the fact that the transfer is to take place, the date or proposed date of the transfer, and the reasons for the transfer;
(b) the legal, economic, and social implications of the transfer for any affected employees;
(c) the measures that it envisages that it will, in connection with the transfer, take in relation to any affected employees or, if it envisages that no measures will be so taken, that fact; and
(d) if the employer is the transferor, the measures, in connection with the transfer, that it envisages the transferee will take in relation to any affected employees who will become employees of the transferee after the transfer by virtue of TUPE 2006, reg 4 or, if it envisages that no measures will be so taken, that fact.

21.231 In relation to (b) above, where the employer genuinely misunderstood the legal effect of a transfer, that did not invalidate the consultation that ensued (on that mistaken belief) (*Communication Workers Union v Royal Mail Group Ltd* [2009] EWCA Civ 1045, [2010] ICR 83, CA).

21.232 If an employer fails to inform and consult with appropriate representatives as to measures, then a complaint may be presented to the tribunal under TUPE 2006, reg 15(1) by the trade union (where the failure relates to trade union representatives), or by the employee representatives, or any of them (where the failure relates to employee representatives), or by any of its employees who are affected employees (where the failure relates to the election of employee representatives and in any other case). TUPE 2006, reg 13 imposes a requirement on the transferor (and indirectly on the transferee) to inform and consult trade union or employee representatives on the matters specified in Transfer of Undertakings (Protection of Employment) Regulations 1981, SI 1981/1794 (TUPE 1981), reg 10(2).

21.233 If the complaint is successful, the tribunal must make a declaration and may order the employer to pay compensation to affected employees (TUPE 2006, reg 15(7)) up to a maximum of 13 weeks' pay each (TUPE 2006, reg 16(3)).

21.234 The transferee and transferor are jointly and severally liable (TUPE 2006, reg 15(9)). Where liability is established, a tribunal is obliged to find the transferee jointly and severally liable with the transferor (*Todd v Strain* UKEAT/0057/10/BI, [2010] All ER (D) 108 (Oct)).

21.235 The amount of the award is determined in the same way as a protective award in redundancy cases (*Susie Radin Ltd v GMB* [2004] IRLR 400 and *Sweetin v Coral Racing* [2006] IRLR 252). In *Todd*, in substituting an award of 13 weeks' pay for seven weeks' pay, Underhill P held that it was wrong in principle to award the maximum 13 weeks' pay in circumstances in which some (although inadequate) information had been given and the measures requiring consultation were of very limited significance.

21.236 A defence to such an award is that there were special circumstances that rendered it not reasonably practicable to comply with the statutory requirements, provided that it took whatever steps to perform the duty as were reasonably practicable (TUPE 2006, reg 13(9)).

21.237 If the employer fails to pay the compensation ordered, the employee may present a complaint to the tribunal under TUPE 2006, reg 15(10).

Collective redundancy

21.238 Employers are under a statutory duty to inform and consult trade unions or employee representatives where it is proposed to make 20 or more employees redundant. The detailed rules are set out in TULR(C)A 1992, s 188. A detailed consideration of those rules lies outside the scope of this book.

The enforcement process of a failure to inform and consult in accordance with these **21.239** provisions is not dissimilar from the rules referred to above in which there is a failure to inform and consult pursuant to TUPE 2006.

TULR(C)A 1992, s 189 provides that, where an employer fails to comply with the **21.240** requirements of s 188, a complaint may be presented to an employment tribunal on that ground. If the employment tribunal finds the complaint to be well founded, it shall make a declaration to that effect and may make a 'protective award' (TULR(C)A 1992, s 189(2)).

A protective award is an award in respect of one or more descriptions of employees **21.241** who have been dismissed as redundant, or whom it is proposed to dismiss as redundant, or in respect of whose dismissal the employee has failed to comply with a requirement of TULR(C)A 1992, s 188 (TULR(C)A 1992, s 189(3)).

The protected period—that is, the period covered by the award—is a period of **21.242** up to 90 days' pay per employee depending on the seriousness of the employer's default (TULR(C)A 1992, s 189(4); see *Susie Radin Ltd v GMB and others* [2004] IRLR 400, CA).

Such a complaint must be presented within a period of three months before the **21.243** date on which the last of the dismissals to which the complaint relates was due to take effect, or, if this is not reasonably practicable, within such further period as the employment tribunal considers reasonable (TULR(C)A 1992, s 189(5)).

A defence to a protected award is that there were special circumstances that ren- **21.244** dered it not reasonably practicable to comply with the statutory requirements (TULR(C)A 1992, s 189(6)).

ICE Regulations 2004

Employees who are dismissed for acting as representatives or candidates for the **21.245** purpose of the ICE Regulations 2004 (or who are selected for redundancy for these reasons) are treated as having been automatically unfairly dismissed by ICE Regulations 2004, reg 30(1)–(4). Similarly, those who are dismissed for seeking to enforce the rights conferred by those Regulations are treated as having been automatically unfairly dismissed by ICE Regulations 2004, reg 30(5). The normal rules on unfair dismissal compensation apply to such complaints.

A detailed consideration of these provisions lies outside the scope of this book, but **21.246** the normal rules on the calculation of unfair dismissal compensation apply to such dismissals.

N. Compensation Claims against Trade Unions

In addition to the rights discussed below, union members or prospective members **21.247** are able to enforce a number of other important statutory rights that do not include a tribunal claim for a compensatory award and so fall outside of the scope of this work.

Right not to be unjustifiably disciplined (TULR(C)A 1992, s 64)

Statutory right

21.248 TULR(C)A 1992, s 64(1) provides that an individual who is or has been a member of a trade union has the right not to be unjustifiably disciplined by the union. The right exists alongside any existing rights (TULR(C)A 1992, s 64(5)), such as common law rights to be dealt with in accordance with the rules of the union and in accordance with natural justice. An individual is 'unjustifiably disciplined' by a trade union if the actual or supposed conduct for which he or she is disciplined falls within one of the categories of conduct falling within TULR(C)A 1992, s 65, or is believed by the union to amount to such conduct. These categories are:

(a) failing to participate in, or support, a strike or other industrial action (whether by members of the union or by others), or indicating opposition to or a lack of support for such action;

(b) failing to contravene, for a purpose connected with such a strike or other industrial action, a requirement imposed on him or her by or under a contract of employment;

(c) asserting (whether by bringing proceedings or otherwise) that the union, any official or representative of it, or a trustee of its property has contravened, or is proposing to contravene, a requirement that is, or is thought to be, imposed by or under the rules of the union or any other agreement or by or under any enactment (whenever passed) or any rule of law (although false assertions made in bad faith are excluded by TULR(C)A 1992, s 65(6));

(d) encouraging or assisting a person:
   (i) to perform an obligation imposed on him or her by a contract of employment; or
   (ii) to make or attempt to vindicate any such assertion as is mentioned in paragraph (c);

(e) contravening a requirement imposed by or in consequence of a determination that infringes the individual's or another individual's right not to be unjustifiably disciplined;

(f) failing to agree, or withdrawing agreement, to the making from his or her wages (in accordance with arrangements between his or her employer and the union) of deductions representing payments to the union in respect of his or her membership;

(g) resigning or proposing to resign from the union or from another union, becoming or proposing to become a member of another union, refusing to become a member of another union, or being a member of another union;

(h) working with, or proposing to work with, individuals who are not members of the union or who are or are not members of another union;

(i) working for, or proposing to work for, an employer who employs or who has employed individuals who are not members of the union or who are or are not members of another union; or

(j) requiring the union to do an act that the union is, by any provision of the Act, required to do on the requisition of a member.

However, conduct that would independently and justifiably lead to the individual being disciplined is excluded. **21.249**

Members are protected from disciplinary action including expulsion, fines, being deprived of benefits or facilities, encouragement or advice to another union not to accept the member, or being subjected to any other detriment (TULR(C)A 1992, s 64(2)). **21.250**

Enforcement

A claim of infringement of the right may be presented in the employment tribunal within three months of the determination complained of (TULR(C)A 1992, s 66(1) and (2)). **21.251**

Remedy

If the claim is established, the tribunal will make a declaration (TULR(C)A 1992, s 66(3)). **21.252**

If such a declaration is made by the tribunal, the claimant may apply for compensation and/or repayment of monies paid by him or her as a result of the unjustified disciplinary action (TULR(C)A 1992, s 67(1)). If the union revokes the unlawful determination or takes all steps necessary to secure the reversal of anything done in order to give effect to the determination, the application for compensation/repayment will be made to the employment tribunal. Otherwise, the application will be made to the EAT (TULR(C)A 1992, s 67(2)). Applications made in the wrong tribunal may be transferred (TULR(C)A 1992, s 67(4)). **21.253**

The amount of compensation will be based on what the tribunal or EAT considers is 'just and equitable' in all of the circumstances (TULR(C)A 1992, s 67(5)), taking into account the duty to mitigate (TULR(C)A 1992, s 67(6)) and any contributory fault (TULR(C)A 1992, s 67(7)). The statutory maximum compensation is the aggregate of: **21.254**

(a) 30 times the maximum week's pay for a basic award in unfair dismissal cases (ERA 1996, s 227—currently £380 from 1 February 2010); and

(b) the maximum compensatory award in such cases (ERA 1996, s 124—currently £65,300 from 1 February 2010).

This gives a maximum award under s 67(8) of £76,700. This is subject to a minimum of £7,200 if application is made to the EAT (TULR(C)A 1992, s 156(1)).

21.255 The compensatory award may include damages for injury to feelings (*Beaumont v Amicus MSF* (2004) 4 August, EAT, unreported).

Right not to be excluded or expelled from union (TULR(C)A 1992, s 174)

Statutory right

21.256 In addition to any existing common law rights, TULR(C)A 1992, s 174 provides the right not to be excluded or expelled from a trade union unless the exclusion or expulsion is permitted by s 174 by falling within one of four categories (TULR(C)A 1992, s 174(1)–(4)):

(a) the individual does not satisfy, or no longer satisfies, an enforceable membership requirement contained in the rules of the union (that is, one that restricts membership solely by reference to one or more of the following criteria: employment in a specified trade, industry, or profession; occupational description; or possession of specified qualifications or work experience);

(b) the individual does not qualify, or no longer qualifies, for membership of the union by reason of the union operating only in a particular part or particular parts of Great Britain;

(c) in the case of a union the purpose of which is the regulation of relations between its members and one particular employer or a number of particular employers who are associated, the individual is not, or is no longer, employed by that employer or one of those employers; or

(d) the exclusion or expulsion is entirely attributable to the individual's conduct, which may not include either conduct consisting of being, ceasing to be, or having been or ceased to be a member of another trade union or of a political party or employed by a particular employer or at a particular place, or conduct falling within TULR(C)A 1992, s 65.

Enforcement

21.257 The claimant must present his or her complaint to the tribunal within six months of the refusal or expulsion.

Remedy

21.258 As with claims under TULR(C)A 1992, s 66, there is two-stage process: first, if the complaint is made out, the tribunal will make a declaration (TULR(C)A 1992, s 176(1)); second, under TULR(C)A 1992, s 176(2) and (3), the claimant cannot apply for compensation until four weeks after the tribunal's declaration. This four-week period is provided to enable the trade union to admit the claimant to membership. If this has been done, then any application for compensation must be made within six months of the tribunal's declaration to the employment tribunal. If the union has not admitted the claimant to membership, then the application must be made to the EAT.

The amount of compensation will be such amount as is considered just and equitable **21.259** in all of the circumstances, but the minimum in the case of an application to the EAT is £6,100. Whether application is made to the tribunal or EAT, the maximum compensatory award is the aggregate of:

(a) 30 times the current limit on the amount of a week's pay for basic award in unfair dismissals (currently £380); and

(b) the current maximum compensatory award in unfair dismissal cases (currently £65,300).

The total maximum is therefore £76,700.

Injury to feelings is recoverable (*Bradley v NALGO* [1991] ICR 359, EAT). **21.260** Arguably the level of injury to feelings should be assessed on the basis of *Vento* (*No 2*) guidelines. Compensation may reduced where the claimant's conduct is found to have contributed to the exclusion or expulsion.

Where the claimant complains of expulsion, he or she can only succeed under **21.261** TULR(C)A 1992, ss 176 or 66, but not both.

Part VI

TRIBUNAL PROCEDURES IN COMPENSATION CLAIMS

22

TRIBUNAL PROCEDURE

A. Introduction

The Employment Tribunals (Constitution and Rules of Procedure) Regulations **22.01** 2004, SI 2004/1861 (ET Regulations 2004), which came into force on 1 October 2004, marked the start of a new era in employment tribunal procedures.

It is perhaps fair to say that the Employment Tribunals (Constitution and Rules of **22.02** Procedure) Regulations 2001, SI 2001/1171 (ET Regulations 2001), and in Scotland, SI 2001/1170, already represented a move away from the previous more informal approach towards giving greater importance to the efficient management of the tribunal system. The ET Regulations 2004 continue this trend. Twenty-three easily understood and largely discretionary rules have been replaced by 61 rules that are, in many cases, prescriptive.

22.03 This chapter looks at how the tribunal's procedural rules impact on compensation claims.

B. General Principles

Overriding objective

22.04 The 'overriding objective' first made its appearance in the ET Regulations 2001.

22.05 ET Regulations 2001, reg 3 provides:

> (1) The overriding objective of these Regulations and the rules in Schedules 1, 2, 3, 4, 5 and 6 is to enable tribunals and Employment Judges to deal with cases justly.
> (2) Dealing with a case justly includes, so far as practicable:
>   (a) ensuring that the parties are on an equal footing;
>   (b) dealing with the case in ways which are proportionate to the complexity or importance of the issues;
>   (c) ensuring that it is dealt with expeditiously and fairly; and
>   (d) saving expense.
> (3) A tribunal or Employment Judge shall seek to give effect to the overriding objective when it or he:
>   (a) exercises any power given to it or him by these Regulations or the rules in Schedules 1, 2, 3, 4, 5 and 6; or
>   (b) interprets these Regulations or any rule in Schedules 1, 2, 3, 4, 5 and 6.
> (4) The parties shall assist the tribunal or the Employment Judge to further the overriding objective.

22.06 It follows that tribunals and the parties are therefore required to give effect to the overriding objective at every stage of the process (including procedural issues relating to compensation).

The claim form

22.07 In the claim form, the claimant is required not only to set out his or her gross and net earnings from employment, but also whether he or she was paid notice and whether he or she was in the employer's pension scheme (section 4), and in an unfair dismissal case, whether the claimant received other benefits from the employer (section 4.5), whether the claimant has found a new job (section 4.6), and, if so, when the new employment commenced (section 4.7) and how much the claimant is earning from the new job (section 4.8), and whether the claimant wishes to be reinstated or re-engaged or seeks only compensation (section 4.9).

22.08 Thus the claim form provides the respondent with all (or nearly all) of the necessary information to quantify a claim for loss of earnings in cases in which the claimant has found a new job.

The claim form perhaps correctly assumes that, where the complaint is also one of **22.09** discrimination arising out of dismissal, it is unnecessary for the claimant to repeat these details. The form does not, however, make provision for financial information arising out of discrimination claims during employment; nor is the claimant required to quantify any claim for injury to feelings or injury to health at this stage.

In other cases, the claimant is required to set out the other payments owed and how **22.10** much is being claimed—for example, unpaid wages, holiday pay, notice pay, or other unpaid amounts (section 5.1).

Response

The respondent is asked whether the details referred to above are correct and, if not, **22.11** to detail what the respondent believes to be the correct figures (section 3). The same process applies to other information (section 6). In breach of contract claims, if the respondent wishes to make a counterclaim, this should be included in the response in a similar way and is treated as a claim.

It should be noted, however, that if the respondent fails to enter a response within **22.12** 28 days of the claim being sent (or if any application is made within that period, such further period as the tribunal considers just and equitable) (ET Regulations 2004, reg 4(1)), it is open to the tribunal to issue a default judgment both in relation to liability and quantum based on the information on the claim. Alternatively, the employment judge may order a remedy hearing that the respondent will not be entitled to participate in (ET Regulations 2004, reg 8(1)–(3)). The respondent may however apply for a review of a judgment entered in default (ET Regulations 2004, reg 33).

C. Schedule of Loss

Where the claimant has not found a job at the time that the claim is presented or **22.13** where there are other issues relating to the loss claimed by the claimant, the employment tribunal is likely to order the claimant to prepare and serve a schedule of loss on the respondent as a standard order (ET Regulations 2004, reg 10).

In more complicated cases, the claimant may be ordered to prepare and serve an **22.14** updated schedule of loss prior to the hearing, and the respondent may be ordered to prepare and serve a counter-schedule.

Prior to the ET Regulations 2004, such orders were not common in ordinary unfair **22.15** dismissal claims. Often, it was necessary to apply for such a direction (which was not always granted). In more recent years, such an order has become a standard direction and is likely to remain so under the new Regulations other than where the loss can be readily quantified from the claim itself.

22.16 Importantly, a tribunal should not award a larger sum than that set out in the schedule of loss without giving both sides an opportunity to make submissions on the matter (*Port of Tilbury (London) Ltd v Birch* [2005] IRLR 92).

22.17 There is currently a variation in tribunal practice in relation to compensation for injury to feelings and injury to health. Some tribunals will require the claimant to include this in the schedule of loss, whereas others take the view that this is a matter for the tribunal to determine and therefore will not require the claimant to particularize the claim in this regard.

Finding out more information

22.18 Taken together, the claim form and the response will normally enable the parties to identify all of the issues relating to compensation in straightforward unfair dismissal cases in which the claimant has found a new job.

22.19 However, where the claimant is out of work or where there is a dispute over benefits or pension loss or, in discrimination cases, where the claimant is claiming compensation for injury to health, the parties may wish to find out more information about their respective claims and counterclaims prior to the hearing.

22.20 It is important to identify what documentary and other evidence may be required in relation to remedy. The standard ways of finding out more information about the claim for compensation is to make a request for additional information (ET Regulations 2004, reg 10(2)(b)), or to make a request for the provision of answers to specific questions put by the tribunal or employment judge (ET Regulations 2004, reg 10(2)(f)), or to make a request for discovery and/or inspection (ET Regulations 2004, reg 10(2)(d))—or a combination of all three.

Checklist in unfair dismissal

The following is a brief checklist of the kind of information that will be relevant to the assessment of compensation in an unfair dismissal case:

- the claimant's personnel file, including contract of employment;
- wage slips from the 'old' job and 'new' job;
- details of changes in rates of pay or hours of work;
- the claimant's P45 and/or P60 (where appropriate);
- details relating to bonus schemes;
- details of commission payments or profit-related pay;
- details of holiday pay;
- details of promotional opportunities;
- details of the pension scheme from both the 'old' job and the 'new' job (it being important that any relevant documentation relating to the previous employer's scheme and any scheme available in the new employment is disclosed at the earliest opportunity, particularly if expert evidence is to be given);

- details of other relevant benefits from the 'old' job and the 'new' job, and how those benefits are valued (relevant examples include methods of valuing company cars, or health insurance or accommodation or other benefits);
- information relating to mitigation of loss (for example, records or other information of the steps that the claimant has taken to look for and apply for a new job, and the outcome of any job applications);
- information relating to the 'state of the labour market', both locally and nationally, or specifically within the industry in question; and
- information relating to the receipts and earnings of any business set up by the claimant in mitigation of loss (for example, business accounts and tax returns), as well as any business development plans.

In addition to the information required in unfair dismissal cases, the following should also be considered in discrimination claims involving an injury to health or disability. **22.21**

Checklist for discrimination cases

- Complete medical records from GP, hospital, and any consultants
- Expert reports—for example, from medical expert, care expert, specialist equipment or information technology expert, equal pay experts, employment consultant, or forensic accountant, etc
- Receipts for all expenses claimed

D. Process for Obtaining Additional Information

In the first instance, requests for such information may be made by letter. There is **22.22**
no reason, in principle, why a request for additional information (previously referred to as 'further particulars'), written answers, and for discovery should not be covered in the same letter. Sometimes, the party making the request will send a copy of the letter to the employment tribunal, but this is unnecessary and tribunals are becoming increasingly critical of parties who follow this practice. The letter will normally set out a time frame within which the information should be provided, after which it may be necessary to apply for an order, but before an order is obtained, it is now necessary to follow the requirements of ET Regulations 2004, reg 11.

In essence, ET Regulations 2004, reg 11 provides that: **22.23**

(a) an application for an order must be made ten days before the date of the hearing (although it is, of course, still possible for applications to be made in the course of the hearing);

(b) unless the employment judge orders otherwise, the application must be made in writing to the employment tribunal and must include:

    (i)   the case number for the proceedings;

    (ii) the reason for the request; and

(iii) if the application is for a case management discussion or a pre-hearing review, any orders sought;

(c) the application must also include an explanation of how the order would assist the tribunal or employment judge in dealing with the proceedings efficiently and fairly; and

(d) where the party is legally represented, a letter should be sent to the other side (or the other side's representative) giving:

(i) details of the application and the reasons why it is sought;

(ii) notification that any objection to the application be sent to the employment tribunal office within seven days of the receipt of the application;

(iii) notification that any objection to the application must be copied both to the tribunal office and all other parties; and

(iv) confirmation in writing to the tribunal that this rule has been complied with. (Where a party is not represented, this task will be undertaken by the Secretary to Tribunals).

Notably, this procedure applies to all applications in proceedings, except that requirement (d) above does not apply to an application for a witness order.

E. Case Management

22.24 One of the most important changes in tribunal procedure in recent years is the greater use of case management discussions to ensure that tribunal claims are properly prepared and the hearing runs smoothly.

22.25 In *Buxton v Equinox Designs Ltd* [1999] IRLR 158, the Employment Appeal Tribunal (EAT) acknowledged, in the context of a discrimination case, that such compensation claims require careful case management and that, to the end, directions may be required involving, amongst other things, an exchange of statements of case and any witness statements. The EAT also anticipated that the same would apply to unfair dismissal once the cap was increased.

22.26 The employment tribunal case management powers are now set out in ET Regulations 2004, reg 10. Amongst the most commonly sought directions in compensation claims are directions for the preparation and exchange of witness statements, expert evidence, preparation of an agreed bundle including orders for discovery and further information including the provision of written answers, and the preparation and updating of a schedule of loss.

Expert evidence in compensation claims

22.27 Provision for a direction for expert evidence is made in ET Regulations 2004, reg 10(2)(t). The provisions of ET Regulations 2004, reg 11 (referred to above) apply to such an application.

The general requirements regarding expert evidence set out in the Civil Procedure **22.28** Rules 1998, SI 1998/3132 (CPR), r 35 also apply to employment tribunals. In particular, the expert's report must state the substance of all material instructions, whether written or oral, on the basis of which the report was written. The instructions are not privileged. At the end of the report, there must be a statement that the expert understands his or her duty to the tribunal and that he or she has complied with which duty (see CPR, r 35.10).

In *De Keyser Ltd v Wilson* [2001] IRLR 324, EAT guidance was given on the use of **22.29** expert evidence in employment tribunals. The main points of this guidance are summarized below.

(a) Careful thought needs to be given before any party embarks upon instructions for expert evidence. It by no means follows that, because a party wishes such evidence to be admitted, it will be. A prudent party will first explore with the employment tribunal at a directions hearing (now a case management discussion hearing) or in correspondence whether, in principle, expert evidence is likely to be acceptable.

(b) Save where one side or the other has already committed itself to the use of its own expert (which is to be avoided in the absence of special circumstances), the joint instructions of a single expert is the preferred course.

(c) If a joint expert is to be instructed, the terms that the parties need to agree include the incidence of that expert's fees and expenses. If one or other party cannot afford these fees, there should at least be an attempt to agree the letter of instruction.

(d) If a joint expert is used, the tribunal may fix a period within which the parties should agree the identity of the expert and the joint letter of instruction, and may also fix the date on which the report should be made available. In cases in which this proves to be impossible, it is open to the tribunal to give formal directions itself.

(e) Any letter of instruction should specify in as much detail as can be given any particular question that the expert should be invited to answer and all more general subjects that the expert is asked to address. Such instructions should avoid partisanship or the use of emotive language. In so far as the expert is required to make assumptions of fact, these should be spelled out and, as stated above, the expert should be reminded that his or her duty is to the tribunal.

(f) Where there is no joint expert, the tribunal should, in the absence of agreement between the parties, specify a timetable for disclosure or exchange of experts' reports and (where there are two or more experts) for meetings between the experts to attempt to identify areas of agreement. Sometimes, experts may be required to produce a schedule of agreed issues and of points of dispute. Any timetable should provide for the raising of supplementary questions with the expert or experts (whether or not there is a joint report) and for the exchange of expert reports in good time before the hearing.

(g) Costs may be awarded where a party fails to comply with any orders (see below) regarding expert evidence.

22.30 The extent to which these guidelines are relevant will depend on the particular circumstances of the case, taking into account the overriding objective. For example, despite the EAT's stated preference that a joint expert should be instructed, tribunals are normally prepared to agree to separate experts being called where there are disputes over quantum.

22.31 Orders for expert evidence should normally be raised at a case management discussion hearing. In the absence of an order for expert evidence, it will be unfair for a party to serve notice of an intention to call expert evidence at a stage in the process at which it is not possible for the other side to call its own expert to challenge the evidence (*Sterlite Industries Ltd v Bhatia* EAT 194/02/MAA).

22.32 In *Hospice of St Mary of Furness v Howard* [2007] IRLR 944, the EAT gave guidance on when a party may call its own expert to contradict the evidence of a joint expert (in that case, on the issue of disability). The EAT ruled that:

> Where there is an issue as to the existence of a physical impairment it is open to a respondent to seek to disprove the existence of such impairment, including by seeking to prove that the claimed impairment is not genuine or is a mental and not a physical impairment.

Expert evidence in unfair dismissal

22.33 Expert evidence will not normally be required in a straightforward unfair dismissal case, but may be necessary in more complex cases. Some examples of the kinds of issues on which expert evidence may be relevant are given below.

Disputes over remuneration

22.34 In unusual circumstances, it may be appropriate to instruct a remuneration consultant to give evidence on pay and benefits. For example, issues may arise under the Employment Rights Act 1996 (ERA 1996), s 123(2) over what bonus payments an employee could have reasonably been expected to receive had he or she not been dismissed. Evidence of industry practice may be relevant. Similarly, expert evidence may be called on the valuation of other benefits.

Disputes over pensions

22.35 Where the calculation of pension loss is based on the *Employment Tribunal Guidelines on Compensation for Loss of Pension Rights*, it will not be necessary to call expert evidence on this issue. However, since there is no duty on an employment tribunal to follow these guidelines and where a party wishes to rely on some alternative method of calculation, it is open to that party to call an expert on the issue of pension loss (see *Port of Tilbury (London) Ltd v Birch* [2005] IRLR 92, EAT).

There may also be a need to call expert evidence to value the benefits that the **22.36** claimant will receive under the new employer's pension scheme.

It is important in instructing the expert to ensure that the expert understands the **22.37** principles on which compensation is to be assessed and for the expert to make clear the methodology used in calculating any loss (including the need to allow for the risk of withdrawal and to give credit for the accelerated nature of the payment).

Disputes over mitigation

In exceptional circumstances, it may be appropriate to call a recruitment consultant **22.38** to give evidence on the issue of mitigation—particularly the state of the job market. This may be particularly relevant if the claimant is employed in some kind of specialist role in a specialist sector or if the market for the particular skills is international.

Experts in discrimination cases

Disputes between medical experts

In the absence of agreement, both sides will often need to call their own medical **22.39** expert to enable the tribunal to resolve disputes in relation to: the correct diagnosis of the medical condition (often by reference to the World Health Organization [WHO] International Classification of Diseases), whether the unlawful discriminatory act caused the condition in question, current symptoms, the need for further treatment, the prognosis, future vulnerability, and fitness for different types of work.

Disputes as to cost of care

In severe injury cases, care experts are often called to assess the past, present, and **22.40** future cost of paid and unpaid care for the claimant, as well as the cost of DIY and gardening.

Disputes over the need for special equipment or adaptations

Where the claimant is severely disabled, aids and equipment experts, such as occu- **22.41** pational therapists or information technology experts, might be required to resolve issues surrounding the need for special items and the costs associated with them.

Disputes over whether work of claimant and comparator is of equal value

In large-scale equal value claims, each party often uses its own expert to support a **22.42** submission that the work in question was, or was not, of equal value.

Disclosure and tribunal documentation

In straightforward cases, the tribunal will make standard orders for disclosure **22.43** (previously known as 'discovery'), inspection, and the agreement of a tribunal bundle under ET Regulations 2004, reg 10(2)(d). In more complex cases, this issue should be raised at a case management discussion and specific order should be made for disclosure by list of documents (in Scotland, referred to as an 'inventory'), inspection, and the production of an agreed bundle. In Scotland, the Employment Tribunals (Scotland) Practice Direction No 1 (2006), issued on 14 December 2006, requires the mutual notification by the parties of the documents (referred to as 'productions') on which each party intends to rely at least 14 days before the hearing.

22.44 Where an application is made for specific disclosure (or for additional information), this should be included in the timetable and allowance should be made for potential applications for orders if voluntary requests are unsuccessful.

22.45 The overriding objective is now the main consideration in determining whether such orders are made by the employment tribunal and the tribunal will be guided by the ordinary Civil Procedure Rules on disclosure (CPR, r 31) and further information (CPR, r 18).

22.46 Additionally, in discrimination cases, the statutory questionnaire procedure can be utilized by claimants to obtain valuable information from the respondent at an early stage of the proceedings.

22.47 The duty of disclosure continues until the conclusion of the proceedings, and if relevant documents come to a party's notice at any time during the proceedings, he or she must immediately notify the other parties (CPR, r 31.11). In *Scott v IRC* [2004] EWCA Civ 400, [2004] IRLR 713, CA, it was held that the employer should have disclosed a change to its retirement policy, which was made after the employee was dismissed, but before the tribunal hearing, because this had a material effect on compensation.

Ogden tables

22.48 The Ogden tables are rarely relevant in quantifying future loss in unfair dismissal claims, although the position in discrimination claims is open to further argument.

22.49 In *Kingston Upon Hull City Council v Dunnachie (No 3)* [2003] IRLR 843, the EAT gave the following guidance on the procedure to be followed if a party does wish to rely on the Ogden tables.

(a) A party should indicate in advance whether it wishes to rely on the Ogden tables and, if so, which table, preferably by way of a schedule submitted within 14 days of the response. Such a schedule should set out the suggested multiplicand, by reference to the relevant 'old job facts' and 'new job facts', the relevant period relied upon, and what, if any, discount is to be made from the multiplier.

(b) The other party upon receipt of such a schedule should submit a counter-schedule within 14 days of receiving the first party's schedule, giving the same particulars.

(c) In a case in which such steps have not been complied with, an employment judge should be robust in issuing orders for further particulars and/or disclosure

well in advance of the hearing, so that each party knows what case is to be met
and what evidence needs to be called.

(d) The tables should not be used by an employment tribunal without giving the
parties the opportunity to put forward their cases.

(e) The use of actuarial evidence (other than to quantify pension loss) outside the
tables should be discouraged.

Exchange of witness statements

Standard orders will also be given on the preparation and exchange of witness state-   **22.50**
ments and, where appropriate, the preparation and exchange of supplementary
witness statements.

This issue may also be raised at a case management discussion. It is always important   **22.51**
to ensure that all of the other evidence is available and complete before finaliz-
ing the timetable for exchange of witness statements, so that the statements are able
to cross-refer to the documentary evidence, preferably by reference to the page
number in the hearing bundle.

Split hearing or single hearing

There is no hard-and-fast rule as to whether liability and remedy should be deter-   **22.52**
mined at a single hearing or at a split hearing, but it is advisable for the parties to
ascertain at an early stage which course the tribunal proposes to adopt.

In Scotland, the normal practice in unfair dismissal cases is for the tribunal to   **22.53**
determine both issues at the same hearing, and the same practice applies in
England and Wales in more straightforward cases. Where this takes place, the parties
should be given an opportunity to call evidence and make submissions on the
question of remedy before a decision is reached (*Duffy v Yeomans & Partners Ltd*
[1993] IRLR 368).

However, in some cases, having regard to the value of the claim and the complexity   **22.54**
of the issues, it will be appropriate to have a split hearing dealing first with liability
and then with remedy. This will often be the case in discrimination claims and
may also apply in more complex unfair dismissal claims in which the amounts
involved are substantial. If the parties consider that a split hearing is appropriate,
this matter should be raised and justified at a case management meeting (because
the normal assumption is that the hearing will cover both liability and remedy).

If the tribunal does direct that a split hearing is to be held, it is important—particu-   **22.55**
larly in unfair dismissal cases—for it to make clear how it proposes to deal with the
issue of contributory fault—that is, whether this is to be considered at the liability
hearing or the remedies hearing (*Dundon v GPT* [1995] IRLR 403)—and at what
stage the relevant witnesses are to be called on this issue. The normal procedure is
that evidence relating to contributory fault and a *Polkey* reduction is given at the

liability hearing, and arguments on quantum are raised at the remedy hearing. But, to avoid confusion, it is advisable to get a clear direction on this issue (*Iggesund Converters Ltd v Lewis* [1984] ICR 544, 552). Similar issues may arise in discrimination cases regarding the application of the principles in *Ministry of Defence v Cannock* [1994] IRLR 509.

Fixing the date and length of the hearing

22.56 A further issue to be addressed is the date and length of the hearing. Dates to avoid of witnesses should be obtained. The time estimate should include sufficient time for evidence, submissions, deliberation, and oral judgments to take place without the need for adjournments.

Enforcing tribunal directions

22.57 It is always open to a party to apply to vary any directions issued by the employment tribunal.

22.58 In the absence of such a variation, the tribunal is empowered to award costs for a failure to comply with a direction (ET Regulations 2004, reg 13(1)) or, if the tribunal makes an 'unless order', to strike out the claim or the response (ET Regulations 2004, reg 13(2)).

F. Tribunal Procedure in Equal Pay Claims

Like work or work rated as equivalent

22.59 If the complaint is that the claimant is employed on 'like work or work rated as equivalent' with a comparator of the opposite sex, then the tribunal first has to decide whether the work is like work or has been properly rated as equivalent under a job evaluation study. Second, the tribunal has to determine whether the respondent has a genuine material factor defence (Equal Pay Act 1970 [EqPA 1970], s 1(3)). Such claims are governed by the ordinary employment tribunal rules contained in Sch 1 to the ET Regulations 2004.

Equal value work

22.60 There is a special procedure applicable to 'equal value' claims that was created by the Equal Pay Act 1970 (Amendment) Regulations 2004, SI 2004/2352, and the Employment Tribunals (Constitution and Rules of Procedure) (Amendment) Regulations 2004, SI 2004/2351, whereby Sch 6 was inserted into the ET Regulations 2004 with effect from 1 October 2004. Comprehensive consideration of the many detailed rules contained in Sch 6 is beyond the scope of this work.

In outline, however, there is now an 'indicative timetable' for dealing with equal value claims whereby: **22.61**

(a) in proceedings in which no independent expert is appointed, there is a 25-week indicative timetable involving a 'Stage 1' equal value hearing within three weeks of the response, with the merits hearing taking place within a further 18 weeks;

(b) in cases in which an independent expert is appointed, the indicative timetable takes 37 weeks and allows for a 'Stage 1' equal value hearing within three weeks of the response, a 'Stage 2' hearing within ten weeks of the Stage 1 hearing, the independent expert's report to be served within four weeks of the Stage 2 hearing, written questions to be put to the expert within four weeks after the report, and the merits hearing then to take place within a further eight weeks.

Stage 1: Equal value hearing

At the Stage 1 equal value hearing, the tribunal will determine whether the claim   **22.62**
should be struck out on grounds that the claimant's work and the comparator's work are not of equal value. If there has already been a job evaluation study that has assessed the work of the claimant as not being of equal value to that of her comparator, the claim will not automatically fail. However, EqPA 1970, s 2A(2A) creates a presumption in favour of upholding the job evaluation study unless the tribunal has reasonable grounds for suspecting that the evaluation was made on a system that discriminates on grounds of gender, or is 'otherwise unsuitable to be relied upon'.

Within 28 days of the Stage 1 hearing, the parties shall provide each other with   **22.63**
written job descriptions for the claimant and any comparator, and shall identify to each other in writing the facts that they consider to be relevant to the question. Then, within 56 days, the parties must present a joint agreed statement covering job descriptions and relevant facts. At least 28 days before the hearing, the parties must submit a statement of facts and issues on which they are in agreement, a statement of facts and issues on which they disagree, and a summary of their reasons for disagreeing. The employer is required to grant access to its premises to the independent expert (ET Regulations 2004, reg 3(1)(d)) or, where there is none, to the claimant and his or her representative (ET Regulations 2004, reg 5(1)(c)). The matter will proceed to a merits hearing if there is no independent expert involved.

Stage 2: Equal value hearing

Where the independent expert has been required to prepare a report, a Stage 2 equal   **22.64**
value hearing will take place to enable the tribunal to 'make a determination of facts on which the parties cannot agree which relate to the question'. The independent expert will then be required to prepare a report on the basis of facts that have either been agreed or resolved by the tribunal. Following amendments to the EqPA 1970, the tribunal may at any time withdraw the requirement on the expert to prepare a report and decide the case for itself.

Equal value merits hearing

22.65 Finally, at the merits hearing, the tribunal will consider (having regard to the expert evidence) whether the work is of equal value with that of a comparator and whether the employer's material factor defence is made out, and will decide upon the remedy if the claim is successful.

G. Reviewing Employment Tribunal Judgments

22.66 The power to review an employment tribunal judgment and decisions is set out in ET Regulations 2004, reg 34. As far as compensation claims are concerned, the two most relevant grounds are:

(a) new evidence has become available since the conclusion of the hearing to which the decision relates, provided that its existence could not have been reasonably known of or foreseen at the time (ET Regulations 2004, reg 34(3)(d)); or

(b) the interests of justice require such a review (ET Regulations 2004, reg 34(3)(e)).

22.67 The two principal examples of a situation in which it may be appropriate to apply to review an award of compensation are:

(a) where the forecast that forms the basis of the award for future loss has been falsified to a sufficiently substantial extent so as to invalidate the assessment; or

(b) new evidence comes to light after the hearing that justifies a variation in the award—for example, in an unfair dismissal case where further evidence of misconduct comes to light that justifies a variation in the award on just and equitable grounds or for contributory fault.

H. Costs in Employment Tribunals

22.68 Ordinarily, legal or other expenses associated with the preparation for a hearing cannot be recovered as part of a compensation claim. The power to award legal costs and expenses in employment tribunals is set out in ET Regulations 2004, regs 13(1)(a) and 38–40.

Failure to comply with orders

22.69 As stated above, costs may be awarded where a party fails to comply with an order or practice direction—for example, an order for discovery or an order for exchange of witness statements.

General power to award legal costs and expenses

22.70 The general power to award costs and expenses is set out in ET Regulations 2004, regs 39 and 40.

A tribunal must make an award of costs or expenses in proceedings for unfair dismissal **22.71** where a hearing has been postponed or adjourned and the claimant has expressed a wish to be reinstated or re-engaged, which has been communicated to the respondent not less than seven days before the hearing, and the postponement or adjournment has been caused by the respondent's failure, without special reason, to adduce reasonable evidence as to the availability of jobs from which the claimant was dismissed or of comparable or suitable employment (ET Regulations 2004, regs 39 and 43).

A tribunal must consider making an award of costs, but is not bound to do so, **22.72** where a party has, in bringing the proceedings—or he or she or his or her representative has, in conducting the proceedings—acted vexatiously, abusively, disruptively, or otherwise unreasonably, or the bringing or conducting of the proceedings by the paying party has been misconceived (ET Regulations 2004, regs 40(3) and 44(3)). The word 'misconceived' is substantially wider than the previous word 'frivolous' used in previous regulations.

Type of award of costs

The ET Regulations 2004 distinguish between situations in which a party is legally **22.73** represented (which is defined to include representation by barristers and solicitors) and situations in which a party is not legally represented.

Where a party is legally represented, the award is strictly limited to legal costs, **22.74** which the paying party (that is, the party who is ordered to pay costs) is ordered to pay to the receiving party.

Where a party is not legally represented, the tribunal may make an order for prepa- **22.75** ratory time costs, which, again, are paid by the paying party to the receiving party.

Importantly, costs are paid by the paying party, not its representative. There is a separate **22.76** power to award wasted costs against representatives in ET Regulations 2004, reg 48.

Amount of costs and expenses

The amount of costs or expenses is determined in one of three ways (ET Regulations **22.77** 2004, reg 41(1)):

(a) such sum as the tribunal may specify up to £10,000;
(b) such sum as may be agreed between the parties. This may exceed £10,000;
(c) such sum as may be determined by way of a detailed assessment in a county court in accordance with the Civil Procedure Rules or, in Scotland, as taxed according to such part of the table of fees prescribed for proceedings in the sheriff court as shall be directed by the order. This may exceed £10,000.

Importantly, in determining both the type of award and the amount of the award, **22.78** the tribunal or the employment judge may take into account the paying party's ability to pay (ET Regulations 2004, reg 41(2)).

Preparation time costs

22.79   The rules on preparation time costs are set out in ET Regulations 2004, regs 42–47. The power and circumstances in which an award may be made are essentially the same as the power to award legal costs. (The relevant references are referred to above.)

22.80   Where the rules differ are in relation to the amount. There is a maximum ceiling of £10,000 (ET Regulations 2004, reg 45(2)) and an hourly rate of £29 per hour as from 6 April 2010 (which is increased annually by £1) (ET Regulations 2004, reg 45(4)). The amount of preparatory time is quantified by evidence of time spent (which may include time spent obtaining legal advice and other preparatory time) and the tribunal's own assessment of what it considers reasonable, with reference to matters such as complexity of the proceedings, the number of witnesses, and documentation required (ET Regulations 2004, reg 45(1)).

22.81   As with legal costs, in determining whether to make an order and the amount to be ordered, the tribunal may take into account the paying party's ability to pay (ET Regulations 2004, reg 45(3)).

Application

22.82   An application for costs can be made at any time during the proceedings, at the hearing, or within 28 days of the receipt of the judgment. This time may be extended where it is considered to be in the interests of justice to do so.

'Without prejudice save as to costs' offers

22.83   There is no equivalent to a 'Part 36' offer in the ET Regulations 2004 and there are doubts as to the extent to which an award for costs will be made against a party who fails to accept an offer that is made 'without prejudice save as to costs'.

22.84   In *Telephone Information Services Ltd v Wilkinson* [1991] IRLR 148, the EAT ruled that an employment tribunal had not misdirected itself in refusing to strike out the employee's complaint of unfair dismissal on the ground that it was frivolous or vexatious when the claimant persisted in pursuing the complaint after his former employer had offered him the then statutory maximum. The EAT reasoned that the claimant had the right to have the question of liability determined by the employment tribunal and that the remedy was not simply a monetary award. The same point might have been made if the employer had applied for costs. It should be noted, however, that this decision was made before the introduction of the overriding objective and before the amendments to the rules on costs.

22.85   More recently, in *Kopel v Safeway Stores Ltd* [2003] IRLR 753, the EAT ruled that the employment tribunal had not erred under ET Regulations 2001, reg 14(1)(a) in awarding costs of £5,000 against an employee who refused to accept an offer of £7,500 'without prejudice as to costs in full and final settlement' in a sex discrimination case. The EAT held that the tribunal was entitled to conclude that part of the claim was 'seriously misconceived' and that the claimant's refusal to accept the employer's offer amounted to unreasonable conduct of the proceedings.

22.86 However, the EAT confirmed that the rule in *Calderbank v Calderbank* [1975] 3 All ER 333 does not apply in employment tribunals as such, although 'an offer of a *Calderbank* type is a factor which an employment tribunal can take into account in deciding whether to make a costs order' in accordance with what is now ET Regulations 2004, reg 40(3).

22.87 The EAT added that a failure to achieve an award in excess of the sum offered would not, of itself, be sufficient to justify an order for costs unless the tribunal considered that the rejection of the offer was unreasonable.

22.88 An important factor in the *Kopel* case was clearly that at least part of the claimant's claim was misconceived and, in principle, this may also apply where the compensation claim was hopelessly inflated or misconceived for some other reason. However, unfortunately, the EAT's earlier ruling in *Wilkinson* does not appear to have been referred to in argument in the *Kopel* case and it must at least be arguable that a claimant is not normally unreasonable to pursue a genuine claim where liability is not admitted. The position may be different where a without-prejudice offer is made after liability has been determined.

I. Enforcement of Awards

22.89 A tribunal judgment ordering the payment of compensation is enforceable as if it were a judgment of the county court. If the judgment is being appealed to the EAT, then if an application to enforce is made to the county court, the paying party will normally be granted a stay of execution pending the determination of the appeal.

22.90 The employment tribunal lacks any power to enforce its own non-compensatory judgments. It can however, order that additional compensation be paid in certain circumstances. For example, in an unfair dismissal case, an additional award may be ordered where the employer has failed to comply with an order for re-employment (ERA 1996, s 117(3)–(5)). Also, in a discrimination case, compensation can be increased where the employer has failed without reasonable excuse to comply with an appropriate recommendation (Equality Act 2010 [EqA 2010], s 124(7)).

22.91 It should be noted that, in *Rank Nemo (DMS) Ltd v Coutinho* [2009] EWCA Civ 454, [2009] IRLR 672, CA, it was held that the failure to pay compensation awarded to a claimant in a discrimination case may be made the subject of a claim of post-termination victimization.

J. Appealing Tribunal Awards

Guidance on appealing tribunal awards

22.92 The Court of Appeal and EAT have given guidance on the principles upon which an appellate court should interfere with the award of a tribunal. An appellate court is entitled to interfere with the assessment of compensation by an employment tribunal where the tribunal has acted on a wrong principle of law or misapprehended the facts, or for other reasons has made a wholly erroneous estimate of the damage suffered (*Coleman v Skyrail Oceanic Ltd* [1981] IRLR 398, [14], CA).

22.93 In *Doshoki v Draeger Ltd* [2002] IRLR 340, the EAT stated that it will overturn awards even if 'correctly categorized' so that its powers are not limited to correcting miscategorized awards. And in *Vento v Chief Constable of West Yorkshire Police* (*No 2*) [2003] ICR 318, [2003] IRLR 102, the Court of Appeal held (at [51]) that an appellate body is not entitled to interfere with the assessment of an employment tribunal simply because it would have awarded more or less than the tribunal has done. In that case, the award of £50,000 for injury to feelings was said to be seriously out of line with the majority of awards made and approved on appeal in reported EAT cases. It was also seriously out of line with the guidelines compiled for the Judicial Studies Board (JSB) and with cases reported in the personal injury field, where general damages have been awarded for pain, suffering, disability, and loss of amenity.

Part VII

SETTLEMENT

23

SETTLEMENT

A. Introduction

'The law loves compromise': so wrote Lord Bingham in his 'Foreword' to David Foskett **23.01** QC, *Law and Practice of Compromise* (4th edn, London: Sweet & Maxwell, 1996; quoted with approval by Mummery LJ in *Dattani v Trio Supermarkets Ltd* [1998] IRLR 240). Moreover, as Lord Bingham also points out, settlement 'may call for as much skill including legal skill, as fighting the action'.

This chapter look at the specific rules that apply to the settlement of employment **23.02** tribunal claims.

B. Settlement of Compensation Claims

The popularity of settlement of employment tribunal claims is borne out by the **23.03** Employment Tribunal and Employment Appeal Tribunal (EAT) Statistics 2009–10 (GB), covering the period 1 April 2009–31 March 2010 and available online at <http://www.tribunals.gov.uk>. The latest statistics show that, of the jurisdictional claims disposed of, 32 per cent were withdrawn, 31 per cent were Advisory, Conciliation, and Arbitration Service (ACAS)-conciliated settlements, and 13 per cent were successful at tribunal.

23.04 For reasons explained below, it is very common for cases that are settled by way of statutory compromise agreement to be recorded as withdrawn.

Reasons for settlement

23.05 Employment tribunal claims are settled for a wide variety of reasons, including the chances of success, the level of awards, the impact of the Employment Protection (Recoupment of Jobseeker's Allowance and Income Support) Regulations 1996, SI 1996/2349 (the Recoupment Regulations) and potential risk of reductions for contributory fault (in unfair dismissal cases), the time and expense of the hearing (the costs of which are still rarely recoverable), the anxiety and stress associated with the hearing itself, and the cost to the employer in business terms.

Preparing for settlement

23.06 Most settlements are for money. This means that, before making an offer, it is essential to assess roughly how much the claim is worth. Having worked out the maximum exposure, it is normal to make allowance for the following factors:

(a) the chances of success;
(b) the prospect of the award being reduced or uplifted;
(c) the effect of the Recoupment Regulations in unfair dismissal cases;
(d) the effect of any *ex gratia* payment on the award;
(e) the effect of tax and interest on the award; and
(f) the cost of fighting the case.

23.07 Obviously, the first factor is the most important because, unless liability is established, no compensation will be payable—for example, the statistics show that, of the total number of claims disposed of, only 13 per cent were successful. It is also important for the parties to have a good idea of the likely breakdown of the award before starting to negotiate. Even if the negotiations are unsuccessful, this may help to identify the issues in relation to the award of compensation and may enable the parties to agree certain heads of compensation in advance of the hearing that will save time and expense at the hearing itself.

23.08 In addition to working out the nature and amount of the claim, it can also be important to consider what other terms should be included in the settlement agreement, such as:

(a) agreed reasons for leaving;
(b) termination date;
(c) resignation from directorships;
(d) agreed reference;
(e) confidentiality clause;

(f) restrictive covenants;

(g) public statements;

(h) tax indemnities;

(i) settlement of other claims;

(j) mechanics of payment (that is, single lump sum or instalments);

(k) parties to the agreement and guarantees;

(l) returning the employer and employee's property;

(m) tribunal order for resolving the dispute; and

(n) legal costs.

(This list is by no means exhaustive.)

Contractual principles

The starting point of any analysis of the law and practice relating to settlement is the **23.09** law of contract because, subject to the special rules that apply to settlement of statutory claims, the ordinary contractual principles apply to the enforceability and interpretation of settlement agreements. Of course, the rules governing statutory compromise agreements do not apply to the settlement of contract claims in the employment tribunal.

A detailed consideration of these principles lies outside the scope of this book, but **23.10** it is important to make sure that all necessary matters are covered, and to express the terms clearly and unambiguously. Issues sometimes arise in relation to the construction and interpretation of such agreements (see, for example, *Brynell v British Telecommunications plc* EAT 0383/04 and *Hinton v University of East London* [2005] IRLR 552, CA; see also The Hon Mr Justice Lewison, *The Interpretation of Contracts* (4th edn, London: Sweet & Maxwell, 2009)).

The courts will make certain presumptions—for example, in the absence of a clear **23.11** express term, it is assumed that the parties do not intend to compromise claims that were not known to exist at the time that the settlement was entered into. It was for this reason that the ACAS-brokered agreements negotiated with the claimants in *Bank of Credit and Commerce International SA (in compulsory liquidation) v Ali and others* [2001] UKHL 9, [2001] IRLR 292, HL (the *BCCI* case) were held not to cover claims for so-called 'stigma damages', because such a claim was not contemplated when the agreements were entered into. Nonetheless, it may be possible to provide for such eventualities by appropriate express words (although, as a matter of policy, ACAS discourages the compromising of future rights in ACAS-conciliated settlements).

C. Binding Settlement of Statutory Claims

A distinguishing feature of all of the statutory claims that can be brought in employment **23.12** tribunals is that a private contractual agreement that purports to exclude or limit an employee's right to make a complaint is of no legal effect. This applies both to the rights that are conferred by the Employment Rights Act 1996 (ERA 1996), s 203, and discrimination law under the Equality Act 2010 (EqA 2010), s 147.

23.13 For example, in *Council of Engineering Institutions v Maddison* [1976] IRLR 389, Mr Maddison was dismissed for redundancy. At the time of his dismissal, he was handed an envelope that contained a cheque for £1,600 and a letter that stated that the cheque constituted a 'lump-sum payment for severance including redundancy payment, the acceptance of which is final settlement leaving you with no outstanding claim against the council'. Neither the tribunal nor the EAT were satisfied that this form of words amounted to a binding agreement, but, even if it did, it was rendered void by what is now the ERA 1996 (see also *Naqui v Stephens Jewellers Ltd* [1978] ICR 631).

23.14 The two principal methods by which an employment tribunal claim can be settled are where an agreement to refrain from instituting or continuing proceedings arises as a result of action taken by a conciliation officer under s 18 of the Employment Tribunals Act 1996 (ETA 1996) or the parties have entered into a statutory compromise agreement.

Statutory conciliation

23.15 Before the presentation of a claim, ACAS merely has the power to provide conciliation services (ETA 1996, s 18(3)). In April 2009, ACAS instituted a new pre-claim conciliation service, which was extended from October 2009 to cover all cases in which it has conciliation powers. Use of this service does not affect the time limits for bringing claims.

23.16 Where a claim has been presented to an employment tribunal and a copy of it has been sent to a conciliation officer, it is the duty of the conciliation officer 'to endeavour to promote a settlement of the proceedings without their being determined by an employment tribunal' if:

(a) he or she is requested to do so by the parties; or
(b) the conciliation officer considers that he or she could act 'with a reasonable prospect of success' (ETA 1996, s 18(2)).

23.17 In discharging the statutory duty imposed by ETA 1996, s 18(2), in alleged unfair dismissal cases, the conciliation officer should first seek 'to promote the reinstatement or re-engagement of the complainant by the employer . . . on terms appearing to the conciliation officer to be equitable' (ETA 1996, s 18(4)(a)). However, where the claimant does not wish to be reinstated or re-engaged, or where such a course is 'not practicable', the conciliation officer is under a duty to 'seek to promote agreement between the parties as to a sum by way of compensation to be paid by the employer to the complainant' (ETA 1996, s 18(4)(b)).

23.18 Anything communicated to a conciliation officer in connection with the performance of his or her functions under ETA 1996, s 18 is not admissible in evidence before a tribunal, except with the consent of the person who communicated it to that officer (ETA 1996, s 18(7)).

In *Clarke v Redcar & Cleveland Borough Council* [2006] IRLR 324, EAT, it was held **23.19** that, in determining whether the conciliation officer exercised her functions in order to effect a valid conciliation contract under the Sex Discrimination Act 1975 (SDA 1975), s 77 (now EqA 2010, s 147), the following principles apply.

(a) The ACAS officer has no responsibility to see that the terms of the settlement are fair on the employee.

(b) The expression 'promote a settlement' must be given a liberal construction capable of covering whatever action by way of such promotion as is applicable in the circumstances of the particular case.

(c) The ACAS officer must never advise as to the merits of the case. It would be quite wrong to say that an ACAS officer is obliged to go through the framework of the legislation. Indeed, it might defeat the officer's very function if he or she were obliged to tell a claimant, in effect, that they might receive considerably more money.

(d) It is not for the tribunal to consider whether the officer correctly interpreted his or her duties; it is sufficient that the officer intended and purported to act under the section.

(e) If the ACAS officer were to act in bad faith or adopt unfair methods when promoting a settlement, the agreement might be set aside and might not operate as a bar to proceedings.

For some time now, ACAS has taken the view that it will not simply rubber-stamp **23.20** binding agreements reached between the parties without any meaningful ACAS involvement. However, a settlement is binding if the conciliation officer has taken action in its promotion even if the conciliation officer's role is a small one. For example, in *Moore v Duport Furniture Products Ltd and ACAS* [1980] IRLR 156, the conciliation officer was called in after Mr Moore had agreed to resign and accept the sum of £300 in settlement of possible statutory liability for unfair dismissal. The conciliation officer recorded the terms of settlement on an ACAS settlement document (COT3—see below) and took the parties through the form, explaining its meaning and its implications. The form was signed by both parties. Mr Moore subsequently commenced proceedings for unfair dismissal. The Court of Appeal ruled that the settlement was binding because the conciliation officer had explained its meaning and consequences to the parties subsequent to the agreement being reached between the parties. He had therefore taken action to effect a binding settlement within the meaning of what is now ERA 1996, s 203(2). The Court of Appeal's decision was later confirmed by the House of Lords (*Moore v Duport Furniture Products Ltd and ACAS* [1982] IRLR 31).

In *Gilbert v Kembridge Fibres Ltd* [1984] IRLR 52, the EAT held that a settlement **23.21** was binding where the parties had reached an oral agreement through ACAS and that Mr Gilbert was bound by the agreement through ACAS even though he or she had subsequently refused to sign the COT3 form.

23.22 In all cases, a conciliation officer will run through the different heads of compensation that can be awarded with both sides, but it has been held that a settlement will still be binding if he or she fails to do this (*Slack v Greenham (Plant Hire)* [1983] IRLR 271).

23.23 A conciliated agreement may be set aside where it is invalid at common law. For example, an 'agreement' will not be binding if a trade union official acts on an employee's behalf without his or her authority (*Gloystarne & Co Ltd v Martin* [2001] IRLR 15, but compare *Times Newspapers Ltd v Fitt* [1981] ICR 637). In addition, an agreement may be set aside if it can be shown that the employee was acting under economic duress at the time of settlement (*Hennessey v (1) Craigmyle & Co Ltd (2) ACAS* [1986] IRLR 300). However, it is unlikely that financial hardship caused by the dismissal itself will be sufficient to amount to economic duress, although it may be prudent to give the claimant some time in which to think about the employer's offer and consider its implications.

Putting the settlement into effect

23.24 The terms of the settlement are recorded on the ACAS form COT3, which should be signed by both parties (although a settlement may still be binding if one of the parties refuses to sign—*Gilbert v Kembridge Fibres Ltd* [1984] IRLR 52).

23.25 The tribunal will normally be notified of the settlement by the conciliation officer, but it is always prudent to check that this has been done. The tribunal will then write to the parties to inform them that the case has been closed.

Wording of COT3

23.26 The conciliation officer will help both parties to word the terms of the settlement and the terms will be recorded on a COT3. The settlement may cover matters that fall outside the tribunal's jurisdiction and, unlike the statutory compromise agreement, the settlement may be all-embracing. For example, the employee may agree to settle all claims arising out of the termination of employment and the employer may agree to give the employee a reference. Where the dispute between the parties does not involve a claim of personal injury or pension rights, ACAS encourages the parties to exclude specifically those matters from an 'all claims' agreement for the sake of clarity and to protect the claimant's future rights. But, ultimately, whether or not these claims are excluded from the settlement is for the parties to decide.

23.27 Settlement may be agreed without admission of liability by the employer or the employer may admit liability, provided that the employee does not claim compensation. More unusually, the parties may agree to settle through ACAS once the issue of liability has been determined by the tribunal (*Courage Take Home Trade Ltd v Keys* [1986] IRLR 427).

> **Example: No admission of liability**
>
> 'The payment is made without any admission of liability.'
>
> **Example: Admission of liability**
>
> 'The respondent admits that it unfairly dismissed the claimant. The claimant agrees not to seek compensation beyond that agreed herein.'

Importantly, it may be prudent for the employee to ensure that the employer agrees **23.28** to pay the compensation within a time limit incorporated into the agreement.

ACAS Arbitration Scheme

Where both parties consent, it is possible for a claim for unfair dismissal or a complaint **23.29** under the statutory flexible working rules to be determined by an ACAS arbitrator under the ACAS Arbitration Scheme (Great Britain) Order 2004, SI 2004/753, and ACAS (Flexible Working) Arbitration Scheme (Great Britain) Order 2003, SI 2004/2333 (ERA 1996, s 203(5)).

The arbitrator will be appointed by ACAS from a panel of arbitrators and sits in **23.30** private. If the claim is upheld, the arbitrator has the power to award the same remedies as an employment tribunal.

Details of the scheme are available from ACAS and online at <http://www.acas. **23.31** org.uk>.

Judicial mediation

Following a pilot scheme in three regions, judicial mediation is now available in **23.32** England and Wales generally under ETA 1996, s 7B (and will be offered in Scotland in the future).

At the moment, judicial mediation is being offered to parties only in cases identified **23.33** by the regional employment judge as being suitable for alternative dispute resolution (ADR) by this means. Generally, due to limited resources, these are cases falling within the discrimination jurisdictions, in which a hearing of three days or more is in prospect, and often in which the employment relationship is continuing or capable of being continued. Judicial mediation is conducted by specially trained employment judges. In Scotland, the President's Practice Direction No 2 (2006) provides for cases to be sisted for possible mediation.

The function of the judicial mediator is to adopt a purely facilitative approach and **23.34** not to offer opinions on the merits of claims or appropriate settlement terms.

Once an employment judge has begun to act as mediator in relation to a disputed **23.35** matter in a case that is the subject of proceedings, the judge may only decide matters in the case with the consent of the parties (ETA 1996, s 7B(3)).

23.36 The facility is provided free of charge to the parties. All parties must agree to a reference to mediation, although there is no guarantee that mediation will be offered. Mediations are normally listed for one day at the tribunal offices. It is essential that a person with authority to agree terms of settlement is in attendance at the mediation. Judicial mediation is conducted in private, and anything said and done is not subsequently admissible in evidence following an unsuccessful mediation. A successful mediation will usually result in the agreed terms being incorporated into an order of the tribunal.

Statutory compromise agreement

23.37 In recent years, it has become increasingly common for the parties to settle employment tribunal claims by way of statutory compromise agreement, which is a settlement agreement that meets the requirements of the relevant statutory provisions—namely:

(a) ERA 1996, s 203(2)(f), (3) and (4);

(b) EqA 2010, s 147;

(c) Part-time Workers (Prevention of Less Favourable Treatment) Regulations 2000, SI 2000/1551 (PTWR 2000), reg 9;

(d) Fixed-term Employees (Prevention of Less Favourable Treatment) Regulations 2002, SI 2002/2034 (FTER 2002), reg 10;

(e) Working Time Regulations 1998 (WTR 1998), reg 35(3)–(7));

(f) National Minimum Wage Act 1998 (NMWA 1998), s 49(4)–(8);

(g) Trade Unions and Labour Relations Act (TULR(C)A 1992), s 288(2A) and (2B); and

(h) Transfer of Undertakings (Protection of Employment) Regulations 2006 (TUPE 2006), reg 8.

The statutory conditions

23.38 The conditions are:

(a) the agreement must be in writing;

(b) the agreement must relate to particular 'proceedings' or the particular 'complaint' (in the case of discrimination and working time complaints);

(c) the employee or worker must have received advice from a relevant independent adviser;

(d) the adviser must be covered by a policy of insurance; and

(e) the agreement must identify the adviser and state that the conditions regulating compromise agreements have been satisfied.

23.39 Below each of these requirements are considered in more detail.

Agreement in writing

23.40 The statutory provisions do not specify any standard form of written agreement provided that the compromise agreement is in writing. In contrast with the ACAS process, a compromise agreement will not be binding until it is reduced to writing.

Agreement must relate to the 'particular proceedings' or 'particular complaint'

As stated above, the phrase 'particular complaint' is used in connection with discrimination claims and claims under the WTR 1998, whereas the phrase 'particular proceedings' is used under the ERA 1996 and other statutory provisions. **23.41**

It is unclear whether any importance should be attached to the distinction. The view of the editors of *Harvey on Industrial Relations and Employment Law* is that there is no difference in substance between these words. **23.42**

The significance of both requirements is that the agreement must relate to the particular complaint or proceedings and that it is not open to the parties to enter into an all-embracing 'full and final settlement' clause of any claim relating to the employment unless the claim has actually been raised between the parties to the complaint. **23.43**

This meaning was confirmed by Viscount Ullswater, the government minister at the time when the provision was originally introduced, when he stated (Hansard, HL, vol 545, col 904, 6 May 1993): **23.44**

> we are proposing that these procedures should only be available in the context of an agreement which settles a particular complaint that has already arisen between the parties to the complaint. They will not allow an individual to compromise his right to present, or to continue with a claim to a tribunal in respect of any matter other than the particular complaint which is the subject of the agreement.

Similarly, in the House of Commons debates, Ann Widdecombe stated: **23.45**

> first the new provisions can be used only in respect of a dispute which has already arisen between the parties and is outstanding. Concerns have reached us from some quarters that the new provisions could be used to encourage individuals to agree not to bring any tribunal claims should disputes arise in the future. I can reassure hon Members that it would not be possible to use the provisions to do that. It is a condition that the agreement should relate to a specific dispute that has already arisen, and, if that condition is not met, the term of the agreement which precludes a tribunal claim will not be enforceable.

A statutory compromise agreement therefore cannot seek to exclude potential complaints that have not yet arisen simply on the basis that such a claim might arise (as could be the case under a properly drafted ordinary contractual agreement or, indeed, could be achieved through ACAS). The statutory compromise agreement therefore can only cover complaints that have been raised by the claimant. **23.46**

However, a number of issues have arisen in relation to the meaning of the words 'relate to' and whether it is necessary to enter into a separate compromise agreement in relation to each particular complaint. The case law confirms that, where a number of different complaints have been raised by the employee either in the employment tribunal claim or in correspondence or orally (*Brynell v British Telecommunications plc* EAT 0383/04) prior to the commencement of the proceedings, these can be settled in one single compromise agreement rather than by way of a separate compromise agreement for each complaint (*Lunt v Merseyside TEC Ltd* [1999] IRLR 458). **23.47**

23.48   The question of whether it is necessary for the compromise agreement itself to refer to the particular statutory complaint raised by the claimant was considered by the Court of Appeal in *Hinton v University of East London* [2005] IRLR 552. In that case, prior to his voluntary redundancy, the claimant raised a number of grievances that amounted to 'protected disclosures' for the purpose of ERA 1996, Pt IV. As part of a voluntary redundancy package, the claimant was required to sign a compromise agreement that settled all claims 'which the employee has or may have arising out of or in connection with or as a consequence of his employment and/or the termination of his employment', as well as certain specific statutory claims. A claim under ERA 1996, s 47B was not amongst those claims specifically identified. Dr Hinton argued that he was entitled to pursue such a claim and the employment tribunal agreed. The Court of Appeal ruled that the words 'relate to the particular proceedings' must be construed as requiring the particular proceedings to which the compromise agreement relates to be clearly identified. Although one document can be used to compromise all of the particular proceedings, it is not sufficient to use a rolled-up expression such as 'all statutory rights' or only to make reference to the statute. Smith LJ held that the claims must be identified either by a generic description, such as 'unfair dismissal', or by reference to the section of the statute giving rise to the claim. Mummery LJ observed that it is good practice for the particulars of 'actual' proceedings and of the particular allegations made in them to be inserted in the compromise agreement in the form of a brief factual and legal description. In the case of 'potential' claims, it is good practice for the particulars of the nature of the allegations and of the statutory or common law basis to be inserted in the form of a brief factual and legal description.

23.49   In *Hilton UK Hotels Ltd v McNaughton* [2006] All ER (D) 327 (May), a part-time pension claim in which the solicitor, when compromising the claim, had not appreciated that the claimant had previously worked part-time, the EAT held that a compromise agreement will not be interpreted as compromising a claim referred to in the agreement if, at the time of the agreement, the claimant did not appreciate that he or she had a possible claim, even though the independent adviser should have advised as to the possibility of such a claim.

Advice from a 'relevant independent adviser'

23.50   There are four categories of 'relevant independent adviser'.

(a) *A qualified lawyer* This includes barristers (whether in practice or employed to give legal advice), and solicitors who hold a practising certificate in England and Wales, and advocates and solicitors who hold a practising certificate in Scotland.

(b) *Trade union officers* This covers an official, employee, or member of an independent trade union who has been certified in writing by the union as competent to give advice and as authorized to do so on behalf of the trade union.

(c) *Advice centre worker* This covers any employee or volunteer at an advice centre who has been certified in writing by the advice centre as competent to give advice and as authorized to do so by the advice centre.

(d) *Other persons as so specified by the Secretary of State* This residual category allows the Secretary of State to add to the list of qualified lawyers by statutory instrument. By virtue of the Compromise Agreements (Description of Person) Order 2004, SI 2004/754, this has been extended to Fellows of the Institute of Legal Executives (ILEX) employed by a solicitors' practice, provided that such a person is supervised by a solicitor when giving such advice.

However, all those recognized as 'relevant independent adviser[s]' for this purpose **23.51** are subject to the general restriction that the adviser must be truly independent—that is, that the adviser must not act for the other party, or be employed by the other party, or be connected with the other party—or, in the case of an advice centre worker, if the claimant pays for the advice (ERA, s 203(3B)). It has been held that this does not preclude an employer from paying for the advice that the claimant receives.

The 'relevant independent adviser' must advise the employee or the worker as to the **23.52** terms and effect of the proposed agreement, and in particular its effect on his or her ability to pursue his or her rights before an employment tribunal (ERA 1996, s 203(3)(c)).

Policy of insurance

When the adviser gives advice, there must be in force a contract of insurance or an **23.53** indemnity provided for members of a professional body covering the risk of claim by the employee or worker in respect of loss arising in consequence of the advice (ERA 1996, s 203(3)(d)).

Identifying the adviser

The agreement must identify the adviser who gave the advice (ERA 1996, s 203(3)(e)). **23.54**

Confirmation that statutory requirements are satisfied

Finally, the agreement must confirm that the statutory conditions referred to above **23.55** have been satisfied (ERA 1996, s 203(3)(f)) and, in particular, that that advice has been given in accordance with the statutory requirements in relation to each of the complaints that the employee or worker has raised (*Lunt v Merseyside TEC Ltd* [1999] IRLR 458). It is not, however, necessary for the adviser to give any warranty to that effect.

In *Palihakkara v British Telecommunications plc* [2007] All ER (D) 131 (Jan), the **23.56** EAT held that a statement that the conditions under ERA 1996, s 203 were satisfied was not sufficient to validate the agreement in so far as it related to discrimination complaints, even though the requirements for such claims to be compromised are the same. Practitioners should be alive to the need to state that the requirements for compromise agreements under each and every statute applicable to each claim intended to be compromised are satisfied.

Effect of agreement

23.57   Once these conditions have been satisfied, there will be a binding agreement and the tribunal will not have jurisdiction to determine any of the matters covered by the agreement.

23.58   The effect of non-compliance with any of these conditions will be to invalidate the agreement in so far as statutory claims are concerned, but the agreement will remain a valid compromise of contractual claims (*Sutherland v Network Appliance Ltd* [2001] IRLR 12).

23.59   In *Rock-It Cargo Ltd v Green* [1997] IRLR 581, EAT, it was held that a tribunal has jurisdiction to enforce a compromise agreement relating to the terms on which employment is to terminate. The combined effect of ETA 1996, s 3(2) and art 3 of the Employment Tribunals Extension of Jurisdiction Order 1994 is to give tribunals jurisdiction to resolve a claim for damages for breach of a contract of employment or other contract connected with employment that arises or is outstanding on the termination of the employee's employment. A compromise agreement as to the terms on which employment is to be brought to an end is a 'contract connected with employment' within the meaning of ETA 1996, s 3(2).

23.60   However, the tribunal's contractual jurisdiction does not extend to breaches of a compromise agreement that was made after the effective date of termination (*Miller Bros and FP Butler Ltd v Johnston* [2002] IRLR 386, EAT).

Role of tribunal

23.61   Where a claim is settled through ACAS, the conciliator will inform the tribunal of the terms of the settlement. On the other hand, where the parties reach a statutory compromise agreement, it will be necessary for the parties to advise the tribunal of the settlement and to decide how they want the tribunal to resolve the matter.

23.62   The tribunal has power to:

(a) record the terms of the settlement;
(b) record that the case has been settled on agreed terms (Employment Tribunals (Constitution and Rules of Procedure) Regulations 2004 [ET Regulations 2004], reg 28(2)); or
(c) dismiss the claim on withdrawal on agreed terms by the claimant (ET Regulations 2004, reg 25), but the latter will only take place on a written application by the employer, which should be made within 28 days of the tribunal being advised of the settlement.

23.63   In the past, it was common for the order to be in form (a) or (b), since a danger of withdrawal is that the tribunal will no longer have jurisdiction to hear the claim if the employer reneges on the settlement (unless the tribunal is willing to review the withdrawal in the interests of justice) whereas, under the other options, provision can be made for the claim to be restored. Another advantage is that, where the decision sets out the terms of settlement, there is no need for a statutory compromise agreement. On the other hand, the Recoupment Regulations will apply where the terms of settlement are recorded in the tribunal's decision, and therefore option (a) may not be considered appropriate in unfair dismissal cases and the parties may not wish the terms of settlement to be made public.

The dangers in option (b) are illustrated by the Court of Appeal's decision in **23.64** *Dattani v Trio Supermarkets* [1998] IRLR 240. In that case, the claimant made a complaint of unfair dismissal in which he raised the allegation that he had not been paid the level of wages that had been agreed. The unfair dismissal claim was settled in the course of the hearing. The terms of settlement, which were referred to in the decision, were that the case 'had been settled on the basis that the respondents pay the applicant the sum of £5,000'. The sum was duly paid, but a year later, the claimant brought a claim in the county court for unpaid wages. The employers said that he was estopped as a result of the settlement reached in the employment tribunal claim. The judge found that the claimant was, in fact, owed £11,800 at the date of termination, but agreed that the claims had been settled as a result of the tribunal's decision. Allowing the appeal, the Court of Appeal ruled that the decision itself did not give rise to an estoppel by reason of *res judicata* that extended to the claim for unpaid wages, partly because there had been no actual determination of the claim by the tribunal, and partly because the terms of settlement were limited to the claim for unfair dismissal and did not cover any claim for unpaid wages. The problem could have been overcome if the claim for unpaid wages had been compromised under a statutory compromise agreement to which the decision referred.

In recent years, it has become more common for the order to be in form (c)—that **23.65** is, that the application is dismissed on withdrawal by the claimant on terms agreed between the parties—because this prevents the terms from being made public. This risk of default can be taken into account by making provision in the settlement agreement that the payment is to be made by a certain date and postponing the withdrawal until after the payment has been made.

It is advisable that, where the terms are not agreed through ACAS, the terms of the **23.66** 'consent' order should be supported by a statutory compromise agreement, because it was argued in *Wilson (HM Inspector of Taxes) Ltd v Clayton* [2005] IRLR 108 that a consent order does not fall within the scope of one of the permitted ways of settling a claim and therefore falls foul of ERA 1996, s 203, although, for technical reasons, the Court declined to rule on the issue. This argument would appear to be even stronger if the claim were to be withdrawn without any determination by the tribunal. Whatever the merits of this argument, the terms agreed between the parties should therefore be set out in a statutory compromise agreement, particularly where other contractual and statutory claims not raised in the tribunal proceedings themselves are to be settled.

Taxation of settlements

23.67   The taxation of settlements is far from straightforward. Much will depend on the basis of settlement and what the settlement is intended to cover. It may be necessary for the parties to take tax advice in the particular circumstances.

23.68   Payments in lieu may fall to be taxed as general earnings under Income Tax (Earnings and Pensions) Act 2003 (IT(EP)A 2003), s 62. It is likely that, following *Richardson v Delaney* [2001] IRLR 663, where a payment equivalent to a payment in lieu is made under the contract, such a payment is taxable in the normal way.

23.69   However, the provisions of IT(EP)A 2003, Pt 6, ch 3 (ss 401–416) may apply to termination payments and, in particular, settlements (whether negotiated through ACAS or through a statutory compromise agreement) in which a lump-sum payment is made to the claimant in settlement of a tribunal claim. This was confirmed by the Court of Appeal in *Wilson* (*HM Inspector of Taxes*) *v Clayton* [2005] IRLR 108, in which it was held that a payment of a tribunal award of £5,060, which was made under a consent order in an employment tribunal (following a finding of unfair dismissal) and consisted of a basic award and payments under ERA 1996, s 114(2)(a), was not taxable under what was Income and Corporation Taxes Act 1988 (ICTA 1988), s 19 (now IT(EP)A 2003, s 62), because neither was made as a payment in return for past services, but to compensate Mr Clayton for unfair dismissal. The Court also rejected the alternative argument that such a payment was a taxable benefit within the meaning of what was ICTA 1988, s 154 (now IT(EP)A 2003, Pt 3) on the ground that a payment made by an employer to an employee pursuant to a fair bargain fell outside the scope of s 154 since:

> where parties at arm's length arrive at a genuine compromise in settlement of hostile litigation, it would be an extremely difficult task for any tribunal or court to unpick the constituent parts of the bargain and put a value on those parts, although the court did not rule out the possibility that a gratuitous benefit would be taxable.

(See also *Mairs v Haughey* (1992) 66 STC 49, a case involving a buyout of an enhanced redundancy payment provision.) In *Clayton*, therefore, the payment was not subject to tax.

23.70   The normal rule, in respect of those elements of the termination package not otherwise chargeable to income tax, is that the first £30,000 is tax-free, whereas any payment over £30,000 is taxable at the graduated rating of 40 per cent, rising to 50 per cent where the payment is in excess of £150,000 (IT(EP)A 2003, s 403(1)). It should be noted, however, that these provisions apply only to termination payments, and that different considerations may apply where the claimant is still in employment and is compensated for the loss of pay and benefits that are taxable under the ordinary rules, and that tax is deductible in the normal way under pay-as-you-earn (PAYE).

Payments into a tax-exempt pension scheme

23.71 The charge does not apply to a payment or benefit received under a tax-exempt pension scheme by way of compensation for loss of employment (IT(EP)A 2003, s 407) or a contribution to a tax-exempt pension scheme pursuant to IT(EP)A 2003, s 408.

23.72 Where pension loss is included as part of the terms of settlement, it may be possible to structure the terms of settlement in such a manner that the employee's pension will be increased in the same way as if he or she had remained in employment during the damages period. Moreover, under HM Revenue and Customs (HMRC) regulations, it will often be possible for an employee to secure tax advantages by augmenting his or her pension up to the maximum permitted by the HMRC (see HMRC Statement of Practice 2/81).

23.73 Liability to tax may therefore be reduced if a contribution is made to a tax-exempt pension scheme. The amount that an employee or former employee is permitted to contribute to such a scheme is likely to change in the tax year 2005–06 and specialist tax advice should be obtained prior to settlement if this is relevant.

Payment for personal injury

23.74 It should also be noted that liability under the statutory provisions only arises in relation to financial payments (or the value of any benefits in lieu) that are made to the claimant. It does not apply to any compensation relating to personal injury, including injury to feelings. This was confirmed by the EAT in *Orthet Ltd v Vince-Cain* [2004] IRLR 857, although this view is not always accepted by the tax authorities. It is open to the parties in a discrimination case to identify a specific sum in the settlement referable to such injury that is not taxable, but the sum must be a reasonable assessment of the loss, because inflated sums may attract the attention of the HMRC.

Tax collection

23.75 The Income Tax (PAYE) Regulations 2003, SI 2003/2682 (the PAYE Regulations) also differentiate between payments made whilst the claimant is in employment and payments made after the employment has terminated. Where the claimant is in employment, any payment made under the compromise agreement will be taxed in the normal manner. Where the claimant's employment has terminated, payments are subject to PAYE at the basic rate (PAYE Regulations, reg 23).

23.76 Provision for the payment of tax is normally included in the compromise agreement.

Personal injuries

23.77 As stated above, where a personal injury claim is not one of the issues between the parties, ACAS encourages them to exclude such a claim from the terms of an 'all claims' settlement for the reasons given above.

23.78 This practice does not, of course, prevent the parties to an ACAS agreement or to a statutory compromise agreement from seeking to settle any claims for personal injury arising during the employment or in connection with its termination, and such a clause is common where compensation for injury to health is being claimed in a discrimination case. But the validity of more general exclusions of actual or potential claims for personal injury is open to doubt, because such a clause could be challenged under the Unfair Contract Terms Act 1977 (UCTA 1977). There is no reported decision on this point. Furthermore, in practical terms, advisers are understandably reluctant to exclude claims that fall outside their authority to act. Sometimes, claimants are asked to warrant that they are unaware of any personal injury claim against their former employer (although the value of such warranties is also questionable).

D. Some Standard Clauses

23.79 It is not uncommon for the parties to concentrate on resolving the financial terms before 'moving on' to the other terms of the agreement, but there are risks in this approach—not least the risk of reaching a binding agreement before the other terms have been raised and addressed. It is therefore better to identify 'any strings' that are to be attached right from the beginning. Below, we highlight some, although by no means all, of the clauses found in settlement agreements.

Full and final settlement clause

23.80 A 'compromise agreement' will always include a clause that is in 'full and final settlement of all claims arising out of or in connection with the employment and termination thereof'. Such a clause may be made with or without admission of liability. As stated above, in relation to statutory claims, for a statutory compromise agreement to be binding, it will be necessary to refer specifically to the particular claims that have been raised by the claimant in the initial complaint.

23.81 Where a claim could have been brought under European Union (EU) law, this should be specifically referred to in the agreement (*Livingstone v Hepworth Refractories plc* [1992] IRLR 63, a case in which a COT3 was held not to preclude the claimant from making complaints under the SDA 1975 or EU law because it failed to refer to the claims under the Equal Pay Act 1970 [EqPA 1970] or the SDDA 1975 or potential claim under European law).

23.82 Each specific complaint should be referred to in the agreement and, as stated above, it is important to ensure that each of the statutory compromise requirements are met in relation to those complaints.

Mechanics of payment

23.83 The agreement should state the sum to be paid and deal with the mechanics of payment—that is, when the payments are to be made and how. Where payments are to be made by instalments and there are doubts about the solvency of the employer, it may be prudent to obtain guarantees for the payment of the compensation.

Confidentiality

The parties, particularly the employer, will often want the terms of settlement to be **23.84** confidential. Views differ on the effectiveness of such gagging clauses. Sometimes, in an effort to strengthen such clauses, the agreement will provide that the settlement monies, or a stated sum, will be repayable on breach, but such clauses may be open to challenge as 'penalty' clauses.

It is also important to be realistic about the scope of confidentiality clauses. It is **23.85** normal for the parties' professional advisers to be excluded from the confidentiality obligation. It is also quite common for a claimant's immediate family members to be excluded—at least to the extent that the claimant is entitled to disclose the terms to a partner or spouse (not least because they will often attend the tribunal and be aware of the details of any settlement). In return for such an exclusion, it is normal for the claimant to undertake that any excluded party to whom the terms are disclosed will agree to keep the terms confidential. Another common restriction is that the confidentiality clause is limited to the terms of settlement rather than the fact of settlement.

A confidentiality clause will not apply where disclosure is required by law or is in **23.86** the public interest. This is normally expressly stated in the clause itself. There are also doubts about the enforceability of such restrictions under 'whistleblowing' legislation where a claimant continues to work for the employer.

Public statements

Related to the issue of confidentiality of the terms of any settlement is the question **23.87** of public statements. Sometimes, an employer will wish to prevent the claimant from making public statements about the former employer, for example, making accusations of discrimination or other critical comments. Similarly, claimants are sometimes anxious to prevent former colleagues from making prejudicial comments about them.

However, such 'gagging' restrictions are subject to the same limitations as confiden- **23.88** tiality clauses.

References

It is common for an agreed form of reference to form part of the compromise agree- **23.89** ment. Provision is normally made for the mechanics of the reference—that is, who is to provide the reference, how it is to be provided, and what is to happen if further information is requested.

23.90 A standard reference is unlikely to be appropriate for more senior professional staff and the settlement agreement may lay down a procedure for such a reference to be given.

23.91 It is also important to bear in mind that certain legal liability may arise in connection with references under the Data Protection Act 1998 (DPA 1998), discrimination law, and the law of tort. A detailed consideration of these potential liabilities lies outside the scope of this book.

Returning property

23.92 The agreement will often make provision for the return of company property, such as credit cards, a company car, laptops, mobile phones, and other electronic equipment or documentation (whether held electronically or otherwise), in the claimant's possession or control.

23.93 Sometimes, it is also necessary for arrangements to be made for the employee to collect his or her personal belongings from the employer.

Restrictive covenants

23.94 The statutory compromise agreement may include restrictive covenants that prevent the former employee from working for a competitor or soliciting or dealing with his or her former employer's customers or suppliers, or seeking to recruit their former colleagues, or using confidential information.

23.95 A detailed consideration of the law relating to restrictive covenants lies outside the scope of this book, but it should be noted that, where the original restrictions were unenforceable for some reason and the former employee enters into any fresh restrictions that restrict the individual's conduct or activities, this will fall within the scope of IT(EP)A 2003, s 225 and therefore a specific taxable sum should be set aside as consideration for entering into such agreements.

Outplacement, training, and counselling

23.96 Sometimes—particularly in redundancy situations or discrimination cases—a compromise agreement may make provision for counselling, outplacement services, or retraining. No liability to income tax arises in respect of the provision of such services in connection with the cessation of employment (see IT(EP)A 2003, ss 310–312).

Legal costs

23.97 It is not uncommon for the agreement to make provision for the payment of the claimant's legal costs. Technically, a sum set aside for the payment of legal costs does fall within the scope of the IT(EP)A 2003, s 401 and this is certainly the view of the HMRC. But the tax liability associated with such costs is the subject of an extra-statutory concession by the HMRC (ESC A81). This provides that:

> in taking legal action to recover compensation for loss of employment, employees may succeed in recovering from the former employer some or all of their legal costs. This may occur either because the employee is successful in the Court action or because a settlement is reached which provides that costs be reimbursed . . . the Inland Revenue have decided that in the following circumstances tax will not be charged on payments of costs to the former employee or office holder.
>
> In cases where the dispute is settled without recourse to the Courts, no charge will be imposed on payments made by the former employer—
>
> - direct to the former employee's solicitor and
> - in full or partial discharge of the solicitor's bill of costs incurred by the employee only in connection with the termination of his employment and under a specific term in the settlement agreement providing for that payment.
>
> In cases where the dispute goes to Court, no charge will be imposed on payments of costs made by the former employer, even where these are made direct to the employee, in accordance with a Court order (whether this is made following judgment or compromise of the action).

23.98 The HMRC's view of this concession is set out in further detail in the Employment Income Manual (EIM) at EIM 13740. It is important to stress that this concession only applies to legal costs (although it may include the costs of a professional expert witness incurred by the employee's legal adviser—EIM 13740), and applies only where the compensation claim exceed £30,000 and the employer pays the costs in strict compliance with the terms of the concession. Nonetheless, a clause in the agreement that provides for the payment of a stated amount of costs in compliance with ESC A81 is a useful way of reducing tax liability.

Tax indemnities

23.99 As stated above, the agreement will normally make provision for the taxation of any payments due to the claimant. Where there are doubts about who is liable to pay the tax, provision may be made for indemnities whereby the claimant agrees to pay any tax due on a sum over £30,000 and agrees to indemnify the employer against any such liabilities.

Appendices

APPENDIX 1

Assessment of Compensation Table for Unfair Dismissal Cases: Tribunal Form*

Unfair Dismissal—Assessment of Compensation			Sheet I	

Additional Award (s. 117(5)(a), (b))

Applicant not reinstated/re-engaged
under Order

Award 26 to 52 weeks' pay		Total D	£ ——	
(a) Monetary Award		Total A	£	
Grand total	£	B	£	
(b) Prescribed Element	£	C	£	
(c) Period of Prescribed Element		D	£ ——	
to				
(d) Excess of (a) over (b)	£	Grand Total £ ——		£ ——
		£		

Basic Award (s. 119)

Less

(a) Unreasonable refusal of reinstatement (s. 122(1))	£		
(b) Conduct before dismissal (s. 122(2) and (3))%	£		
(c) Redundancy award/payment (s. 122(4))	£ ——	——	
Net Basic Award		A	——

Compensatory Award (s. 123)

Loss of wages to date of hearing/promulgation
(after allowing for failure to mitigate)

Net average wages £   p.w.

From   to   (weeks)

Less

(a) Post-dismissal earnings/money in lieu of notice	£	£	
(b) Any balance of (i) and (ii) not deducted from C below	£	£ ——	

(Continued)

(Continued)
Less

Contributory fault (s. 123(6)) and/or
conduct before dismissal (s. 123(1))   %

Prescribed Element   B   £ _____

(1) Estimated future loss of wages (after
allowing for failure to mitigate)   £

Net average wages £   p.w. for   weeks   £

(2) Loss of other benefits (before and after
hearing)   £

(3) Loss of statutory industrial rights   £

(4) Loss of redundancy rights in excess of
statutory entitlement: (s. 123(3))   £

(5) Loss of pension rights   £

(6) Expenses incurred   £ _____

Total (1) to (6)   £ _____

Less

(i) Any other payment by respondent   £

(ii) Excess of redundancy payment over
Basic Award (s. 123(7))   £ _____   £ _____

Less

Contributory fault (s. 123(6)) and/or
Conduct before dismissal (s. 123(1))   %   £ _____

Total C   £ _____

* *Author's note:* This form assumes that a full award of compensation is made. Where a *Polkey* reduction is made pursuant to ERA, s 123(1) (see Chapter 12), it should be made after the loss is calculated, but before the reduction for contributory fault in accordance with the EAT's ruling in *Digital Equipment Ltd v Clements (No 2)*. For application of a *Polkey* reduction to redundancy payments on *ex gratia* payments, see Chapter 15. The tables also assume that the compensatory award is not increased or reduced. Where there is an increase or reduction, this takes place before any reduction for contributory fault (see **10.12** and **12.58**).

APPENDIX 2

Schedule of Loss Pro Forma

PART A	**Basic Award**			
	No need to set this out as it follows set formula			

PART B   **Compensatory Award**

a) **Loss of Wages**

    (i)   net average wage per week from [   ](the date of dismissal)   £

        to [   ] (the date new employment secured or today's date, whichever is the earlier)

    Less

    (i)   pay in lieu: earnings in new /   £

    (ii) alternative work: (give full details)   £

                                      sub total: £

                                                net loss of earnings   £

b) **Loss of benefits e.g. company car; bonus; share option scheme;**
life insurance (give full details)   +   £

c) **Loss of pension**
(give full details)   +   £

d) **Expenses incurred in looking for**
work (give full details)   +   £

                                                  sub total   £

<u>LESS</u>

Any extra payment received from Respondent   -   £

                                                TOTAL   £
                                              NET

APPENDIX 3

Appendices 3–7 from Employment Tribunal Guidelines, *Compensation for Loss of Pension Rights* (3rd edn)

Appendix 3
State Earnings-Related Pension Scheme (SERPS) and State Second Pension (S2P)

SERPS

Since April 1978, employees who have paid national insurance contributions on earnings over the lower earnings limit have been entitled to an earnings-related additional pension payable by the State and generally referred to as the State Earnings-Related Pension Scheme (SERPS). Since April 2000 employees earning between the lower earnings limit and the primary threshold for National Insurance contributions are treated as having paid the necessary NI contributions and hence qualified for SERPS accrual. Earnings between the lower earnings and upper earnings limits in any tax year ('relevant earnings') are revalued in line with the general level of increase in earnings up to the year before that in which state pension age is attained. These revalued earnings are then averaged over the period from age 16, or April 1978 if later, to the end of the year preceding state pension age. The retirement pension is payable from state pension age and is indexed after that age in line with the general level of prices.

State pension age for men is 65. State pension age is age 60 for women retiring up to 5 April 2010. For women retiring from 6 April 2020 onwards state pension age will be 65, as it is for men. Between these dates, state pension age for women will increase by one month in every two month interval as set out in Table 3.1.

Table 3.1 State pension age for women—adjustments

Date of birth	State pension age (year. month)	Pension date	Date of birth	State pension age (year. month)	Pension date
06.03.50	60.0	06.03.2010	06.10.52	62.7	06.05.2015
06.04.50	60.1	06.05.2010	06.11.52	62.8	06.07.2015
06.05.50	60.2	06.07.2010	06.12.52	62.9	06.09.2015
06.06.50	60.3	06.09.2010	06.01.53	62.10	06.11.2015
06.07.50	60.4	06.11.2010	06.02.53	62.11	06.01.2016
06.08.50	60.5	06.01.2011	06.03.53	63.0	06.03.2016
06.09.50	60.6	06.03.2011	06.04.53	63.1	06.05.2016
06.10.50	60.7	06.05.2011	06.05.53	63.2	06.07.2016
06.11.50	60.8	06.07.2011	06.06.53	63.3	06.09.2016
06.12.50	60.9	06.09.2011	06.07.53	63.4	06.11.2016
06.01.51	60.10	06.11.2011	06.08.53	63.5	06.01.2017
06.02.51	60.11	06.01.2012	06.09.53	63.6	06.03.2017

(Continued)

Table 3.1 *Continued*

Date of birth	State pension age (year. month)	Pension date	Date of birth	State pension age (year. month)	Pension date
06.03.51	61.0	06.03.2012	06.10.53	63.7	06.05.2017
06.04.51	61.1	06.05.2012	06.11.53	63.8	06.07.2017
06.05.51	61.2	06.07.2012	06.12.53	63.9	06.09.2017
06.06.51	61.3	06.09.2012	06.01.54	63.10	06.11.2017
06.07.51	61.4	06.11.2012	06.02.54	63.11	06.01.2018
06.08.51	61.5	06.01.2013	06.03.54	64.0	06.03.2018
06.09.51	61.6	06.03.2013	06.04.54	64.1	06.05.2018
06.10.51	61.7	06.05.2013	06.05.54	64.2	06.07.2018
06.11.51	61.8	06.07.2013	06.06.54	64.3	06.09.2018
06.12.51	61.9	06.09.2013	06.07.54	64.4	06.11.2018
06.01.52	61.10	06.11.2013	06.08.54	64.5	06.01.2019
06.02.52	61.11	06.01.2014	06.09.54	64.6	06.03.2019
06.03.52	62.0	06.03.2014	06.10.54	64.7	06.05.2019
06.04.52	62.1	06.05.2014	06.11.54	64.8	06.07.2019
06.05.52	62.2	06.07.2014	06.12.54	64.9	06.09.2019
06.06.52	62.3	06.09.2014	06.01.55	64.10	06.11.2019
06.07.52	62.4	06.11.2014	06.02.55	64.11	06.01.2020
06.08.52	62.5	06.01.2015	06.03.55	65.0	06.03.2020
06.09.52	62.6	06.03.2015	06.04.55	65.0	06.04.2020

Following the Social Security Contributions and Benefits Act 1992 the additional pension was eventually to be 20 per cent of revalued earnings as defined above and could be regarded as accruing uniformly over the working life between age 16 and the end of the tax year preceding state pension age. For those over 16 in April 1978 when the accrual of additional pension commenced, the working life was taken to be between April 1978 and the end of the tax year preceding state pension age.

For people reaching state pension age after April 1999, the accrual rate will be 25/N per cent in respect of earnings up to April 1988, where N is the number of tax years in the earner's working life from April 1978 or age 16, if later, to the end of the one preceding state pension age. However, the accrual rate in respect of earnings after April 1988 depends on the year in which state pension age is attained as follows … :

Year of retirement	Percentage accrual rate for period 1988–89 onwards
2003–04	23/25
2004–05	22.5/26
2005–06	22/27
2006–07	21.5/28
2007–08	21/29
2008–09	20.5/30
2009–10	20/31
2010–11	20/32
…	…
2027–28 and later	20/49

THE STATE SECOND PENSION

The Child Support, Pensions and Social Security Act 2000 introduced a number of changes to additional pension, which is now known as The State Second Pension (S2P). The main changes, which took effect from the tax year 2002–03, were:

- The introduction of three different accrual rates on different bands of earnings
- Treating those earning between the annualized lower earnings limit (the qualifying earnings factor or QEF set to be £4,004 in 2003–04) up to the 'low earnings threshold'—£11,200 in terms of 2003–04 earnings—as though they earned the low earnings threshold
- Treating qualified carers and people with long-term disabilities who have no earnings or earnings below the annual lower earnings limit, as if they had earnings at the level of the low earnings threshold.

S2P will accrue on earnings (actual or treated as earned) between the lower earnings limit and the upper earnings limit. These earnings ('relevant earnings') will initially be divided into three bands. Band 1 will be from the annual lower earnings limit to the low earnings threshold (LET). Band 2 will be from the low earnings threshold plus £1 to an amount equal to 3 × LET *less* 2 × QEF. This would be £25,600 in terms of 2003–04 earnings. Band 3 will be from the top of the second band plus £1 to the upper earnings limit. The lower and upper earnings limits and the low earnings threshold will be revalued from year to year.

The S2P accrual rates will be double, half and equal to the SERPS accrual rates on bands 1, 2 and 3 of earnings respectively. Thus, for example, for retirements in 2009–10 and later the S2P will be based on 40%, 10% and 20% of earnings in bands 1, 2 and 3 respectively.

POTENTIAL LOSS OF S2P

S2P will be accrued by all employees earning over the lower earnings limit who are in pension arrangements which are not contracted-out of the S2P. Thus, for any employee who is not a member of an occupational scheme or is a member of an occupational pension scheme which was not contracted out of S2P (circumstances which currently apply to about three-quarters of the private sector working population, but to only a small proportion of public sector workers) there is a potential loss of rights in relation to S2P.

The value of the loss of future accrual of S2P can be obtained by using the relevant factor from Table 3.2 of this appendix which reflects the value of one year's accrual of S2P by age and sex. To obtain the value of the loss of S2P rights, the appropriate factor is taken from Table 3.2 according to the applicant's age at the date of dismissal and sex. The gross earnings of the applicant at the date of dismissal are then multiplied by this factor to give the value of one year's accrual of S2P. The resulting amount should then be multiplied by the length of the period, in years, for which the loss is being valued. The basis used for calculating the factors is described in Appendix 2 [of these Guidelines].

Table 3.2 Factor to be applied to gross earnings for valuing loss of future accruals of S2P for one year

QEF = 4004   LET = 11200   UEL = 30940   (2003–2004)

	Salary																	
	5,000	6,000	7,000	8,000	9,000	10,000	11,000	12,000	13,000	14,000	15,000	20,000	25,000	30,000	35,000	40,000	45,000	50,000
Men (age)																		
20	9.2%	7.7%	6.6%	5.8%	5.1%	4.6%	4.2%	3.9%	3.8%	3.6%	3.5%	3.0%	2.7%	2.8%	2.5%	2.2%	1.9%	1.7%
25	9.7%	8.1%	6.9%	6.0%	5.4%	4.8%	4.4%	4.1%	4.0%	3.8%	3.6%	3.2%	2.9%	2.9%	2.6%	2.3%	2.0%	1.8%
30	10.2%	8.5%	7.3%	6.4%	5.7%	5.1%	4.7%	4.4%	4.2%	4.0%	3.9%	3.3%	3.0%	3.1%	2.7%	2.4%	2.1%	1.9%
35	10.9%	9.1%	7.8%	6.8%	6.0%	5.4%	4.9%	4.7%	4.4%	4.3%	4.1%	3.6%	3.2%	3.3%	2.9%	2.5%	2.3%	2.0%
40	11.5%	9.6%	8.2%	7.2%	6.4%	5.8%	5.2%	4.9%	4.7%	4.5%	4.3%	3.8%	3.4%	3.5%	3.1%	2.7%	2.4%	2.2%
45	13.5%	11.3%	9.7%	8.5%	7.5%	6.8%	6.1%	5.8%	5.5%	5.3%	5.1%	4.4%	4.0%	4.1%	3.6%	3.2%	2.8%	2.5%
50	16.2%	13.5%	11.6%	10.1%	9.0%	8.1%	7.4%	7.0%	6.6%	6.4%	6.1%	5.3%	4.8%	4.9%	4.3%	3.8%	3.4%	3.0%
55	19.9%	16.6%	14.2%	12.4%	11.1%	10.0%	9.1%	8.5%	8.1%	7.8%	7.5%	6.5%	5.9%	6.0%	5.3%	4.7%	4.1%	3.7%
60	26.0%	21.6%	18.5%	16.2%	14.4%	13.0%	11.8%	11.1%	10.6%	10.2%	9.8%	8.5%	7.7%	7.8%	6.9%	6.1%	5.4%	4.9%
63	32.5%	27.1%	23.2%	20.3%	18.1%	16.3%	14.8%	13.9%	13.3%	12.7%	12.3%	10.6%	9.6%	9.8%	8.7%	7.6%	6.8%	6.1%
Women (age)																		
20	10.2%	8.5%	7.3%	6.4%	5.7%	5.1%	4.7%	4.4%	4.2%	4.0%	3.9%	3.3%	3.0%	3.1%	2.7%	2.4%	2.1%	1.9%
25	10.8%	9.0%	7.7%	6.7%	6.0%	5.4%	4.9%	4.6%	4.4%	4.2%	4.1%	3.5%	3.2%	3.2%	2.9%	2.5%	2.2%	2.0%
30	11.3%	9.5%	8.1%	7.1%	6.3%	5.7%	5.2%	4.9%	4.6%	4.4%	4.3%	3.7%	3.4%	3.4%	3.0%	2.7%	2.4%	2.1%
35	12.0%	10.0%	8.6%	7.5%	6.7%	6.0%	5.5%	5.2%	4.9%	4.7%	4.5%	3.9%	3.6%	3.6%	3.2%	2.8%	2.5%	2.3%
40	12.7%	10.6%	9.0%	7.9%	7.0%	6.3%	5.8%	5.4%	5.2%	5.0%	4.8%	4.1%	3.7%	3.8%	3.4%	3.0%	2.6%	2.4%
45	14.7%	12.3%	10.5%	9.2%	8.2%	7.4%	6.7%	6.3%	6.0%	5.8%	5.6%	4.8%	4.4%	4.4%	3.9%	3.4%	3.1%	2.8%
50	20.7%	17.2%	14.8%	12.9%	11.5%	10.3%	9.4%	8.9%	8.4%	8.1%	7.8%	6.7%	6.1%	6.2%	5.5%	4.8%	4.3%	3.9%
55	31.8%	26.5%	22.7%	19.9%	17.7%	15.9%	14.4%	13.6%	13.0%	12.5%	12.0%	10.4%	9.4%	9.6%	8.5%	7.4%	6.6%	5.9%
58	39.4%	32.8%	28.1%	24.6%	21.9%	19.7%	17.9%	16.9%	16.1%	15.4%	14.9%	12.9%	11.7%	11.9%	10.5%	9.2%	8.2%	7.4%

Example

A male employee is dismissed in 2003–04 at age 50 from private sector employment with gross earnings of £35,000 a year and no prospect of reemployment before state pension age of 65. The claimant was not a member of any pension arrangements run by the employer and hence was accuring S2P since his earnings are above the lower earnings limit. The loss for future accrual of S2P is assessed as

$$£35,000 \times 0.043 \times 15 = £22,575$$

where the factor of 0.043 is taken from Table 3.2 at age 50 for males with gross earnings of £35,000.

If the employee was a member of a pension arrangement which was contracted out of the Additional Pension under SERPS and/or S2P, there will be a potential loss of state pension benefits under S2P for members of employer contracted-out final salary schemes and contracted-out money purchase schemes with earnings below 3 × LET *less* 2 × QEF (= £25,600 in 2003–04 terms) and for employee members of Appropriate Personal Pensions with earnings below the Lower Earnings Threshold (= £11,200 in 2003–04 terms). Had the member not been dismissed, a top-up pension would have been paid by the State from the state pension age equal to the amount of S2P the member would have accrued less the amount of SERPS the member would notionally have accrued. The loss of the SERPS accrual is effectively allowed for in the assessment of the loss of occupational pension rights, as discussed in section 5 et seq. [of these Guidelines]. Hence, the loss of state pension benefits in respect of future service which are not allowed for elsewhere can be assessed as the value of the S2P which would have been paid in respect of future service less the value of the amount of SERPS the member would notionally have accrued. However, the value of this top-up is complex to calculate and is usually small relative to the value of the loss of pension from the pension scheme. In keeping with the aim of simplifying the calculations as far as possible, it is recommended that no award of compensation be made in respect of the potential loss of any top-up pension payable to members of contracted out pension arrangements.

There may be cases where the employee was a member of a company occupational pension scheme which was not contracted out. This means that there are two potential losses which have to be assessed separately; one under S2P and the second under the occupational pension scheme. The methods for assessing this second loss are discussed in Chapters 5, 6, 7 and 8 [of these Guidelines]. An employee who was not previously a member of an occupational pension scheme will not suffer a loss of future pension rights (other than those payable by the State) unless the employer was contributing to a personal pension or stakeholder pension on behalf of the employee, in which case the loss can be measured as the loss of that contribution (see Chapter 7 [of these Guidelines]).

In general, the lower and upper earnings limits and the lower earnings threshold will be uprated at the beginning of each tax year. Thus the figures in Table 3.2 will need to be revised on an annual basis; in calculating the value of the S2P loss on dismissal, factors relevant to the tax year in which dismissal took place should be applied to the gross earnings as at the date of dismissal.

Where the factors are used to value the S2P accruing from some future employment, the table of factors for the latest available tax year should be used and applied to the assessed gross earnings in the new employment.

Appendix 4
Tables of multipliers to be applied to the deferred annual pension to assess compensation for loss of enhancement of accrued pension rights
(Chapter 5 [of these Guidelines])

Table 4.1 Men in private sector schemes

Age last birthday at dismissal	Normal retirement age—men			Age last birthday at dismissal	Normal retirement age—men		
	55	60	65		55	60	65
20 and under	5.62	5.22	4.63	43	2.85	3.31	3.37
21	5.55	5.18	4.60	44	2.65	3.16	3.28
22	5.49	5.13	4.57	45	2.45	3.02	3.17
23	5.41	5.09	4.55	46	2.23	2.86	3.07
24	5.34	5.03	4.51	47	2.01	2.70	2.96
25	5.25	4.98	4.48	48	1.77	2.53	2.84
26	5.17	4.92	4.44	49	1.53	2.36	2.72
27	5.08	4.86	4.41	50	1.28	2.18	2.59
28	4.98	4.80	4.37	51	1.01	1.99	2.46
29	4.88	4.73	4.32	52	0.74	1.79	2.32
30	4.78	4.66	4.28	53	0.45	1.58	2.18
31	4.67	4.58	4.23	54	0.15	1.37	2.03
32	4.55	4.50	4.18	55		1.14	1.87
33	4.43	4.42	4.12	56		0.91	1.71
34	4.30	4.33	4.06	57		0.66	1.54
35	4.17	4.24	4.00	58		0.40	1.37
36	4.03	4.14	3.94	59		0.14	1.18
37	3.88	4.03	3.87	60			0.99
38	3.73	3.93	3.79	61			0.79
39	3.57	3.81	3.72	62			0.57
40	3.40	3.70	3.64	63			0.35
41	3.22	3.57	3.55	64			0.12
42	3.04	3.44	3.47				

Table 4.2 Men in public sector schemes

Age last birthday at dismissal	Normal retirement age—men			Age last birthday at dismissal	Normal retirement age—men		
	55	60	65		55	60	65
20 and under	6.26	5.91	5.33	43	3.10	3.65	3.80
21	6.19	5.85	5.30	44	2.88	3.49	3.69
22	6.10	5.80	5.26	45	2.66	3.33	3.57
23	6.02	5.74	5.22	46	2.42	3.15	3.45
24	5.92	5.68	5.18	47	2.17	2.97	3.32
25	5.83	5.61	5.14	48	1.92	2.78	3.18
26	5.73	5.54	5.09	49	1.65	2.59	3.05
27	5.62	5.47	5.05	50	1.38	2.39	2.90
28	5.51	5.39	4.99	51	1.09	2.18	2.75

(Continued)

423

Table 4.2 (*Continued*)

Age last birthday at dismissal	Normal retirement age—men			Age last birthday at dismissal	Normal retirement age—men		
	55	60	65		55	60	65
29	5.39	5.31	4.94	52	0.79	1.96	2.59
30	5.27	5.22	4.88	53	0.49	1.73	2.43
31	5.14	5.13	4.82	54	0.16	1.49	2.26
32	5.01	5.04	4.76	55		1.24	2.09
33	4.87	4.94	4.69	56		0.99	1.90
34	4.72	4.83	4.62	57		0.72	1.71
35	4.57	4.72	4.54	58		0.44	1.52
36	4.41	4.61	4.47	59		0.15	1.31
37	4.25	4.49	4.38	60			1.10
38	4.08	4.36	4.30	61			0.87
39	3.90	4.23	4.21	62			0.64
40	3.71	4.10	4.11	63			0.39
41	3.51	3.96	4.01	64			0.13
42	3.31	3.81	3.91				

Table 4.3 Women in private sector schemes

Age last birthday at dismissal	Normal retirement age—women			Age last birthday at dismissal	Normal retirement age—women		
	55	60	65		55	60	65
20 and under	5.89	5.54	4.96	43	2.98	3.50	3.61
21	5.83	5.49	4.94	44	2.77	3.35	3.50
22	5.75	5.44	4.91	45	2.56	3.19	3.39
23	5.68	5.39	4.88	46	2.33	3.02	3.28
24	5.59	5.34	4.84	47	2.10	2.85	3.16
25	5.51	5.28	4.81	48	1.85	2.68	3.04
26	5.42	5.22	4.77	49	1.60	2.49	2.91
27	5.32	5.15	4.73	50	1.33	2.30	2.77
28	5.22	5.09	4.68	51	1.06	2.09	2.63
29	5.12	5.01	4.63	52	0.77	1.88	2.48
30	5.00	4.94	4.58	53	0.47	1.67	2.33
31	4.89	4.85	4.53	54	0.16	1.44	2.17
32	4.77	4.77	4.47	55		1.20	2.00
33	4.64	4.68	4.42	56		0.95	1.83
34	4.50	4.58	4.35	57		0.69	1.64
35	4.36	4.48	4.28	58		0.42	1.46
36	4.21	4.38	4.21	59		0.14	1.26
37	4.06	4.27	4.14	60			1.05
38	3.90	4.16	4.06	61			0.84
39	3.73	4.03	3.98	62			0.61
40	3.55	3.91	3.89	63			0.37
41	3.37	3.78	3.80	64			0.13
42	3.18	3.64	3.71				

Table 4.4 Women in public sector schemes

Age last birthday at dismissal	Normal retirement age—women			Age last birthday at dismissal	Normal retirement age—women		
	55	60	65		55	60	65
20 and under	6.53	6.22	5.68	43	3.23	3.84	4.04
21	6.45	6.17	5.65	44	3.00	3.67	3.92
22	6.36	6.11	5.61	45	2.76	3.49	3.79
23	6.27	6.04	5.57	46	2.51	3.31	3.66
24	6.18	5.98	5.52	47	2.26	3.12	3.53
25	6.08	5.91	5.48	48	1.99	2.92	3.38
26	5.97	5.83	5.43	49	1.72	2.72	3.24
27	5.86	5.75	5.38	50	1.43	2.50	3.08
28	5.74	5.67	5.32	51	1.13	2.28	2.92
29	5.62	5.59	5.26	52	0.82	2.05	2.75
30	5.49	5.49	5.20	53	0.50	1.81	2.58
31	5.36	5.40	5.14	54	0.17	1.56	2.40
32	5.22	5.30	5.07	55		1.30	2.21
33	5.07	5.19	4.99	56		1.03	2.02
34	4.92	5.08	4.92	57		0.75	1.81
35	4.76	4.97	4.84	58		0.46	1.60
36	4.59	4.85	4.75	59		0.15	1.38
37	4.42	4.72	4.66	60			1.16
38	4.24	4.59	4.57	61			0.92
39	4.05	4.45	4.48	62			0.67
40	3.86	4.31	4.37	63			0.41
41	3.66	4.16	4.27	64			0.14
42	3.44	4.00	4.16				

Appendix 5
Tables of multipliers to be applied to the estimated final annual pension to assess value of pension arising from service to Normal Retirement Age (Chapter 8 [of these Guidelines])

Table 5.1 Men in private sector schemes

Age last birthday at dismissal	Normal retirement age—men			Age last birthday at dismissal	Normal retirement age—men		
	55	60	65		55	60	65
20 and under	12.79	10.83	8.91	43	16.24	13.75	11.29
21	12.92	10.94	9.00	44	16.42	13.89	11.41
22	13.05	11.05	9.09	45	16.60	14.04	11.53
23	13.19	11.16	9.18	46	16.78	14.20	11.66
24	13.32	11.28	9.27	47	16.97	14.35	11.78
25	13.46	11.39	9.36	48	17.16	14.51	11.91
26	13.60	11.51	9.46	49	17.35	14.67	12.04
27	13.74	11.63	9.56	50	17.55	14.84	12.17

(Continued)

425

Table 5.1 (*Continued*)

Age last birthday at dismissal	Normal retirement age—men			Age last birthday at dismissal	Normal retirement age—men		
	55	*60*	*65*		*55*	*60*	*65*
28	13.88	11.75	9.66	51	17.76	15.01	12.30
29	14.02	11.87	9.76	52	17.97	15.18	12.44
30	14.17	11.99	9.86	53	18.19	15.36	12.58
31	14.32	12.12	9.96	54	18.42	15.55	12.72
32	14.47	12.25	10.07	55		15.74	12.87
33	14.62	12.37	10.17	56		15.95	13.03
34	14.77	12.50	10.28	57		16.16	13.19
35	14.93	12.64	10.39	58		16.38	13.36
36	15.08	12.77	10.50	59		16.61	13.54
37	15.24	12.90	10.61	60			13.73
38	15.40	13.04	10.72	61			13.93
39	15.57	13.18	10.83	62			14.14
40	15.73	13.32	10.95	63			14.37
41	15.90	13.46	11.06	64			14.62
42	16.07	13.60	11.18				

Table 5.2 Men in public sector schemes

Age last birthday at dismissal	Normal retirement age—men			Age last birthday at dismissal	Normal retirement age—men		
	55	*60*	*65*		*55*	*60*	*65*
20 and under	15.97	13.65	11.36	43	20.26	17.31	14.40
21	16.13	13.79	11.47	44	20.48	17.50	14.55
22	16.30	13.93	11.59	45	20.70	17.68	14.70
23	16.46	14.07	11.71	46	20.93	17.88	14.86
24	16.63	14.21	11.82	47	21.16	18.07	15.02
25	16.80	14.36	11.95	48	21.40	18.27	15.18
26	16.98	14.51	12.07	49	21.64	18.48	15.35
27	17.15	14.66	12.19	50	21.89	18.69	15.52
28	17.33	14.81	12.32	51	22.15	18.90	15.69
29	17.51	14.96	12.44	52	22.41	19.12	15.87
30	17.69	15.12	12.57	53	22.69	19.35	16.05
31	17.87	15.27	12.70	54	22.97	19.59	16.24
32	18.06	15.43	12.84	55		19.83	16.44
33	18.25	15.59	12.97	56		20.09	16.64
34	18.44	15.75	13.11	57		20.35	16.85
35	18.63	15.92	13.24	58		20.63	17.07
36	18.82	16.08	13.38	59		20.92	17.30
37	19.02	16.25	13.52	60			17.55
38	19.22	16.42	13.66	61			17.81
39	19.42	16.60	13.80	62			18.08
40	19.63	16.77	13.95	63			18.38
41	19.83	16.95	14.10	64			18.70
42	20.05	17.13	14.24				

Table 5.3 Women in private sector schemes

Age last birthday at dismissal	Normal retirement age—women			Age last birthday at dismissal	Normal retirement age—women		
	55	60	65		55	60	65
20 and under	13.26	11.32	9.37	43	16.74	14.28	11.81
21	13.39	11.43	9.47	44	16.92	14.43	11.93
22	13.53	11.55	9.56	45	17.10	14.58	12.05
23	13.67	11.67	9.66	46	17.28	14.73	12.18
24	13.80	11.78	9.75	47	17.47	14.89	12.30
25	13.94	11.90	9.85	48	17.66	15.05	12.43
26	14.08	12.02	9.95	49	17.85	15.21	12.56
27	14.23	12.14	10.05	50	18.05	15.38	12.70
28	14.37	12.27	10.15	51	18.25	15.55	12.84
29	14.52	12.39	10.26	52	18.46	15.72	12.98
30	14.66	12.51	10.36	53	18.67	15.90	13.12
31	14.81	12.64	10.46	54	18.89	16.08	13.27
32	14.96	12.77	10.57	55		16.27	13.42
33	15.11	12.90	10.67	56		16.47	13.58
34	15.27	13.03	10.78	57		16.67	13.74
35	15.42	13.16	10.89	58		16.88	13.91
36	15.58	13.30	11.00	59		17.10	14.09
37	15.74	13.43	11.11	60			14.27
38	15.90	13.57	11.22	61			14.46
39	16.07	13.71	11.34	62			14.66
40	16.23	13.85	11.45	63			14.88
41	16.40	13.99	11.57	64			15.10
42	16.57	14.13	11.69				

Table 5.4 Women in public sector schemes

Age last birthday at dismissal	Normal retirement age—women			Age last birthday at dismissal	Normal retirement age—women		
	55	60	65		55	60	65
20 and under	16.48	14.19	11.91	43	20.81	17.91	15.01
21	16.64	14.33	12.02	44	21.02	18.09	15.16
22	16.81	14.48	12.15	45	21.25	18.28	15.32
23	16.98	14.62	12.27	46	21.47	18.48	15.48
24	17.15	14.77	12.39	47	21.70	18.67	15.64
25	17.32	14.92	12.51	48	21.94	18.87	15.81
26	17.50	15.07	12.64	49	22.18	19.08	15.98
27	17.68	15.22	12.77	50	22.42	19.28	16.15
28	17.86	15.37	12.90	51	22.67	19.50	16.33
29	18.04	15.53	13.03	52	22.93	19.72	16.51
30	18.22	15.69	13.16	53	23.19	19.94	16.69
31	18.40	15.85	13.29	54	23.46	20.17	16.88
32	18.59	16.01	13.43	55		20.41	17.08
33	18.78	16.17	13.56	56		20.65	17.28
34	18.97	16.33	13.70	57		20.90	17.48

(Continued)

Table 5.4 (*Continued*)

Age last birthday at dismissal	Normal retirement age—women			Age last birthday at dismissal	Normal retirement age—women		
	55	60	65		55	60	65
35	19.16	16.50	13.84	58		21.16	17.70
36	19.36	16.67	13.98	59		21.43	17.92
37	19.56	16.84	14.12	60			18.15
38	19.76	17.01	14.26	61			18.40
39	19.96	17.18	14.41	62			18.65
40	20.17	17.36	14.56	63			18.92
41	20.38	17.54	14.70	64			19.21
42	20.59	17.72	14.86				

Appendix 6
Tables of multipliers to be applied to the deferred annual pension to assess value of deferred pension (Chapter 8 [of these Guidelines]

Table 6.1 Men in private sector schemes

Age last birthday at dismissal	Normal retirement age—men			Age last birthday at dismissal	Normal retirement age—men		
	55	60	65		55	60	65
20 and under	7.17	5.61	4.28	43	13.39	10.44	7.92
21	7.37	5.76	4.40	44	13.76	10.73	8.14
22	7.57	5.92	4.51	45	14.15	11.03	8.36
23	7.77	6.08	4.63	46	14.55	11.33	8.59
24	7.98	6.24	4.76	47	14.96	11.65	8.83
25	8.20	6.41	4.88	48	15.38	11.98	9.07
26	8.43	6.59	5.02	49	15.82	12.31	9.32
27	8.66	6.77	5.15	50	16.28	12.66	9.57
28	8.90	6.95	5.29	51	16.75	13.02	9.84
29	9.14	7.14	5.43	52	17.24	13.40	10.12
30	9.39	7.34	5.58	53	17.74	13.78	10.40
31	9.65	7.54	5.73	54	18.27	14.19	10.69
32	9.92	7.74	5.89	55		14.60	11.00
33	10.19	7.96	6.05	56		15.04	11.32
34	10.47	8.18	6.22	57		15.50	11.65
35	10.76	8.40	6.39	58		15.97	12.00
36	11.06	8.63	6.56	59		16.47	12.36
37	11.36	8.87	6.74	60			12.74
38	11.68	9.11	6.92	61			13.14
39	12.00	9.36	7.11	62			13.56
40	12.33	9.62	7.31	63			14.02
41	12.67	9.89	7.51	64			14.50
42	13.03	10.16	7.71				

Table 6.2 Men in public sector schemes

Age last birthday at dismissal	Normal retirement age—men			Age last birthday at dismissal	Normal retirement age—men		
	55	60	65		55	60	65
20 and under	9.71	7.74	6.03	43	17.16	13.66	10.59
21	9.95	7.93	6.18	44	17.60	14.00	10.86
22	10.19	8.13	6.33	45	18.05	14.36	11.13
23	10.45	8.33	6.48	46	18.51	14.72	11.41
24	10.71	8.54	6.64	47	18.99	15.10	11.70
25	10.97	8.75	6.81	48	19.48	15.49	12.00
26	11.25	8.97	6.97	49	19.99	15.89	12.30
27	11.53	9.19	7.15	50	20.51	16.30	12.62
28	11.82	9.42	7.32	51	21.06	16.73	12.94
29	12.11	9.65	7.50	52	21.62	17.17	13.27
30	12.42	9.89	7.69	53	22.20	17.62	13.62
31	12.73	10.14	7.88	54	22.81	18.10	13.98
32	13.05	10.40	8.08	55		18.59	14.35
33	13.37	10.66	8.28	56		19.10	14.74
34	13.71	10.92	8.49	57		19.63	15.14
35	14.05	11.20	8.70	58		20.19	15.56
36	14.41	11.48	8.91	59		20.78	15.99
37	14.77	11.76	9.14	60			16.45
38	15.14	12.06	9.36	61			16.94
39	15.53	12.36	9.60	62			17.45
40	15.92	12.67	9.84	63			17.99
41	16.32	12.99	10.08	64			18.57
42	16.73	13.32	10.34				

Table 6.3 Women in private sector schemes

Age last birthday at dismissal	Normal retirement age—women			Age last birthday at dismissal	Normal retirement age—women		
	55	60	65		55	60	65
20 and under	7.37	5.79	4.41	43	13.76	10.79	8.20
21	7.57	5.94	4.53	44	14.15	11.08	8.42
22	7.78	6.11	4.66	45	14.54	11.39	8.66
23	7.99	6.27	4.78	46	14.95	11.71	8.90
24	8.21	6.44	4.91	47	15.37	12.04	9.14
25	8.43	6.62	5.05	48	15.80	12.37	9.40
26	8.67	6.80	5.18	49	16.25	12.72	9.66
27	8.90	6.99	5.33	50	16.71	13.08	9.93
28	9.15	7.18	5.47	51	17.19	13.45	10.21
29	9.40	7.38	5.62	52	17.69	13.84	10.49
30	9.66	7.58	5.77	53	18.20	14.23	10.79
31	9.92	7.79	5.93	54	18.73	14.65	11.10

(Continued)

Table 6.3 (*Continued*)

Age last birthday at dismissal	Normal retirement age—women			Age last birthday at dismissal	Normal retirement age—women		
	55	60	65		55	60	65
32	10.20	8.00	6.09	55		15.07	11.42
33	10.48	8.22	6.26	56		15.52	11.75
34	10.77	8.45	6.43	57		15.98	12.10
35	11.06	8.68	6.61	58		16.46	12.45
36	11.37	8.92	6.79	59		16.96	12.83
37	11.68	9.16	6.97	60			13.22
38	12.00	9.41	7.16	61			13.63
39	12.34	9.67	7.36	62			14.05
40	12.68	9.94	7.56	63			14.50
41	13.03	10.21	7.77	64			14.98
42	13.39	10.49	7.98				

Table 6.4 Women in public sector schemes

Age last birthday at dismissal	Normal retirement age—women			Age last birthday at dismissal	Normal retirement age—women		
	55	60	65		55	60	65
20 and under	9.94	7.97	6.22	43	17.58	14.07	10.97
21	10.19	8.17	6.38	44	18.03	14.42	11.24
22	10.45	8.37	6.54	45	18.49	14.79	11.53
23	10.71	8.58	6.70	46	18.96	15.16	11.82
24	10.97	8.79	6.87	47	19.45	15.55	12.12
25	11.25	9.01	7.04	48	19.95	15.95	12.43
26	11.53	9.24	7.21	49	20.46	16.36	12.74
27	11.82	9.47	7.39	50	20.99	16.78	13.07
28	12.11	9.70	7.58	51	21.54	17.22	13.41
29	12.42	9.94	7.76	52	22.11	17.67	13.75
30	12.73	10.19	7.96	53	22.69	18.13	14.11
31	13.05	10.45	8.16	54	23.29	18.61	14.48
32	13.37	10.71	8.36	55		19.11	14.86
33	13.71	10.98	8.57	56		19.62	15.26
34	14.05	11.25	8.78	57		20.15	15.67
35	14.40	11.53	9.00	58		20.70	16.10
36	14.77	11.82	9.22	59		21.28	16.54
37	15.14	12.12	9.45	60			17.00
38	15.52	12.42	9.69	61			17.48
39	15.91	12.73	9.93	62			17.98
40	16.31	13.05	10.18	63			18.51
41	16.72	13.38	10.44	64			19.07
42	17.15	13.72	10.70				

Appendix 7

Tables of factors to be applied to the standard contribution rate to assess the age specific contribution rate

Table 7.1 Men

Age last birthday at dismissal	Normal retirement age—men			Age last birthday at dismissal	Normal retirement age—men		
	55	*60*	*65*		*55*	*60*	*65*
20 and under	0.77	0.74	0.71	43	1.09	1.04	1.00
21	0.78	0.75	0.72	44	1.11	1.06	1.01
22	0.79	0.76	0.73	45	1.12	1.08	1.03
23	0.80	0.77	0.74	46	1.14	1.09	1.05
24	0.82	0.78	0.75	47	1.16	1.11	1.06
25	0.83	0.79	0.76	48	1.18	1.13	1.08
26	0.84	0.81	0.77	49	1.20	1.15	1.09
27	0.85	0.82	0.78	50	1.22	1.16	1.11
28	0.87	0.83	0.80	51	1.24	1.18	1.13
29	0.88	0.84	0.81	52	1.26	1.20	1.15
30	0.89	0.86	0.82	53	1.28	1.22	1.17
31	0.91	0.87	0.83	54	1.30	1.24	1.18
32	0.92	0.88	0.84	55		1.27	1.20
33	0.93	0.90	0.86	56		1.29	1.22
34	0.95	0.91	0.87	57		1.31	1.24
35	0.96	0.92	0.88	58		1.33	1.27
36	0.98	0.94	0.90	59		1.36	1.29
37	0.99	0.95	0.91	60			1.31
38	1.01	0.97	0.93	61			1.34
39	1.02	0.98	0.94	62			1.37
40	1.04	1.00	0.95	63			1.39
41	1.06	1.01	0.97	64			1.42
42	1.07	1.03	0.98				

Table 7.2 Women

Age last birthday at dismissal	Normal retirement age—women			Age last birthday at dismissal	Normal retirement age—women		
	55	*60*	*65*		*55*	*60*	*65*
20 and under	0.77	0.74	0.70	43	1.09	1.04	0.99
21	0.78	0.75	0.71	44	1.11	1.06	1.00
22	0.79	0.76	0.72	45	1.12	1.08	1.02
23	0.81	0.77	0.73	46	1.14	1.09	1.03
24	0.82	0.78	0.75	47	1.16	1.11	1.05
25	0.83	0.80	0.76	48	1.18	1.13	1.07
26	0.84	0.81	0.77	49	1.20	1.14	1.08
27	0.86	0.82	0.78	50	1.21	1.16	1.10
28	0.87	0.83	0.79	51	1.23	1.18	1.12
29	0.88	0.85	0.80	52	1.25	1.20	1.14

(*Continued*)

Table 7.2 (*Continued*)

Age last birthday at dismissal	Normal retirement age—women			Age last birthday at dismissal	Normal retirement age—women		
	55	*60*	*65*		*55*	*60*	*65*
30	0.90	0.86	0.81	53	1.28	1.22	1.15
31	0.91	0.87	0.83	54	1.30	1.24	1.17
32	0.92	0.88	0.84	55		1.26	1.19
33	0.94	0.90	0.85	56		1.28	1.21
34	0.95	0.91	0.86	57		1.30	1.23
35	0.96	0.92	0.88	58		1.33	1.25
36	0.98	0.94	0.89	59		1.35	1.27
37	0.99	0.95	0.90	60			1.30
38	1.01	0.97	0.92	61			1.32
39	1.02	0.98	0.93	62			1.35
40	1.04	1.00	0.95	63			1.37
41	1.06	1.01	0.96	64			1.40
42	1.07	1.03	0.97				

APPENDIX 4

Compensatory Limits

The table below sets out the statutory limits on compensatory awards for breaches of certain statutory rights.

The limits are varied from 1 February each year by statutory instrument.

The current limits are governed by the Employment Rights (Revision of Limits) Order 2009 (SI 2009 No 3274) with effect from 1 February 2010.

It should be noted that the use of the Retail Prices Index formula in relation to the limit on a week's pay used to calculate redundancy payments and the unfair dismissal basic award, among other things, was suspended following a one-off increase in October 2009. The limit on weekly pay for these purposes will remain at £380 until February 2011 at the earliest. Where the February 2010 value is the same as per October 2009, this is indicated by an asterisk.

Type of award	£ New max amount of a wk's pay (old max)	£ New statutory cap (old cap)	Statutory provision	Relevant date
Unfair dismissal: basic award	£400* (£380) max amount of a week's pay	£12,000* (£11,900) This is subject to a minimum basic award of £5,000 (£4,700) if the principal reason for dismissal is: carrying out activities as a **health and safety rep** (s. 100(1), ERA 1996); carrying out functions as a **trustee of an occupational pension scheme** (s. 102(1), ERA 1996); performing functions or activities as an **employee rep** (ss. 101A(d) and 103, ERA 1996); and **union membership or activities** (ss. 152(1) and 153, TULR(C)A 1992	s. 227(1)(a), ERA 1996	Effective date of termination
Unfair dismissal: compensatory award	—	£68,400 (£65,300)	s. 124(1), ERA 1996	Effective date of termination
Unfair dismissal: additional award for between 26 and 52 weeks' pay where the employer has failed to comply with an order of reinstatement or re-engagement	£400* (£380) max amount of a week's pay	£20,800* (£19,760) Additional award is set at between 26 and 52 weeks' pay (s. 117(3)).	s. 227(1)(b), ERA 1996	Date by which reinstatement or re-engagement order should have been complied with
Redundancy pay	£380* (£350) max amount of a week's pay	£12,000* (£11,400)	s. 227(1)(c), ERA 1996	Effective date of termination. This is subject to ss. 145 and 153, ERA 1996
Guarantee pay during short time or temporary lay-off	£22.80 (£21.20) max amount of a day's pay during short time or temporary lay-off	£111 (£106) Guarantee pay is set at a maximum of five days' pay (s. 31(3)) in any period of three months (s. 31(2))	s. 31(1), ERA 1996	Day for which guarantee pay is claimed
Failure to comply with right to be accompanied	—	£800* (£760) This is set at a maximum of two week's pay	s. 11(3), ERelA 1999	Date of failure or threatened failure

Type	Max amount of a week's pay	Total amount	Statutory reference	Date
Insolvency debt repayments by Sec State: arrears of pay	£400* (£380) max amount of a week's pay for recoverable debts (s. 186(1))	£3,800* (£3,040) Arrears of pay is set at between one and eight weeks' pay (s. 184(1))	s. 184(1)(a), ERA 1996	Date of employer's insolvency
Insolvency debt repayments by Sec State: statutory notice pay	£400* (£380) max amount of a week's pay for recoverable debts (s. 186(1))	£4,800 (£4,560)	s. 184(1)(b), ERA 1996	Date of employer's insolvency or effective date of termination (whichever is the later)
Insolvency debt repayments by Sec State: holiday pay	£400* (£380) max amount of a week's pay for recoverable debts (s. 186(1))	£2,400 (£2,280) Holiday pay is set at a maximum of six weeks' pay (s. 184(1)(c)(i))	s. 184(1)(c), ERA 1996	Date of employer's insolvency
Insolvency debt repayments by Sec State: basic award	£400* (£380) max amount of a week's pay for recoverable debts (s. 186(1))	£12,000 (£11,400)	s. 184(1)(d), ERA 1996	Date of employer's insolvency or effective date of termination or date on which the award was made (whichever is the later)
Unjustifiable discipline by union: basic award + compensatory award	£400* (£380) max amount of a week's pay	£8,400 (£76,700) This is subject to a minimum of £7,600 if application is made to the EAT	s. 67(8), TULR(C)A 1992 ss. 176(6A) and 67(8A), TULR(C)A	Date of determination by union
Refusal of employment on grounds related to union membership		£68,400 (£69,300)	s. 140(4), TULR(C)A 1992	Date of refusal
Unreasonable exclusion/expulsion from union: basic award + compensatory award	£400 (£350) max amount of a week's pay	£80,400 (76,700 from Feb 09). This is subject to a minimum of £7,600 if application is made to the EAT	s. 176(6), TULR(C)A 1992 ss. 176(6A) and 67(8A), TULR(C)A	Date of refusal of application for or expulsion from membership
Failure to consult with union on training		£800* (£760) This is set at a maximum of two weeks' pay per person	s. 70C(4), TULR(C)A 1992	Date of failure

INDEX